AF800719

European Yearbook of International Economic Law

Special Issue

Series Editors

Jelena Bäumler, Lüneburg, Germany

Christina Binder, Neubiberg, Germany

Marc Bungenberg, Saarbrücken, Germany

Markus Krajewski, Erlangen, Germany

Giesela Rühl, Berlin, Germany

Christian J. Tams, Glasgow, UK

Jörg Philipp Terhechte, Lüneburg, Germany

Andreas R. Ziegler, Lausanne, Switzerland

Assistant Editor

Judith Crämer, Lüneburg, Germany

Advisory Editors

Armin von Bogdandy, Heidelberg, Germany

Thomas Cottier, Bern, Switzerland

Mary Footer, Nottingham, UK

Stefan Griller, Salzburg, Austria

Armin Hatje, Hamburg, Germany

Christoph Herrmann, Passau, Germany

Meinhard Hilf, Hamburg, Germany

Locknie Hsu, Singapore, Singapore

William E. Kovacic, Washington, USA

Gabrielle Marceau, Geneva, Switzerland

Ernst-Ulrich Petersmann, Florence, Italy

Hélène Ruiz Fabri, Luxembourg, Luxembourg

Bruno Simma, München, Germany

Rudolf Streinz, München, Germany

Tania Voon, Melbourne, Australia

The European Yearbook of International Economic Law (EYIEL) is a Springer-publication in the field of International Economic Law (IEL), a field increasingly emancipating itself from Public International Law scholarship and evolving into a fully-fledged academic discipline in its own right. With the yearbook, editors and publisher make a significant contribution to the development of this "new" discipline and provide an international source of reference of the highest possible quality.

The EYIEL covers all areas of IEL, in particular WTO Law, External Trade Law of major trading countries, important Regional Economic Integration agreements, International Competition Law, International Investment Regulation, International Monetary Law, International Intellectual Property Protection and International Tax Law.

EYIEL publishes articles following a substantive review by the editors and external experts as appropriate.

The editors have published extensively in the field of IEL and European Law alike. They are supported by an international Advisory Board consisting of established scholars of the highest reputation.

Series Editors

Marc Bungenberg, Saarbrücken, Germany

Markus Krajewski, Erlangen, Germany

Christian J. Tams, Glasgow, UK

Jörg Philipp Terhechte, Lüneburg, Germany

Andreas R. Ziegler, Lausanne, Switzerland

The European Yearbook of International Economic Law (EYIEL) is an annual publication in International Economic Law, a field increasingly emancipating itself from Public International Law scholarship and evolving into a fully-fledged academic discipline in its own right. With the yearbook, the editors and publisher intend to make a significant contribution to the development of this "new" discipline and provide an international reference source of the highest possible quality. The EYIEL covers all areas of IEL, in particular WTO Law, External Trade Law for major trading countries, important Regional Economic Integration agreements, International Competition Law, International Investment Regulation, International Monetary Law, International Intellectual Property Protection and International Tax Law. In addition to the regular annual volumes, EYIEL Special Issues routinely address specific current topics in International Economic Law.

Alexandr Svetlicinii • I-Ju Chen
Editors

The EU-China Comprehensive Agreement on Investment

Towards a Binding Investment Liberalisation

Springer

Editors
Alexandr Svetlicinii
Faculty of Law
University of Macau
Macao, Macao

I-Ju Chen
School of Law
University of Exeter
Exeter, UK

ISSN 2510-6880 ISSN 2510-6899 (electronic)
Special Issue
ISSN 2364-8392 ISSN 2364-8406 (electronic)
European Yearbook of International Economic Law
ISBN 978-3-031-66861-6 ISBN 978-3-031-66862-3 (eBook)
https://doi.org/10.1007/978-3-031-66862-3

© The Editor(s) (if applicable) and The Author(s), under exclusive license to Springer Nature Switzerland AG 2024
This work is subject to copyright. All rights are solely and exclusively licensed by the Publisher, whether the whole or part of the material is concerned, specifically the rights of translation, reprinting, reuse of illustrations, recitation, broadcasting, reproduction on microfilms or in any other physical way, and transmission or information storage and retrieval, electronic adaptation, computer software, or by similar or dissimilar methodology now known or hereafter developed.
The use of general descriptive names, registered names, trademarks, service marks, etc. in this publication does not imply, even in the absence of a specific statement, that such names are exempt from the relevant protective laws and regulations and therefore free for general use.
The publisher, the authors and the editors are safe to assume that the advice and information in this book are believed to be true and accurate at the date of publication. Neither the publisher nor the authors or the editors give a warranty, expressed or implied, with respect to the material contained herein or for any errors or omissions that may have been made. The publisher remains neutral with regard to jurisdictional claims in published maps and institutional affiliations.

This Springer imprint is published by the registered company Springer Nature Switzerland AG
The registered company address is: Gewerbestrasse 11, 6330 Cham, Switzerland

If disposing of this product, please recycle the paper.

Acknowledgements

The research for this book benefited from discussions and feedback received by the contributors at the hybrid conference "The EU-China Comprehensive Agreement on Investment" held on 11 July 2022 at the University of Birmingham. We are grateful to the colleagues who served as session chairs and discussants: Henok Asmelash (Birmingham Law School), Pasha L. Hsieh (Singapore Management University), Chukwuma Okoli (Birmingham Law School), Bryan Mercurio (Chinese University of Hong Kong), Chen Wei Zhu (Birmingham Law School), Jie (Jeanne) Huang (University of Sydney), Georgia Antonopoulou (Birmingham Law School), Geraldo Vidigal (University of Amsterdam).

Several other individuals deserve an acknowledgement for their friendship, support and collaboration in this research project, which greatly benefited from their feedback and efforts in publicizing the research findings: Martin Trybus, Paul McConnell, Heng Wang, Velimir Zivkovic.

Special thanks go to Laura Hofmann for patiently guiding us through the publication process.

We are also grateful to Jess Farr-Cox who helped improve the language quality of the manuscripts and Monica Chan for her editorial assistance.

The work on this volume was supported by the Asia Europe Comparative Studies Research Project—Academic Research Grant 2021 awarded by the Institute of European Studies of Macau.

5 May 2024 Alexandr SvetliciniiI-Ju Chen

Contents

Introduction: The EU-China Comprehensive Agreement on Investment and a Thorny Path Towards Investment Liberalisation . . . 1
Alexandr Svetlicinii and I-Ju Chen

Part I Geopolitical Origins and Negotiations of the EU-China Comprehensive Agreement on Investment

The Political Economy of the EU-China Comprehensive Agreement on Investment: Balancing the European Union's Economic Interests . . . 15
Duncan Freeman

The Political Economy of China and the EU-China Comprehensive Agreement on Investment . . . 37
Sohyun Zoe Lee

The European Union and China: In Search of Positioning and Exercising Normative Power in the Comprehensive Agreement on Investment . . . 51
I-Ju Chen

Part II EU-China Comprehensive Agreement on Investment: Substantive Issues

Pre-Entry National Treatment in EU-China Comprehensive Agreement on Investment: An Open Sesame to the Chinese Market? . . . 71
Xueji Su

The Disciplines of State-Owned Enterprises in the China-EU Comprehensive Agreement on Investment: Assessment, Implications and Directions . . . 95
Wei Yin

The EU-China Comprehensive Agreement on Investment: Disciplining Competition Law Enforcement in China? 121
Alexandr Svetlicinii

Intellectual Property Dimension of the EU-China Comprehensive Agreement on Investment: The EU Approach Against Non-Market-Mediated International Technology Transfer 143
Danny Friedmann

Regulating Subsidies in the EU-China Comprehensive Agreement on Investment: Implications for Global Subsidies Reform 169
Ben Czapnik

Disputing Personal Data in the EU-China Comprehensive Agreement on Investment 187
Mark McLaughlin

Part III EU-China Comprehensive Agreement on Investment: Procedural Issues

The Future of Investor-State Dispute Settlement in the EU-China Comprehensive Agreement on Investment 211
Ming Du

A New Dish of "CAI" for State-to-State Dispute Settlement in the EU-China Comprehensive Agreement on Investment 233
Anran Zhang

Never Fear to Negotiate: Options for Non-Adversarial Dispute Resolution in the EU-China Comprehensive Agreement on Investment 253
Sara Migliorini and Naina Gupta

Introduction: The EU-China Comprehensive Agreement on Investment and a Thorny Path Towards Investment Liberalisation

Alexandr Svetlicinii and I-Ju Chen

The negotiations on the EU-China Comprehensive Agreement on Investment (CAI) were launched by the parties in 2014 and concluded in principle on 30 December 2020, after thirty-five rounds of negotiations.[1] On that occasion, Ursula von der Leyen, the President of the European Commission, vowed that the CAI "will provide unprecedented access to the Chinese market for European investors, enabling our businesses to grow and create jobs".[2] The euphoria from the successfully completed negotiations didn't last long, as on 22 March 2021 the EU made use of its recently adopted EU Global Human Rights Sanctions Regime[3] and imposed sanctions on four Chinese officials and one entity in connection with the human rights situation in the Xinjiang Uyghur Autonomous Region.[4] In response, China moved

[1] See European Commission, EU-China agreement: Milestones and documents. https://policy.trade.ec.europa.eu/eu-trade-relationships-country-and-region/countries-and-regions/china/eu-china-agreement/milestones-and-documents_en.

[2] European Commission, EU and China reach agreement in principle on investment (30 December 2020), IP/20/2541. https://ec.europa.eu/commission/presscorner/detail/en/ip_20_2541.

[3] Council Regulation 2020/1998 of 7 December 2020 concerning restrictive measures against serious human rights violations and abuses, OJ L 410 I/1, 7 December 2020.

[4] Council Implementing Regulation 2021/478 of 22 March 2021 implementing Regulation (EU) 2020/1998 concerning restrictive measures against serious human rights violations and abuses, OJ L 99 I/1, 22 March 2021.

A. Svetlicinii (✉)
University of Macau, Faculty of Law, Macao SAR, China
e-mail: alexandrs@um.edu.mo

I.-J. Chen
School of Law, University of Exeter, Exeter, UK

© The Author(s), under exclusive license to Springer Nature Switzerland AG 2024

A. Svetlicinii, I.-J. Chen (eds.), *The EU-China Comprehensive Agreement on Investment*, European Yearbook of International Economic Law,
https://doi.org/10.1007/978-3-031-66862-3_1

to impose sanctions on "ten individuals and four entities on the EU side that severely harm China's sovereignty and interests and maliciously spread lies and disinformation".[5] As a result, the European Parliament concluded that its ability "to duly analyse the CAI is significantly hindered by the Chinese sanctions" and decided "that any consideration of the EU-China Comprehensive Agreement on Investment (CAI), as well as any discussion on ratification by the European Parliament, has justifiably been frozen because of the Chinese sanctions in place".[6]

Despite the current stalemate in the conclusion and ratification of the CAI, its importance cannot be underestimated, as it is the first bilateral investment treaty between the two major economic powerhouses and international norm entrepreneurs. The published texts of the agreement in principle and the parties' schedules of commitments and reservations[7] allow for a scholarly assessment of how "comprehensive" the CAI is in securing market access and competitive conditions for European investors doing business in China, the major declared objective pursued by the EU in the CAI negotiations. Such an assessment should provide an estimation of the "added value" of the CAI that was negotiated in the background of China's unilateral opening-up and liberalisation of its regulatory framework for foreign investment progressing in parallel with the EU's search for "strategic autonomy" and its attempts to ensure the "level playing field" for its companies both in the EU's own internal market and overseas. The CAI also merits an assessment in its capacity of being a type of a "WTO-extra"[8] or "BIT-extra" agreement covering a range of issues that are not addressed, at least between these parties, within the existing multilateral economic governance frameworks. Finally, as both the EU and China actively participate in international rule-making, the scrutiny of the CAI and the ascertaining of the compromise the parties have managed to achieve on a wide range of issues of investment regulation should provide a valuable reflection on the emerging developments in international economic law.

---

[5] Ministry of Foreign Affairs of the People's Republic of China, Foreign Ministry Spokesperson Announces Sanctions on Relevant EU Entities and Personnel (22 March 2021). https://www.fmprc.gov.cn/mfa_eng/xwfw_665399/s2510_665401/2535_665405/202103/t20210322_9170814.html. The sanctions were imposed on: Reinhard Butikofer (MEP, the Greens), Michael Gahler (MEP, European People's Party), Raphaël Glucksmann (MEP, Progressive Alliance of Socialists and Democrats), Ilhan Kyuchyuk (MEP, Renew Europe) and Miriam Lexmann (MEP, European People's Party), Sjoerd Wiemer Sjoerdsma (Dutch Parliament), Samuel Cogolati (Belgian Federal Parliament), Dovile Sakaliene (Seimas of the Republic of Lithuania), Adrian Zenz (Victims of Communism Memorial Foundation), Björn Jerdén (Swedish Institute of International Affairs), the Political and Security Committee of the Council of the European Union, the Subcommittee on Human Rights of the European Parliament, the Mercator Institute for China Studies, and the Alliance of Democracies Foundation.

[6] European Parliament resolution of 20 May 2021 on Chinese countersanctions on EU entities and MEPs and MPs (2021/2644(RSP)), para 10. See also Svetlicinii (2022a), pp. 217–239.

[7] European Commission, EU-China agreement in principle. https://policy.trade.ec.europa.eu/eu-trade-relationships-country-and-region/countries-and-regions/china/eu-china-agreement/eu-china-agreement-principle_en.

[8] See Horn et al. (2010), p. 1567.

With the aforementioned assessment objectives in mind, we have organized the discussion on the CAI along the following three themes, which correspond to the respective parts of this volume: (1) the outline of the strategic objectives and negotiating positions of the parties that would set one of the benchmarks for the assessment of the CAI's accomplishments; (2) the scrutiny of the substantive provisions of the CAI in order to ascertain their "added value" for investment liberalisation in relation to the existing bilateral and multilateral frameworks where both the EU and China participate; and (3) the analysis of the dispute resolution methods available to the parties under the CAI that would reflect on the overall effectiveness and enforceability of the agreement.

Following the established narrative, Part I of the book explores the geopolitical origins and negotiations of the CAI. It includes three contributions covering distinct elements of the negotiation process and analyzing the multiple objectives of the parties, with a special focus on market access, investment liberalisation, and the "level playing field" pursued by the EU. As Freeman notes in chapter "The Political Economy of the EU-China Comprehensive Agreement on Investment: Balancing the European Union's Economic Interests", "as EU policy documents make clear, the penetration of the market in China by European companies has been a central goal of the EU". In the aftermath of the 2008 global financial crisis, the investment relationships between the two sides appeared unbalanced in favor of China. As a result, the CAI was pursued by the EU to achieve reciprocity and a "level playing field". It was certainly not about the enhanced protection of European investments in China, as at the time of negotiations of the CAI, all but one EU Member State had BITs with China. The CAI's primary goal for the EU was to expand European FDI in China. The EU side frequently framed the lack of reciprocity in terms of existing regulatory barriers in China that precluded further expansion of EU-originating investments. European enterprises doing business in China have been frequently reporting various regulatory barriers that hinder or retard their investments. Consequently, the EU viewed the CAI as a tool for binding investment liberalisation, imposing on China enforceable obligations regarding openness towards FDI originating from the EU. The EU demanded from China "significantly improved market access for foreign companies as well as a level playing field and fair competition for business and investment, benchmarked at the level of openness provided for all companies operating in the EU market".[9] On the other hand, Freeman argues that the drive for CAI from the EU side cannot be explained by mere reciprocity concerns but rather by the increasing dependence of the EU companies on their investments in China, which compensated their losses on domestic and other foreign markets.

In chapter "The Political Economy of China and the EU-China Comprehensive Agreement on Investment", Lee argues that, for the Chinese government, incorporating higher investment standards in the CAI was equally pressing, as the

[9] Commission Communication (2016, June 22) Elements for a new EU strategy on China, JOIN 30 final, p. 5.

Transatlantic Trade and Investment Partnership (TTIP) had been progressing between the US and the EU since 2013 and the rigorous standards of the TTIP were expected to have negative repercussions for Chinese investors abroad. Lee demonstrates, among others, that the CAI has been largely driven by Beijing's conventional political and economic objectives at both domestic and international levels. The liberalisation obligations and comprehensive scope of CAI provisions would have pushed forward domestic reforms and strengthened the Chinese government's determination in relation to liberalising foreign investments in China.[10] At the international level, the CAI exhibits China's ambitions to take a greater role in shaping international investment rules, driven by intense global power dynamics.

Furthermore, Chen, in chapter "The European Union and China: In Search of Positioning and Exercising Normative Power in the Comprehensive Agreement on Investment", explores China's and the EU's respective positions in competing for normative power in international economic governance. The EU's and China's decades-long bilateral and, by now, strategic partnership has progressed to a high level of complexity. The two partners have developed diverging approaches according to their interpretations and prioritizations of international principles, norms, and values. The CAI appears to be a place where the EU and China demonstrate and exercise normative power in international economic governance. Chen argues that the conclusion of the CAI enabled the EU to re-construct its normative power identity, especially during the post-Brexit period.

Part II of the book discussing the substantive issues of the CAI starts with one of the most apparent manifestations of the EU's drive for binding investment liberalisation: the pre-establishment national treatment obligations. The 2015 report "Assessing "National Treatment (NT)" as a Basis for Securing Market Access"[11] prepared for the Commission identified several market access restraints that could be remedied by pre-entry national treatment obligations: market entry, government approvals, equity requirements, and technology transfer. China adopted its new Foreign Investment Law (FIL)[12] in 2019, which introduced several major changes to the existing regulatory framework: (1) the Foreign Investment Catalogue scheme was abrogated and superseded by the Negative List for Foreign Investment; (2) the corporate form restrictions on foreign-invested enterprises were repealed; and (3) the *ex ante* case-by-case authorization scheme was replaced by the pre-establishment national treatment and an *ex post* reporting mechanism. Nevertheless, despite this "partial opening-up", several attractive sectors remained closed for foreign investors, various administrative checks, including security reviews, persisted, the dominance of the SOEs undergoing consolidations[13] further increased market entry

[10] See also Wei (2018), pp. 170–202.

[11] Covington and Burling LLP, Assessing "National Treatment" as a Basis for Securing Market Access Under a Comprehensive Agreement on Investment with the PRC. Report prepared for the European Commission Directorate-General for Trade, 2015.

[12] Law of the People's Republic of China on Foreign Investment, adopted at the Second Session of the Thirteenth National People's Congress on 15 March 2019, came into force on 1 January 2020.

[13] See also Svetlicinii (2022c), pp. 17–28.

barriers for newcomers. This led to doubts about the added value of the pre-establishment NT in the CAI. As shown in the chapter "Pre-Entry National Treatment in EU-China Comprehensive Agreement on Investment - An Open Sesame to the Chinese Market?" authored by Su, the binding NT commitments provided in the CAI could at least secure the current level of market access for European investors. However, as argued by the author, these commitments have limited value in dealing with restrictions applicable to both domestic and foreign investors. One of such limitations concerns the invocation of NT in relation to the competitive advantages of SOEs that can be derived from various sources and justified on the grounds of security and public policy.[14]

Aware of the aforementioned limitations, the EU insisted on the inclusion of special SOE-tailored disciplines in the CAI. This move corresponds to the EU's emerging treaty practices and policy initiatives, such as the one jointly launched with the US and Japan,[15] referring to "unfair competitive conditions" created by the SOEs. In chapter "The Disciplines of State-Owned Enterprises in the China-EU Comprehensive Agreement on Investment: Assessment, Implications and Directions" on CAI's approach to regulating the SOEs, Wei distinguishes between "SOE-relevant rules" and "SOE-specific rules". The first group contains competitive neutrality obligations imposed on the government regulating the conduct of various market players, including SOEs. The second group of rules is directly applicable to the conduct of SOEs. The author examines the following "SOE-specific rules" included in the CAI: commercial considerations, non-discrimination, and transparency. Wei concludes that effective enforcement of these rules remains questionable given the lack of certainty associated with the interpretation of the concepts used therein, including "covered entities" and "commercial activity".

Another major irritant in EU-China economic relations is the issue of market-distorting subsidies. In the CAI negotiations, the EU was demanding both subsidies disciplines and greater transparency to facilitate the anti-subsidy investigations. As Czapnik notes in chapter "Regulating Subsidies in the EU-China Comprehensive Agreement on Investment: Implications for Global Subsidies Reform", bilateral agreements can sometimes serve as "building blocks" for multilateral reform in trade regulations. However, subsidies are not the type of issue that could be properly addressed in bilateral negotiations, as their effects are diffused globally and are not limited to a specific bilateral relationship. Explaining the relatively modest subsidies regulations included in the CAI, Czapnik concludes that it is not realistic to expect that the EU would have achieved all or even most of its broader subsidies-related objectives in the negotiations of a bilateral investment treaty.

Another frequently discussed issue related to the "level playing field" for European companies doing business in China concerns the competitive conditions on the Chinese markets. The SOEs dominate numerous economic sectors in China,

---

[14] Su (2022), pp. 545–571.

[15] Joint Statement on Trilateral Meeting of the Trade Ministers of the United States, Japan, and the European Union, 31 May 2018. https://ustr.gov/about-us/policy-offices/press-office/press-releases/2017/december/joint-statement-united-states.

acting as both trading partners and competitors for European investors, making the enforcement of competition law especially relevant. At times, the Chinese authorities enforcing the Anti-Monopoly Law (AML)[16] were accused of using competition rules strategically by targeting foreign companies while shielding domestic enterprises, especially the SOEs, from enforcement. As discussed in chapter "The EU-China Comprehensive Agreement on Investment: Disciplining Competition Law Enforcement in China?" by Svetlicinii, the CAI attempts to discipline the market conduct of the SOEs as potential suppliers or purchasers of foreign investors through the commercial considerations obligation applied to the "covered entities". The competition law would cover the market conduct of SOEs competing with foreign investors. However, as China's AML contains multiple objectives, protection of competitive conditions being only one of them, it appears problematic for the CAI provisions to effectively constrain the discretion of the Chinese enforcement authorities when applying competition rules in individual cases.[17] As a result, according to Svetlicinii, without formally discriminating among different enterprises, the AML provides the Chinese authorities with sufficient decision-making space for the protection of national economic interests that may be *de facto* discriminatory against foreign investors for the mere reason that the latter do not play the same role in China's economy as the domestic SOEs and private companies.

The ensuing chapter "Intellectual Property Dimension of the EU-China Comprehensive Agreement on Investment: The EU Approach against Non-Market-Mediated International Technology Transfer", authored by Friedmann, addresses China's "market-for-technology strategy", which refers to non-market-mediated technology transfer. Being an issue of high concern for China's major trading partners, the US and the EU, prohibitions against forced technology transfer were included in the US-China Economic and Trade Agreement,[18] and then in the CAI. Pressured by the EU and US, China explicitly prohibited forced technology transfer in its Foreign Investment Law and Administrative License Law[19] in 2019. The EU insisted on the inclusion of the relevant obligations in the CAI. However, as argued by Friedmann, the CAI lacks a monitoring and enforcement system that would ensure compliance with the respective provisions. In addition, the CAI is lacking a dedicated section on the protection and enforcement of intellectual property rights, which could create further uncertainties in the interpretation of the scope of the IPRs and enforcement procedures relevant to technology transfers.

[16] Anti-Monopoly Law of the People's Republic of China, adopted by the National People's Congress on 30 August 2007, came into force on 1 August 2008.

[17] See also Svetlicinii (2022b), pp. 37–72.

[18] Economic and Trade Agreement between the Government of the USA and the Government of the PRC (Phase One), concluded on 15 January 2020, came into effect on 14 February 2020.

[19] Administrative License Law of the People's Republic of China, adopted at the 4th session of the Standing Committee of the 10th National People's Congress on 27 August 2003, amended at the 10th Session of the Standing Committee of the Thirteenth National People's Congress on 23 April 2019.

Chapter "Disputing Personal Data in the EU-China Comprehensive Agreement on Investment" on data flows under the CAI, authored by McLaughlin, considers these issues in light of China's current regulatory framework, comprising of 2017 Cybersecurity Law,[20] the 2021 Data Security Law,[21] and the 2021 Personal Information Protection Law.[22] The author contrasts the EU's rights-based approach to the protection of personal data embedded in the General Data Protection Regulation[23] with China's securitization of the data protection regime. Overall, the CAI leaves personal data protection in the regulatory space of its signatories. The author's interpretation of the CAI provisions leads to the conclusion that data and data flows would be included within the ambit of protection in the CAI and thus subject to the same substantive protections as other assets. Under certain conditions, the national data regulations could be found inconsistent with the NT commitments or prohibition of setting performance requirements for foreign investors. McLaughlin then reviews the aforementioned requirements through the lens of the public policy exceptions. Given the lack of agreement on data regulation across jurisdictions, the CAI serves as the most prominent illustration of individual states securing the regulation of data flows in cross-border trade and investment.[24]

Part III of the book addresses the enforceability of the CAI obligations by assessing the available dispute resolution mechanisms. In chapter "A New Dish of "CAI" for State-to-State Dispute Settlement in the EU-China Comprehensive Agreement on Investment", Zhang introduces the state-to-state dispute settlement (SSDS) mechanism between the EU and China within the existing international investment regime. CAI establishes a comprehensive, detailed, and step-by-step arbitration mechanism compared with other investment treaties signed between China and the EU Member States. Zhang argues that the specified SSDS was designed with political expectations and shows a joint effort from both the EU and China to develop a reformative mechanism for the resolution of investment-related disputes.

The CAI does not include substantive investment protection standards as well as the corresponding investor-state dispute settlement (ISDS). While reaching an agreement in principle, the parties committed to continue negotiations on these issues and "endeavor" to conclude them within two years from the signature of the CAI. In chapter "The Future of Investor-State Dispute Settlement in the EU-China Comprehensive Agreement on Investment", Du explores the future of ISDS in the

---

[20] Cybersecurity Law of the People's Republic of China, adopted by the Standing Committee of the National People's Congress on 7 November 2016, came into force on 1 June 2017.

[21] Data Security Law of the People's Republic of China, adopted by the Standing Committee of the Thirteenth National People's Congress on 10 June 2021, came into force on 1 September 2021.

[22] Personal Information Protection Law of the People's Republic of China, adopted by the Standing Committee of the Thirteenth National People's Congress on 20 August 2021, came into force on 1 November 2021.

[23] Regulation (EU) 2016/679 of the European Parliament and of the Council of 27 April 2016 on the protection of natural persons with regard to the processing of personal data and on the free movement of such data, and repealing Directive 95/46/EC, OJ L 119, 4 May 2016.

[24] See also Chaisse (2023), pp. 73–89.

CAI. He argues that the divergence between the approaches to ISDS reform in the EU and China may not be unbridgeable. In view of the EU's proposed two-tier International Investment Court System (ICS) in the EU free trade agreements, Du shows that it is possible for China to agree on a two-tier ICS in the CAI. Du also states that "there are no strong reasons for China to oppose the EU's multilateral investment court (MIC) proposal, in particular after the EU indicated that the MIC proposal could take an open architecture".

Finally, in chapter "Never Fear to Negotiate: Options for Non-Adversarial Dispute Resolution in the EU-China Comprehensive Agreement on Investment", by Migliorini and Gupta, the two scholars explore the CAI model of the non-adversarial investment dispute resolution methods: negotiation, conciliation, and mediation. The authors find, *inter alia*, that the CAI provisions on non-adversarial dispute resolution generally follow the recent treaty practice of both signatories to include the respective dispute settlement methods in their trade and investment agreements. Nevertheless, the actual application of the consensual dispute settlement under the CAI will depend on whether the parties will be able to transform the current geopolitical tensions into a long-term strategy of peaceful cooperation, engagement, and dialogue that would make this dispute resolution venue more attractive.

Drawing upon the insights on investment liberalisation elaborated in the individual chapters, this book contributes to the understanding of the CAI as an example of international rule-making aimed at addressing investment-related issues in bilateral economic relations and setting the precedent for multilateral negotiations. First, both the EU and China are interested in maintaining investment liberalisation on a global scale and will continue engaging in international economic governance to promote these interests. Second, the CAI entails a type of "WTO-extra" or "BIT-extra" agreement covering a range of issues that are not addressed, at least between these parties, in the existing multilateral and bilateral economic governance frameworks. Finally, the CAI reveals both the opportunities and limitations concerning the enforceability of its binding commitments through the envisaged investment dispute settlement mechanisms, including the SSDS and a range of non-adversarial dispute resolution methods.

Despite the delay in the signing of the CAI, the Chinese officials continuously maintained that it "is a win-win deal reached by the two sides through consultation on the basis of many years of mutually beneficial cooperation and mutual trust. It is an economic and trade agreement with the highest level of openness, lowest market access threshold and the widest range of areas to date on the part of China. It is good for China, and even better for Europe".[25] From the EU's side, the European Parliament insisted in 2022 that the ratification of the CAI cannot proceed until the Chinese sanctions on the MEPs are lifted, while noting that "the CAI alone would not solve all issues ailing our economic and political relationship, and therefore has to be considered in the context of a strengthened and more assertive EU toolbox of

[25] Ministry of Foreign Affairs of the People's Republic of China, Foreign Ministry Spokesperson Wang Wenbin's Regular Press Conference on 30 March 2022. https://www.fmprc.gov.cn/mfa_eng/xwfw_665399/s2510_665401/202203/t20220330_10657752.html.

unilateral measures".[26] Speaking before the Mercator Institute for China Studies in 2023, shortly before her official visit to the PRC, the Commission's President von der Leyen remarked: "we have to recognise that the world and China have changed in the last three years – and we need to reassess CAI in light of our wider China strategy".[27]

In the absence of political progress on CAI, the two sides have continuously engaged in dialogue, discussing various aspects of their trade and investment relations.[28] For example, at the 24th EU-China Summit in 2023, the EU officials focused on the trade deficit with China and, without any references to the CAI, expressed an "expectation that China takes concrete action to improve market access and the investment environment for EU investors and exporters".[29] This approach yielded certain results, as exemplified by China's decision to facilitate European companies' compliance with the applicable cross-border data transfer regulations.[30]

At the same time, while acknowledging Beijing's shift from "reform and opening" to "security and control", the EU elevated the importance of its own economic security and national security in trade and investment relations with China. Following the start of the Russia-Ukraine war, the EU embarked on a path of strengthening its economic resilience and reducing dependency on China for supplies of certain products and raw materials,[31] tightening FDI screening in the critical sectors[32] and considering the adoption of an outbound investment control mechanism.[33]

---

[26] European Parliament resolution of 16 September 2021 on a new EU-China strategy (2021/2037(INI), OJ C 117/40, 11 March 2022, para 56.

[27] European Commission, Speech by President von der Leyen on EU-China relations to the Mercator Institute for China Studies and the European Policy Centre, 30 March 2023, SPEECH/23/2063, https://ec.europa.eu/commission/presscorner/detail/en/speech_23_2063.

[28] See European Commission, EU-China: Commission and China hold second High-level Digital Dialogue, 18 September 2023, IP/23/4488, https://ec.europa.eu/commission/presscorner/detail/en/ip_23_4488.

[29] European Council, 24th EU-China Summit: engaging to promote our values and defend our interests, 7 December 2023, https://www.consilium.europa.eu/en/press/press-releases/2023/12/07/24th-eu-china-summit-engaging-to-promote-our-values-and-defend-our-interests/.

[30] See European Commission, EU calls for greater market access and fair competition at EU-China High-Level Dialogue, 25 September 2023, IP/23/4609, https://ec.europa.eu/commission/presscorner/detail/en/ip_23_4609.

[31] See Regulation (EU) 2024/1252 of the European Parliament and of the Council of 11 April 2024 establishing a framework for ensuring a secure and sustainable supply of critical raw materials and amending Regulations (EU) No 168/2013, (EU) 2018/858, (EU) 2018/1724 and (EU) 2019/1020, OJ L 2024/1252, 3 May 2024.

[32] See European Commission, Proposal for a Regulation on the screening of foreign investments in the Union and repealing Regulation (EU) 2019/452 of the European Parliament and of the Council, COM(2024) 23 final, 24 January 2024.

[33] See European Commission, Speech by President von der Leyen at the European Parliament Plenary on the need for a coherent strategy for EU-China relations, 18 April 2023, SPPECH/2333, https://ec.europa.eu/commission/presscorner/detail/en/speech_23_2333.

During President Xi's visit to France in 2024, the Commission's President von der Leyen raised a number of issues in EU-China economic relations, including subsidized Chinese products on European markets, subsidized public tender bids, and first investigations under the International Procurement Instrument, as well as trade agreements with third countries to ensure supply of critical raw materials.[34] Speaking before the European Parliament's International Trade Committee in March 2024, the Commission's Executive Vice President Dombrovskis remarked that out of 184 trade defense measures in place, almost two thirds concerned China.[35] All of these are "defensive" trade policies that are leading away from the mutual opening up in terms of trade and investment. Naturally, the Chinese side reacted with dissatisfaction to the aforementioned trade defense measures, which reduced the confidence of the Chinese enterprises in carrying out trade and investment activities in Europe.[36] In their meetings with the European business community in China, the PRC officials attempted to enhance the confidence of foreign investors in China despite the "securitization" of certain areas.[37] Various governmental policies[38] attempted to instill confidence in foreign investors in times of geopolitical confrontations, albeit with limited success.

Regardless of the exact future trajectory of the CAI in terms of its prospective ratification, re-consideration, or abandonment following the EU's "de-coupling" or "de-risking" policy towards China, it sets an important benchmark for international economic rule-making. Therefore, it is our hope that the present volume will inform policy-making and rule-making activities in the domain of investment regulation and contribute to the mutually beneficial economic relationship between the two economic and normative power houses.

---

[34] European Commission, Press statement by President von der Leyen following the trilateral meeting with French President Macron and President of the People's Republic of China Xi Jinping, 6 May 2024, STATEMENT/24/2464, https://ec.europa.eu/commission/presscorner/detail/en/statement_24_2464.

[35] European Commission, Speech by Executive Vice-President Dombrovskis at the European Parliament International Trade (INTA) Committee, 21 March 2024, SPEECH/24/1643, https://ec.europa.eu/commission/presscorner/detail/en/speech_24_1643.

[36] See Ministry of Commerce of the PRC, The head of the Trade Remedy Bureau of the Ministry of Commerce made representations to the European side on the EU's investigation of foreign subsidies from China and other issues, 11 April 2024, http://www.mofcom.gov.cn/article/xwfb/xwsjfzr/202404/20240403501854.shtml.

[37] See e.g. Ministry of Commerce of the PRC, Ministry of Commerce holds European business symposium, 10 February 2023, http://www.mofcom.gov.cn/article/xwfb/xwbldhd/202302/20230203384261.shtml; Ministry of Commerce of the PRC, Ministry of Commerce holds roundtable with Belgian enterprises, 15 January 2024, http://www.mofcom.gov.cn/article/xwfb/xwbldhd/202401/20240103466536.shtml.

[38] See e.g. Notice by the General Office of the State Council of Issuing the Action Plan for Steadily Advancing High-level Opening up and Making Greater Efforts to Attract and Utilize Foreign Investment, No. 9 [2024] 28 February 2024.

References

Chaisse J (2023) 'The Black Pit': power and pitfalls of digital FDI and cross-border data flows. World Trade Rev 22:73–89
European Commission (2020, December 30) EU and China reach agreement in principle on investment, IP/20/2541. https://ec.europa.eu/commission/presscorner/detail/en/ip_20_2541
European Commission (2023, March 30) Speech by President von der Leyen on EU-China relations to the Mercator Institute for China Studies and the European Policy Centre. https://ec.europa.eu/commission/presscorner/detail/en/speech_23_2063
European Commission, EU-China agreement: milestones and documents. https://policy.trade.ec.europa.eu/eu-trade-relationships-country-and-region/countries-and-regions/china/eu-china-agreement/milestones-and-documents_en
European Commission, EU-China agreement in principle. https://policy.trade.ec.europa.eu/eu-trade-relationships-country-and-region/countries-and-regions/china/eu-china-agreement/eu-china-agreement-principle_en
European Parliament (2021, May 20) Resolution of 20 May 2021 on Chinese countersanctions on EU entities and MEPs and MPs (2021/2644(RSP))
European Parliament (2022, March 11) Resolution of 16 September 2021 on a new EU-China strategy (2021/2037(INI), OJ C 117/40
Horn H, Mavroidis PC, Sapir A (2010) Beyond the WTO? An anatomy of EU and US preferential trade agreements. World Econ 33(11):1565–1588
Ministry of Foreign Affairs of the People's Republic of China (2022, March 30), Foreign Ministry Spokesperson Wang Wenbin's Regular Press Conference on 30 March 2022. https://www.fmprc.gov.cn/mfa_eng/xwfw_665399/s2510_665401/202203/t20220330_10657752.html
Su X (2022) Liberalising the Chinese market: state-owned enterprise disciplines in the EU-China comprehensive agreement on investment. JWIT 23:545–571
Svetlicinii A (2022a) China's defense against secondary sanctions: lessons from the EU blocking statute. J Int Trade Law Policy 21(3):217–239
Svetlicinii A (2022b) China's merger control: competition assessment or foreign investment screening? KLRI J Law Legisl 12(1):37–72
Svetlicinii A (2022c) Consolidation of the state-owned enterprises in China: a missed opportunity for the EU merger control? JECL Pract 13(1):17–28
Wei Y (2018) Challenges, issues in China-EU investment agreement and the implication on China's domestic reform. APLR 26(2):170–202

Part I
Geopolitical Origins and Negotiations of the EU-China Comprehensive Agreement on Investment

The Political Economy of the EU-China Comprehensive Agreement on Investment: Balancing the European Union's Economic Interests

Duncan Freeman

Abstract The EU's pursuit of the CAI with China was based on economic interest. Since the initiation of formal relations between the EEC and China in 1975, economic interest has been the core of EU policy, and as EU policy documents make clear, the penetration of the market in China by European companies has been a central goal of the EU. In its initial period the EU-China relationship was dominated by trade, both in terms of policy and real economic exchanges. In the 2010s investment moved to the top of the EU agenda, and the EU became the demandeur for the CAI. In the EU's view, the relationship with China, including FDI, was unbalanced in favour of the latter. The relationship required rebalancing through what the EU called reciprocity and a level playing field. The CAI was a tool through which the imbalance between the open EU investment regime and the restrictive Chinese regime could be altered in favour of the interests of EU companies. However, this view of the lack of reciprocity in the EU-China relationship does not explain the EU's pursuit of the CAI, which must be understood in a wider context of political economy. The centring of FDI in EU policy occurred following the crisis of 2008 in which China became the driver of global economic growth while the EU economy stagnated. While on the surface investment between the EU and China was small, EU investment in China became increasingly important to European economies and companies. Rather than being driven by the exclusion of EU FDI in China, the EU pursuit of the CAI was driven by increasing dependence of EU economies and companies on investment in China. However, the penetration of the market in China was not equally distributed among EU member states, with some benefitting much more than others.

D. Freeman (✉)
ICHEC Brussels Management School, Brussels, Belgium
e-mail: dfreeman@ichec.be

© The Author(s), under exclusive license to Springer Nature Switzerland AG 2024

A. Svetlicinii, I.-J. Chen (eds.), *The EU-China Comprehensive Agreement on Investment*, European Yearbook of International Economic Law,
https://doi.org/10.1007/978-3-031-66862-3_2

1 Background

The EU spent eight years negotiating what it called a Comprehensive Agreement on Investment (CAI) with China, which was provisionally concluded by both sides in December 2020. The EU was the demandeur of the CAI, and made the agreement the centrepiece of its China policy during the years that it was being negotiated. From the EU side, pursuit of the CAI was justified by clear economic interest arguments. When the CAI was being negotiated their economic relationship had become highly important for both the EU and China. As was repeatedly pointed out on both sides, EU-China trade had become one of the most important trading relationships in the global economy. For the EU, China had become the largest single source of imports, and a growing market for exports second only to the US, while for China the EU was a second-largest single market after the US, as well as a significant source of imports. The importance of the trading relationship was emphasised in the statement often repeated by EU officials in the 2010s that the EU-China trade was valued at over one billion euros a day.[1]

Despite their high degree of interdependence, the EU claimed that its interests and those of its economic actors were not being served in the relationship. The CAI negotiation took place in a context of increasingly dominant negative views of the EU-China economic relationship in European policy, business and media circles. The view that the relationship was unbalanced was widely adopted in Europe, and in the EU-China relationship the benefits flowed to only the Chinese side. According to the EU, market penetration through investment by its companies in China had been very limited. Investment flows between the EU and China were indeed much smaller than trade flows. Over several years during the 2010s the EU investment flows to China declined from their earlier peak, which could be contrasted with a rise in FDI flows from China to the EU in the same period. In the European view, the disparity was attributed to the regulatory environments in the EU and China: while the EU has an open investment regime, that in China is highly restrictive, hence the need to create a level playing field.

Thus, the EU sought a "rebalancing" of the economic relationship which was framed in terms of reciprocity, and a level playing field in which the CAI was a central policy tool. The negotiation of the CAI was intended not merely to increase FDI flows to China, but also to achieve a fundamental change in China's policy on FDI, which in turn would have implications for the foundations of not only its external trade and investment relations but also for its entire economic system. While from a European point of view it did not resolve all outstanding problems, the agreed CAI text was welcomed by the EU, business organisations and member states,[2] most importantly Germany, which was the strongest supporter of its finalisation.[3] By contrast, the signing of the agreement was criticised by, politicians and

[1] European Commission (2019).

[2] European Commission (2020), ESF (2020), EUCCC (2020).

[3] BDI (2021).

NGOs who believed that it did not address important concerns such as environmental and labour rights with sufficient strength.[4]

The CAI touches on immediate questions of the role of FDI in the EU-China economic relationship and why the European side at the level of the EU and certain member states made the agreement central to their China strategy. The political economy of the CAI also raises general questions of why FDI occurs and what is the role of the state (or, in the case of the EU, a supra-national polity) in FDI. Although couched in the language of modern economic diplomacy, the EU pursuit of the CAI placed itself within the long European history of state policy seeking to penetrate global markets and restructure how the global economy functions in its favour.[5] Market penetration in China has been a longstanding policy goal of the EU dating to the early days of contemporary EU-China relations. European states have a history of hundreds of years of seeking market penetration in Asia, in which China was considered the greatest prize, reaching back to the beginning of the modern global economy and the establishment of the Portuguese maritime empire in Asia in the sixteenth century.[6] This reached its apogee in the nineteenth century after European powers, led by Great Britain, forced the opening of China's trading system in the Opium Wars.[7] While China's efforts to halt imports of opium were the proximate cause of war, the underlying problem was the large trade imbalance between the East India Company and China, which led to flows of specie to China, to which export of opium from India was the solution. The Opium Wars were the culmination of British efforts at rebalancing economic relations with China through policies intended to end the restrictive Canton system and fundamentally change how China conducted its commerce. The wars in China were only one example of nineteenth-century British free trade imperialism, which sought not just to open markets but to do so on the basis of a specific set of economic principles into which the world economy would be integrated, by force if necessary.[8] The recent policy of the EU and its member states has historical precedent, although in the past European and EU policy has generally given priority to trade in penetration of the China market. The recent priority of the EU given to investment focused on the CAI is historically a new development.

Many scholars argue that the EU adopts foreign economic policies based on the aggregation of demands of different interests or societal preferences.[9] The question of why demands are made at either the member state or societal level is central. The explanation of what today is called foreign direct investment (FDI) and its link to state policy has been a concern of political economy since the emergence of the

[4] ETUC (2021), Zhang (2021).

[5] Bartels (2007).

[6] Russell-Wood (1992), Kamen (2004), Wolf (2010).

[7] Cain and Hopkins (1980), Cain (1999), Arrighi (2010), Wolf (2010), Buzan and Lawson (2015), Ferguson (2018).

[8] Arrighi (2010), Wolf (2010), Buzan and Lawson (2015).

[9] Woolcock (2012), Young and Peterson (2014).

modern global capitalist economy. The question was addressed by classical political economists from Adam Smith onwards. In the later nineteenth century, Marxist political economy, most famously exemplified by VI Lenin, sought to explain the phenomenon. These political economists explained outward investment through variations of a common theme of a decline in return on capital or the rate of profit in the source economy.[10] There was however, another dimension to their discussion, as they were not only explaining investment, but also why states engaged in the acquisition of colonies in the case of Smith or imperialism in the case of Hobson and Lenin.[11] The late Victorian period was a golden age of cross-border investment, and also imperialism.[12]

The emergence of a new stage of global investment in the post-war period brought renewed efforts to explain outward investment.[13] Many models that have sought to explain FDI flows that have been proposed focus on different features of the phenomenon.[14] In these, the action of states was largely eliminated by models based on the firm and markets. This was reinforced by the prevailing ideology in the West in which market liberalism came to dominate. Historically, the imposition of controls on investment flows has been a feature of the development of industrialised economies. Indeed, it has been argued that it is key to successful development and industrialisation, in Europe, the US as well as East Asia.[15] However, the removal of state intervention from domestic and international economic transactions became the prevailing orthodoxy in developed economies of the West, whose corporations also dominated global trade and investment flows, and the removal of barriers to trade and investment the recommended policy prescription for all economies. In the late twentieth century, this culminated in proliferation of belief in ideas such as a borderless world, and the decline of the role of the state in the international economy.[16]

The EU policy focuses on one particular determinant of FDI flows in the form of regulatory barriers. Arguably, by focusing on regulatory barriers the EU is following an analysis based in institutional economics, which has become common in attempts to explain FDI flows,[17] much of which is derived from the work of North on institutions which was based on transaction costs.[18] The EU analysis is less sophisticated than this and is based on a more simplistic view than the work of North on institutions. Leaving aside its somewhat simple policy framework, the

[10] Smith (1976), Hobson (1902), Lenin (1933).

[11] Hobson (1902), Lenin (1933).

[12] Arrighi (2010), Wolf (2010), Buzan and Lawson (2015).

[13] Kindleburger (1969), Vernon (1971),

[14] Johanson and Vahlne (1977), Hennart (2000), Dunning (2001), Blonigen (2005), Cantwell et al. (2010).

[15] Chang (2004).

[16] Vernon (1971), Strange (1988, 1996), Ohmae (1995), Evans (1997).

[17] Dunning and Lundan (2008), Peng et al. (2008), Marinova et al. (2012), Stoian (2013).

[18] North (1981, 1984, 1990, 1994).

question of why the EU chose this particular focus of rebalancing one regulatory element in the EU-China relationship touches on the problem of the role of the state in the international economy.

Despite the orthodoxy of the Washington Consensus that states and markets are, or can be, separate, and the role of the state in the economy should be minimised, states have been central actors in the market and international economy.[19] Those states that have espoused the ideology of free trade since the nineteenth century, or more recently the Washington Consensus or neoliberalism, continued to expand the realm of the market in the global economy, even if this is now usually through economic diplomacy rather than gunboat diplomacy. The CAI was an opportunity for the EU to attempt to exert what scholars have called its market or trade power[20] or normative power[21] and achieve an ambitious agenda in China.[22] The imperialist policies of the nineteenth century were abandoned, and trade and investment agreements (multilateral, plurilateral or bilateral) and other instruments proliferated in order to remove the barriers, accomplished by economic diplomacy or foreign economic policy.

In the standard account that the EU offers of the pursuit of the CAI based on the necessity rebalancing and reciprocity, EU policy remains unexplained beyond this elementary justification. According to this account of the EU-China economic relationship, FDI has been a minor part of the exchange that has been imbalanced in favour of China. Thus, there was a need for reciprocity to increase European FDI penetration in China. As will be discussed below, in fact this was not the case, as EU FDI in China had become an essential element of the relationship. The necessity of the CAI cannot be explained by the lack of market penetration or an imbalance in favour of China. There is a considerable difference between reciprocity in terms of regulation and barriers to investment and the real economy that is not revealed in the basic statistics on investment flows usually cited to support this argument. Both the importance and nature of the investment relationship and the balance of the benefits are very different from how they are normally portrayed in the EU. This became fundamental to the relationship in the period following the North Atlantic crisis of 2008 and when the EU began focusing on FDI and negotiation of the CAI with China. The investment relationship between the EU and China and the need for the CAI became systemically significant in the structure of the real economic relationship in the post-crisis period. The state-led opening of investment in China by the EU and its member states through the CAI was necessary to maintain the viability of EU economies and companies in the post-2008 crisis period. At the same time, the CAI became the tool with which the EU believed systemic change in the Chinese economy could be pursued.

---

[19] Smith (1976), List (1909), Hirschman (1945), Krasner (1976), Weiss (1998), Palan et al. (1999).

[20] Damro (2012), Meunier and Nicolaidis (2005).

[21] Whitman (2011).

[22] European Commission (2016, 2019).

2 EU-China Policy Context: The Primacy of Economic Interests

The EU pursuit of the CAI was rooted in its longstanding policy of seeking market access in China, but the negotiation of the agreement took place in a rapidly changing economic and political context. The CAI has usually been justified in Europe by the need for reciprocity in the bilateral relationship, but both global and domestic factors were also important in determining the context in which the EU and its member states conducted policy on the CAI. From the 1990s domestic and external EU economic policy focused on removing barriers to trade and investment. Domestically this brought about the creation of the single market that removed barriers to flow of goods, services, capital and people, and the application of regulatory principles that limited the role of the state in the economy. Externally the EU abandoned the idea of creating a protectionist fortress Europe in favour of the pursuit of "liberal" market norms in international trade and investment.[23] This was manifested in the EU's external economic policy conducted through the means of multilateralism at the WTO and other fora. Later, following the failure of mulitateralism, this focused on regional and bilateral agreements.

Since the European Economic Community (EEC) and China established diplomatic relations in 1975, China has emerged as a major global economy which has become central to an evolving relationship with the EU.[24] The EU-China relationship was defined by economics in their trade agreements of 1978 and 1985,[25] which became the formal basis of their relations. These placed economic interest at the core of their relationship, with the expectation that the exchange would be mutually beneficial. In policy documents on China issued in the 1990s, the growing importance of China was recognised and the development of the Chinese economy was seen as positive for the EU. This was not just because of the growth of the Chinese economy, but also its process of reform, which entailed liberalisation and opening. The EU expected that the Chinese economy would transition through the domestic reform process in which Brussels would be an active partner. The European Commission stated that 'China's market could become the largest in the world in many high-tech sectors, from telecommunications to aircraft and from computers to energy. An active role for EU business in China, where US and Japanese competition is already fierce, is essential'.[26]

The EU policy was intended to create greater market access for its companies in China,[27] to be achieved through multilateral means and also bilateral negotiation.[28] At this stage, the EU was committed to multilateralism, and the strategic tool of its

[23] Hanson (1998).

[24] Naughton (2007), Breslin (2007), Brandt and Rawski (2008), Ash (2007).

[25] EEC (1978), EEC (1985).

[26] European Commission (1995).

[27] Ibid.

[28] European Commission (1995, 1998).

policy was WTO accession for China. The ultimate goal was the integration of China into the global economy as it was conceived in the EU.[29] Imbalances in the relationship were recognised but were downplayed in favour of prioritising long-term goals. The trade relationship, and its imbalance, far outweighed the significance of investment, but market penetration through improving the climate for European investment in China, even at this stage, was stated as one of the EU's objectives.[30]

While China's WTO accession in 2001 was a major policy success for the EU, the subsequent rapid emergence of China as an economic power began to weigh on EU policy-making. On the one hand, in 2003, the two sides initiated a Comprehensive Strategic Partnership (CSP), which might be considered a high point in the relationship, and in policy documents on China the two sides acknowledged their importance to each other.[31] On the other, even as the EU recognised that its economic interests were linked to growth in China, it also believed that there were imbalances in trade that were the result of China's growth model, which required China to open its market to 'fair competition'.[32] In the earlier period the EU had been content to support the structural transition of the Chinese economy, but by the 2000s, despite the transformation that had occurred, the structure of the Chinese economy began to be considered a problem in Europe.[33] Thus, the later framing of the relationship was prefigured, as the Commission stated that 'driving a fair bargain with China will be the central challenge of EU trade policy in the decade to come'.[34] This introduced the idea of the need to level the playing field, even if at this time the gains continued to be seen as outweighing the losses in the relationship.[35]

These concerns presaged a much greater shift, precipitated by the financial and economic crisis that originated in the US and the EU in 2008, although its impact was largely unspoken in EU policy documents on China. The EU continued to recognise the economic importance of China, and the linkage between EU prosperity and growth in China,[36] but by this time the way in which this was framed had changed. According to the EU there was a fundamental imbalance that required correction. The policy document issued by the EU in 2016 gave high priority to promoting what it called 'reciprocity, a level playing field and fair competition across all areas of co-operation'.[37] This was an elevation of the themes of the need for EU access to China, including specifically for investment, expressed in previous policy documents. The problem was to be addressed through the new instrument of the

[29] European Commission (1995, 1998, 2001, 2003).

[30] European Commission (1998).

[31] European Commission (2003), Ministry of Foreign Affairs (2003).

[32] European Commission (2006a).

[33] European Commission (2006a, 2006b).

[34] European Commission (2006a).

[35] European Commission (2006b).

[36] European Commission (2016).

[37] Ibid.

CAI, the negotiation of which was initiated in 2013, and which became the tool to achieve EU policy goals in China.

The use of reciprocity is not new to international economic policy. The idea dates back at least to nineteenth-century Britain, and it has been used by other states, notably by the US in its trade conflicts with Japan.[38] The argument for reciprocity is usually used by states that have adopted free trade policies when they are faced with states that fail to adopt free trade. Arguments based on reciprocity have constituted a response to trade barriers, to bring about policy change and open markets. While the EU use of reciprocity as a policy goal is applied generally to China, in this case, the focus has been increasingly on investment through the CAI.

The basic goals of the EU remained largely unchanged and were defined as market access, a level playing field and fair competition for business and investment.[39] According to the EU, these should be 'benchmarked' at the level of openness of the EU market,[40] while the previously existing positives of the relationship no longer existed, and this was linked with the unprecedented scale and speed of China's development. In parallel with this the EU increasingly focused on what it claimed was the failure of China to pursue reforms that would open its economy to foreign companies. In 2019 the EU again placed the question of balance at the forefront of its policy. The policy document issued in 2019 by the Commission indicated even more clearly that there had been a significant change in the relationship and the distribution of benefits, stating that 'there is a growing appreciation in Europe that the balance of challenges and opportunities presented by China has shifted'.[41] This change in language and priorities was reinforced by the fact that the document included an entire section on what it called a balanced and reciprocal trade and investment relationship.[42] Thus the CAI emerged in this broad context, and became the foundation stone of the policy of rebalancing and reciprocity.

From the early period of the formal relationship between the EU and China, the main policy focus was on goods trade, as reflected in the early trade agreements.[43] This was natural enough, as goods trade constituted by far the most important part of their economic relationship and, as the EU policy documents themselves often noted, it was also where there were significant imbalances and frictions, which grew with the bilateral trade. While not abandoning the goods trade agenda, EU policy shifted toward other areas, notably services and investment, which became marked in the 2010s[44] and recognised important elements in the economic relationship that had been previously neglected. Services were a key sector for the EU economy where its companies held significant advantages, the EU being the world's largest

[38] Bhagwati and Irwin (1987).

[39] European Commission (2016).

[40] Ibid.

[41] European Commission (2019).

[42] Ibid.

[43] EEC (1978), EEC (1985).

[44] Brenton (2000).

importer and exporter of services,[45] and where access to the market in China was restricted. Foreign direct investment was a fundamental element of the global economy and globalisation but where the EU-China flows were insignificant.

Foreign Direct Investment, which, unlike trade under the WTO, has no global regulatory regime, has generally been governed internationally by regional and bilateral agreements. When the CAI negotiation was initiated all but one of the then 27 EU member states had a Bilateral Investment Treaty (BIT) with China. These were agreements that European states had begun signing with China in the 1980s after it initiated the policy of economic reform and opening, in which FDI was central from the beginning. In 1979 China adopted the Equity Joint Venture Law, and the first Special Economic Zones, designed to attract foreign investment, were established in 1980. One common explanation for such agreements, which were pursued by China and other developing countries, was that they provided a substitute for what was considered to be institutional weaknesses in developing countries, although their impact on actual investment flows generally has been shown to be marginal.[46] Several of these agreements with European governments were renewed and upgraded in the years before the CAI negotiations were commenced. The CAI would replace individual EU member state agreements, going beyond the traditional investment protection of BITs as a "comprehensive" agreement and driven by what the EU called an "ambitious agenda" centred on reciprocity.

While the term reciprocity had been used previously in describing the EU policy goals, in the post-crisis period the term and its apparent synonym of a level playing field were increasingly deployed in European rhetoric that was linked to questions of market access in China. The lack of reciprocity was framed in the EU as a question of regulatory barriers: China's barriers to trade and investment were contrasted with the EU's openness. According to this argument, the real economic relationship was imbalanced because of the regulatory inequality. The rebalancing was to be achieved through creating reciprocity and a level playing field and the CAI was a tool through which this agenda could be advanced.

3 Trade and Investment: Context and Consequences

The negotiation of the CAI was initiated in a period of dramatic change in the bilateral and global economic context that is generally unacknowledged in official EU policy documents on China. Following the formal agreements of 1978 and 1985, trade expanded rapidly, notably from the 1990s, but the greatest period of expansion occurred in the 2000s. This was a period of growing integration of China in the world economy after its WTO accession and creation of global supply chains when multinational companies were investing in increasingly complex production

[45] Eurostat (2017).

[46] Guzman (1997), Tobin and Rose-Ackerman (2005), Neumayer and Spess (2005), Ginsburg (2005).

systems, and was a high point of globalisation when international trade and investment flows were growing rapidly.

The expansion of economic exchange between the EU and China and the latter's rising global economic role was the result of policies of reform and opening adopted under Deng Xiaoping in the late 1970s without which China would not have been an active actor in globalisation. Opening to foreign investment was a central feature of the policy, initiated by the adoption of the Equity Joint Venture Law in 1979 and establishment of the first Special Economic Zones in 1980, intended to attract capital, technology and know-how to modernise the Chinese economy,[47] although FDI inflows only became significant for China in the 1990s.

The opening of China coincided with a period when what has been variously described as the Washington Consensus, neoliberalism or globalisation, which sought to expand trade and investment flows, was being pursued by major Western economic powers. The early 2000s were the apogee of the post-Cold War period of globalisation and Western global military, political and economic power that commenced with the fall of the Berlin Wall in 1989 and the subsequent collapse of the Soviet Union. China's WTO accession in 2001 was apparently symbolic of the dominance of the West in structuring the global economy and the integration of China in the system. Following China's WTO accession, its economic rise measured by domestic growth accelerated, bringing with it an increasing role in the global economy through expanded trade and inward investment.

At the time of China's WTO accession, EU policy-makers generally considered that its deficit on bilateral trade was not large enough to pose a significant macroeconomic problem in Europe. As a whole, the external trade and current account of the EU was more or less in balance, or even in surplus. Nevertheless, views of the economic relationship with China were often divided on a national and sectoral basis. Member states with an ideological propensity toward free trade policies and those economic sectors that were not severely impacted by competition from China or that benefited from trade and investment flows tended to emphasise the benefits of the relationship, while those with less ideological commitment to free trade and industries that suffered from competition adopted more strongly protectionist positions. The EU position was generally supportive of trade with China, but the outcome on specific trade defence issues often depended on the positions of key member states and sectors.[48] At this time the apparent negative consequences of trade with China could be balanced by arguments for the positive effects, notably for consumers, and the actual and potential benefits of the growing Chinese market. Furthermore, in the 2000s, the outlook for the EU, its economy and position in the world appeared positive. Steps toward European integration, and notably the creation of the euro, seemed to have established a global economic power that was enjoying stronger economic performance than in the 1990s. The EU was playing a leading role in the construction of a globalised economy based on the free-market

[47] Chen (2018).

[48] De Bièvre and Eckhardt (2010), Eckhardt (2011).

capitalism that it advocated and from which it would be a major beneficiary and in which China would be integrated on terms determined by the West.

Historically, Europe has been an exporter of capital in the global capitalist economy. Europe, above all Britain, was a major exporter of capital in the nineteenth century, financing investment not only in its own Empire but also elsewhere.[49] In the post-World War II period, while the US was the primary global investor, Europe nevertheless re-emerged as an investor when its economy recovered and in the period of globalisation beginning in the 1980s the EU became a major source of investment. The expansion of globalised investment flows from the 1980s took place in a successor of the global economic system established at Bretton Woods for the post-war period, which was dominated by the US. Intended to avoid the failures of pre-WWWorld War II policy that led to the Great Depression of the inter-war years, outside the Soviet bloc the US sustained the system and global economic growth. But the system was not sustainable in the long term and the US delinking the dollar from gold in 1973 brought an end to Bretton Woods. Europe, which had depended on inflows of American capital and its market for exports in the post-war years, had benefited from the system centred on the US. After the demise of the Bretton Woods system, dependence endured into the 1990s and 2000s with the US continuing as the EU's largest single export market. By then the twin government and current account deficits of the US were linked through imports of goods and capital in which the trans-Atlantic relationship with Europe played a central role.

This was the period in which the growth of major Western economies including the EU was sustained by rising levels of debt and financialisation, manifested in the EU by increasing imbalances between surplus and deficit member states in the eurozone.[50] The capital and goods flows between surplus and deficit states became a central driver of growth within the EU, especially in the eurozone as credit flows to member states in the north to southern Europe created demand for German exports in particular.[51] China, by providing cheap imports and helping to keep inflation and interest rates low, was a factor in sustaining the system in which rising levels of debt and asset inflation replaced wage and productivity increases as the means by which living standards were maintained. This occurred at a time of increased global capital flows dominated by those between Europe and the US.[52] China, while it had become a significant destination for FDI, and the largest in the developing world, nevertheless remained a relatively minor element in these global capital flows.

The system of capital and trade flows within the EU and across the Atlantic broke down in the crisis of 2008. As Tooze points out, the crisis was North Atlantic in its genesis, although the origins in the US and EU were different.[53] In the EU, the crisis

[49] Cain and Hopkins (1980), Cain (1999), Arrighi (2010), Wolf (2010), Buzan and Lawson (2015), Ferguson (2018).

[50] Stiglitz (2016), Varoufakis et al. (2011), Tooze (2018).

[51] Varoufakis et al. (2011), Tooze (2018), p. 105.

[52] Tooze (2018).

[53] Tooze (2018), p. 5.

was rooted in the creation of the euro, which was a structurally flawed economic and political project.[54] In the early years of its existence the euro performed relatively well, and European growth accelerated,[55] although it was not evenly distributed and even in Germany, the dominant EU economy, it remained weak.[56] The fundamental flaws in the design of the euro remained unresolved, resulting in the system almost collapsing in the crisis years after 2008.

The North Atlantic crisis of 2008 was a watershed for the global economy. Nowhere was this more the case than the domestic EU economy, but the crisis was also a watershed its relationship with China. The policy choices of the US and EU in responding to the crisis diverged considerably.[57] The solution adopted in the EU was austerity and structural reform imposed on debtor member states by the "Troika" of the International Monetary Fund, European Central Bank and European Commission and backed by lenders, of which Germany was the most important. The US adopted a policy of stimulus that led to a moderate economic recovery after 2009, while the austerity policy adopted in the EU was '[o]ne of the worst self-inflicted economic disasters on record' that extended and deepened the crisis.[58] The result was that the structural failings of the EU, especially those of the euro, internal division over policy and the imposition of austerity policies after the crisis weakened the position of the EU in the global economy.[59]

The long-term weakening of the Transatlantic economy decisively accelerated the shift of the global economic centre of gravity to East Asia, centred on China. Both the US and EU were major export markets for China, and the contribution of exports to growth had been important to China's economic development from the 1980s, and especially in the 2000s when it peaked prior to the crisis. The collapse of markets in the EU and US in the crisis had a direct negative impact on the Chinese economy through the trade vector. The Chinese government's policy of economic stimulation mitigated the short-term negative consequences of the decline in its key markets, but had the longer-term result that China became the single most important driver of global growth. Tooze argues that China's response to the crisis it imported from the West was of world historic proportions, dramatically accelerating the shift of the global balance of economic activity toward East Asia.[60] China's stimulus package was one of largest in world, both in relative and absolute terms and not only had a domestic impact, but aided all of its trading partners.[61] The crisis and the policy response also shifted China's economic development pattern away from what had been relatively high reliance on exports to domestic investment and increasing

---

[54] Stiglitz (2016), Sinn (2014), Varoufakis et al. (2011), Tooze (2018).

[55] Tooze (2018).

[56] Stiglitz (2016).

[57] Stiglitz (2016), Varoufakis et al. (2011), Tooze (2018).

[58] Tooze (2018).

[59] Ibid.; Varoufakis et al. (2011), Stiglitz (2016).

[60] Tooze (2018), p. 7.

[61] Ibid., p. 255.

consumption, although this was accompanied by increased levels of debt in the economy.

China's response contrasted with the policies of austerity adopted in the EU, which failed to restart economic growth. Even though the EU eventually recovered from the worst of the economic and financial crisis, growth in many member states has generally remained weak. China, while negatively impacted by the immediate crisis in its major export markets, did not suffer to the same degree. The stimulus policy enabled China to continue strong growth, and this had important consequences for the EU's relationship with China that became central in the negotiation of the CAI. Broadly, these can be described as increased EU dependence on Chinese growth, and more specifically greatly increased importance of investment in the bilateral relationship. Furthermore, the specifics of how this occurred were major factors in determining the relationship of individual member states with China. The importance that the EU attached to the CAI and its ambitious agenda of market penetration can be placed in this post-crisis context.

Post-crisis, the growth of EU exports to China accelerated as imports were drawn in by the stimulus programmes implemented by the Chinese government. According to Eurostat statistics, EU exports to China doubled from €72.4 billion in 2008 to €145.1 billion in 2014.[62] As a result of increased demand, China became the second-largest EU export destination after the US, and the EU trade deficit with China ceased growing at the same rate as prior to the crisis. Nevertheless, the benefits were not equally distributed across all EU member states and economic sectors: the primary beneficiary was Germany, which enjoyed rapid expansion of its exports to China from €34.0 billion in 2008 to €74.9 billion in 2014, accounting for roughly half of EU exports to China, and its trade balance moved into surplus, which has been sustained ever since.[63] Other major EU economies all enjoyed export growth to China in the post-crisis period, but this was significantly less than Germany, and their trade balances mostly continued to be in deficit. The acceleration of EU export growth to China was most obvious in the period immediately following the crisis, and has tailed off since then, including for Germany, but China has remained the EU's second-largest export destination, despite disruption of the global economy by COVID.

The EU export growth to China in the post-crisis period was the most obvious immediate effect of the shift in their economic relationship. On the surface, statistics on FDI appear to show, as has been argued by the EU, that it is far less important than trade in the EU-China relationship and from an EU perspective actually declined in importance after reaching a peak in 2013. As Fig. 1 shows, in 2008 EU FDI flows to China were €5.9 billion and in 2013 EU 27 FDI flows to China reached a peak of €21.4 billion, but fell in subsequent years, and were only €2.8 billion in 2020.[64] Of this, Germany accounted for the largest share of EU FDI going to China,

[62] https://ec.europa.eu/eurostat/data/database. International Trade In Goods.

[63] https://ec.europa.eu/eurostat/data/database. European Union Direct Investments.

[64] Ibid.

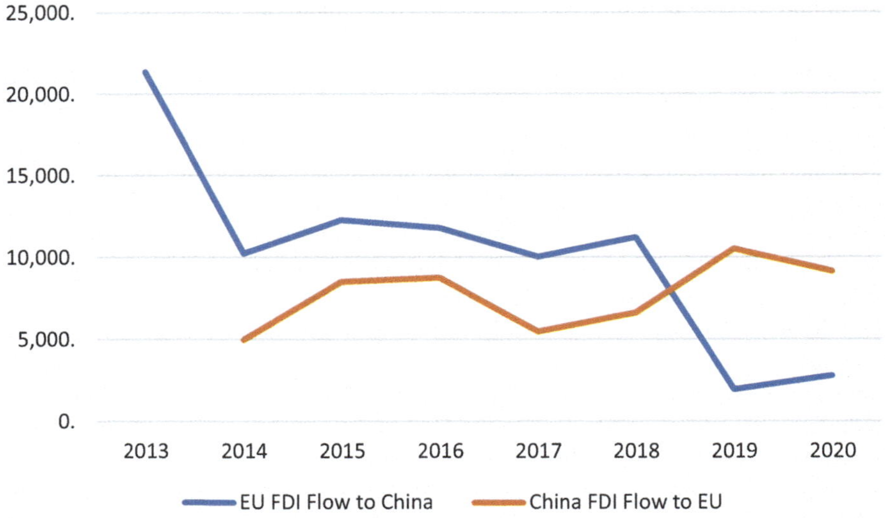

Fig. 1 EU-China FDI Flows (€ million). Source: Eurostat

with €9.4 billion of the flows in 2013, and €3.4 billion in 2019. Among the other major EU economies, France contributed €1.6 billion and Italy €402.1 million in 2013, while in 2020 flows from France were €1.3 billion and from Italy they were €1.6 billion.[65] By contrast, in 2014 FDI inflows from China were €5.0 billion, and fluctuated in subsequent years, but were €9.2 billion in 2020 (Fig. 1).[66]

As a consequence, the EU FDI stock in China has increased. According to Eurostat, as Fig. 2 shows, in 2019 the stock of EU investment in China was €201.2 billion, compared with €120.2 billion in 2013,[67] and had increased every year in the intervening period. Of this, Germany once again dominated, accounting for an FDI stock of €84.6 billion in 2019.[68] Nevertheless, this remained a relatively small amount compared to the total EU outward FDI stock, and also the stock of investment in countries such as the US which was €2.1 trillion in 2020. In addition to being the largest single trade partner and export market, the US has also been the largest source and destination of FDI to and from the EU.

The FDI flows and stocks do not tell the whole story of EU investment in China. In the post-crisis period, both exports and investment in China have become vitally important to the EU economy. Indeed, investment in China has arguably displaced trade as the most important part of the relationship. This is demonstrated by the turnover of affiliates of EU companies in China (those entities in China with EU investment). As Fig. 3 shows, according to Eurostat statistics the turnover of EU

[65] Ibid.

[66] Ibid.

[67] Ibid.

[68] Ibid.

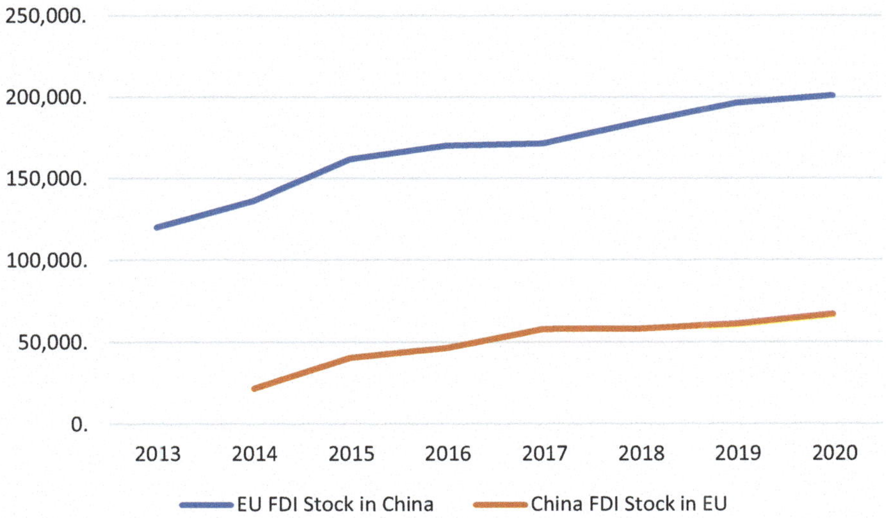

Fig. 2 EU-China FDI Stock(€ million). Source: Eurostat

affiliates in China increased from €192 billion in 2010 to €383.4 billion in 2018 (Chart 3).[69] By 2017, the turnover of EU affiliates in China was greater than EU exports to China. While investment flows to China are still significantly less than those to the US, in the post-crisis period the turnover of EU affiliates in China has grown much more rapidly than that of affiliates in the US. There was, however, a huge difference between member states. As Fig. 4 shows, the turnover of Germany's affiliates in China rose from €74.1 billion in 2010 to €192.5 billion in 2019 and was close to the amount they received from the US, for French affiliates turnover increased from €40.0 billion in 2010 to €77.8 billion in 2019, while that for Italian affiliates from €9.8 billion in 2010 to €15.7 billion in 2019.[70]

EU investment income from China has also grown rapidly, and while the amount does not match that from the US, China has become a significant source of income in some member states. In the case of Germany, over the post-crisis period investment income from China has matched that from the US. According to Eurostat statistics, in 2020 Germany's direct investment income from China was €11.0 billion, while for France investment income from China was €1.2 billion and Italy also €1.2 billion.[71] By comparison, the figures for direct investment income from the US were €13.4 billion for Germany, €7.9 billion for France and €1.4 billion for Italy.[72] Even though FDI stocks in China are relatively small, investment income is high because the return on investment in China has been amongst the highest of any EU

[69] https://ec.europa.eu/eurostat/data/database. Foreign Controlled Enterprise Statistics.

[70] Ibid.

[71] https://ec.europa.eu/eurostat/data/database. European Union Direct Investments.

[72] Ibid.

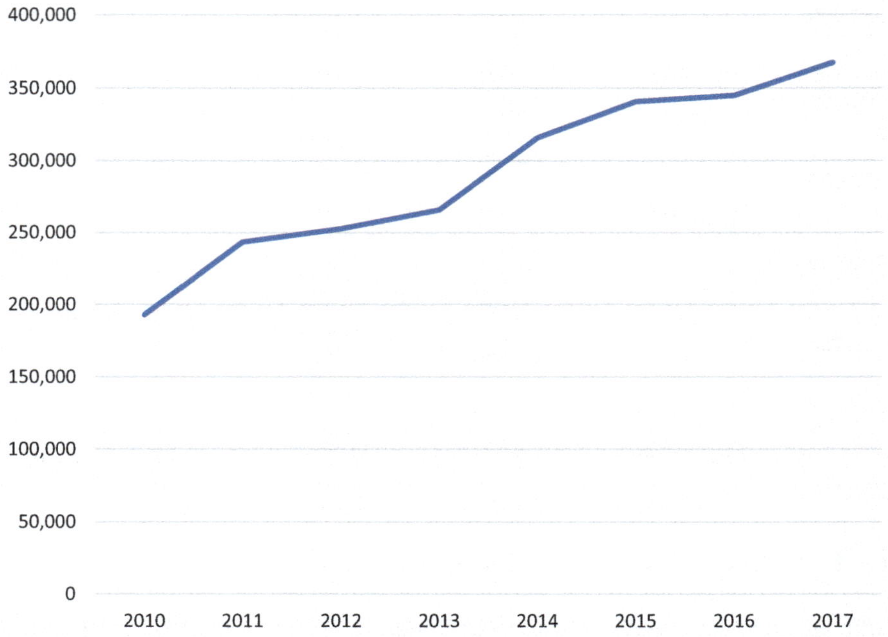

Fig. 3 Turnover of EU Affiliates in China (€ million). Source: Eurostat

FDI destination in the world. The result has been that, for many EU companies, notably those from Germany, China has become the most important source of growth since the crisis. Exports have been an important factor in this growth, but very often this has been achieved through investment.

The changes that took place in trade and investment following the crisis of 2008 in the North Atlantic economy are evidence of the consequent change in the structure of the EU-China-China economic relationship. While the initial effects were primarily seen in trade, over the longer-term the bigger impact was in investment. On the surface, China continued to be a relatively minor destination for EU FDI, but underlying this was a huge increase in the benefits that the EU derived from investment in China. Furthermore, even though the benefits derived from investment in China were spread across EU member states, this was not evenly distributed, with by far the biggest beneficiary being Germany.

4 Conclusion

The pursuit of the CAI was adopted as the central goal of EU policy on China and it was negotiated in a period when the European view of the relationship between the EU and China was increasingly negative. The EU officially declared the relationship was unbalanced in favour of China, and investment was considered to be a

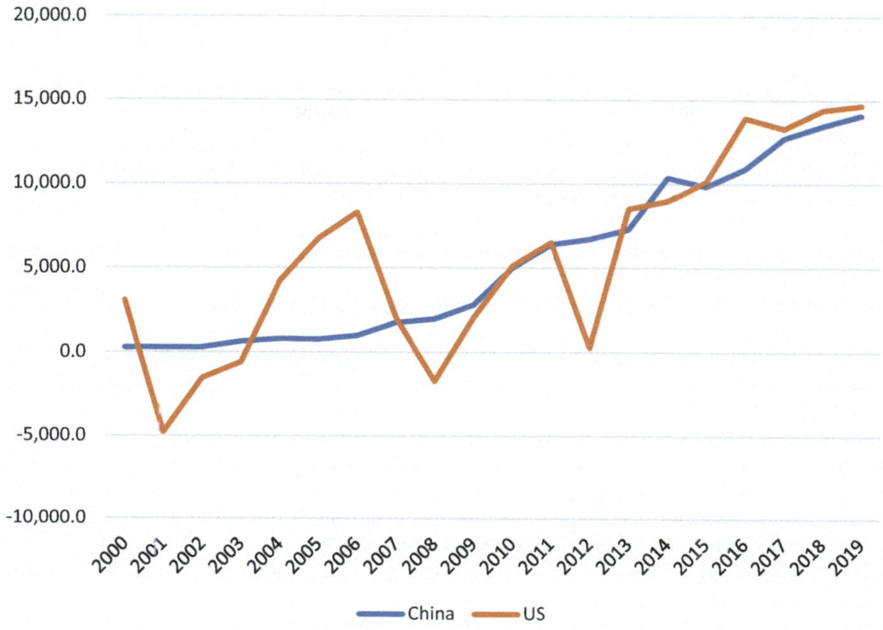

Fig. 4 Germany Primary Investment Income from FDI (€ million). Source: Eurostat

key factor in the imbalance, including investment flows being small compared to merchandise trade. The open regulatory regime for FDI in the EU was contrasted with Chinese restrictions. By achieving the EU's "ambitious agenda" the CAI was intended to achieve market penetration for EU companies by removing investment restrictions and in doing so change China's control of FDI.

This justification does not fit the facts. The focus on investment in EU policy occurred following the crisis of 2008 in the US and Europe, which caused the collapse of traditional export markets of the EU and long-term weakness in its domestic markets. The stimulus policy of the Chinese government in response to the crisis contrasted with the austerity measures adopted in the EU. Chinese policy created demand for EU exports, but also in the longer term for EU investors in China. This resulted in considerably increased dependence of EU companies on demand from China, including through their investments. Despite the restrictions on investment, the reality was that EU companies drew enormous benefits from their FDI in China, which compensated for their losses in other international and domestic markets. The apparent lack of reciprocity and small size of FDI flows to China contrasts with the real dependence of EU companies on investment in China. The pursuit of the CAI is not explained by reciprocity, but by this dependence which became critical for EU member states and their companies, which explains their support for the CAI, although this dependence and benefits were not distributed evenly.

References

Arrighi G (2010) The long twentieth century: money, power and the origin of our times. Verso, London
Ash R (2007) Europe's commercial relations with China. In: Shambaugh D, Sandschneider E, Zhou H (eds) China-Europe relations: perceptions, policies and prospects. Routledge, Abingdon
Bartels L (2007) The trade and development policy of the European Union. Eur J Int Law 18(4):715–756
Bhagwati JN, Irwin DA (1987) The return of the reciprocitarians—US trade policy today. World Econ 10(2):109–130
Blonigen BJ (2005) A review of the empirical literature on FDI determinants. Atlantic Econ J 33:383–403
Brandt L, Rawski T (2008) (eds) China's great economic transformation. CUP, Cambridge
Brenton P (2000) The changing nature and determinants of EU trade policies. CEPS Working Document No. 150
Breslin S (2007) China and the global political economy. Palgrave, Basingstoke
Buzan B, Lawson G (2015) The global transformation: history, modernity and the making of international relations. CUP, Cambridge
Cain PJ (1999) Economics and empire: the metropolitan context. In: Porter A (ed) The Oxford history of the British empire, vol III. OUP, Oxford, pp 31–52
Cain PJ, Hopkins AG (1980) The political economy of British expansion overseas, 1750–1914. Econ Hist Rev 33(4):463–490
Cantwell J et al (2010) An evolutionary approach to understanding international business activity: the co-evolution of MNEs and the institutional environment. J Int Bus Stud 41:567–586
Chang H (2004) Regulation of foreign investment in historical perspective. Eur J Dev Res 16(3):687–715
Chen C (2018) The liberalisation of FDI policies and the impacts of FDI on China's economic development. In: Garnaut R et al (eds) China's 40 years of reform and development: 1978–2018. Australian National University Press, Acton, pp 595–617
Damro C (2012) Market power Europe. J Eur Public Policy 19(5):682–699
De Bièvre D, Eckhardt J (2010) The political economy of EU anti-dumping reform. ECIPE Working Paper, No. 03/2010
Dunning JH (2001) The eclectic (OLI) paradigm of international production: past, present and future. Int J Econ Bus 8:173–190
Dunning JH, Lundan SM (2008) Institutions and the OLI paradigm of the multinational enterprise. Asia Pacific J Man 25:573–593
Eckhardt J (2011) Firm lobbying and EU trade policy making: reflections on the anti-dumping case against Chinese and Vietnamese shoes (2005–2011). J World Trade 45(5):965–991
EEC (1978) Trade agreement between the European economic community and the People's Republic of China. European Commission, Brussels
EEC (1985) Agreement on trade and economic cooperation between the European economic community and the People's Republic of China. European Commission, Brussels
ETUC (2021) ETUC Statement on EU-China Comprehensive Agreement on Investment, 9 February
European Commission (1995) Communication of the Commission, A Long-Term Policy for China-Europe Relations
European Commission (1998) Communication from the Commission, Building a Comprehensive Partnership with China, 25 March
European Commission (2001) Communication from the Commission to the Council and the European Parliament, EU Strategy Towards China: Implementation of the 1998 Communication and Future Steps for a More Effective EU Policy, 15 May

European Commission (2003) Commission Policy Paper for Transmission to the Council and the European Parliament, A Maturing Partnership – Shared Interests and Challenges in EU-China Relations, 10 September
European Commission (2006a) Communication from the Commission to the Council and the European Parliament, EU-China: Closer Partners, Growing Responsibilities, 24 October
European Commission (2006b) Commission Working Document, Competition and Partnership, 24 October
European Commission (2016) European Commission and High Representative of the Union for Foreign Affairs and Security Policy, Joint Communication to the European Parliament and the Council, Elements of a New EU Strategy on China, 22 June
European Commission (2019) European Commission and High Representative of the Union for Foreign Affairs and Security Policy, Joint Communication to the European Parliam9ent, the European Council and the Council, EU-China-Strategic Outlook, 12 March
European Commission (2020) EU and China Reach Agreement in Principle on Investment, Press Release, Brussels, 30 December
European Services Forum (ESF) (2020) European Services Forum Welcomes the EU-China Comprehensive Agreement on Investment, Press Release, Brussels, 30 December
European Union Chamber of Commerce in China (EUCCC) (2020) European Chamber Stance on the Political Agreement of the EU-China Comprehensive Agreement on Investment, 30 December 2020. https://www.europeanchamber.com.cn/en/press-releases/3304/european_chamber_stance_on_the_political_agreement_of_the_eu_china_comprehensive_agreement_on_investment. Accessed 17 August 2022
Eurostat (2017) Globalisation patterns in EU trade and investment, Luxembourg, Eurostat
Evans P (1997) The eclipse of the state? Reflections on stateness in an era of globalisation. World Polit 50(1):62–87
Federation of German Industries (BDI) (2021) EU-China Comprehensive Agreement on Investment: What does German Industry Gain? Position Paper, Berlin, 3 May
Ferguson N (2018) Empire: how Britain made the modern world. Folio Society, London
Ginsburg T (2005) International substitutes for domestic institutions: bilateral investment treaties and governance. Int Rev Law Econ 25(1):107–123
Guzman A (1997) Why LDCs sign treaties that hurt them: explaining the popularity of bilateral investment treaties. Virginia J Int Law 38:640–688
Hanson B (1998) What happened to fortress Europe? External trade policy liberalization in the European Union. Int Org 52(1):55–85
Hennart J (2000) Transaction costs theory and the multinational enterprise. In: Pitelis C, Sugden R (eds) The nature of the transnational firm. Routledge, London, pp 127–149
Hirschman A (1945) National power and the structure of foreign trade. University of California Press, Berkeley
Hobson J (1902) Imperialism: a study. James Pott & Company, New York
Johanson J, Vahlne J-E (1977) The internationalization process of the firm—a model of knowledge development and increasing foreign market commitments. J Int Bus Stud 8:23–32
Kamen H (2004) Empire: how Spain became a world power 1492–1763. Harper Collins, New York
Kindleburger C (1969) American business abroad: six lectures on direct investment. YUP, New Haven
Krasner S (1976) State power and the structure of international trade. World Polit 28(3):317–347
Lenin V (1933) Imperialism: the highest stage of capitalism. Lawrence & Wishart, London
List F (1909) The national system of political economy. Longmans, Green & Co., London
Marinova S et al (2012) Institutional field for outward foreign direct investment: a theoretical extension? Inst Theory Int Bus Man Adv Int Man 25:233–261
Meunier S, Nicolaidis K (2005) The European Union as a trade power. In: Hill C, Smith M (eds) International relations of the European Union. OUP, Oxford, pp 209–234
Ministry of Foreign Affairs (2003) Policy Paper on the European Union, Beijing, 13 October
Naughton B (2007) The Chinese economy: transitions and growth. MIT Press, Cambridge

Neumayer E, Spess L (2005) Do bilateral investment treaties increase foreign direct investment to developing countries? World Dev 33(10):1567–1585
North DC (1981) Structure and change in economic history. WW Norton & Co., London
North DC (1984) Government and the cost of exchange in history. J Econ Hist 44:255–264
North DC (1990) Institutions, institutional change and economic performance. CUP, Cambridge
North DC (1994) Economic performance through time. Am Econ Rev 84:359–368
Ohmae K (1995) The end of the nation state: the rise of regional economies. The Free Press, New York
Palan R et al (eds) (1999) State strategies in the global political economy. Pinter, London
Peng M et al (2008) An institution-based view of international business strategy: a focus on emerging economies. J Int Bus Stud 39:920–936
Russell-Wood AJR (1992) The Portuguese empire, 1415–1808: a world on the move. Johns Hopkins University Press, Baltimore
Sinn H (2014) The euro trap: on bursting bubbles, budgets, and beliefs. OUP, Oxford
Smith A (1976) An enquiry into the nature and causes of the wealth of nations. Liberty Press, Indianapolis
Stiglitz J (2016) The euro and its threat to the future of Europe. Allen Lane, London
Stoian C (2013) Extending Dunning's investment development path: the role of home country institutional determinants in explaining outward foreign direct investment. Int Bus Rev 22:615–637
Strange S (1988) States and markets. Pinter Press, London
Strange S (1996) The retreat of the state: the diffusion of power in the world economy. CUP, Cambridge
Tobin J, Rose-Ackerman S (2005) Foreign direct investment and the business environment in developing countries: the impact of bilateral investment treaties. Yale Law & Econ Research Paper No. 293
Tooze A (2018) Crashed: how a decade of financial crises changed the world. Allen Lane, London
Varoufakis Y et al (2011) Modern political economics: making sense of the post-2008 world. Routledge, Abingdon
Vernon R (1971) Sovereignty at bay: the multinational spread of US enterprises. Basic Books, New York
Weiss L (1998) The myth of the powerless state: governing the economy in a global era. Polity Press, Cambridge
Whitman RG (ed) (2011) Normative power Europe: empirical and theoretical perspectives. Palgrave Macmillan, Basingstoke
Wolf E (2010) Europe and the people without history. University of California Press, Berkeley
Woolcock S (2012) European Union economic diplomacy: the role of the EU in external economic relations. Routledge, Abingdon
Young A, Peterson J (2014) Parochial global Europe: 21st century trade politics. OUP, Oxford
Zhang J (2021) The EU–China investment Deal is a missed opportunity for sustainable development, China Dialogue, 9 March

Duncan Freeman has a BA in Politics and Modern History from the University of Manchester, an MSc in Chinese Politics from the School of Oriental and African Studies, University of London, a Postgraduate Diploma in Economic Principles from the School of Oriental and African Studies, University of London and a PhD completed at the Vrije Universiteit Brussel (VUB) on domestic institutional factors in determining China's outward investment. He currently lectures at the Brussels Management School (ICHEC). He has previously been Research Fellow at the EU-China Research Centre of the College of Europe. Prior to this he was Research Fellow and taught and carried out research on China's economic and policy development in addition to EU-China relations at the VUB. He has also lived and worked in Beijing and Hong Kong for a total of 17 years and is fluent in Chinese. During his time in Hong Kong he was the editor and publisher of several leading publications on the Chinese legal and tax systems and their impact on international businesses operating in China. His co-edited volume, The Evolving Relationship between China, the EU and the USA: A New Global Order?, published by Routledge, was named as one of the Choice Outstanding Academic Titles for 2021 of the American Library Association. Among his areas of research are the political economy of EU-China relations, especially in the area of trade and outward investment, energy and climate policy, the mutual external impacts of the EU's and China's domestic development and the EU-China political relationship.

The Political Economy of China and the EU-China Comprehensive Agreement on Investment

Sohyun Zoe Lee

Abstract This chapter examines China's political economy rationale for the EU-China Comprehensive Agreement on Investment (CAI). Since reform and opening up, Beijing has frequently utilized economic policies not only to promote domestic reforms, but also to achieve security goals and to elevate China's status in the global political economy. Given China's emphasis on economic statecraft, to what extent is the EU-China CAI consistent with China's conventional economic diplomacy? What were the key drivers that motivated China to negotiate the CAI? Examining the development of CAI demonstrates that the agreement has been driven in large part by Beijing's conventional political and economic objectives. At the domestic level, the high liberalization standards and comprehensive scope of provisions adopted in the CAI have been utilized to lock in domestic reforms and strengthening the Chinese government's legitimacy. At the international level, the CAI demonstrates China's ambitions to raise its status and to take a greater role in shaping global rules of investment, driven by intense global power dynamics.

1 Introduction

This chapter examines China's political economy rationale in the EU-China Comprehensive Agreement on Investment (CAI). Since the reform and opening up of 1978, China has witnessed a rapid rise in its international investment flows. From 1980 to 2020, China's foreign direct investment (FDI) inflows have risen from US$ 57 million to US$ 149.3 billion,[1] becoming the world's second-largest FDI recipient

[1] UNCTAD Stat (n.d.).

S. Z. Lee (✉)
Queen's University Belfast, Belfast, Ireland
e-mail: sohyun.lee@qub.ac.uk

© The Author(s), under exclusive license to Springer Nature Switzerland AG 2024

A. Svetlicinii, I.-J. Chen (eds.), *The EU-China Comprehensive Agreement on Investment*, European Yearbook of International Economic Law,
https://doi.org/10.1007/978-3-031-66862-3_3

after the US.[2] At the same time, FDI outflows have rapidly increased from US$ 44 million in 1982 to US$ 132.9 billion in 2020, which indicate an expansion in Chinese investment abroad.[3] To support the increasing role of FDIs in the Chinese economy, China has actively engaged in negotiating bilateral investment treaties (BITs). The first such BIT was negotiated with Sweden, which was signed and entered into force in March 1982. Throughout the 1980s, China negotiated numerous BITs with European countries including Germany, France, the Belgium-Luxembourg Economic Union (BLEU), Finland, Norway, Italy, Denmark, Netherlands, Austria, the UK, and Switzerland, as well as with non-European economies, such as Thailand, Singapore, Japan, Australia, New Zealand, and Kuwait.[4]

After the Asian financial crisis of 1997–1998, many East Asian governments began to negotiate free trade agreements (FTA) in an effort to recover from the crisis and to overcome the slow progress of the multilateral negotiations at the World Trade Organization (WTO). Joining this trend, China also began to take part in shaping the regional and global economy through government-driven trade initiatives. China's accession into the WTO in 2001 signposted this trend. Since then, China has become an active negotiator of FTAs with both regional and cross-regional partners, including Hong Kong, Macao,[5] ASEAN, Pakistan, Chile New Zealand, Singapore, Peru, Costa Rica, Iceland, Switzerland, South Korea, Australia Georgia, the Maldives, Mauritius, Cambodia, and the members of RCEP.[6] In terms of BITs, China began adopting new standards that accommodated more universally accepted practices, which was considered significant progress for Chinese foreign economic policies.[7] By the end of 2022, China had 125 BITs and 18 FTAs signed or in effect. The lowering of tariff and non-tariff barriers through these initiatives had a reinforcing impact on facilitating the flows of FDIs in and out of China.[8]

In contemporary China, both FTAs and BITs have become vital tools for its statecraft. It was in this context that China, represented by Premier Wen Jiaobao, and the EU, represented by the European Council's President Herman Van Rompuy and the European Commission's president José Manuel Barroso, officially agreed on the launch of the EU-China CAI negotiations in February 2012.[9] In November 2013, the two parties announced the launch of the CAI negotiations, while further

---

[2] UNCTAD (n.d.).

[3] UNCTAD Stat (n.d.).

[4] Some of the early BITs have expired. For a full list of China's BITs, see UNCTAD Investment Policy Hub (n.d.).

[5] China uses the term 'Closer Economic Partnership Arrangement' with Hong Kong and Macao instead of FTAs. However, they are listed as FTAs by the Ministry of Commerce. For further detail, see: http://fta.mofcom.gov.cn/english/index.shtml.

[6] At the end of 2022, eight additional FTAs were underway, including China-Gulf Cooperation Council (GCC) FTA, China-Japan-Korea FTA, China-Sri Lanka FTA, China-Israel FTA, China-Norway FTA, China-Moldova FTA, China-Panama FTA, and China-Palestine FTA.

[7] Cohen and Schneiderman (2017), pp. 110–128.

[8] Schill (2007), pp. 73–79.

[9] Council of the European Union (2012b, February 14).

agreeing to initiate the feasibility study of the EU-China FTA 'at an appropriate time.'[10] Hence, the first round of CAI negotiations began in January 2014. The negotiations continued over seven years, involving 35 rounds in total. Meanwhile, however, the EU-China FTA did not progress. An agreement for CAI was finally reached in December 2020 after pressing calls from both sides.[11]

Since reform and opening up, Beijing has frequently utilized economic policies to achieve both domestic reforms and security goals, and to elevate China's status in the global political economy. Given China's emphasis on economic statecraft, to what extent is the EU-China CAI consistent with China's conventional economic diplomacy? What were the key drivers that motivated China to negotiate the CAI? Was it a coincidence that the agreement was reached at the end of 2020, when US-China tensions continued to shape the dynamics of the global political economy while the presidential transition of US president-elect Joe Biden was taking place? Why did the CAI progress and not the FTA? These questions are important in understanding the complex relationship between the EU and China, as the two parties' mutual economic gains from the CAI cannot be isolated from their political interests. As the European Commission describes, to the EU, China is 'simultaneously a cooperation partner, an economic competitor in pursuit of technological leadership, and a systemic rival promoting alternative models of governance.'[12] Hence, this chapter explores China's political economy rationale in the CAI. Examining China's motivations, it demonstrates that the agreement has been driven in large part by Beijing's conventional political and economic objectives, consistent with its existing economic diplomacy.

This chapter is organized as follows. The following section provides a background to China's economic statecraft. The third section investigates China's political and economic motivations behind the EU-China CAI. The final section concludes the findings of this chapter and assesses the implications of the CAI in the context of China's broader economic diplomacy and the global political economy.

2 The Political Economy of China's Foreign Economic Policies

China has become a major actor in the global political economy since Deng Xiaoping's open-door policy in 1978. With the end of the Cold War and its accession to the WTO in 2001, China has accelerated its engagement with the global economy through bilateral, regional, and multilateral initiatives. In this regard, BITs and FTAs have been some of China's key foreign economic policy instruments to achieve strategic goals, rather than simply to increase economic returns. Considering

[10] Xin (2014, March 18).

[11] European Commission (2020, December 30).

[12] European Commission (2019, March 12).

China's controversial position in the international order, the use of such policies was considered a compelling device to raise China's domestic political legitimacy and diplomatic status. With this backdrop, this section examines how China has utilized its foreign economic policies to achieve its political and economic objectives at both domestic and international levels.

At the domestic level, BITs have been considered a means to enhance the government's political legitimacy through economic performance. As with China's other foreign economic policies, such as the Belt and Road Initiative (BRI), one of the Chinese government's major goals in its foreign economic policies has revolved around sustaining economic growth and employment.[13] Chinese authorities have thus demonstrated a strong commitment to opening up the Chinese economy through active engagement in the global economy, for instance through the adoption of the 'Going Global' strategy in 1998[14] and joining the WTO in 2001. Similarly, China's extensive involvement in BITs and FTAs demonstrate the government's attempt to reflect the trends of international investment governance and to lock in domestic reforms. In this regard, the government's endeavors to upgrade China's BITs and FTAs have been essential in dealing with domestic economic problems such as growing inequality, problems of SOEs, and economic slowdown.

For instance, China runs trade deficits with most of its existing FTA partners.[15] Nevertheless, the Chinese leadership has attempted to negotiate high standard FTAs for greater integration into the world economy by exposing domestic producers and SOEs to greater competition, which would ultimately result in sustained economic growth. In other words, it has sought a long-term solution to the sluggish economic growth, rather than an immediate result.[16] Its willingness to tolerate short-term domestic costs is reinforced by its highly centralized decision-making process.[17] Similarly, China has signed BITs with democratic and advanced countries with which China does not have powerful bargaining leverage; the rationale is largely economic, as assuring foreign investors is essential in attracting foreign capital to China.[18] Likewise, higher standard BITs since the late 1990s reflect China's growing interdependence with the global economy, and the need to provide greater protection for both inward and outward foreign investment.[19] China's promotion of BITs and upgraded BIT standards have been considered mutually beneficial for the Chinese and the foreign investors; Chinese investment abroad may take advantage of greater protection, while foreign investors can also gain greater confidence to invest in the Chinese market.[20] As such, China has pursued rigorous BITs when

[13] Yu (2018), p. 225.

[14] Bickenback et al. (2015).

[15] Eckhardt and Wang (2021), pp. 588–590.

[16] Ibid.

[17] Zeng (2016), pp. 119–120.

[18] Han et al. (2019), pp. 1–38.

[19] Zeng (2016), p. 116.

[20] Schill (2007), pp. 73–118.

undertaking domestic reforms, which indicates that foreign economic policies have been considered a vital means to lock in the government's commitment in addressing pressing domestic economic agenda.[21]

At the international level, China's domestic goals are closely linked with its external goals of extending its global influence and raising China's diplomatic status. China has utilized both BITs and FTAs to expand its capacity to shape global trade and investment governance and gaining acceptance of its diplomatic status from partner countries. For instance, an examination of China's existing FTAs demonstrates that Beijing has frequently shown 'big country morality' by offering greater concessions to the counterpart to gain Market Economy Status.[22] Because BITs do not extensively involve domestic interest groups as FTAs do, BITs can be more readily utilized as a lower-cost foreign policy means to establish a friendly relationship with strategically significant partners.[23] In this respect, the US has also used BITs to strengthen political relationship with the partner states, and often political incentives were greater than economic benefits.[24]

Along the same lines, one of the key aims of China's efforts to strengthen its economic ties with the rest of the world since the end of the Cold War was to handle international pressure.[25] Building upon its outward-oriented strategy, the Chinese government has upgraded its BITs since the late 1990s so that they adhere to the standard ISDS provision that cover disputes in all respects and adopt national treatment for foreign investors.[26] During this period, China's BIT partner choices were also predominantly focused on developed European countries.[27] While China was a latecomer to FTAs like its East Asian neighbors, its FTA strategies, coupled with BITs, have become increasingly proactive in the recent years, seeking higher-quality agreements with developed countries. In the early 2000s, China's FTAs were heavily focused on developing countries. Since the late 2000s and throughout the 2010s, however, China began negotiating FTAs with developed economies and pushing for upgrades in the quality of its FTAs, while pursuing BITs with the US[28] and the EU, to demonstrate China's conformity with the international standards and to enhance China's diplomatic position and power in the global market.[29]

Having explored political and economic motivations of China's BITs and FTAs, the next section will examine how these motivations have played out in the China-EU CAI.

---

[21] Zeng (2016), pp. 112–129.

[22] Jiang (2010), pp. 253–255.

[23] Bonnitcha et al. (2017), pp. 181–207; Tobin and Busch (2010), pp. 1–42.

[24] Chilton (2016), pp. 614–642.

[25] Cohen and Schneiderman (2017), pp. 110–128.

[26] Ibid.; Schill (2007), p. 80.

[27] Cohen and Schneiderman (2017), pp. 110–128.

[28] The first attempt to negotiate a BIT between China and the US failed in the 1980s. Contemporary BIT negotiations between the two parties began in 2008. However, the negotiations are yet to be concluded at the time of writing (April 2023).

[29] Chi (2017), pp. 478–479; Chow (2015), pp. 102–137.

3 China's Political and Economic Motivations in the CAI

Prior to China's official engagement with the CAI negotiations, China already had individual BITs with all the EU member states, except for Ireland.[30] The CAI, which was announced at the 14th EU-China Summit in February 2012, was therefore meant to supplement the existing 26 BITs, at least until the parties could agree on a standard of protection and investor-state dispute settlement (ISDS). At the Summit, China and the EU mutually recognized that the EU-China economic relations have deepened through increasing trade and FDIs, and therefore, an investment agreement would further provide increased protection and greater certainty to companies and investors engaging in each other's markets. The two parties further recognized the potential creation of a trade pact, considering the deepening of the two parties' economic relations and to prevent global protectionism in trade and investment with the lack of progress at the WTO.[31]

While the call for the CAI had been in part driven by steadily increasing investment flows in both directions, the CAI was more a result of cooperation at the institutional level between China and the EU, rather than entirely market-driven. Since the 2000s, FDIs have steadily increased between China and the EU in both directions; China's FDI in the EU grew from US$ 0.18 billion in 2005 to US$ 10.2 billion in 2017, while the EU's FDI in China grew from US$ 4.1 billion in 1997 to US$ 8.2 billion in 2017.[32] However, these FDIs, in terms of proportions, were very low; the EU's FDI accounted for approximately 5% of global FDI inflows into China from 2007 to 2017, while China's FDI to the EU accounted for 0.6% of global inbound FDI in the EU from 2009 to 2015.[33] Thus, the two parties specifically aimed to reduce barriers to bilateral investment flows and enhancing protections for investors when entering each other's markets.[34]

The launch of the CAI negotiations was announced in November 2013, and the two parties reconfirmed their potential interest in the EU-China FTA in the long-term. China and the EU, at the time of this announcement, had estimated that the CAI negotiations would take two-and-a-half-years at the longest.[35] The beginning of the CAI negotiations also coincided with President Xi Jinping's launch of the BRI and the Asian Infrastructure Investment Bank (AIIB) in the latter half of 2013, which would further boost China's outward FDIs in Eurasia and Africa. Given this background, the promotion of new generation BITs, including the CAI, was expected to provide greater protection to China's growing outbound investment.[36]

[30] Note, Belgium and Luxembourg jointly negotiated a BIT with China, unlike the rest of the EU member states that negotiated independent bilateral deals.

[31] Council of the European Union (2012a, February 14).

[32] Li and Bian (2020), pp. 1–2.

[33] Ibid.

[34] Council of the European Union (2013, October 18).

[35] Ibid.

[36] Li and Bian (2020), pp. 3–4.

China's active engagement in the outward-oriented foreign economic policies not only reflected China's geopolitical interests in extending its global influence, but also in coping with the slowdown of the domestic economy.[37] In other words, China's greater engagement with more in-depth, higher-standard BITs and FTAs had become crucial in augmenting China's role in the global investment and trade governance while securing the legitimacy of the Chinese government.

The first round of CAI negotiations began in January 2014. On the surface, harmonizing existing BITs was expected to reduce the costs attached to utilizing these BITs. Even though China's BIT standards were upgraded since the late 1990s to reflect international standards, there were still significant variances across the 26 BITs, for instance, in the scope of most favored nations treatment or application of the ISDS provisions.[38] Furthermore, there was much room for improvement in these individual BITs as the existing BITs only protected foreign investments after they have entered into host states. This granted the host state substantial room to regulate foreign investments; thus, the CAI could provide an increased protection to private investors, by introducing new regulatory measures that would protect foreign investments prior to being admitted to the host state.[39] Also, the CAI would include elements of new generation BITs, which address more specific and comprehensive provisions. According to Berger, these issues included 'more detailed and restrictive fair and equitable treatment or indirect expropriation clauses, exclusion of ISDS from the scope of the MFN clause, public policy exceptions, or rules on environmental and labour issues.'[40] For the Chinese government, incorporating these high standards into the CAI was pressing, as the Transatlantic Trade and Investment Partnership (TTIP) had been progressing between the US and the EU since February 2013 and its rigorous standards were expected to have negative repercussions for Chinese investors abroad.[41]

Because the EU-China CAI would be the most ambitious BIT China has ever concluded, it was considered a foreign economic policy tool to enhance China's image and strategic position in the rulemaking of global investment and trade governance while locking in domestic reforms. China's emphasis on the CAI also reflected its shifting focus in the choice of investment and trade partners since the 2010s; China has become increasingly interested in negotiating higher quality BITs and FTAs with developed countries, while actively engaging in negotiating the Regional Comprehensive Economic Partnership (RCEP), facing the competitive rise of mega-regional FTAs.[42] In this respect, China introduced an unprecedentedly high level of market access, pre-establishment (rather than post-establishment) of national treatment, comprehensive rules to ensure a level playing field, and a

[37] Yu (2017), pp. 355–356.

[38] Bickenback et al. (2015), p. 3.

[39] Berger (2020), pp. 1–2.

[40] Ibid, pp. 17–18.

[41] Ibid, p. 20.

[42] Chi (2017), pp. 476–477.

negative list approach to the negotiations, while additionally addressing environmental and labour issues. The negative-list approach of negotiations was adopted for the first time in China's BITs, which is more liberalizing than a positive-list approach as all sectors (including services and non-services), unless stated otherwise, are liberalized.[43] Beijing's economic and political intentions in the CAI were supported by the official position of the Chinese government. As Xiang Xia, Mission of the People's Republic of China to the EU states:

> CAI will inject new impetus to China's reform and opening up. Over the past 40-plus years of reform and opening up, China has lifted 800 million people out of poverty, and has come a long way in economic and social development. Reform and opening up is the shared commitment of the 1.4 billion Chinese people. CAI defines obligations for high-level opening up and offers a new driving force for China's shift from factors-based opening to institutional opening. This is the solemn commitment made by China to the EU and the world in the form of an international treaty. China's development may not be free of problems and difficulties. Yet we keep moving in the right direction step by step, from reform and opening up to building a socialist market economy, from joining the WTO to concluding the CAI.[44]

By the same token, China reiterated its desire to negotiate an FTA with the EU. An FTA with the EU would reinforce domestic reform while enhancing China and the Chinese government's image, showing that China's socialist market economy pursues open markets and innovation.[45] Since the beginning of the CAI negotiations, however, the EU side was pessimistic about an FTA with China, considering existing obstacles to market access and competition in China.[46] In essence, the EU felt that China did not meet the EU's high standards in FTAs. Also, the EU already had a high trade deficit with China, and therefore, did not want further liberalization in merchandise trades; however, it was more open to liberalizing services sectors.[47] The EU's position that a premature FTA with China would have negative implications to the EU was repeatedly confirmed during the negotiations. Hence, in 2016, Cecilia Malmström, then-EU Commissioner for Trade, specified that the EU would only launch the FTA once the following conditions were established:

- A good outcome on the investment negotiations. This will show China is committed to the kind of ambitious trade and investment agreements that the EU negotiates.
- Progress on China's internal reforms, most importantly the goal of giving the market a more decisive role. Signing up to a European-style FTA would mean making real changes. The state would need to be a regulator not an economic

[43] Xia (2021), pp. 507–509.

[44] Ibid, p. 508.

[45] Shi and Chen (2021), pp. 80–99; Wang (2021b), pp. 51–63.

[46] Bilby (2013, May 12).

[47] Basedow (2021a, July 13).

operator; allow inefficient companies to go bankrupt, and make adjustments to reduce overcapacity.[48]

Facing tensions with the US since the Trump administration, Beijing's strategic interests for the CAI were further strengthened. With the US withdrawing from the Trans-Pacific Partnership (TPP) and the initiation of the US-China trade war, Beijing began positioning itself as a benign power that adheres to the liberal investment and trade governance, in contrast with the US. Beijing has since emphasized that the CAI would benefit both China and the EU, as well as the global economy, as the world faces growing uncertainty.[49] Against this backdrop, at the 21st EU-China Summit, held in April 2019, European Commission President Jean-Claude Juncker and Premier Li Keqiang agreed that the CAI be concluded by 2020. In recognition of the delay to negotiations after having failed to meet the earlier deadline of the CAI negotiations, the two parties reconfirmed their willingness to expedite the negotiations to realize a high-level CAI that addresses the economic interests of the two parties. The EU also reaffirmed its one-China policy.[50] Despite this agreement, however, negotiations proceeded at a slow pace due to the EU's concerns about human rights violations in Xinjiang.

The CAI negotiations took a sharp turn in the last week of December 2020, when President Xi offered a significant concession to the EU on two contentious areas: labour standards and climate change.[51] The EU was also motivated to reach an agreement with China, as it was in the EU's interests to take the lead in shaping global investment and trade governance and reinvigorating multilateralism by engaging the US in these efforts. To quote Sabine Weyand, Director General for Trade of the European Commission:

> Through the CAI, the EU is trying to engage with China on the issue of levelled playing field, which is something that China has not yet want to engage at the WTO or any other partner before...The CAI will be a building block for a rules-based regulation of globalization and we hope to engage with likeminded countries, like the US, to launch issues at the WTO that will have strong systemic impact.[52]

Furthermore, as Valdis Dombrovskis the EU's trade commissioner remarked, the EU would gain from the CAI by 'levelling up' with the United States, regarding the phase one trade deal that was reached between the United States and China in January the same year.[53]

The timing of the announcement was considered by the media and pundits as highly political and diplomatic, as the inauguration of President Joe Biden was due to take place on January 20, 2021; hence, the conclusion of the CAI was considered

[48] Malmström (2016, February 25).

[49] Shen (2018), pp. 799–840; Chen (2020, September 16).

[50] Delegation of the European Union to China (2019, October 4).

[51] Elmer (2020, December 24); Le Corre (2021, March 24).

[52] Lai (2021, February 23).

[53] Hutt (2020, December 31).

a reflection of the two parties' intentions to pressure the US.[54] China's foreign ministry immediately argued against this speculation, emphasizing that China's focus has been consistent in enhancing the EU-China relations at a steady pace.[55] Nevertheless, US discontent regarding the immanent conclusion of the CAI visualized the power politics amongst China, the EU, and the US. The incoming national security adviser Jake Sullivan cautioned the EU regarding the CAI: 'The Biden-Harris administration would welcome early consultations with our European partners on our common concerns about China's economic practices.'[56] Likewise, China's state councillor Wang Yi repeatedly emphasized to the EU that it should uphold 'strategic autonomy' for 'the formulation and implementation of the correct policies towards China.'[57]

Despite these power dynamics amongst the EU, the US, and China, the EU-China CAI was concluded on 30 December 2020. As this chapter is being drafted, however, it is unclear whether the CAI will enter into force in the foreseeable future as the international political environment complicates the ratification of the agreement. After the CAI schedules were released in March 2021,[58] EU-China relations quickly deteriorated due to the two party's disputes concerning China's human rights issues. Adding to this concern was the stepping down of Angela Merkel as Chancellor or Germany, who had been a strong supporter of the CAI. Furthermore, there were no signs of improvement in EU-China relations throughout 2022 as new political issues emerged, including China's refusal to condemn Russia's invasion of Ukraine and China's disagreement with the EU regarding Taiwan.[59]

Nevertheless, China continues with its charm offensive, emphasizing the significance of the CAI through the rhetoric such as "win-win" cooperation and the CAI's positive implications for the world. As China's Ministry of Commerce underlines, economic cooperation between China and the EU will facilitate the recovery of the global economy, and such cooperation has become vital to overcome the global economic downturn that has been aggravated by the Covid-19 pandemic.[60] Likewise, at the 23rd EU-China Summit, held in July 2021, President Xi highlighted China's upholding of multilateralism and its adherence to the international system, norms, and the UN convention. President Xi further urged that 'China and the EU should

---

[54] Ibid.; Basedow (2021b, March 23).

[55] *Global Times* (2020, December 22).

[56] Sullivan (2021, December 22).

[57] Embassy of the People's Republic of China in the United Kingdom of Great Britain and Northern Ireland (2020, November 23); CGTN (2021, June 22).

[58] European Commission (2021, March 12).

[59] In November 2021, a Taiwan Representative office was opened in Lithuania. Beijing considered that the use of "Taiwan" instead of "Taipei" went against the One China policy, thereby taking measures to sanction Lithuania. The EU initiated a dispute against China at the WTO in January 2022, regarding China's economic sanction on Lithuania or those nations with links to Lithuania. The EU's relationship with China further stagnated throughout 2022 as the EU announced the plans to upgrade its trade and investment relations with Taiwan.

[60] Liu (2021, July 9).

correctly view each other's differences and rationally deal with divergences', implying Beijing's position that the EU's strategy should be promoted independent from US influence.[61] In addition, China has been drawing support from a number of Central and Eastern European Countries (CEECs)[62] and Greece, countries that have substantially benefitted from China's BRI, as the CAI is expected to complement BRI projects in these countries.[63] As Poland's Minister of Foreign Affairs Zbigniew Rau stated, the CAI is 'the best choice that suits the interests of the two sides…Poland upholds an independent diplomatic policy, understands and respects China's legitimate rights and interests and will make active efforts for the healthy development of EU-China relations and cooperation between China and CEECs.'[64]

Such implications of the CAI are also closely linked with China's broader domestic and international goals. For instance, as specified in the Dual Circulation Strategy announced in 2020 and China's formal application to enter the Comprehensive and Progressive Agreement for TPP (CPTPP) in September 2021.[65] For Beijing, the key value of the EU-China CAI lies in deepening China's domestic reform and opening up while establishing a stepping stone for greater engagement in the international investment and trade governance, which in turn will consolidate the Chinese government's position and leadership.

4 Conclusion

This chapter has demonstrated China's political and economic motivations in the EU-China CAI through an extensive examination of the CAI negotiations. It has shown that China's motivations in the EU-China CAI are consistent with China's conventional economic diplomacy. The high liberalization standards and comprehensive scope of provisions adopted in the CAI have been utilized to raise China's status in the global economy while locking in domestic reforms and strengthening the Chinese government's legitimacy. Over the years of the CAI negotiations, China desired to further promote an FTA with the EU. However, the EU was hesitant to embark on an FTA with China, due to its high trade deficit and concerns that China's political and economic circumstances do not meet the EU's FTA standards nor values. In the meanwhile, a major turning point for CAI came in December 2020, when China agreed to make a concession to the EU on labour standards and environmental measures. President Xi's offering of these terms led to the long overdue conclusion of the CAI. However, the timing of the agreement raised suggestions that the

[61] Chen et al. (2021, July 5).

[62] Note, not all CEECs support China. See note 61 for further detail.

[63] Wang (2021a, February 11).

[64] Embassy of the People's Republic of China in the Republic of Indonesia (2021, May 29); *Global Times* (2021, May 30).

[65] Shi and Chen (2021), pp. 98–99; Wang (2021b), p. 59.

agreement was driven by intense global power competition between China, the EU, and the US rather than solely by economic motivations.

China's ambitions to take a greater role in shaping global rules of investment and trade are also clearly demonstrated by its recent engagement in the mega-regional FTAs, with the conclusion of RCEP in November 2020 and its application for membership of CPTPP in September 2021. Similar to China's engagement with CAI, these international goals are closely tied to the domestic goals of increasing domestic consumption and promoting innovation, specified by the Dual Circulation Strategy or industrial programs such as Made in China 2025. Balancing these domestic and international goals are a priority for the Chinese government, not only to avoid the middle-income trap, but also to internationalize the Chinese economy to ultimately ensure the government's survival. In this respect, the CAI is a significant apparatus for Beijing to accelerate these momentums and opportunities.

References

Basedow R (2021a, July 13) Is the EU's China policy sustainable? Research event at Chatham House, online. https://www.chathamhouse.org/events/all/research-event/eus-china-policy-sustainable

Basedow R (2021b, March 23) Putting the China-EU investment agreement in perspective – and assessing the lessons for the UK. European Politics and Policy, London School of Economics and Political Science. https://blogs.lse.ac.uk/europpblog/2021/03/23/putting-the-china-eu-investment-agreement-in-perspective-and-assessing-the-lessons-for-the-uk/

Berger A (2020) The China-EU investment agreement negotiations. In: Li Y, Qi T, Bian C (eds) China, the EU and international investment law. Routledge, London and New York, pp 11–25

Bickenback F, Liu W-H, Li G (2015) The EU-China bilateral investment agreement in negotiation: motivation, conflicts, and perspectives, kiel. Policy Brief 95

Bilby E (2013, May 12) Exclusive: EU says Chinese FTA possible, but wants market opening. Reuters. https://www.reuters.com/article/us-eu-china-investment-idUSBRE94K11A20130521

Bonnitcha J, Skovgaard Poulsen LN, Michael Waibel M (2017) The political economy of the investment treaty regime. OUP, Oxford

CGTN (2021, June 22) Wang Yi urges Europe to adhere to strategic autonomy, multilateralism. https://news.cgtn.com/news/2021-06-22/Wang-Yi-urges-Europe-to-adhere-to-strategic-autonomy-multilateralism-11idrMOeOu4/index.html

Chen Q, Hu Y, Wan L (2021, July 5) Update: Xi's call for correct views on differences between China, EU 'a timely guidance' for ties amid downward spiral: experts. Global Times https://www.globaltimes.cn/page/202107/1227891.shtml

Chen W (2020, September 16) Xi's remarks on China-EU ties applauded. China Daily. https://www.chinadaily.com.cn/a/202009/16/WS5f6169eca31024ad0ba79c9d.html

Chi M (2017) The China-EU BIT as a stepping stone towards a China-EU FTA: a policy analysis. In: Bungenberg M, Krajewski M, Tams C, Terhechte JP, Ziegler AR (eds) European yearbook of international economic law. Springer, Cham, Switzerland, pp 475–490

Chilton AS (2016) The political motivations of the United States' bilateral investment treaty program. Rev Int Polit Econ 23(4):614–642

Chow DCK (2015) Why China wants a bilateral investment treaty with the United States. Boston Univ Int Law J 33:102–137

Cohen T, Schneiderman D (2017) The political economy of chinese bilateral investment treaty policy. Chinese J Comp Law 5(1):110–128

Council of the European Union (2012a, February 14) Joint Press Communiqué of the 14th EU-China Summit

Council of the European Union (2012b, February 14) Political agreement between the EU and China to launch negotiations. European Commission. http://eeas.europa.eu/archives/docs/china/summit/summit_docs/120214_joint_statement_14th_eu_china_summit_en.pdf

Council of the European Union (2013, October 18) Press Release

Delegation of the European Union to China (2019, October 4) Joint statement of the 21st EU-China summit. https://eeas.europa.eu/delegations/china_en/60836/Joint%20statement%20of%20the%2021st%20EU-China%20summit

Eckhardt J, Wang H (2021) China's new generation trade agreements: importing rules to lock in domestic reform? Regul Gov 15:581–597

Elmer K (2020, December 24) What is the China-EU CAI and how is an investment deal different from a trade deal? South China Morning Post. https://www.scmp.com/news/china/diplomacy/article/3115199/what-china-eu-cai-and-how-investment-deal-different-trade-deal

Embassy of the People's Republic of China in the Republic of Indonesia (2021, May 29) Wang Yi Holds Talks with Polish Foreign Minister Zbigniew Rau. https://www.mfa.gov.cn/ce/cesb//eng/zgyw_12/t1879784.htm

Embassy of the People's Republic of China in the United Kingdom of Great Britain and Northern Ireland (2020, November 23) Wang Yi Speaks with High Representative of the EU for Foreign Affairs and Security Policy Josep Borrell on the Phone. https://www.mfa.gov.cn/ce/ceuk//eng/zgyw/t1835385.htm

European Commission (2019, March 12) EU-China – A strategic outlook, European Commission and HR/VP contribution to the European Council

European Commission (2020, December 30) EU and China reach agreement in principle on investment. European Commission. https://trade.ec.europa.eu/doclib/press/index.cfm?id=2233

European Commission (2021, March 12) Commission publishes market access offers of the EU-China investment agreement. https://trade.ec.europa.eu/doclib/press/index.cfm?id=2253

Global Times (2020, December 22) FM refutes report on EU-China CAI; steady bilateral relations benefit world. https://www.globaltimes.cn/page/202012/1210654.shtml

Global Times (2021, May 30) China-EU CAI a best choice that benefits both sides: Poland FM. https://www.globaltimes.cn/page/202105/1224841.shtml

Han D, Chen Z, Tian Y (2019) To sign or not to sign: explaining the formation of China's bilateral investment treaties. Int Relat Asia Pac 0:1–38

Hutt D (2020, December 31) EU-China deal may give Biden's team more options. Asia Times. https://asiatimes.com/2020/12/eu-china-deal-may-give-bidens-team-more-options/

Jiang Y (2010) China's pursuit of free trade agreements: is China exceptional? Rev Int Polit Econ 17(2):238–261

Lai K (2021, February 23) Primer: EU-China Comprehensive Agreement on Investment. IFLR. https://www.iflr.com/article/b1qp5tynld2h1h/primer-eu-china-comprehensive-agreement-on-investment

Le Corre P (2021, March 24) Europe's Tightrope Diplomacy on China, Carnegie Endowment for International Peace. https://carnegieendowment.org/2021/03/24/europe-s-tightrope-diplomacy-on-china-pub-84159

Li Y, Bian C (2020) Introduction. In: Li Y, Qi T, Bian C (eds) China, the EU and international investment law. Routledge, London and New York, pp 1–8

Liu Z (2021, July 9) China-EU agreement will benefit world, says MOC. China Daily. https://www.chinadaily.com.cn/a/202107/09/WS60e785fea310efa1bd660acb.html

Malmström C (2016, February 25) The EU and China: trade and investment in the global economy, European Commission – Speech. https://trade.ec.europa.eu/doclib/html/154322.htm

Schill SW (2007) Tearing down the great wall: the new generation investment treaties of the People's Republic of China. Cardozo J Int Comp Law 15(1):73–118

Shen W (2018) Evolution of non-discriminatory standards in China's BITs in the context of EU-China BIT negotiations. Chinese J Int Law 17(3):799–840

Shi J, Chen X (2021)《中欧全面投资协定》：我国商签经贸条约的新范式 [The Paradigm Shift in China's Negotiating Investment Treaty: A Commentary on the China-EU Comprehensive Agreement on Investment]. 国际法研究 5:80–99

Sullivan J (2021, December 22). Twitter post. https://twitter.com/jakejsullivan/status/1341180109118726144?lang=en-GB

Tobin JL, Busch ML (2010) A BIT is better than a lot: bilateral investment treaties and preferential trade agreements. World Polit 62(1):1–42

UNCTAD (n.d.) World Investment Report 2020. https://unctad.org/webflyer/world-investment--report-2020. Accessed 1 Feb 2022

UNCTAD Investment Policy Hub (n.d.) International Investment Agreements by Economy, China. https://investmentpolicy.unctad.org/international-investment-agreements/countries/42/china. Accessed 1 Feb 2022

UNCTAD Stat (n.d.) Foreign direct investment: Inward and outward flows and stock, annual. UNCTAD Stat. https://unctadstat.unctad.org/. Accessed 18 Dec. 2021

Wang M (2021a, February 11) Xi's Commitment to European Ties Hailed. China Daily. https://global.chinadaily.com.cn/a/202102/11/WS602476fba31024ad0baa8b05.html

Wang Y-H (2021b) 中欧CAI达成的背景、影响与中国策略选择. [The Background and Influence of China-EU CAI and China's Strategic Choice]. 中国流通经济 (7):51–63

Xia X (2021) Seize opportunities and jointly advance China-Eu economic and trade relations. Asia Eur J 19:507–509

Xin C (2014, March 18) The EU's dilemma with China: free trade or bilateral investment? The Parliament. https://www.theparliamentmagazine.eu/news/article/the-eus-dilemma-with-china-free-trade-or-bilateral-investment

Yu H (2017) Motivation behind China's 'One Belt, One Road' initiatives and establishment of the Asian infrastructure investment bank. J Cont China 26(105):353–368

Yu J (2018) The belt and road initiative: domestic interests, bureaucratic politics and the EU-China relations. Asia Eur J 16:223–236

Zeng K (2016) Understanding the Institutional Variation in China's Bilateral Investment Treaties (BITs): the complex interplay of domestic and international influences. J Cont China 25(97):112–129

Sohyun Zoe Lee is a Lecturer in International Political Economy at Queen's University Belfast. Her scholarly interests lie in the broad field of international relations and international political economy, with a more specific focus on the political economy of free trade agreements (FTAs) and economic integration in the Asia-Pacific and Indo-Pacific regions. She is particularly interested in the processes and practices involved in FTA negotiations through the examination of interactions among various domestic stakeholders. Dr. Lee also collaborates closely with policymakers, providing expertise in trade policies. Her work has appeared in the Pacific Review and Contemporary Politics, among others. From 2018 to 2021, she served as a postdoctoral fellow at the Institute of International Relations, China Foreign Affairs University. During her sabbatical leave in fall 2023, she was a visiting fellow at the World Trade Institute in Geneva, funded by AHRC. Dr. Lee holds a PhD in International Relations from the London School of Economics and Political Science (2018), an AM in Regional Studies—East Asia from Harvard University (2012), and a BA in International Studies from Korea University (2009).

The European Union and China: In Search of Positioning and Exercising Normative Power in the Comprehensive Agreement on Investment

I-Ju Chen

Abstract The EU and China, two of the most externally integrated global economies, have much in common in the context of international economic governance. However, these two partners have developed different models according to their interpretations and prioritisations of international principles and values. The EU focuses more on its own internal problems, and China expands its reach around the world after its accession to the WTO (the World Trade Organisation) in 2001. Both the EU and China have emerged as ambitious leaders or even normative powers in international economic governance. The EU-China strategic partnership has reached a new equilibrium based on which they manage their contending normative self-understanding. Their four-decade-long bilateral and by now strategic partnership has progressed to a level of complexity whereby their impacts on each other are mutual and inevitable. The principal conclusion of the CAI has advanced in bringing these two major economic powers together. This chapter identifies opportunities that the EU and China have in the negotiation of the CAI despite challenges from current global, regional, and bilateral political issues. Nevertheless, considering EU and China's individual limits as normative powers and the necessity to cooperate in re-constructing the economy after the pandemic, this "frenemy" situation could last for years with the concluded and eventually enforced CAI serving as a legal foundation and guidance for EU-China policy implementation.

1 Introduction

The foreign and economic relationship between the EU and China not only illustrates a strategic partnership but also a great power competition in the twenty-first century. Debate has intensified on both the EU's capacity as a normative power to

I.-J. Chen (✉)
School of Law, University of Exeter, Exeter, UK
e-mail: i.chen2@exeter.ac.uk

© The Author(s), under exclusive license to Springer Nature Switzerland AG 2024

A. Svetlicinii, I.-J. Chen (eds.), *The EU-China Comprehensive Agreement on Investment*, European Yearbook of International Economic Law,
https://doi.org/10.1007/978-3-031-66862-3_4

maintain and extend its global relevance and China's increasing capacity as an emerging global actor to generate development. This chapter examines how the EU and China exercise their normative power in the context of the CAI. It also describes the EU's and China's position as normative foreign policy actors in international economic governance by employing a constructivist approach which emphasises the role of recognition and context in identity formation.

The CAI, initially launched for negotiation in the EU-China Political Agreement in 2012, has opened a greater level of market access for EU firms to invest in China. By contrast, China is becoming more committed to ensuring fair treatment for EU companies. Therefore, EU firms can compete on a more level playing field in China. This is considered a breakthrough in the relationship between these two global major economic powers as well as for these two powers to reconcile their different principles and value. However, there is a question regarding these two economic powers' competition in international economic governance. In other words, the relationship between the EU and China begs a critical question about these two economic entities being friends or foes to compete for a normative power identity. Over the past thirty years, international relations scholars have studied how certain ideas attain the status of norms bringing about changes in the behaviour of states and other actors in international politics. Examinations of the agenda-setting process tend to focus on specific actors.[1]

This chapter adopts a doctrinal approach to examine three questions. The first seeks out the positions of the EU and China's individual normative power developments in international economic governance in the last twenty years. This inquiry is an examination of the engagement between the EU and China in accordance with the concept of normative power put forward by Ian Manners.[2] In international relations scholarships, normative power remains the dominant conceptual framework in exploring the explanation of Beijing's increasing influence in international economic governance due to the following reasons.[3] On the one hand, owing to the perceived complexity of the EU, Asian scholars have been rather passive to engage with the propositions and concepts of European international relations. On the other, European international relations scholars have generated and expanded minimal efforts to translate and transform the applicability of their terminology to non-EU actors and contexts.[4] Kavalski points out that 'this is both because of the all-pervasive nature of the EU and also because of the positioning of Asian studies outside the traditional international relations curriculum'.[5] As a consequence, this chapter also demonstrates the concept of normative power by establishing an encounter with its 'Chinese characteristics', which arises from witnessing a 'rise of

[1] Davies and True (2017), p. 702.

[2] Manners (2002), p. 236–252.

[3] Kavalski (2017), p. 150.

[4] Ibid.

[5] Ibid.

normative powers' in global politics.[6] The main aim of this chapter is to contribute to bridging differences between the EU and China and further to a more relational knowledge-production in international relations scholarships.

The second question in this chapter is about limits, opportunities, and challenges arising from the CAI. This chapter also explores an exercise of norm entrepreneurship performed by the EU and China through shaping international economic governance. The final question explores whether multilateralism still matters for international economic governance whilst there is economic power competition between the EU and China.

2 The EU, China, and Normative Power

The definition of normative power has taken political theorists a considerable amount of time to determine. Political elites have attempted to set up frames to channel public perception of this definition in a specific direction. This makes framing analysis a useful instrument to discover and underline the central organising ideas on normative foreign policy actors (NFPAs). NFPAs are derived from 'a framework for exploring how its image is constructed in three related steps: an actor evaluates an issue; takes up a position; and locates itself in relation to other actor's.[7]

This section will first delineate the theoretical framework of normative power, followed by demonstrating the EU's and China's engagement with the framework.

2.1 The Theoretical Framework of Normative Power

Normative power, contrary to military or economic power, is in general defined by how the relations of asymmetry are managed and a focus on building a more secure, organised, and prosperous world.[8] However, Manners conceptualises the power as follows: '[t]he ability to change the concept of 'normal' in international affairs through the diffusion of an actor's norms externally'.[9]

With the emergence of China as an economic significant power and gradual growth of military strength in the Asia-Pacific region, it is crucial to investigate the status of China as a normative power. China is seen as facing the challenges from the Western-dominated international society. China does not seem to want to conform to the Western standard of civilisation or the neo-liberal order and has its own distinctive features in establishing itself as a normative power.

[6] Ibid., p. 149.

[7] Wunderlich (2020a), p. 1111.

[8] Kavalski (2014), p. 306.

[9] Manners (2002), p. 251.

However, studies on normative power are scarce and of 'recent provenance', and this topic has 'hardly been broached in the analysis of Asian international affairs'.[10] Addressing caveats, to date, there appears 'insufficient systematic analysis of the impact of interests on norms and norm diffusion in the normative power scholarship. Some studies contend that normative power is indeed based on the exclusion of interests in norm diffusion'.[11] It is suggested that '[i]n multilateral institutions, normative power can be exercised by shaping the norms of the institution with the norms preferred by an actor to obtain control over the institutional processes'.[12]

2.2 *The EU: A Global Actor and Long-Term Normative Power with the Rule-of-Law Traditions*

The EU has been considered a normative power; an *idee force*; and a global actor by exemplifying and implementing the ideals for which it advocates.[13] To differentiate with other significant powers in the world (e.g., the US), the EU aims to establish its identity by becoming a different kind of power and a collective force by way of 'the promotion of universal values, shared interests, and the powers of attraction and persuasion'.[14] According to Art. 21(1) TEU, the EU's relations with the rest of the world are shaped to advance 'democracy, the rule of law, the universality and indivisibility of human rights and fundamental freedoms, respect for human dignity, the principles of equality and solidarity, and respect for the principles of the United Nations Charter and international law'.[15]

EU's external policies have grown in ambition, scope and stature. However, historically, the EU has never excelled in hard-power governance and struggled to gain leverage on the foundation of its economic weight. Eeckhout points out that the trajectory of EU's external relations and policies is neither unproblematic nor linear.[16] His critical opinion addresses that the EU's constitutional ambition, as expressed in the EU Treaties, is difficult to realise.[17] For instance, the Lisbon

[10] Kavalski (2013), p. 247; Kavalski (2014), p. 303.

[11] Peng (2020), p. 43.

[12] Ibid.

[13] Ferenczy (2019), p. 1.

[14] Manners (2002), p. 252.

[15] Consolidated version of the Treaty on European Union—Title V: General Provisions on the Union's External Action and Specific Provisions on the Common Foreign and Security Policy—Chapter 1: General provisions on the Union's external action.

[16] Eeckhout (2015), p. 219.

[17] Ibid.

Treaty—Art. 3(5) TEU and the full version of Art. 21[18]—was a thinly veiled attempt to further constitutionalise the founding Treaties concerning EU's external policies.[19]

'When it comes to external policies, the EU is best understood as a conglomerate of the EU institutions and Member States. Specifically, the EU seeks to become an ever more significant and engaging global actor',[20] not just in economic governance but across and beyond the range of its internal competences and policies. By contrast, the EU today is constantly challenged by internal economic, social, and political crises. Moreover, EU citizens and the world question the EU's ability to uphold the values that it affirms as fundamental to strengthen its existence.[21] Regardless of commitment as a global actor, the EU and the values that it and its Member States stand for have gradually fallen into an identity crisis. The EU's existence is affected by EU-scepticism and the possibility of disintegration.[22] The UK's withdrawal from the EU also amplified the identity crisis. Thus, EU's normative blueprints and ambitions incorporated in its China-related politics have unavoidably been impacted.[23]

Many legal scholars have been critical of the attempt to constitutionalise the values and objectives of the EU.[24] The idea of normative power Europe (NPE) was first defined by Manners in 2002[25] and underpinned by political theorists' conceptualisations.[26] A basis of the concepts of normative power investigates the EU in global politics and conceptualises the EU as a global actor. The concept of an NPE illustrates the EU's external relations as influenced by normative principles and embraced beliefs, which are at the core and codified in various places in the *acquis commauntaire*. Therefore, 'the EU's self-understanding has significant implications for the persona the EU aims to project externally'.[27] The EU aims to diffuse its own model, thereby normalising its own legal and rules-based approach to global

[18] 'The Union's action on the international scene shall be guided by the principles which have inspired its own creation, development and enlargement, and which it seeks to advance in the wider world: democracy, the rule of law, the universality and indivisibility of human rights and fundamental freedoms, respect for human dignity, the principles of equality and solidarity, and respect for the principles of the United Nations Charter and international law. The Union shall seek to develop relations and build partnerships with third countries, and international, regional or global organisations which share the principles referred to in the first subparagraph. It shall promote multilateral solutions to common problems, in particular in the framework of the United Nations.'

[19] Eeckhout (2015), p. 219.

[20] De Búrca (2013), p. 43.

[21] Ferenczy (2019), p. 1.

[22] Ibid.

[23] Ibid., p. 2.

[24] Eeckhout (2015), p. 224.

[25] Manners (2002), p. 235.

[26] Duchêne (1972), Galtung (1973) and Bull (1982) developed the earliest conceptualisations of the European Community's global role.

[27] Manners (2006), pp. 81–82.

governance.[28] An NPE is associated with the wider attempt to construct a post-cold-war European identity.[29]

The rule of law, long-standing applied in the EU, has also been a central element of EU's China policies since early times. 'Building a Comprehensive Partnership with China', supporting China's transition to the rule of law and respect for human rights has been one of Europe's five priorities and long-term objectives.[30] To enhance the practical implementation of the EU's normative power, several key steps are suggested.[31] These include ensuring that the systematic value mainstreaming prescribed by the EU's official discourse and aligning with the ideal type of NPE is practically realised. Nevertheless, in line with the essential standards in the EU, these steps are likely to counter the discourses that challenge value mainstreaming and shape the behaviour and/or practices of officials from the EU Commission and the European External Actions Services. Furthermore, such steps would foster common ground between EU officials and between the EU and Chinese sides in terms of increasing mutual understanding on values and standards.[32]

2.3 *China: An Emerging Economic and Normative Power Seeks Its Global Position*

When it comes to the rise of China—arguably, the most significant geopolitical challenge in the twenty-first century—this might appear to be the case particularly with China's sprawling Belt and Road Initiative (BRI).[33] Launched in 2013, the BRI is recognised as Xi's initiative for his 'Chinese dream'.[34]

The rapid transformation of China's economic potential is in the global limelight. China is increasingly influencing norms in international economic governance. A scholar in China urges for 'the general principals' to be resolved when viewing the economy of China and praises China's unique model of the combination of socialism and market economy as the 'first time in human history' that this has happened.[35] For instance, there is a new term, the "China model", in digital

[28] Tocci (2008), p. 3.

[29] Diez (2005), pp. 616–617.

[30] European Commission, Building a Comprehensive Partnership with China, 1998. The other objectives of the EEAS consist of support to stability, promotion of human rights and democracy. See EU Strategy towards China, https://eur-lex.europa.eu/legal-content/EN/TXT/HTML/?uri=LEGISSUM:r14205&from=EN and Commission Policy Paper for Transmission to the Council and the European Parliament, 'A maturing partnership, shared interests and challenges in the EU-China relation' 2003.

[31] Taylor (2019), p. 304.

[32] Ibid.

[33] Wu (2016), p. 261; Erie and Streinz (2021), p. 3.

[34] Chaisse and Matshshita (2018), pp. 165–70.

[35] Wong (2018), p. 16.

governance.[36] Engaging with difference has been at the core of a number of recent international relations publications that aim to de-centre and decolonise scientific knowledge and academic practice.[37] This inquiry offers productive means of overcoming the Eurocentric master narrative of the discipline by not only 'provincialising' its ratiocination but also urging international relation knowledge-production to take account of the 'specificities of its historical and local contexts'.[38]

With regards to China's rise in the context of international economic governance, the World Trade Organisation (WTO) regulations are not fully equipped to handle the range of economic problems associated with its rise. China gradually became an emerging power after its accession to the WTO in 2001. During this short period, the Chinese economy underwent an impressive transformation. China's emergence is thus reconfiguring WTO dispute settlement in a potentially worrying manner, given that 'China's economy is fundamentally different — even unique'.[39] 'The Chinese economy embraces market-oriented dynamics, yet it is not strictly a free-market capitalist system'.[40] The Chinese Communist Party, a separate political actor that plays an active role in the management of state-owned enterprises (SOEs) in China, is another influencing factor.

The current state of China is described in popular beliefs that see the "dragon" is emerging and trying to establish hegemony. There is an increasingly widespread belief that China is progressing and developing itself on the global stage as an important player, which would make China become a normative power. Specifically, the vision is 'the great rejuvenation of the Chinese nation' with the ultimate aim of standing strong as a power capable of shaping global events, capturing the yearning of 1.4 billion Chinese citizens.[41] Therefore, the challenge is to create a sense of unity around this vision. Beijing's going-out policy (2001), followed by initiatives such as the 16+1 Platform (2012), the BRI (2013) and Going Global 2.0, have come to be perceived as strong examples of an assertive China, getting ready to be a world leader as a 'fully developed, rich and powerful' nation by the 100th anniversary of the People's Republic of China in 2049.

The Chinese model of normative power suggests that to have normative power is to utilise it.[42] China holds various and simultaneous identities of a developing

---

[36] Erie and Streinz (2021), p. 3.

[37] Kavalski (2017), p. 151.

[38] Ibid., pp. 151–152.

[39] Wu (2016), p. 264.

[40] Ibid.

[41] Li Haiqing, Confidence in history important to achieve national rejuvenation China Daily, October 22nd 2022, https://www.chinadaily.com.cn/a/202210/22/WS6353414ea310fd2b29e7de76.html. Xi Jinping: Always act for people and rely on them in everything we do, embrace great rejuvenation of Chinese nation on all fronts through Chinese path to modernization https://www.fmprc.gov.cn/eng/zxxx_662805/202210/t20221024_10791244.html Ministry of Foreign Affairs, the People's Republic of China.

[42] Kavalski (2017), p. 164.

country, an emerging economy, and a significant economic power.[43] At the core of China's normative priorities is its emphasis on a communitarian concept of sovereignty: '[t]hat each country ought to develop its own political and economic system and norms without undue outside interference'.[44] This Westphalian reading of sovereignty premised on non-interference represents the essence of China's external identity, which is that of an alternative normative power to the West. It further forms part of Zhou Enlai's Five Principles of Peaceful Coexistence[45] and of China's international positioning as an NFPA. As the emergence of China gradually imposes pressure on the West, contested sovereignty is a hurdle for China to become a recognised normative power. As a result, China is attempting to exhibit and exercise its normative strength through constructive engagement by setting up the Asia Investment Infrastructure Bank (AIIB), BRI, and the New Development Bank. For instance, the AIIB will 'significantly enhance China's normative power in international society'.[46]

The Chinese model of economic development emphasises the key role played by government planning, which involves significant investment in infrastructure and industrial policy. As the Chinese economy grew increasingly competitive, China gained confidence in its economic model and started to promote it as an alternative to development models advocated by the US-dominated Bretton Woods systems. China attempts to establish new markets for Chinese products, which markets are governed by a combination of private contracts and treaties, underpinned by novel dispute settlement mechanisms. The development stimulates economic integration that creates new bonds with Beijing. In law and development circles, this model is based on what is referenced as a "Beijing consensus" or "Beijing model," constituting a rival to the so-called neoliberal "Washington consensus".[47]

Concerning the rule of law, it is largely conceptualised by the Chinese Communist Party's one-party rule. Therefore, in China's governance, rule of law is usually framed under the slogan 'socialist rule of law with Chinese characteristics' and distinguished from a Western context. Nevertheless, this Chinese Communist Party's rule of law also signals openness to embrace and learn from other countries' practices.[48]

[43] Breslin (2013), p. 617.

[44] Ibid.

[45] Ibid., p. 631; Womack (2008), p. 266.

[46] Peng and Tok (2016), p. 736.

[47] Shaffer and Gao (2020), p. 610.

[48] Ferenczy (2019), p. 92.

3 The EU and China: Exercising Normative Power in the CAI and/or Performing Norm Entrepreneurships in the Negotiations of the CAI?

The CAI is a bilateral investment agreement between the EU and China. Compared to the EU's earlier trade agreements (with Korea and Vietnam), the CAI has several notable features, 'especially as far as the commitments accepted by China are concerned'.[49] Therefore, the bilateral EU-China investment agreement could be useful for a future multilateral agreement in areas where current WTO rules do not provide sufficient disciplines for countries such as China.[50]

Through maintaining bilateral dialogues with EU Member States, Beijing has engaged with individual legal systems in the context of European legal pluralism. 'Legal pluralism' as a concept is marked by deep conceptual confusion. Therefore, diverse, competing, crossing, and overlapping legal orders appear to be proliferating. In the European case, it entails an official legal system and supranational framework linked to an institutionalised legal apparatus with legislatures and enforcement agencies.[51] For the Chinese case, the appeal of legal pluralism with the EU could be regarded as an incentive for a rule of law dialogue. Alternatively, emulating other legal systems could also damage Chinese advancement, because there is no template that China can copy, no predecessor to show the way; rather, the Chinese Communist Party must find the right balance in its legal reforms, and Chinese rule of law must remain capable of positive growth and change.[52]

EU-China foreign and economic relations are one of the most important and complex global partnerships. They are influencing and further shaping their regions, such as discourse in addressing global challenges and finding solutions. As a result, the implications of their relationship are far-reaching in regional and international development. Ferenczy points out that Europe is a globally more aloof and inward-looking region, whereas China is a more engaging and outward-looking country.[53] Thus, debate has intensified on how the two sides actually shape each other's perspectives and development. China, as an emerging actor seeking international recognition, has also voiced its determination to pursue its own economic and political interests, by means of navigating between embrace and dismissal of international laws, norms, and standards. The EU will seek to help bring China in line with international relations and norms. Nevertheless, the overall optimism towards China's future appears to be a great contrast to Western scholars' view. The comparative study of normative power Europe and normative power China (both *acquis communautaire* and *guanxi,* translated as 'social relations' in English) bespeak distinct

---

[49] Mavroidis and Sapir (2022), p. 1.

[50] Ibid.

[51] Ferenczy (2019), p. 92.

[52] Ibid.

[53] Ibid., p. 1.

modes of international outreach and indicate that the former suggests a "rule-based" system, while the latter outlines a relationship framework for the management of a dynamic and interactive environment.[54] For this kind of comparative analysis, the argument is that such distinct points of departure have led to the evolution of distinct concepts and practices of normative power. The required qualification is a parallel examination that focuses on the ideal types implicit in the normative powers of the EU and China.[55]

The CAI appears to be a place where the EU and China exhibit and attempt to exercise normative power in international economic governance. After eight years of negotiations, the EU and China signed in December 2020 a bilateral investment agreement. If ratified, this agreement will have significant economic effects because of the economic size of the two players and the difference in their economic systems. The CAI will be the largest Global-North-and-South investment agreement between a developed and an emerging economy, and between a market and a non-market economy.[56]

Negotiation of the CAI also seems to reflect the EU and China's norms around entrepreneurship. Norm entrepreneurs is a concept arising from constructivist international relations research on norms.[57] Entrepreneurs, including 'individual and collective actors who eagerly strive to promote the establishment, diffusion, and institutionalisation of norms',[58] are the main driving forces during norm socialisation processes.[59] It is argued that norm entrepreneurs—both external and internal—have been essential for bringing social norms, such as human rights, to the EU's attention.[60] Jenichen finds that the importance of norm entrepreneurs lies in making the EU aware of international political developments, including the persecution of religious and/or sexual minorities in other parts of the world and in overcoming internal resistance by soliciting a positive self-image of the EU and international obligations of its Member States.[61] For instance, the CAI is not just about investment liberalisation but primarily concerned with two narrower issues: the environment and labour rights protection. The CAI reaffirms the parties' 'right to regulate', requires parties to strive to ensure laws provide for 'high levels' of environmental standards and labour protection, and recognises that it is 'inappropriate' to promote investment by reducing environmental or labour rights protection. These latter two clauses concerning sustainable development enshrine EU principles.[62] Thus, this shows that the negotiation of the CAI appears to be a platform for norm

[54] Kavalski (2017), p. 152.

[55] Ibid.

[56] Mavroidis and Sapir (2022), p. 1.

[57] Jenichen (2022), p. 1300.

[58] Wunderlich (2020b), p. 22.

[59] Ibid., p. 15.

[60] Jenichen (2022), p. 1299.

[61] Ibid., p. 1300.

[62] Cotula (2021), p. 363.

entrepreneurs in the EU to influence China, particularly due to the inclusion of sustainable development regulations protecting the environment and labour rights. This is underpinned in Wunderlich's research, which addresses the fact that the institutional setting of norm negotiation processes would influence the content of the norm.[63]

3.1 *Limits, Opportunities, and Challenges Faced by the EU and China in the Negotiation of the CAI*

This section identifies limits, opportunities, and challenges. First of all, EU's limits in exercising normative power fall in its abiding commitments in promoting universal values stipulated in Arts. 3(5) and 21 in TEU. Regarding China's limits, it takes time for China to move closer in line with international standards.[64]

Secondly, the EU can utilise the CAI to extend its level playing field with China, which would enable China to be closer to international neoliberal standards. With regards to foreign investment, the EU has a liberal attitude. The Lisbon Treaty gave the EU competence over foreign investment policy. The CJEU declared that 'direct investment' indeed falls within the competence of the EU, yet portfolio investment, investor protection and Investor-State Dispute Settlement (ISDS) frameworks do not.[65] As a result, the EU has become an active member of the global investment community.[66] Thus, this chapter believes that the CAI will provide opportunities for the EU to re-construct its normative power image and an active global actor identity.

More than twenty years after China's accession to the WTO, the CAI could be a significant step in the relationship between China and its trading and investment partners.[67] The CAI poses opportunities to implement China's Go Global investment strategy, launched in 2001. Chinese observers acknowledge the importance of arrangements concerning market access, level playing field, and dispute resolution stipulated in the CAI.[68] At the first China Investment and Trade Fair held in Xiamen in 2001, the Chinese Government officially launched a two-way investment strategy as a prelude to all-around integration into the global economy. At that time, the previous Chinese Vice Premier Wu Bangguo pointed out that the outbound investment strategy will be integrated with continuous effort to promote foreign capital inflow to boost China's overall involvement in global economic cooperation. It was believed to be an important decision by the Chinese Government to meet the

[63] Wunderlich (2020b), p. 32.

[64] Ferenczy (2019), p. 8.

[65] EU Opinion 2/15.

[66] Woolcock (2010), p. 22.

[67] Mavroidis and Sapir (2022), p. 19.

[68] Chang and Pieke (2018), p. 323.

demands of international and domestic situations as well as to support China's economic development.[69]

Finally, further challenges to officially conclude the CAI arise from the war between Russia and Ukraine in February 2022 after the European Parliament froze the CAI ratification in 2021. The recent EU trade policy review communication recognises China and India as 'indispensable partners for WTO reform discussions' and notes that '[d]iscussions with China and India should help to better understand our respective perspectives, including on the issues for which progress should be achieved at MC12 and beyond'.[70]

3.2 *EU vs. China: Friends or Foes in International Economic Governance?*

Upon celebrating forty years of bilateral relations, both the EU and China agreed to establish an EU-China Legal Affairs Dialogue for policy exchanges, mutual learning and cooperation in legal affairs.[71] The announced exchange on legal affairs is expected to lead to the establishment of new dialogue mechanisms.[72] There was no mention, however, of the establishment of an actual dialogue dedicated to the rule of law in the document, or in any other joint statement. Ferenczy found that China refused to establish a rule of law dialogue with the EU.[73] Rather, Beijing maintains individual dialogues with EU Member States, which indicates China's general preference to work with Member States and signals its divide-and-rule approach.[74] It is worth addressing that the fragmentation of EU governance has remained critical in shaping EU's rule of law policy towards China. Additionally, the impacts of EU Member States' individual actions on EU's joint action can further damage EU's credibility and undermine its power internally.[75]

Prior to the contemporary issues between the EU and China, both the EU and China were neither systemic rivals nor strategic competitors. EU-China bilateral relations have deteriorated, notably related to a growing number of incidents, such as China's countermeasures to EU sanctions on human rights and China's position

---

[69] "Go Global" Investment Strategy Needed for Chinese Enterprises, http://www.china.org.cn/english/GS-e/19033.htm.

[70] European Commission (2021), Trade Policy Review – An Open, Sustainable and Assertive Trade Policy. Annex: Reforming the WTO: Towards a Sustainable and Effective Multilateral Trading System. COM(2021) 66 final, p. 16.

[71] European External Action Service, 2015, The Way Forward after Forty Years of EU-China Cooperation. First China-EU Legal Affairs Dialogue, 2016 https://ec.europa.eu/newsroom/just/items/34106.

[72] Ibid.

[73] Ferenczy (2019), p. 94.

[74] Ibid.

[75] Ibid.

on the war in Ukraine. Nevertheless, the EU remains committed to engagement and cooperation with China due to China's crucial role in addressing global and regional challenges. Simultaneously, the EU will continue to deal with China as a strategic partner for cooperation and negotiation, an economic competitor and a systemic rival.[76]

The two adopt open strategies when facing challenges. For example, common goals of the EU and China indicate that 'EU-China cooperation should not be seen as an end in itself, but as a stepping stone to wider global governance cooperation and reform'.[77] Therefore, there was much overlap between the EU and China concerning fundamental strategic outlook and trajectory, including a desire for effective multilateralism to be at the heart of international economic governance.[78] For instance, the Chinese Foreign Minister called for true multilateral win-win cooperation at G20 meeting held in July 2022.[79]

The author thinks that the CAI bridges the gap between the EU and China much more closely than before. The negotiation of the CAI has enabled the EU-China strategic partnership to enter a new phase. This newfound equilibrium is arguably due to the EU's 'decreasing expectations *vis-à-vis* China that concern China's internal democratisation and the EU confining discussions on human rights solely to the EU-China Human Rights Dialogue'.[80]

While COVID has overshadowed several other crises, post-pandemic reconstruction remains one of the world's most urgent challenges.[81] Considering this pressing issue, China needs Europe to re-construct the national developments, regional integration, and global economy. The impact of China's rise on the EU is diverse mainly because EU Member States have different interests *vis-à-vis* China. The varying engagement of Member States with China includes the uneven economic impact of trade and investment relationships or the lack of an agreement on normative principles or strategic priorities. As a result, deeper engagement with China is likely to exacerbate these differences amongst EU Member States. This might bring about opportunities to intensify cooperation between the EU and China, both bilaterally and in the context of multilateral institutions. However, the rise of China also causes risks to the EU—not least that it may become more difficult for the EU to manage external relations with other global powers whilst maintaining a semblance of unity among Member States.[82]

---

[76] EEAS, EU-China Relations factsheet (April 1st 2022), https://www.eeas.europa.eu/eeas/eu-china-relations-factsheet_en.

[77] Garcia-Herrero et al. (2017), p. 55.

[78] Ferenczy (2019), pp. 36–38.

[79] Chinese FM calls for true multilateralism, win-win cooperation at G20 meeting, http://en.people.cn/n3/2022/0709/c90000-10120978.html.

[80] Michalski and Nilsson (2019) p. 445.

[81] Wang and Miao (2020), p. 226–227.

[82] Christiansen and Maher (2017), p. 131.

4 Beyond the Normative Power Competition Between the EU and China in International Economic Governance: Does Multilateralism Still Matter?

Many provisions in the CAI are fundamentally WTO-plus in nature.[83] Substantively, the CAI represents an important negotiating outcome on a range of contested investment issues that include market opening issues.[84] This chapter argues that multilateralism plays a key role in international economic governance amidst the normative power contest between the EU and China.[85] Concerning the function of the WTO, which is composed of 164 members, the author is convinced that the existence of the WTO is a recognised forum for countries from Global North and South to negotiate measures to confront global challenges in relation to trade. Superpowers' competition would inevitably cause impacts on global trade governance. Given such tensions, the multilateral trading system, its goals and rules will amplify collective efforts to mitigate impacts arising from the superpower rivalry. Moreover, the dispute settlement mechanism, widely considered the jewel in the crown of the WTO, has been used by China, US, and the EU. This reflects the value and benefit of a multilateral trading system regardless of suspending the function of Appellate Body (AB). Effective dispute settlement mechanisms are critical to sustain trade cooperation. Resolving the AB crisis requires the commitment of all stakeholders, especially the major trade powers, to agree on reform of WTO dispute settlement. This is to ensure conflict resolution continues to be apolitical.[86] The EU initiated the establishment of an interim appeals mechanism that WTO members can use while the AB remains unable to function - this interim mechanism is called Multi-Party Interim Appeal Arbitration Arrangement (MPIA). China joined the EU in supporting this initiative. The EU and China have recently renewed their commitments to international adjudication by participating in the MPIA and the CAI.[87]

Regarding the recent proposal of a multilateral investment court (MIC), the EU tried to gain support for its cause from other stakeholders to put public pressure on opponents of the MIC. Lobbying is an example of coalition-building in international organisations that can be complex and involve public and private negotiation.[88] Therefore, the proposed MIC re-affirms the essential role of a multilateral institution in international economic governance.

---

[83] Kurtz and Gong (2021), p. 207.

[84] Ibid.

[85] There are a number of discussions on this topic. See Mavroidis and Sapir (2022); Hoekman et al. (2021).

[86] Liao and Mavroidis (2021), p. 61.

[87] Ibid., pp. 71–72.

[88] Svoboda (2022), p. 23.

5 Conclusion

EU-China bilateral economic relations have undergone a significant transformation. The signing of the CAI is certainly promising for developments of international trade and investment, regardless of the suspended ratification of the agreement at the European Parliament. It has also attracted much academic attention in law, international relations, and political science.

As Kavalski notes, it seems that an unintended outcome of the post-Cold War global order and the focus in world affairs has been gradually shifting from West to East.[89] Thus, commentators in the early 1990s were pondering how far Western norms would spread, whereas nowadays, the debate tends to be about how far Asian (and, especially, Chinese) ideas or values will reach to the other side of the world.[90] The principal conclusion of the CAI reflected a shift towards a more harmonious development and recognition of the need to invest in reducing the East–West dividends in international economic governance. The negotiation process of the CAI also represents a model referred to as a "Beijing consensus" and constitutes a rival to the so-called neoliberal "Washington consensus".

In line with Manners's definition, this chapter has attempted to locate the positions of the EU and China in the normative power competition in the context of the CAI. This chapter found that EU and China exercise their normative power through very different approaches. Such a difference might result from EU's rule-of-law foundations and China's preferred relationship framework for governance. The negotiation of the CAI also seems to reflect the EU and China's norm entrepreneurships exercise. A vivid example is the EU's usual inclusion of sustainable development chapters in its bilateral trade agreements and also in the CAI with the aim of protecting the environment and labour rights. This European norm and value incorporated into the CAI bridges the normative gap between the EU and China. CAI additionally brings about opportunities to enhance EU and China's normative power identity. Nevertheless, the pending ratification of the CAI in the EU as well as impacts from the Russia-Ukraine War have caused the EU and China's strategic relationship to deteriorate. Thus, now the EU simultaneously sees China as an economic competitor, a systemic rival, and a partner for cooperation and negotiation.

References

Breslin S (2013) China and the global order: signalling threat or friendship? Int Aff 89(3):615–634
Bull H (1982) Civilian power Europe: a contradiction in terms? J Common Mark Stud 21(2):149–164
Chaisse J, Matsushita M (2018) China's "Belt and Road" initiative: mapping the world trade normative and strategic implications. J World Trade 52(1):163–185

89 Kavalski (2017), p. 164.

90 Ibid.

Chang VKL, Pieke FN (2018) Europe's engagement with china: shifting Chinese views of the EU and the EU-China relationship. Asia Eur J 6:317–331

Chinese FM calls for true multilateralism, win-win cooperation at G20 meeting, http://en.people.cn/n3/2022/0709/c90000-10120978.html Accessed 10 Aug 2024

Christiansen T, Maher R (2017) The rise of China—challenges and opportunities for the European Union. Asia Eur J 15:121–131

Cotula L (2021) EU–China comprehensive agreement on investment: an appraisal of its sustainable development. Bus Human Rights J 6(2):360–367

Davies SE, True J (2017) Norm entrepreneurship in foreign policy: William Hague and the prevention of sexual violence in conflict. Foreign Policy Anal 13(3):701–721

De Búrca G (2013) EU external relations: the governance mode of foreign policy. In: Van Vooren B, Blockmans S, Wouters J (eds) The EU's role in global governance – the legal dimension. OUP, Oxford, pp 39–58

Diez T (2005) Constructing the self and changing others: reconsidering 'Normative Power Europe', millennium. J Int Stud 33(3):613–636

Duchêne F (1972) Europe's role in world peace. In: Mayne R (ed) Europe tomorrow: sixteen Europeans look ahead. Fontana, London, pp 32–47

Eeckhout P (2015) A normative basis for EU external relations? Protecting internal values beyond the single market. In: Krajewski M (ed) Services of general interest beyond the single market. Springer, Switzerland, pp 219–232

Erie MS, Streinz T (2021) The Beijing effect: China's Digital Silk Road as transnational data governance. NY Univ J Int Law Polit 54(1):1–92

Ferenczy Z (2019) Europe, China, and the limits of normative power. Edward Elgar, Cheltenham

Galtung J (1973) The European community: a superpower in the making. Allen & Unwin, London

Garcia-Herrero A, Kwok KC, Liu X, Summers T, Zhang Y (2017) EU-China economic relations to 2025: building a common future, a joint report by Bruegel, Chatham House, China Centre for International Economic Exchange and the Chinese University of Hong Kong.

"Go Global" Investment Strategy Needed for Chinese Enterprises, http://www.china.org.cn/english/GS-e/19033.htm. Accessed 10 Aug 2024

Hoekman B, Wolfe R (2021) Reforming the World Trade Organization: Practitioner Perspectives from China, the EU, and the US. China & World Economy 29(4):1–34

Jenichen A (2022) The politics of normative power Europe: norm entrepreneurs and contestation in the making of EU external human rights policy. JCMS 60(5):1299–1315

Kavalski E (2013) The struggle for recognition of normative powers: normative power Europe and normative power China in context. Cooperat Confl 48(2):247–267

Kavalski E (2014) The shadows of normative power in Asia: framing the international agency of China, India, and Japan. Pac Focus 29(3):303–328

Kavalski E (2017) Normative power Europe and normative power China compared: towards a relational knowledge-production in international relations. Korean Pol Sci Rev 51(6):147–170

Kurtz J, Gong B (2021) The EU–China comprehensive agreement on investment: A model for investment coverage in the world trade organization? Global Governance Programme, RSC Working Paper 2021/58

Li H (2022) Confidence in history important to achieve national rejuvenation. China Daily, October 22nd https://www.chinadaily.com.cn/a/202210/22/WS6353414ea310fd2b29e7de76.html. Accessed 10 Aug 2024

Liao S, Mavroidis PC (2021) China, the European Union, and the WTO dispute settlement crisis. In: Hoekman B, Tu X, Wang D (eds) Rebooting multilateral trade cooperation: perspectives from China and Europe. Centre for Economic Policy Research Press, London, pp 61–73

Manners I (2002) Normative power Europe: a contradiction in terms. J Common Mark Stud 40(2):235–258

Manners I (2006) Normative power Europe reconsidered: beyond the crossroads. J Eur Public Policy 13(2):182–199

Mavroidis PC, Sapir A (2022) What is so special about CAI? Asia Pac Law Rev 30(2):348–366

Michalski A, Nilsson N (2019) Resistant to change? The EU as a normative power and its troubled relations with Russia and China. Foreign Policy Anal 15(3):432–449
Peng Z (2020) A comparative analysis of the normative power of the EU and China. University of Melbourne, PhD thesis
Peng Z, Tok SK (2016) The AIIB and China's normative power in international financial governance structure. Chinese Pol Sci Rev 1:736–753
Shaffer G, Gao H (2020) A new Chinese economic law order? J Int Econ Law 23(3):607–635
Svoboda O (2022) UNCITRAL Working Group III and Multilateral Investment Court –Troubled Waters for EU Normative Power
Taylor MR (2019) Seeking common ground: assessing the practical implementation of the EU's normative power in EU-China Dialogues, University of Bath PhD
Tocci N (2008) Profiling normative foreign policy: the European Union and its global partners. In: Tocci N (ed) Who is a normative foreign policy actor: the European Union and its global partners. Centre for European Policy Studies, Brussels, pp 1–23
Wang H, Miao L (2020) In this together: China-EU relations in the COVID-19 Era. Asia Eur J 18:223–226
Womack B (2008) China as a normative foreign policy actor, CEPS Working Document No.282
Wong L (2018) China as a future normative power: a Chinese cultural perspective. ABC Res Alert 6(1):15–24
Woolcock S (2010) EU trade and investment policymaking after the lisbon treaty. Intereconomics 45:22–25
Wu M (2016) The "China, Inc." challenge to global trade governance. Har Int Law J 57(2):261–324
Wunderlich C (2020b) Rogue States as norm entrepreneurs: black sheep or sheep in wolves' clothing? Springer, Switzerland
Wunderlich J-U (2020a) Positioning as normative actors: China and the EU in climate change negotiations. JCMS 58(5):1107–1123
Xi JP (2022) Always act for people and rely on them in everything we do, embrace great rejuvenation of Chinese nation on all fronts through Chinese path to modernization. https://www.fmprc.gov.cn/eng/zxxx_662805/202210/t20221024_10791244.html Ministry of Foreign Affairs, the People's Republic of China

I-Ju Chen is Lecturer in Law at the University of Exeter, School of Law. Prior to joining University of Exeter, she was Teaching Fellow at the University of Birmingham, where she obtained her funded PhD and the Fellowship in Advance HE for her teaching qualification. She holds an LLM in EU competition law from University College London. She was Visiting Scholar at Doshisha University Faculty of Law in 2024. She was Jean Monnet Visiting Scholar at Singapore Management University Yong Pung How School of Law (2023) and Visiting Scholar of the Centre for Chinese Law and Policy at Durham University (2021). Her research interests lie in international economic law, in particular WTO law, EU external economic relations law, and international financial law. She is a Rapporteur of headnotes in Oxford International Organizations (OXIO). She published in renowned journals, for example, *Chinese Journal of Comparative Law (OUP), Asian Journal of WTO and International Health Law and Policy*, and European Federation for Investment Law and Arbitration (EFILA).

Part II
EU-China Comprehensive Agreement on Investment: Substantive Issues

Pre-Entry National Treatment in EU-China Comprehensive Agreement on Investment: An Open Sesame to the Chinese Market?

Xueji Su

Abstract Since its inception, the EU-China Comprehensive Agreement on Investment (CAI) has prioritised the goal of market liberalisation. To this purpose, the EU has proposed that the CAI should include, among other market liberalisation disciplines, a pre-establishment national treatment requirement with a narrow list of exemptions. However, China's 2019 legislative overhaul in the sphere of foreign investment regulation, which introduced pre-establishment national treatment for foreign investment and repealed its long-standing case-by-case clearance procedure, casts doubt on the value of the EU's proposal. At the same time, despite the new regulations, market access difficulties for foreign investors have not been eliminated entirely, and new issues have emerged from China's reforms and increasingly politicised investment settings. This chapter examines the effects and limitations of the pre-establishment national treatment discipline alongside the negative list approach in the CAI, in light of persistent and emerging concerns with market access in China.

1 Introduction

In 2020, with the passage of a 'in principle' draft text, the long-awaited negotiations on the Comprehensive Agreement on Investment (CAI) between the European Union (EU) and China were finally completed.[1] As it stands, this agreement contains a variety of market liberalisation terms, but lacks conventional investment protection elements such as fair and equitable treatment, norms for expropriation, and

[1] Council of the European Union, Joint Press Communiqué of the 14th EU-China Summit, Beijing, 14 February 2012.

X. Su (✉)
University of Macau, Faculty of Law, Macao, China
e-mail: xuejisu@um.edu.mo

© The Author(s), under exclusive license to Springer Nature Switzerland AG 2024

A. Svetlicinii, I.-J. Chen (eds.), *The EU-China Comprehensive Agreement on Investment*, European Yearbook of International Economic Law,
https://doi.org/10.1007/978-3-031-66862-3_5

the full protection and security standard. As two exceptions, the national treatment and most-favourable-nation treatment criteria are both provided under Section II of the agreement, which however also aim to achieve investment liberalisation rather than investment protection.

This chapter explores the CAI's national treatment standard—which covers the pre-entry stage—and its effects on market liberalisation. The pre-establishment national treatment standard is initiated by the EU for the purpose of further liberalizing the Chinese market for European investment. Although the EU first placed national treatment at the core of its negotiations, subsequent changes have pushed it to resort to other deep trade disciplines. The most significant of these changes has been China's overhaul of its foreign investment regulation, which has introduced pre-entry national treatment for foreign investment and revoked the long-standing case-by-case approval mechanism.[2] These changes have not only eliminated some investment barriers and thus obviated the value of national treatment standard in the CAI, but also created new obstacles to market access. Considering the persistent and emerging market access issues in China, this chapter evaluates the adequacy of the pre-establishment national treatment and the negative list approach in the CAI.

The chapter is structured as follows. Section 2 examines the *raison d'être* of the EU-China CAI, and in particular the expectations of the EU with regard to market liberalization and the recalibration of its strategy. Section 3 looks at the changing landscape in foreign investment law and regulation in China as well as the residual and novel market access issues in spite of the advances. Section 4 overviews pre-establishment national treatment standard and negative list approach in a broader landscape of treaty making practice and in the CAI. Section 5 assesses the effects, the limits and the scope of pre-entry national treatment clause and the negative list vis-à-vis the standing market access barriers for potential foreign investors.

2 Market Liberalisation as Major Driving Force in the Negotiations

The decade-long EURO crisis, which result in a glaring fault line for European nations' liquidity and capital,[3] provides a significant incentive for searching investments from outside Europe.[4] The desire of European states and enterprises to tap

[2] In particular, the adoption of 中华人民共和国外商投资法 (Foreign Investment Law of China), adopted on 15 March 2019, effective on 1 January 2020,中华中华人民共和国外商投资法实施条例 (Implementing Regulation of the Foreign Investment Law of China), adopted on 26 December, effective on 1 January 2020, and 外商投资准入特别管理措施 (负面清单)(Negative List for Foreign Investment), firstly published in 2017 and renewed annually.

[3] Godement et al. (2011).

[4] Ewert (2016).

into China's economic potential for recapitalization, in turn, has induced a cacophony of competition among indebted EU Member States.[5]

On 7 July 2010, with a view to reconciling investment measures of the Member States and preparing the EU for its newly-acquired exclusive competence over third country investment, the Commission adopted the Communication 'Towards a comprehensive European international investment policy'. The Communication outlines several important tasks for future EU investment policy as well as the fundamental criteria for certain imminent activities in this domain. In addition, the Communication singled out strategic trading partners with whom new investment agreements were considered particularly desirable, including the People's Republic of China.[6] The Commission notes in the Communication that in the selection of its future bilateral investment treaty negotiating partners, regard should be given to the following criteria: (a) 'the interests of our stakeholders'; (b) the character of the EU's future negotiating partners and; (c) 'the nature of the existing agreements of Member States with any given third country'.[7] While further clarification is lacking in the Communication, these factors all manifest in the following impact assessment of the EU-China CAI produced by the Commission.[8]

In the impact assessment, the criteria 'the interests of stakeholders' and 'the character of the EU's future negotiating partners' are translated into two enquires – where European capital is destined,[9] and where European enterprises face impediments in terms of entry and operation. Given the importance of public opinion on the selection of desirable treaty partners, in May 2011, the EU launched public consultation.[10] Around 60% of respondents named China as a strategic market for EU businesses.[11] The respondents cited '[t]The proximity to the clients/market, the reduced labour costs, the costs of resources, and the productivity' as the Chinese market's most appealing features.[12]

While this analysis demonstrates the significant desire of European investors to enter the Chinese market, their frustration is equally evident.[13] European enterprises frequently report various regulatory barriers in China that hinder their investment. According to the Business Confidence Survey 2013,[14] published by the European Union Chamber of Commerce in China (EUCCC), 45% of EU companies lost

[5] Hallinan (2016), p. 31; Godement and Stanzel (2015), p. 7.

[6] Copenhagen Economics (2012), p. 17.

[7] European Commission (2010), p. 343.

[8] European Commission (2013).

[9] See 'Comprehensive European International Investment Policy', p. 6.

[10] European Commission (2011), p. 3.

[11] Ibid.

[12] Tenuta (2015), p. 13.

[13] According to Li and Bian, foreign investors find the Chinese market attractive for two reasons: (1) relatively high investment returns; and (2) low production costs and high production efficiency. See Li and Bian (2022), p. 4.

[14] The data from 2013 is presented here, as relevant to the period in which negotiations were launched.

business opportunities due to market access and regulatory barriers.[15] Moreover, EUCCC reported an upward trend in unfair treatment of foreign companies in successive years.[16] In parallel, Copenhagen Economics also distributed questionnaires during the CAI's agenda-setting phase to acquire a better understanding of the requirements of European business operators pertinent to the agreement.[17] The analysis revealed that, out of 214 identified barriers, over half (114) were considered to raise the cost of accessing the Chinese market, with 34 limiting the scope of EU firms' activities in China, and 29 adding to the cost of functioning in China. Additionally, 26 impediments directly hamper investment, while 11 barriers increase the risk associated with investing in China.[18] International investment is restricted in a significant number of critical areas for the Chinese economy. Other industries are only partially accessible, as foreign investors face numerous limitations and incidents of maltreatment, such as the prohibition on creating entirely foreign-owned enterprises, restrictive local rules and regulations, and cumbersome and opaque administrative procedures.[19]

The Commission summarizes all these issues as 'two main challenges of the current investment relationship – the lack of market access and discriminatory treatment of foreign investors'.[20] To address these two challenges, the EU determined that a comprehensive legal framework is warranted.[21] After examining the status of existing agreements with China, the Commission expected that,

> by negotiating a single EU-China BIT to replace the current 26 BITs a number of advantages could occur that would make the option attractive: (1) improve the level of protection for EU investors in China originating in countries with a 'weaker' BIT with China (and non in the case of Ireland) and grant protection to investors in such EU Member States with an equivalent or higher level of protection granted in the 'strongest' of the current BITs; (2) a consolidation could also improve and simplify the investment protection regime for Chinese investors in Europe by replacing the current 25 different agreements with one single agreement. Finally, it may be argued that the Commission could be expected to have increased negotiation power vis-à-vis China when negotiating on behalf of the entire union, and thereby perhaps leverage on that negotiation power to obtain better investment protection including provisions not covered in the current BITs.[22]

As regards investment protection, the following specific requirements come to prominence: (1) avoiding forced technology transfers; (2) removing discriminatory authorisation procedures; (3) ensuring that state-owned enterprises compete on equal terms and act on the basis of commercial considerations; and (4) improving

---

[15] European Union Chamber of Commerce in China (2013).

[16] European Union Chamber of Commerce in China (2017).

[17] Copenhagen Economics (2012), p. 10.

[18] Ibid., p. 70.

[19] Ibid.

[20] European Commission (2013).

[21] Ibid.

[22] Copenhagen Economics (2012), p. 37; 'Comprehensive European International Investment Policy', pp. 6–7.

transparency regarding subsidies to Chinese companies.[23] In a nutshell, the EU's priorities regarding the CAI negotiations can be reduced to two goals: investment liberalization (i.e., ensuring both improved market access and effective enforcement of investors' rights) and investment protection (i.e., reconciling the competing investment policies of the Member States and unifying investment protection standards).[24]

In accordance with the market liberalisation objective, when the mandates for the EU-China CAI were presented, the Commission entrusted Covington & Burling LLP to conductan empirical research to determine the efficacy of the national treatment norm. The results of the study were published as 'Assessing "National Treatment" as a Basis for Securing Market Access' (hereinafter 'NT report'). This report bears out the EU's initial intention of using pre-establishment national treatment standard plus the negative list approach as a principal means to liberalizing the Chinese market.[25] The 'NT report' identified four types of 'pre-establishment' restraints that thwart free access for foreign investment into China: market entry, government approval, equity requirements, and technology transfer.[26] According to the report, the first goal, resting on the idea of reciprocity, is to significantly reduce China's Catalogue for foreign investments and to expand the treatment beyond China's special economic zones to its whole territory.[27] Furthermore, the analysis determined that the implementation of the pre-entry national treatment standard would lead to a reduction in the stringency of approval procedures. It was also anticipated that the incorporation of national treatment standard would reduce or eliminate performance requirements and forced technology transfer. At the outset of the discussions, the national treatment and the exchange of market access offers were the foundations of the CAI talks.

However, it was reported in 2019 that, during the negotiations 'the European Union has raised additional requirements and expectations of political changes over the course of recent talks, including state subsidies', and 'some of the demands of the EU transcend the competence of Chinese negotiating team'.[28] The gravity of the negotiations shifted to three aspects of the level playing-field rules (state-owned enterprises, transparency rules for subsidies and rules tackling forced technology transfers). The European side bemoaned a lack of ambition and engagement from high-level politicians in Beijing, while China reiterated that the EU should meet it 'half way'.[29] As a result, the virtual 22nd EU-China Summit in July 2020 ended without the usual joint statement and press conference, and was instead marked by a rather critical speech from Commission President Ursula von der Leyen,

[23] European Commission (2019).

[24] Hallinan (2016); Bickenbach et al. (2015), p. 20.

[25] See also Li (2014).

[26] Tenuta (2015), p. 13.

[27] Covington and Burling LLP (2015).

[28] Wu (2020).

[29] Ibid.

emphasizing a need for 'more ambition on the Chinese side in order to conclude negotiations on an investment agreement'.[30] However, the report on the 31st round of the negotiations, held from 20 to 24 July 2020, indicated a U-turn and noted significant progress on the three aspects of level playing-field rules, reflecting 'the Parties commitment during the EU-China Summit on 22 June to advance discussions in this area'.[31] Nevertheless, the eighth EU-China High-level Economic Dialogue, which took place on 28 July 2020, once again emphasized the significant remaining tasks related to market access in several specific sectors, including telecommunications, health, biotechnology, new energy vehicles, and sustainable development.

These ebbs and flows have to do with the changing political climate. The most significant change was the phase one trade deal reached between China and the US in January 2020, which was swiftly criticized by Europe for China's distraction from the CAI discussions.[32] At the same time, China's concessions in the trade deal become a reference for European negotiators and business groups in evaluating the CAI.

Another critical change was China's adoption of its new Foreign Investment Law (FIL) in 2019, which entered into force in January 2020. It was suggested that the amendments were made in compliance with China's commitments in the phase one trade deal.[33] A variety of adjustments were made to China's foreign investment policy, addressing some of the most pressing concerns of international investors. One salient example is the implementation of a pre-entry national treatment and negative list regulation framework. Despite these positive changes, however, new market access barriers have emerged in China, which have led European investors to report "promise fatigue".[34]

Owing to these shifts, the market access issues confronting European negotiators are remarkedly different from those portrayed in the 'NT' report. More importantly, due to the institution of a pre-entry national treatment and negative list regulation framework in China, the EU's initial proposal to include such standards in the CAI now appears to be somewhat redundent. To lay the groundwork for evaluating the efficacy and reamining benefits of national treatment in the CAI in relation to market liberalization, the following section sets forth market access hurdles in China for foreign investors prior to and after the enactment of China's new FIL.

---

[30] European Commission (2020b).

[31] European Commission (2020a).

[32] Wu (2020).

[33] Li and Bian (2022).

[34] Bermingham (2020).

3 Foreign Investment Regulatory Landscape in China and Market Access Issues

3.1 *Market Access Issues in Pre-FIL Period*

Market access issues before the adoption of FIL, as demonstrated in the analysis of Copenhagen Economics, EUCCC survey, and the NT report, primarily derived from China's stringent and multi-layered foreign investment regulation. In the pre-FIL era, the entry of foreign investment is contingent on the following conditions: (a) the types of approval and licenses required for the specific investment and business activities; (b) the criteria for approval and other restrictions provided in pertinent laws, regulations and policies; and (c) whether administrative discretion is exercised in a non-arbitrary, non-discriminatory manner.

In general, China's regulatory framework for foreign investment follows a dual-track approach, merging foreign investment supervision with investment promotion and facilitation policy.[35] Indicative of this approach is the Catalogue of Industries Guiding Foreign Investment (Foreign Investment Catalogue).[36] Under this Catalogue, foreign investment is categorised as the encouraged, the restricted, and the prohibited investment.[37] Being placed on the encouraged list allows foreign investors to enjoy special rights and policy privileges, while those on the forbidden list are denied access entirely. For those who would like to invest in the restricted sectors, market access is subject to specific requirements, such as joint venture formation and shareholding limits.[38] Investment in sectors that are not mentioned on the restricted and prohibited lists is, in theory, permitted; however, national treatment is not guaranteed. As a result, permissible foreign investment could also face various restrictive and discriminatory rules and burdensome administrative requirements.

Besides the Catalogue, foreign investors are also subject to strictures regarding corporate forms[39] and multi-layered approval schemes for entry and accession.[40] Some of these controls are overt, but more are covert. For instance, the admission of foreign investment hinges on two additional controls compared to domestic invest-

[35] Huang (2003), p. 14; Potter (1995).

[36] 外商投资指导目录 (Catalogue of Industries for Guiding Foreign Investment) first issued in 1995 and amended in 2002, 2004, 2007, 2011, 2015 and 2017.

[37] China-Hong Kong CEPA Investment Agreement (concluded and signed 28 June 2017), Art. 5; Regional Comprehensive Economic Partnership (signed 15 November 2020, not yet effective), Art. 10.3.

[38] See Mahony (2015).

[39] Before the FIL, foreign investment was regulated under three primary laws: the Law on Sino-Foreign Equity Joint Ventures (中华人民共和国中外合资经营企业法), the Law on Wholly Foreign-Owned Enterprises (中华人民共和国外资企业法), and the Law on Sino-Foreign Contractual Joint Ventures (中华人民共和国中外合作经营企业法). These three laws predate China's first company law and work in tandem with the latter. See Mahony (2015), pp. 3–5.

[40] See Li and Bian (2022), p. 46.

ment—a case-by-case foreign investment approval by the Ministry of Commerce or its local subsidiaries and a national security review by an inter-ministerial panel.[41] As another example, the fixed-asset investment approval procedure, which is administered by National Development and Reform Commission or a local Development and Reform Commission, necessitates ex ante approval for inbound foreign investment across a diverse array of project categories.[42] In this regard, foreign investment that is subject to local scrutiny is more susceptible to administrative arbitrariness and unpredictability as a result of the widespread regional and provincial protectionism.[43]

This business climate has propelled the EU towards its national treatment strategy at the beginning of the CAI negotiations. By pushing for the national treatment standard and a narrow range of exemptions, the EU aimed to address the abovementioned issues and level the playing field for European investors seeking to enter the Chinese market.

3.2 Advances and New Market Access Issues in Post-FIL Period

3.2.1 National Treatment in China's Foreign Investment Regulation

The enactment of the FIL has altered the context, resulting in three significant changes to market access in China: first, the Foreign Investment Catalogue scheme was abrogated and superseded by the Negative List for Foreign Investment (Negative List). Second, corporate restrictions on foreign-invested enterprises were repealed together with three primary foreign investment laws that embody them. The Chinese Company Law and the Partnership Enterprise Law now cover both foreign-invested and domestic enterprises. More importantly, the FIL institutes a pre-establishment national treatment strandard and an *ex post* information reporting mechanism, replacing the former *ex ante* case-by-case authorization.[44]

By instituting pre-establishment national treatment rules, China pledged to abolish market access requirements that differentiate between domestic and foreign investors.[45] Furthermore, the FIL commits to granting equal treatment to foreign enterprises in respect of funding, land supply, tax reduction, licencing, standard setting, project application, human resources policies, and the application process of these policies.[46] However, such commitments are not, and can never be, absolute.

[41] Ibid.

[42] Covington and Burling LLP (2015).

[43] Mahony (2015).

[44] Li and Bian (2022), p. 48.

[45] Zhang (2020).

[46] FIL Implementing Regulation (2019), Art.6; See Li and Bian (2022), p. 65.

Certain exemptions are provided in the form of the Negative List,[47] specifying several sectors where foreign investment is either prohibited or restricted.[48] Unlike the Foreign Investment Catalogue, however, a negative list appended to the national treatment standard indicates that any foreign investment outside the list should automatically enjoy national treatment. China's first domestic Negative List was released in 2017, which has been amended annually and now contains 31 prohibited and restricted items.[49] Furthermore, as pointed out, China's commitment to investment liberalization 'is not only reflected in the sheer diminishing numbers of prohibited and restricted items, 'but also the gradual openness to strategic sectors.'[50] Financial sectors, for instance, are thus open to foreign investors as a result of the reform.[51]

3.2.2 Outstanding and Emerging Hindrances

As mentioned in Sect. 2, China's new FIL was received with ambivalence by foreign business community.[52] This section sets out the remaining and emerging grievances of foreign investors.

Firstly, according to EUCCC, many items removed from the Negative List are of limited importance for European investors, whereas the remainder covers a broad spectrum of significant sectors, such as legal and telecommunications services.[53] Further, due to intensified politicization in recent years, China has enacted or reinvigorated several overarching legal instruments bearing on foreign investment, such as the national security review, the Unreliable Entity List, and the Countermeasure List.[54] These laws, regulations, and measures provide grounds for derogations from national treatment and again call into doubt the stability and predictability of China's domestic investment control system.[55] In China's 2020 Measures for National Security Review of Foreign Investment, several critical concepts, including the notion of national security, are left undefined. In addition, the extensive list of relevant areas implies that every foreign investment has the potential to undergo assessment.[56] Similarly, the provisions provided in the Unreliable Entity List[57] and

[47] Ibid., pp. 51–54.

[48] Equal treatment is granted to sectors outside of the Negative List. FIL (2019), Art. 28.

[49] China's Foreign Investment Negative List 2021 Edition.

[50] Li and Bian (2022), p. 62.

[51] European Chamber of Commerce in China (2021a).

[52] Zhou (2020).

[53] European Chamber of Commerce in China (2020).

[54] See an in-depth analysis in Li and Bian (2022), p. 102.

[55] Li (2016).

[56] This is a common state practice. 外商投资安全审查办法 (Measures for the National Security Review of Foreign Investment), adopted 19 December 2021, effective 18 January 2021; Arts. 35 and 40 of the FIL (2019). See also Jensen (2010).

[57] 不可靠实体清单规定 (Provisions on the Unreliable Entity List), adopted 19 September 2020.

the Anti-Foreign Sanctions Law,[58] which are almost carte blanche, have profound implications for foreign investment.[59]

Secondly, market access barriers that apply equally to foreign and domestic investors persist. Thus, laws and regulations that are non-discriminatory but restrictive have remained, involving sector-based approval and licensing, registration of establishment with local administration for market regulation, and fixed-asset investment approval, approval for land use rights, environmental impact assessment, and zoning approval.[60] As noted, China's legal framework regarding market entry is now undergoing a shift from nationality-based to sector-based assessment and from subject supervision to conduct inspection.[61] In 2016, China adopted the first Negative List for Market Access applicable to both domestic and foreign investment. The list covers 130 broadly defined items. Several prohibited and restricted items removed from the Negative List for Foreign Investment are now placed on this new national list. In the face of various administrative procures related to the restricted sectors, European business operators reported 'being twice as likely to face such indirect barriers compared to direct ones'.[62] One telling example concerns the newly opened financial sector. Despite the easing of restrictions, to incorporate a new bank in China, business operators must seek a license from the authorities pursuant to the 2020 Negative List for Market Access.[63] EUCCC complained that the standards for review remain beyond international norms. As a result, only a handful of foreign banks have successfully obtained operating licenses.[64] It should be mentioned that the misalignment between Chinese national standards and international standards is regarded to have been crafted by China to shield Chinese companies in certain sectors—for instance, the automobile and IT sectors—from foreign competition.[65] Although the FIL has finally included foreign investors in compulsory national standard-setting, the establishment of voluntary national standards, local-government-issued standards or market-issued standards remain outside China's commitments.

Lastly, concerns also abound about Chinese state-owned enterprises (SOEs) and their competitive advantages, which are now deemed as a systematic market access

[58] 中华人民共和国反外国制裁法 (Anti-Foreign Sanctions Law), adopted 10 June 2021. Similar examples could be found in 阻断外国法律与措施不当域外适用办法 (The Rules on Counteracting Unjustified Extra-Territorial Application of Foreign Legislation an Measures), adopted 9 January 2021 and 中华人民共和国出口管制法(Export Control Law of China), adopted 17 October 2020.

[59] Li and Bian (2022).

[60] Ibid., pp. 51–54.

[61] Ibid., pp. 6, 57; see also Kong (2019).

[62] European Chamber of Commerce in China (2020).

[63] Li and Bian (2022), p. 57.

[64] The EUCCC noted that recent announcements from the China Securities Regulatory Commission signify a positive change.

[65] See Du (2020).

barrier for foreign investors.[66] As market obstacles are reduced, it is expected that the problem of SOEs would become more prominent.[67] In addition, the new round of SOE reforms in China, which was heralded alongside the FIL reform, have arguably fuelled dismay among foreign investors. The reforms amalgamated several massive Chinese SOEs and strengthened their economic might.[68] As EUCCC proclaimed, due to China's capricious 'selective opening-up',[69] when restrictions for a market are finally lifted, foreign investors often find the market already saturated with Chinese SOEs, thus dissuading potential investors.[70]

To recapitulate, although Chinese foreign investment regulation has already shifted to pre-establishment national treatment, indirect market barriers that vex foreign investors linger. Several significant sectors appealing to foreign investors remain closed; administrative procedures that might give rise to discretion, incoherency and rent-seeking persist; security-based exceptions are of mounting concern; and SOEs are growing exponentially and bearing down on competitive sectors. In light of these old and new issues, the next section considers the limits of national treatment standard in relation to market access in China.

4 Pre-entry National Treatment Standard in Treaty Practice

4.1 Pre-entry National Treatment Standard at a Glance

The practice of including market liberalisation standards in preferential trade agreements (PTAs) is not novel, either in international treaty making landscape or in the EU's treaty practice. At the international level, attempts to address 'behind-the-border' issues (Singapore issues) encountered major setbacks with the fallout of the Doha Round negotiations. Under the influence of 'variable geometry', recourse has been shifted to bilateral and plurilateral treaty-making.[71] Therefore, despite the debate on the pros and cons of plurilateralism, PTAs proliferate.[72] International investment agreements (IIAs) and investment chapters within PTAs are widely recognized as effective legal tools for attracting foreign investment and, sometimes, for encouraging the opening up of foreign markets.[73] In this context, the US and Canada have spearheaded in incorporating market liberalisation clauses into PTAs.[74] Two

[66] See Su (2022).

[67] See the criticisms of SOE reform in Lardy (2019).

[68] Ibid.

[69] See China's selective approach in Gallagher and Shan (2009), p. 28.

[70] European Chamber of Commerce in China (2020).

[71] Warwick Commission (2007); Leal-Arcas (2011).

[72] Hoekman (2018).

[73] Salacuse (2013), p. 359.

[74] Gomez-Palacio and Muchlinski (2012), p. 446.

sets of disciplines are emblematic of this trend: the prohibition on market performance requirements, which are modelled on the General Agreement on Trade in Services (GATS), and the pre-establishment national treatment and negative list approach.[75] However, the latter is currently only available in a small number of IIAs. [76]

The EU's treaty-making experience in relation to market liberalisation has evolved in tandem. Prior to the Lisbon treaty, the EU had only incidental competence in relation to investment matters. The distribution of competence on this score was described as follows: while the Member States 'focused on the promotion and protection of all forms of investment, the Commission elaborated a liberalisation agenda focused on market access for direct investment'.[77] This distribution results in the EU's main focus on a 'liberalisation agenda',[78] which finds telling expression in the so-called 'EU Minimum Platform on Investment', a negotiating template for EU FTAs.[79] In contrast, most BITs negotiated by the EU Member States follow the 'controlled-entry' model with little regard to conditions of entry.[80] With the coming into force of the Lisbon Treaty and the conferral of exclusive competence over foreign investment, the European Union desires an independent role in norm-setting for investment.[81] In this context, the EU is poised to fill the gap at the 'entry' or 'admission' phase for European investment via multilateral and bilateral pacts.[82] As with the US and Canada, the EU has turned to the pre-establishment national

---

[75] See in general Collis (2014).

[76] According to the statistics of the United Nations Conference on Trade and Development (UNCTAD), only 168 of 2,575 international investment agreements national treatment standard covers pre-establishment phase. UNCTAD, International Investment Navigator, Mapping of IIA Content, Standards of Treatment, National Treatment. https://investmentpolicy.unctad.org/international-investment-agreements/iia-mapping. However, it is observed that BITs incorporating pre-establishment phase is on the rise. See for example Vandevelde (2016).

[77] 'Comprehensive European International Investment Policy', p. 10.

[78] Gomez-Palacio and Muchlinski (2012).

[79] Titi (2015).

[80] See investment control model in UNCTAD, International Investment Agreements: Key Issues-Volume, UNCTAD/ITE/IIT/2004/10 (2004), pp. 148–153.

[81] The EU's general objective on investment liberalization derives from the TFEU, Art. 3(1) €, which establishes the EU's exclusive competence for the common commercial policy. Art. 206 provides that 'the Union shall contribute to progressive abolition of restrictions on foreign direct investment'. Art. 207(1) TFEU sets out the need for uniform principles including for FDI and liberalisation measures.

[82] At the multilateral level, the General Agreement on Trade in Services (GATS) provides for a framework for undertaking commitments on the supply of services through a commercial presence (defined as 'mode 3' by GATS Article I). At the bilateral level, the Union has concluded negotiations with Korea on a Free Trade Agreement, which includes provisions on market access for investors and establishments. See also Shan and Wang (2015).

treatment plus negative list approach, which are provided in the EU-Canada Comprehensive Economic and Trade Agreement (CETA)[83] and the CAI.[84]

China, on its part, had successive generations of national treatment clauses. Notably, China has begun to reduce the limitations placed on foreign investments in order to attract international money and stimulate foreign investment. However, the moves to lift restrictions have been conducted cautiously and progressively, as demonstrated by China's reluctance to accept full-scale national treatment provision.[85] Gallagher and Shan considered the incorporation of a national treatment norm, together with unrestricted access to international arbitration, as distinguishing features of the third phase of Chinese BIT practice.[86] Of all the standing Chinese BITs, less than half grant national treatment standard.[87] Moreover, the national treatment provisions in Chinese BITs are usually either grandfathered or subject to domestic law.[88] More recent Chinese BITs are brought closer to the full-scale formula by stating in a non-exhaustive manner that the national treatment obligation applies to 'the investors and their investments with respect to the management, conduct, operation, maintenance, use, sale, liquidation, or other forms of disposal of such investments'.[89] In certain instances, China committed to refraining from enhancing discriminatory treatment and to making an effort to gradually eliminate non-conforming

[83] National Treatment, Draft CETA Investment Text, Art. X.7, 21 November 2013. The CETA adopted a 'negative list' approach with respect to the 'establishment, acquisition (and possibly expansion) of investment'. Most EU Member States' BITs provide for 'unqualified' NT and MFN, but applicable only post-establishment. See for instance the EU-South Korea FTA, the EU-Colombia-Peru FTA and the EU-Singapore FTA, which follow the GATS-type 'positive list' approach with respect to market access provisions and NT. EU-South Korea FTA, Art. 7.11.

[84] Ünekbaş (2021).

[85] The China–UK BIT of 1986, the first Chinese BIT to include a NT clause, provides a 'best effort' approach. See Shan et al. (2012).

[86] Gallagher and Shan (2009), pp. 39–43. See the six different types of national treatment identified in ibid., 166–171.

[87] Germany-China BIT, Art. 3(2). The only exception in China's BIT practices seems to be that sometimes the national treatment standard is extended to the 'expansion' of existing investments. See, for example, the China-Korea BIT of 2007, Art. 3(1).

[88] See the former in the China-Portugal BIT (signed 9 December 2005, entered into force 26 July 2008);China-Spain BIT (signed 14 November 2005, entered into force 1 July 2008); China-Belgo-Luxembourg BIT (signed 6 June 2005, entered into force 1 December 2009); China-Czech Republic BIT (signed 8 December 2005, entered into force 1 September 2006); China–Finland BIT (signed 15 November 2004, entered into force 15 November 2006); China–Germany BIT (signed 1 December 2003, entered into force 11 November 2005); China-Netherlands BIT (signed 26 November 2001, entered into force 1 August 2004). See the latter (which is exceptional in China-EU Member States BITs) in China-France BIT (signed 26 November 2007, entered into force 20 August 2010). The former is more liberal as it imposes constraints on the making of new measures or changing of existing measures that are contradictory to national discrimination. See Shan et al. (2012), p. 135.

[89] The Agreement of Investment of the Framework Agreement on Comprehensive Economic Cooperation Between the Association of Southeast Asian Nations and the People's Republic of China (The China-ASEAN Treaty).

measures.[90] However, none of the 26 investment accords that are signed between China and the EU Member States speak of a pre-establishment phase national treatment.[91]

The shifting stance of China on pre-establishment national treatment and negative list approach could be traced back to its negotiations of a BIT with the US, when China for the first time hinted at a possibility of including a pre-establishment national treatment clause with a negative list.[92] However, the negotiations eventually failed, so did China's stated commitment to pre-establishment national treatment standard. In 2017, a pre-establishment national treatment provision with a negative list finally manifested in the China-Hong Kong Closer Economic Partnership Arrangement Investment Agreement. In the newly-concluded Regional Comprehensive Economic Partnership, China again gave its consent to this standard.[93]

4.2 *Pre-entry National Treatment Standard plus Negative List Approach in the CAI*

The national treatment standard provided in the CAI includes both pre-establishment and post-establishment phases. Article 4 under Section II mandates:[94]

> [e]ach Party shall accord to investors of the other Party and to covered enterprises treatment no less favourable than the treatment it accords, in like situations, to its own investors and to their enterprises, with respect to establishment and operation in its territory.

Moreover, it stipulates that the protocol 'shall not be constructed as preventing a Party from prescribing ordinary formalities, such as a requirement to provide authenticated documents or official translations, or information requirements for statistical purposes', without prejudice to the national treatment obligation.[95]

The rule is subject to a Chapeau of Section II and thus does not cover subsidies, government procurement, and activities supplied in the exercise of governmental authority.[96] Besides, both Parties exclude certain sensitive industries and measures

---

[90] Germany-China BIT, Additional Protocol, Art. 3(2); see also Mexico-China BIT, Art.3. See also Berger (2013).

[91] See on a summary of national treatment in China-EU Member States' BITs in Shen (2018), p. 802 et seq.

[92] In the chapter on cross-border trade in services under the China-Australia FTA, China consents to market access and NT yet with a 'positive list' approach, whereas Australia applies a 'negative list'.

[93] Li and Bian (2022), p. 59.

[94] EU-China CAI, Section II, Art. 4.1.

[95] Ibid.

[96] EU-China CAI, Section II, Art. 1.

from the national treatment obligation through the negative list.[97] On 12 March 2021, soon after the discharge of the 'in principle' text of the CAI, the European Commission published the list, bearing the title of market access offers. China's market access offers follow a 'hybrid model', composed of four major parts (Annexes I–IV). Annexes I and II adopts a negative list approach in respect of national treatment, most-favoured nation treatment, prohibited performance requirements, and requirements on senior management and boards of directors. Annex III, which concerns the commitments on performance requirements, follows a positive list approach. Annex I contains a limited number of 36 entries, including the following sectors: publication; radio and television; film; culture and recreation; network audio-visual service, internet culture operation; and atomic energy. Annex II comprises 17 entries, covering the specific sectors, subsectors, or activities for which China may maintain existing measures or adopt new and more restrictive measures.[98]

5 Pre-entry National Treatment for Liberalizing the Chinese Market

To assess the efficacy of pre-establishment national treatment in the CAI, it is imperative to understand how the standard addresses market access issues. Furthermore, as Chinese domestic investment law already provides pre-establishment national treatment, another valid question is whether and how the inclusion of the standard in the CAI might contribute to a 'better-off' situation.

5.1 The Operational Mechanism of the Approach

National treatment obligation is a 'relative standard'. According to the idea of national treatment, international investors should be given the same treatment as local investors. Equal treatments refer not only to the same level of market access possibility but also to the same national preferential policies, such as preferential fiscal and financial policies, taxation, and land use. In the words of Sonarajah, screening laws also 'would have to be dismantled at least to the extent that they are inconsistent with the pre-entry national treatment provision.'[99] Thus, the treatment of local investors acts as a gauge and limit for the treatments that international investors are eligible for.[100]

---

[97] Shan and Wang (2015).

[98] EU-China CAI, China's schedule of commitments and reservations.

[99] Sornarajah (2021), p. 422.

[100] Host countries may accord foreign investors treatments more favourable than those of their domestic investments, subjecting to their discretion and domestic policies. Kurtz (2010).

In practice, countries could and often circumscribe the national treatment commitments by carving out certain sectors and policy areas.[101] This may take the forms of either positive or negative lists. The latter is held to be more liberal, as it is succinct and indicates an 'in principle' open market. The difference between the positive and the negative list is particularly prominent in the case of emerging industries.[102] Apart from the negative list of non-conforming measures, other provisions in IIAs could also confine the scope of application of the national treatment standard. One way is through the definition of investment and investor. If an activity does not meet the definition established in an International Investment Agreement (IIA), it is not covered by the national treatment protection. As for the definition of 'investment', most Chinese BITs require investment to be made 'in accordance with national law'.[103] In CAI, however, this qualification is not present, which means the CAI provides 'unqualified' national treatment. Another restriction lies in the general and security exceptions, which are stipulated in the CAI. Such exceptions could exonerate the host country from liabilities arising from discrimination based on policy grounds such as health, public order, safety and security.[104]

5.2 *Effect Analysis: Liberalising the Chinese Market*

As national treatment represents a 'relative standard', to establish a violation thereof, differential treatment must be present. In adjudication, tribunals usually ascertain the violations of national treatment by inquiring into three aspects: (1) whether the situations are alike; (2) whether the treatment is differential; and (3) whether there is justification.[105] As mentioned, foreign investors continue to encounter indirect investment barriers 'such as ambiguous rules, conflicting regulations, unequal treatment of foreign companies and favouritism of SOEs'. However, many of these issues affect both foreign investors and Chinese domestic investors. First of all, foreign investment is now governed by a number of Chinese rules and regulations that apply to both domestic investors and foreign investors,[106] and thus no discrimination de jure should arise, no matter how arbitrary, ambiguous or inconsistent the implementation might be. Nevertheless, foreign investors might

[101] Sornarajah (2021), p. 423; Shan and Wang (2015).

[102] As hardly legislators can foretell industrial advances and iterations and carve them out in advance, in principle national treatment will automatically apply to an emerging industry with a negative list in place.

[103] Korea-China BIT (2005), Arts. 3(4) and 5(1); Japan-China BIT (1988), Art. 4.

[104] Art 4., Section VI.

[105] See Pop & Talbot Inc. v. Government of Canada, Award on the Merits of Phase 2, para 181 (Apr 10, 2001).

[106] Negative List for Market Access (2019 edition). Covington and Burling LLP (2015); The European Union Chamber of Commerce in China, 'Negative List Reductions are Welcome, But Regulatory Reforms are Crucial' (1 July 2019).

take recourse to the national treatment standard if it is possible to prove that they are treated differently from domestic investors. In this situation, one hurdle lies in the 'black box' operation of approval and other administrative proceedings. It would be onerous for foreign investors to demonstrate the disparities in treatment and the presence of discrimination de facto. This is not, however, to suggest that the CAI as a whole neglects this issue. Provisions with regard to licensing, qualification requirements and procedures, and other administrative proceedings are provided in Section III,[107] which sets out the following requirements on the making of ordinance and bylaws: '(a) clear; (b) objective and transparent; (c) pre-established, made public in advance and accessible.'[108] In addition, the procedures 'shall be clear, as simple as feasible'.[109] However, these requirements are provided in an obscure and hortatory manner, and hence it remains to be seen how they will be implemented.

As Chinese private enterprises are themselves in a disadvantageous competitive position relative to SOEs, the choice of comparator becomes another issue. First of all, in the CAI, SOE sectors are not carved out as a whole by way of non-conforming measures. Therefore, SOEs in non-reserved sectors could potentially be used as comparators. Yet, in this case, it is still difficult to demonstrate and assess the second element—distinctions in treatment, as discussed above. Furthermore, since the discrimination at question does not rest on the grounds of nationality, it is also worth asking whether a violation of the national treatment standard could only derive from nationality-based discrimination.[110] The past arbitral tribunal's decisions do not seem to support this argument. In *Marvin Roy Feldman Karpa v. United Mexican States*, a comparison was drawn between the treatment that the claimant received and the 'best treatment' conferred on at least one domestic investor.[111] Therefore, as demonstrated in this case, the fact that other domestic investors also receive less favourable treatment does not impede the establishment of discrimination.[112] Even if market access is denied by the Chinese approval authorities on the grounds that are ostensibly applicable to both foreign and domestic investors, the denial could nonetheless lead to a breach of national treatment obligation insofar as the restrictions effectively lead to discriminatory results.[113] Nevertheless, as regards the determination of the 'like situation' element, which is present in the CAI, jurisprudence shows the lack of consistency or *stare decisis*.[114] Therefore, given the public duties that SOEs undertake in the Chinese economy and governance, whether foreign

[107] EU-China CAI, Section III, Arts. 2 and 3.

[108] EU-China CAI, Section III, Art. 2.1.

[109] EU-China CAI, Section III, Art. 3.1.

[110] See DiMascio and Pauwelyn (2008).

[111] See in general Grieson-Weiler and Laird (2008), p. 293.

[112] Marvin Roy Feldman Karpa v. United Mexican States, ICSID Case No. ARB(AF)/99/1 (2002), at 181.

[113] Collis (2014), pp. 169–170.

[114] See in general Kotuby and Egerton-Vernon (2015).

investors are similarly placed remains contestable.[115] Even if this element could be established, the more favourable treatment for SOEs might also be justified on sound policy grounds.[116] A practical issue in this respect is that Chinese SOEs derive their competitive advantages from eclectic sources, including monopoly rights, subsidization, and in general a distorted business environment. For instance, financial institutions in China, be they public or private, arguably prefer SOEs over private enterprises in granting loans.[117] As a result, SOEs receive a vast amount of off-the-record financial support and subsidy.[118] Nevertheless, the decisions of these financial institutions are more commercial than political, which are made in view of SOEs' government favouritism, better corporate governance, and credit ratings relative to Chinese private companies. In the CAI, as the government monopoly is exempted, it is hard to attribute the commercial favouritism of market entities to the Chinese state.

The overall picture aside, several critical sectors merit particular attention. As European investors stated, the industries open to them may not align with their economic interest. These complaints are reminiscent of China's Free Trade Zones (FTZs) practice. It is an established practice in China to use FTZs as pilots to test the possibility of its domestic governance transition, and thus prior to the adoption of its FIL, China had already widely tested the Negative List approach in these areas.[119] However, as EU and US investors are unsatisfied with the lengthiness of these negative lists, they have received limited positive feedback.[120] Therefore, as regards carve-outs, not only the modality but also the length and the specific sectors matter. During the CAI negotiations, deliberations centre on telecommunications, information and communication technology, health, financial services, and manufacturing.[121] When releasing the 'in principle' text, the EU also touted the market access offers by citing China's substantial concessions in roughly the same sectors.[122] The following analysis therefore compare China's domestic Negative List with the CAI market access offers with a view to assessing the latter's contribution.

---

[115] See the comparability issue when SOEs act as investors in Wang (2016). Wang points out that in United Parcel Service (UPS) v. Canada [United Parcel Service of America Inc v. Government of Canada (UPS v Canada), UNCITRAL, Award (24 April 2007)], the majority opinion of the tribunal was that, as the SOE at issue assumed special duties, UPS should not be considered as similarly placed.

[116] Marvin Roy Feldman Karpa v. United Mexican States, at 318; Gami Investment v. Mexico (2004) 44 ILM 545.

[117] See Li and Bian (2022), p. 69.

[118] Ibid; See also, Lardy (2019), Figure 4.1.

[119] Huang (2015).

[120] Bickenbach (2015), p. 1; Zhang (2015).

[121] European Commission (2019).

[122] Ibid.

Firstly, the Commission highlighted China's commitments in the CAI in terms of the manufacturing of transportation equipment.[123] In this regard, the CAI provides that the limitation for traditional fuel-powered motor vehicles does not apply to the acquisition of existing traditional fuel-powered motor vehicle enterprises. Further, the limitation for new energy vehicles does not apply if the total investment amount for the project is no less than USD 1 billion. This seems to be a hallmark of the CAI's market liberalisation agenda. However, in fact, since the 2020 Negative List has removed the equity caps for commercial vehicle, there has been no more restriction in China's domestic acts on the three major pillars of motor vehicles. The only remaining restriction is that in the case of foreign investment in the manufacture of complete automobiles (passenger cars), the shareholding percentages of the Chinese party shall not be less than 50%. The same requirement is also present in China's schedule attached to the CAI.[124] Furthermore, in the 2021 version of the Negative List, this requirement was also removed, making China's domestic law even more preferential than the CAI in this regard.[125]

Overall, China's general manufacturing sectors are by and large open to foreign investors. Since the 2020 list lifted the prohibitions on nuclear energy sectors, what remain on the list (besides the manufacture of transportation equipment) are only the printing of publications, which is required to be controlled by the Chinese Party, investing in processing techniques and the production of confidential prescription products of proprietary Chinese medicines, and satellite television broadcast ground receiving facilities. China's CAI schedule includes the first (i.e., printing of publications)[126] and the second (i.e., Chinese Traditional Medicine) items.[127] The third requirement is not on the schedule and has also been removed from China's own 2021 version of Negative List.

Another sector in the spotlight is telecommunications. Pursuant to Chinese domestic law, only the service types listed in its Telecoms Catalogue are permitted.[128] According to EUCCC, among the various types of value-added telecoms services (VATS) under the 2015 revision of the Telecoms Catalogue,[129] internet resources collaboration (IRC) is the one in which foreign players take the greatest interest. To provide IRC service within China, an IDC/IRC license is required. According to the Negative List, China has only agreed to open the telecom sectors listed in China's WTO schedules of specific commitments, excluding a number of service types needed to provide VATS. In China's CAI schedule, its reservation on this score does not repeat identically the expression in the domestic Negative List.[130] Besides

[123] Ibid.

[124] EU-China CAI, Schedules of China, Annex I Entry 6.

[125] Ibid., Annex I Entry 5.

[126] Ibid., Annex I Entry 5 – Printing of Publications.

[127] Ibid, Annex II Entry 5 – Chinese Traditional Medicine.

[128] Telecoms Catalogue, MIIT, adopted 28th December 2015.

[129] Ibid.

[130] EU-China CAI, Schedules of China Annex I, Entry 12 – Telecommunication Services.

prohibitions on internet services, only shareholding restrictions are imposed, which potentially opens the door for cloud service supply.[131] However, all these concessions could already be found in several free trade or service pilot zones including the Hainan free trade port. It has also been submitted that, even in these pilots, where restrictions on shareholding structure do not apply, foreign companies nonetheless face other restrictions, such as licensing requirements, and those who intend to apply for a license receive no guidance.[132]

These examples demonstrate that the EU has indeed obtained some achievements via the CAI.[133] However, these achievements by and large reconcile with China's own industrial policy and liberalization pace. The sectors liberalized by the CAI might be open anyway even in the absence of the CAI. The virtue of the CAI for market liberalisation, therefore, is not how many and which sectors it manages to open, but that it freezes China's liberalisation commitments, generating the so-called standstill effect. As discussed above, foreign investors are ambivalent about China's 'selective opening-up' strategy, which allows China to manipulate its market power. Without being bound by international legal requirements, a country has considerable freedom to create and modify its own laws and policies regarding domestic investments.[134] Thus, whatever China has unilaterally promised in its domestic law, that is not fixed. This is where an international commitment could make a difference. As national treatment in the CAI is unqualified, China essentially recognizes that international commitments on liberalized sectors would take primacy over its domestic negative list. Thus, binding commitments provided in the CAI could at least secure the current level of market access for foreign investors.[135]

Nevertheless, uncertainty looms as the presence of general and security exceptions in the CAI allows for the use of emerging security-based measures.[136] It is worth noting that the security exceptions provided in the CAI do not contain a provision referring to the avoidance of abuse.[137] Therefore, the operation and admission of foreign investment remain susceptible to national measures adopted on security or public policy grounds. The latter could be observed in China's recent responsive measures for Covid-19 pandemic, which substantially hampered foreign investment

[131] European Chamber of Commerce in China (2021b), p. 330. Generally, only companies that are less than 49 per cent foreign-invested can apply for a Basic Telecoms Services licence. Only companies that are less than 50 per cent foreign-invested can apply for a VATS licence, with the exception of limited sectors such as online data processing and transaction processing services (operating e-commerce), domestic multiparty communications services, store-and-forward services and call centre services.

[132] Ibid.

[133] Similar examples could also be found in the fields of medical services, aviation, real estate and other business services, and financial services.

[134] Dolzer et al. (2012), p. 87.

[135] European Commission (2013).

[136] EU-China CAI, Section VI, Art. 4. It is worth noting that besides security exception, a 'necessity' defence might also exonerate security, emergency-based measures.

[137] Contrast it with the Korea-China-Japan Trilateral Investment Treaty of 2012, Art. 18.2.

and commercial activities. It is also important to note that there has not been an investment arbitration award ruling on a state's violation of a pre-establishment national treatment promise.[138] In practice, although the national treatment clause has evolved in the recent generations of Chinese BITs, it has hitherto never been evoked by foreign investors to counter procedural unfairness or preferential treatments of SOEs.[139] Moreover, none of the earlier EU FTAs that include market access provisions allow disputes concerning market access to be resolved under the investor state dispute settlement (ISDS) mechanism. Instead, state-to-state dispute settlement is often preferred.[140] In the EU-Canada CETA, for instance, disputes with respect to pre-establishment commitments are excluded from the ISDS.[141] Technically speaking, compensation for a treaty breach of pre-establishment national treatment would also be difficult to ascertain: the fact that the affiliated investors have no record of operation in the host state renders any claims of lost profits speculative. For the time being, the CAI only provids state-to-state dispute settlement mechanism, which, albeit governs national treatment obligations, does not accord to individual business operators much autonomy. Therefore, practically speaking, pre-establishment national treatment obligation in the CAI remains mainly hortatory.

6 Conclusion

The purpose of the EU-China CAI discussions is to facilitate market liberalization. This objective is based on the EU's commitment to market access and its new competence over foreign investment. At the outset of the negotiations, the EU opted for a pre-establishment national treatment plus negative list strategy, imitating the treaty practice of the US and Canada in this regard. However, as the new Chinese FIE come into being, which established national treatment standard alongside a negative list for foreign investment, the added value of pre-establishment national treatment in the CAI was called into doubt. At the same time, market access difficulties, such as costly and opaque administrative procedures, selective opening-up, and prohibitions on entry into several attractive industrial sectors, continue to frustrate European investors. The standards for licensing and qualifications are now sector-based rather than hinges on nationality. Concurrently, new market challenges have

[138] In UPS v. Canada, the issue of pre-establishment national treatment was brought out but received no decision.

[139] One of the reasons is, as mentioned earlier, that China carefully confines the applicable scope of NT obligation and the absence of full-scale NT.

[140] Shan and Wang (2015).

[141] The ISDS EU-Canada Compromised Table (17 May 2013). A report on the state of play of the EU-Canada CETA by the European Commission expressed that both the EU and Canada agreed on the non-application of the ISDS to pre-establishment. See also the EC–Chile Association Agreement.

emerged, such as security-based investment inspection and Chinese SOEs as a systemic market barrier across both monopolistic and competitive sectors. This chapter has evaluated the efficacy of pre-establishment national treatment in the CAI in light of these lingering and increasing market access hindrances.

Firstly, national treatment is a relative standard and, as such, has limited value in dealing with restrictions applicable to both domestic and foreign investors. Its effectiveness is further tempered by sector-wide or policy-based exemptions in the CAI. In this regard, China's market access offers in the CAI do not substantially exceed its domestic commitments as outlined in the national Negative Lists. Therefore, in areas that allow foreign investment, local businesses that already dominate the market may maintain their advantage, while foreign companies, who have to go through complicated administrative processes, may lose their competitive edge. In addition, the CAI's exceptions for security and public policy offer ample room for China to maintain and implement new security-based measures. Despite these deficiencies, the vaule of national treatment lies in a standstill or no rollback effect. Countries that accept unqualified national treatment are no longer left free to alter the terms of liberalization commitments. A full-scale national treatment plus a relatively narrow negative list in the CAI—in line with its unilateral investment liberalisation pledges—is China's assent to binding international responsibilities that would prevent it from manipulating market dynamics by deploying a selective-opening strategy.

References

Berger A (2013) Investment rules in Chinese preferential trade and investment agreements: is China following the global trend towards comprehensive agreements? Deutsches Institut für Entwicklungspolitik Discussion Paper <http://edoc.vifapol.de/opus/volltexte/2014/5035/pdf/DP_7.2013.pdf>

Bermingham F (23 July 2020) China-EU investment treaty talks hit crunch time, as Europeans bemoan seven years of "Promise Fatigue"'. South China Morning Post

Bickenbach F et al. (2015) The EU-China bilateral investment agreement in negotiation: motivation, conflicts and perspectives. Kiel Policy Brief 95

Collis D (2014) National treatment in emerging market investment treaties. In: Kamperman Sanders A (ed) The principle of national treatment in international economic law: trade, investment and intellectual property. Edward Elgar, London, pp 161–182

Copenhagen Economics (2012) EU-China Investment Study: Final Report

Covington and Burling LLP (2015) Assessing "National Treatment" as a Basis for Securing Market Access Under a Comprehensive Agreement on Investment with the PRC. Report prepared for the European Commission Directorate-General for Trade

DiMascio N, Pauwelyn J (2008) Nondiscrimination in trade and investment treaties: worlds apart or two sides of the same coin? Am J Int Law 102:48

Dolzer R et al (2012) Principles of international investment law. OUP, Oxford

Du M (2020) The regulation of product standards in world trade law. Hart Publishing, London

European Chamber of Commerce in China (2013) European Business in China: Business Confidence Survey <www.europeanchamber.com.cn/en/publications-business-confidence-survey/

European Chamber of Commerce in China (12 May 2017) 2016 Annual Report

European Chamber of Commerce in China (23 Sept 2021a) Banking and Securities Working Group Position Paper 2021/2022
European Chamber of Commerce in China (23 Sept 2021b) Executive Position Paper, 2021/2022, Information and Communication Technology Working Group
European Commission (2010) Directorate General for External Policies, Towards a Comprehensive European International Investment Policy (Communication) 343
European Commission (2011) Summary of contributions to the European Commission's public consultation on "The future investment relationship between the EU and China"
European Commission (2013) Commission Staff Working Document: Impact Assessment Report on the EU-China Investment Relations Accompanying the Document Recommendation for a Council Decision Authorising the Opening of Negotiations on an Investment Agreement Between the European Union And the People's Republic Of China.
European Commission (19 Dec 2019) EU to Evaluate Chinese Offer for European Investors, Brussels
European Commission (22 June 2020a) Statement by President Von Der Leyen at the Joint Press Conference with President Michel Following the EU-China Summit Videoconference, Brussels
European Commission (28 July 2020b) Report of the 31st round of negotiations on the EU-China Comprehensive Agreement on Investment, Brussels
Ewert I (2016) The EU–China bilateral investment agreement: between high hopes and real challenges. Security Policy Briefs 68
Gallagher N, Shan W (2009) Chinese investment treaties: policy and practice. OUP, Oxford
Godement F, Stanzel A (2015) The European interest in an investment treaty with China. European Council on Foreign Relations (ECFR)
Godement F, Parello-Plesner J, Richard A (2011) China's scramble for Europe. ECFR
Gomez-Palacio I, Muchlinski P (2012) Admission and establishment. In: Muchlinski P et al (eds) The Oxford handbook of international investment law. OUP, Oxford, pp 227–258
Grieson-Weiler TJ, Laird IA (2008) Standard of treatment. In: Muchlinski P et al (eds) The Oxford book of international investment law. OUP, Oxford, pp 259–304
Hallinan D (2016) The EU–China bilateral investment treaty: a challenging first test of the EU's evolving BIT model. China-EU Law J 5(1):31
Hoekman B (2018) Revitalizing multilateral governance at the world trade organization: report of the high-level board of experts on the future of global trade governance, RSC research reports. European University Institute http://hdl.handle.net/1814/60580
Huang J (2015) Challenges and solutions for the China-US BIT negotiations: insights from the recent development of FTZs in China. J Int Econ Law 18:307
Huang Y (2003) One country, two systems: foreign-invested enterprises and domestic firms in China. China Econ Rev 14:404
Jensen E (2010) Balancing security and growth: defining national security review of foreign investment in China. Pac Rim Law Policy J 19:161
Kong Q et al (2019) 《中华人民共和国外商投资法》解读 (An interpretation of the foreign investment law of the People's Republic of China). Law Press, Beijing
Kotuby CT Jr, Egerton-Vernon JA (2015) Apotex Holdings Inc and Apotex Inc v the government of the United States of America: the adoption by international tribunals of a substantive/transactional approach to Res Judicata—a new paradigm in international dispute resolution? ICSID Rev 30:486
Kurtz J (2010) The merits and limits of comparativism: national treatment in international investment law and the WTO. In: Schill S (ed) International investment law and comparative public law. OUP, Oxford, pp 243–278
Lardy NR (2019) The state strikes back: the end of economic reform in China? PIIE Publication, Washington DC
Leal-Arcas R (2011) The fragmentation of international trade law: is now the time for variable geometry? J World Invest Trade 2:145
Li J (22 January 2014) China, EU talking investment. China Daily usa.chinadaily.com.cn/epaper/2014-01/22/content_17251o1.htm

Li X (2016) National security review in foreign investments: a comparative and critical assessment on China and US laws and practices. Berkeley Bus Law J 13:255
Li Y, Bian C (2022) China's foreign investment legal regime: progress and limitations. Routledge, London
Mahony T (2015) Foreign investment law in China: regulation, practice and context. Tsinghua University Press, Beijing
Potter PB (1995) Foreign investment law in the People's Republic of China: Dilemmas of state control. China Q 141:155
Salacuse JW (2013) The three laws of international investment. OUP, Oxford
Shan W, Wang L (2015) The China–EU BIT and the emerging 'Global BIT 2.0'. ICSID Rev 30:260
Shan W, Gallagher N, Zhang S (2012) National treatment for foreign investment in China: a changing landscape. ICSID Rev 27:120
Shen W (2018) Evolution of nondiscriminatory standards in China's BITs in the context of EU-China BIT negotiations. Chinese J Int Law 17:799
Sornarajah M (2021) The international law on foreign investment, 5th edn. CUP, Cambridge
Su X (2022) Liberalising the Chinese market: state-owned enterprise disciplines in the EU-China comprehensive agreement on investment. J World Invest Trade 23:545
Tenuta F (2015) The motivations behind the EU-China bilateral investment treaty negotiations. 3.15 EU-China Observer.
Titi C (2015) International investment law and the European Union: towards a new generation of international investment agreements. Eur J Int Law 26:639
Ünekbaş S (2021) Scaling the great wall: the EU-China comprehensive agreement on investment and market access. J World Invest Trade 22:347
Vandevelde KJ (2016) The liberal vision of the international law on foreign investment. In: Chin Leng lim (ed) Alternative visions of the international law on foreign investment: essays in honour of Muthucumaraswamy Sornarajah. CUP, Cambridge, pp. 43-68.
Wang L (2016) Non-discrimination treatment of state-owned enterprise investors in international investment agreements? ICSID Rev 31:45
Warwick Commission (2007) The multilateral trading regime: which way forward? University of Warwick
Wu W (25 December 2020) China insiders see "No Progress" on ending subsidies, as clock ticks on EU investment deal talks. South China Morning Post
Zhang M (2020) Change of regulatory scheme: China's new foreign investment law and reshaped legal landscape. UCLA Pacific Basin Law J 37:179
Zhang X (2015) Treading carefully in the minefield of the EU-China investment treaty. Europe's World Spring http://europesworld.org/2015/04/01/treading-carefullyminefield-eu-china-investment-treaty/#.VhZf7U3oulg
Zhou C (25 June 2020) China eases restrictions on foreign investors, but is it too little too late? South China Morning Post

Xueji Su is Research Assistant Professor at the University of Macau. She specializes in international economic law, European Union law, interdisciplinary studies of international law and global governanceand, law and technology. Dr. Xueji Su has also served as visiting fellow/researcher at The Hague Academy of International Law, Max Planck Institute Luxembourg for Procedural Law, the Macao Economic & Trade Office to the European Union (EU), and various international organizations including the United Nations Commission on International Trade Law (UNCITRAL) and the International Institute for the Unification of Private Law (UNIDROIT).

The Disciplines of State-Owned Enterprises in the China-EU Comprehensive Agreement on Investment: Assessment, Implications and Directions

Wei Yin

Abstract Considerable attention has been paid to the activities of state-owned enterprises (SOEs), due to their state ownership and active role in the international market. Tailored SOE disciplines incorporated in recent negotiated or signed trade and investment agreements aim to direct the transnational conduct of SOEs and achieve a level playing field. This chapter analyses the SOE disciplines contained in the text of key provisions of the China-EU Comprehensive Agreement on Investment (CAI), assesses the implication of these SOE specific rules and discusses whether the CAI will shape SOE-specific rules globally. In disciplining SOEs, CAI provides a definition of covered entities, delivers on requirements of acting in accordance with commercial consideration, avoiding discriminatory treatment and ensuring transparency. This chapter recognises the merits and remaining issues of these SOE-specific rules in CAI as a potential model in regulating SOEs in other regional and multilateral negotiations.

1 Introduction

The negotiations on the China-EU Comprehensive Agreement on Investment (hereinafter referred to as the CAI or the Agreement) were officially launched in 2013 and concluded in principle on 30 December 2020, after 35 rounds of negotiations. Given the long-term stagnation of negotiations in the WTO, regional investment and trade agreements have been widely valued by many economies.[1] Several recent agreements provide strong evidence of this trend, e.g., the Comprehensive Progressive Trans-Pacific Partnership (CPTPP), the Regional Comprehensive Economic Partnership (RCEP) and those treaties signed between the EU and third

[1] Hoekman (2013), p. 245.

W. Yin (✉)
Southwest University of Political Science and Law, Chongqing, China

© The Author(s), under exclusive license to Springer Nature Switzerland AG 2024

A. Svetlicinii, I.-J. Chen (eds.), *The EU-China Comprehensive Agreement on Investment*, European Yearbook of International Economic Law,
https://doi.org/10.1007/978-3-031-66862-3_6

countries. The CAI is the first stand-alone investment agreement concluded by the EU since the Lisbon Treaty extended EU competence to foreign direct investment (FDI).[2] For China, the CAI and RCEP represent two milestones in China's recent international economic treaties. Apart from those rules that offer greater levels of market access, the Agreement ensures the discipline of state-owned enterprises (SOEs), transparency of subsidies, prohibits forced technology transfer,[3] as well as including provisions on sustainable development. It is also the most important bilateral legal document in the China-EU economic and trade relations since the China-EU Trade and Economic Cooperation Agreement of 1985.

In the early stages of negotiations, the EU and China did not make SOE disciplines the main focus of discussion. It was not until the 24th round that dialogue on SOE rules began. However, issues concerning SOEs from market access and competition perspectives were major areas of disagreement during the CAI negotiations. Different perceptions of 'fair competition' and SOEs adopted by the EU and China contributed. Recent EU treaty practices and joint statements released with the US and Japan indicate the EU's attitude towards disciplining SOEs[4] and also highlight the EU's attention to address the 'distortive practices' of SOEs in the international arena. SOE disciplines can be found in EU-Japan EPA and EU-Vietnam FTA,[5] although these agreements focus on trade-related issues rather than investment. In recent years, the increasing presence of SOEs and sovereign wealth funds (SWFs) in the global markets has prompted challenges and concerns,[6] regarded as a new round of 'state capitalism'.[7] This can be partly attributed to the rise and development of emerging and developing economies, where state ownership plays a critical role. Particular attention has been paid to China and the upsurge of Chinese SOEs in overseas investment.[8] Projects promoted by the Belt and Road Initiative (BRI)

---

[2] The Treaty of Lisbon differentiates between three types of competence: exclusive competence, where the EU alone can legislate and Member States only implement; shared competence; and supporting competence. See <https://www.europarl.europa.eu/ftu/pdf/en/FTU_1.1.5.pdf> Accessed 1 January 2022.

[3] Provisions in relation to SOEs, forced technology transfers and transparency in subsidies are treated as rules to ensure the level playing field. Kassas (2022); Morbiato (2021).

[4] The joint statement on 12 December 2017 stated that three Ministers agreed on the need for a level global playing field to enhance close cooperation on SOEs and other issues. The joint statement on 31 May 2018 mentioned that 'the Ministers concurred on the need to deepen and accelerate discussions regarding possible new rules on industrial subsidies and SOEs so as to promote a more level playing field for our workers and businesses'. The joint statement on 14 January 2020 focuses on industrial subsidies and claims that the interpretation of 'public body' by the WTO Appellate Body undermines the effectiveness of WTO subsidy rules.

[5] SOE definition (Art. 13.1), scope (Art. 13.2) and substantive provisions concerning SOEs, i.e., commercial considerations and non-discriminatory treatment (Art. 13.5) and transparency (Art. 13.7) are incorporated in Japan-EU EPA. In the EU-Vietnam FTAs, definition of SOEs (Art. 11.1), scope of application (Art. 11.2) and substantive provisions, i.e., non-discrimination and commercial considerations (Art. 11.4) and transparency (Art. 11.6) can also be found.

[6] Guluzade (2019); Zhang and Yin (2020).

[7] Lyons (2007).

[8] Drake (2013).

also place Chinese SOEs in the spotlight.[9] The increasing investments made by Chinese SOEs in energy and infrastructure in Europe led to concerns, i.e., threats to national security and market distortion.[10] However, SOE-relevant rules are rare in China's investment treaties, perhaps because the extensive structural and institutional reforms required in these provisions would be inconsistent with the roles of SOEs in the Chinese economy.[11] China's specific commitments on SOE-related rules appear only and mainly in its WTO accession protocol.[12] In the report on China's accession to the WTO, the commercial consideration and non-discriminatory were confirmed by the representative of China:

> China would ensure that all state-owned and state-invested enterprises would make purchases and sales based solely on commercial considerations, e.g., price, quality, marketability and availability, and that the enterprises of other WTO Members would have an adequate opportunity to compete for sales to and purchases from these enterprises on non-discriminatory terms and conditions.[13]

Although national security concerns have attracted attention from not only the US but also the EU, it is not a core issue in CAI negotiations; rather, the issue of a level playing field between SOEs and private-owned enterprises (POEs).[14] The national security concerns raised by SOE investments hope to be addressed via introducing EU Foreign Investment Screening Regulation unilaterally. The EU, via treaty negotiation, seeks to ensure more market opening and liberalisation for EU companies and investors,[15] and reduce favourable treatment to SOEs and restrictions to EU investors in China.

It is worth noting that SOEs are not new to the EU. In Europe, SOEs prominently feature in some 15 Member States, such as France, Italy and Sweden, and the scope of public ownership in various sectors of the economy is particularly extensive in some of the new Member States such as Romania, Poland, Slovenia and Croatia.[16] The EU usually treats the regulation of SOEs as a matter of corporate governance

---

[9] Chinese SOEs are the main participants in the BRI and play a leading role in implementation, which can be regarded as a continuation of China's 'going out' strategy. Zhang and Yin (2019).

[10] The EU argues that SOEs do not follow market principles fully and this undermines market efficiency (García-Herrero and Xu (2017), but it is important to note that the proportion of Chinese investment in the Europe is smaller than investment from the EU and the US. In 2019, the share of SOEs plummeted, to a mere 11% of aggregate investment. See Kratz et al. (2020); for more discussion of national security issue of Chinese SOEs in the field of international investment, see McLaughlin (2020).

[11] Yin (2018), p. 185.

[12] China's accession to the WTO was expected to both regulate the conduct of the government and accelerate SOE reform. Li and Xu (2015), p. 193; Levy (2017); Zhou et al. (2019).

[13] WTO, Report of the Working Party on the Accession of China, WT/ACC/CHN/49. 1 October 2001, p. 8.

[14] Yin (2017), p. 12

[15] Delegation of the European Union to the People's Republic of China (2021).

[16] European Commission (2016).

that focuses on improving transparency, predictability and accountability.[17] Neutrality or non-discrimination between SOEs and POEs is rooted in Art. 345 of the Treaty on the Functioning of the European Union (TFEU).[18] The EU and its Member States regulate SOEs based on the principle of competitive neutrality, to maintain a level playing field.[19] This is in line with the rules embedded in the covered entities clause in the CAI. In the context of EU merger control, SOEs are viewed as market players with other POEs.[20] However, the current merger control regime is criticised for having less impact on targeting foreign subsidies provided to, by or via SOEs that distort competition in the internal market. This results in an attempt to introduce new rules, i.e., EU Foreign Subsidies Regulation, aiming to address investment subsidies.[21]

Compared with SOEs in EU member states, Chinese SOEs are larger, involve a wide range of industries, and are more concentrated in industry rather than agricultural and service sectors, with close relations with the Chinese government.[22] It was argued that the Chinese government's preferential policies for SOEs have weakened the competitiveness of EU companies.[23] At the same time, Chinese SOEs encounter regulatory scrutiny when they invest in the Europe market, especially merger control review and national-security based reviews involving mergers and acquisitions.[24] Chinese companies complain that they have been discriminated against and are subject to onerous administrative requirements, including the need to provide EU Member States or the EU with documents issued by China's State Council or State-Owned Assets Supervision and Administration Commission (SASAC).[25] Therefore, China also intends to clarify the relevant provisions through the CAI negotiations, so as to reduce the burdensome administration faced by Chinese companies investing in the EU.

[17] European Commission, 'Communication of the Commission to the European Parliament, the Council, the European Economic and Social Committee and the Committee of the Regions of 27 February 2008 — A Common European Approach to Sovereign Wealth Funds' COM (2008) 115 final. See also Thatcher (2012), p. 6.

[18] Art. 345 of the TFEU states that EU law should not prejudice 'the rules in Member States governing the system of property ownership'.

[19] OECD (2018).

[20] In EU merger control, the term 'undertaking' is used as a neutral expression, to highlight the neutrality of ownership. For more discussion of the legal status of SOEs under EU merger control, see Svetlicinii (2020), pp. 4–5.

[21] Clarke (2021).

[22] China's largest firms in most industries are SOEs, and 91 of the 124 Chinese members in the latest Fortune Global 500 are SOEs. See Kennedy (2020).

[23] Garcia-Herrero and Wolff (2020).

[24] Merger control, FDI screening and control of foreign subsidies are regarded as 'Three Great Mountains' that Chinese SOEs cannot avoid when investing in the Europe. See Svetlicinii (2021).

[25] As the EU continues to tighten scrutiny of foreign investment, discriminatory treatment of Chinese companies investing in Europe has increased. A proportion of SOEs report longer review processes and more complex review requirements than enterprises from other countries. See Academy of China Council for the Promotion of International Trade (2021).

It is with the idea of addressing these concerns that SOE discipline was discussed within the CAI negotiations. The CAI represents the first mega-regional investment treaty in which China commits to incorporate SOE-relevant rules and ensure a level playing field, compared with the recent RCEP, which does not emphasise SOE-specific rules. The structural design and provision-drafting of the CAI indicate that it is a non-traditional, new model of investment treaty.[26] Given the role of the signatories, the CAI is the first investment treaty signed by two large, influential economies, where SOEs are active and bear social value. Furthermore, the CAI is the first investment treaty signed by China after the implementation of a new round of SOE reform, i.e., the mixed ownership reform.[27] Although the CAI ratification process has been temporarily put on hold, it is undeniable that the SOE discipline (the 'covered entities' clause) is an important treaty for China in regulating SOEs and will have a significant impact on Chinese SOEs and domestic reform. However, the vagueness of several essential terms leaves much rooms for interpretation; the existence of some exceptions also makes the actual effect of the discipline questionable.

This chapter aims to analyse the elements of SOE rules in the CAI and three main disciplines of SOEs, i.e., non-discriminatory treatment, commercial considerations and transparency. It also assesses the implication of these rules for the Contracting Parties and for developing or shaping international rules on SOEs. It intends to shed some light on the current discussion and debate of regulating 'state capitalism' in the field of international economic law.

2 SOE Rules in CAI

2.1 The Narrative of SOE Rules

The narrative of SOE rules mainly stems from relevant discussion of regulating transnational activities of SOEs. Increasing claims raised by several economies on disciplining SOEs are arguably due to the concern that competitive advantages of SOEs distort the market and disturb fair competition, but not because of the ownership or existence of SOEs.[28] Rules or obligations are introduced to ensure a level playing field, especially from the EU perspective and reflected in several OECD documents.

There are usually two types of rules when discussing SOE rules or promoting fair competition, i.e., SOE-relevant rules and SOE-specific rules. By 'SOE-relevant

---

[26] A traditional investment treaty includes investment liberalisation, investment protection, and dispute resolution provisions. However, the current text of CAI does not include investment protection or ISDS. It features rules concerning disciplining SOEs, transparency of subsidies and provisions on sustainable development, which are key points usually addressed by trade agreement.

[27] Yin (2021).

[28] Willemyns (2016), pp. 661–663; Omran (2004), p. 1038.

rules', this chapter means that designed requirements or obligations are imposed on the government or the state in ensuring competitive neutrality. By 'SOE specific rules', this chapter means that obligations are put on SOEs *per se*, rather than the government. The WTO framework incorporates both SOE-relevant rules and -specific rules, i.e., disciplines on SOEs and on governments. The GATT, GATS, the Agreement on Government Procurement, Agreement on Subsidies and Countervailing Measures, impose some requirements on governments' practice of providing unfair advantages to SOEs e.g., preferential regulatory treatment and subsidies, and on SOEs' discriminatory behaviour in both goods and services. The conduct of SOEs is also regulated through the general international law principles of attribution,[29] captured in Arts. 5 and 8 of the ILC Draft Articles.[30] The existing soft-law instruments adopt an alternative way to regulate SOEs by introducing corporate governance guidelines for SOEs, e.g., *OECD Guidelines on Corporate Governance of State-Owned Enterprises*, and *Sovereign Wealth Funds Generally Accepted Principles and Practices*. The transparency requirement, as a prerequisite for regulating SOEs, is embedded in these guidelines. However, the effective enforcement of these soft laws is usually questioned by scholars, and some are outside the scope of existing hard laws.[31]

Scholars who advocate the specific regulation for SOEs, argue that five main elements must be incorporated in disciplines on SOEs, i.e., a clear definition and broad scope; a general obligation and rights; specific disciplines on trade-distortive practices by SOEs and specific exception; provisions to improve transparency; and rules regarding enforceability and dispute settlement.[32] Current SOE rules do not contain all of these elements. CPTPP is regarded as a new starting point for regulating SOEs by introducing WTO-plus disciplines on SOEs and government intervention.[33] SOE-specific rules in the CPTPP include definition, the scope of application, commercial considerations and non-discriminatory treatment, transparency requirements and non-commercial assistance. Non-discriminatory treatment and commercial considerations are regarded as general obligations, while non-commercial assistance is regarded as specific to SOEs.[34] There are also various kinds of exceptions and dispute settlement mechanisms for addressing conflicts or issues arising from these SOE rules. These rules are specific to SOE conduct rather than general requirements for governments.

CAI incorporates provisions ensuring a level playing field, which in this chapter means that it includes both SOE-relevant rules (imposing requirements on government) and SOE-specific rules (imposing requirements directly on SOEs). Provisions

---

[29] For discussions of attribution rules and SOEs, see Hobér (2008); Du (2021); Schonsteiner (2019).

[30] Although SOEs entail complexities in terms of state responsibility, the status and conduct of SOEs can hardly be addressed by Art. 4 of ILC Draft Articles on state organs. See Lee (2015), p. 147.

[31] Kawase and Ambashi (2018), p. 5.

[32] Willemyns (2016), p. 658.

[33] Nawawi (2021), p. 138.

[34] Willemyns (2016), pp. 667–669.

concerning SOEs, forced technology transfer and transparency in subsidies are regarded as key commitments to make investment fair.[35] This chapter focuses on SOE-specific rules or disciplines. Unlike the CPTPP, and other EU-led FTAs, e.g., EU-Japan EPA and EU-Vietnam FTA, CAI does not employ the wording of 'state-owned enterprises' as a section or provision title, but 'covered entities'. Using such language expands the scope of requirements on the basis of SOEs. The 'covered entities' clause is in the Investment Liberalisation Section of Chapter II of the CAI. Compared with the suggested five elements of any specific SOE regulations and the practice of CPTPP, the CAI covers the definition, the scope of application and general requirements. Key SOE-specific disciplines (or general requirements) of CAI refer to commercial considerations, non-discrimination and transparency (i.e., providing requested information for assessment of whether particular SOEs are complying with their obligations).

2.2 *Definition in CAI*

Footnote 5 of the CAI highlights that the list of covered entities in this section is for the purpose of framing the scope of application. Therefore what is meant by targeted entities in Art. 3bis (Covered Entities) is broader, including not only the traditional sense of SOEs, but also POEs with monopoly status or other entities controlled directly or indirectly by the government. Wholly state-owned enterprises (*Guo You Du Zi*) and State-controlled enterprises (or state-owned holding enterprises, *Guo You Kong Gu*) in the usual sense can be covered by this definition, while entities for which the government controls its decision-making by holding a minority stake, or holds no rights and interests but controls its decision-making through instructions in accordance with the law, also satisfy the definition. In addition, public or private enterprises with a monopoly position in the relevant market due to the designation by the government of one Contracting Party also fall into the scope of application of the relevant rules.

Covered entities consist of those entities where the government has: (1) de facto control;[36] (2) de jure control;[37] or (3) delegates monopoly rights.[38] This means that the government's potential economic power and legal or statutory intervening power in certain entities are considered in the CAI. As far as the nature of the entities is concerned, this formulation softens concern about 'state ownership' and instead adopts an expression consistent with the notion of 'ownership neutrality'.[39] However,

---

[35] Baruzzi (2021).

[36] CAI, Art. 3bis (1) (a).

[37] CAI, Art. 3bis (1) (b).

[38] CAI, Art. 3bis (1) (c) (d).

[39] The basic characteristic of an ownership neutral structure is that all players should be on the same level playing field, none having special privileges and should be regulated with the same gover-

this also indicates that the coverage of this clause is broader than SOE-alone provisions and the subject that this clause attempts to regulate is not limited to SOEs.

2.3 Scope and Exceptions

The 'Covered Entities' clause reiterates and emphasises non-discrimination with respect to ownership from the outset. It indicates that covered entities are not prevented from being established or maintained due to their different ownership or corporate forms. The main purpose of this clause is to regulate and restrain governmental intervention in the economic activities of these entities, exerting distortive impacts or providing privileges or preferential treatment based solely on 'state ownership'.

The 'Covered Entities' clause should be read with exceptions and carve-outs. Five exceptions to the application of 'Covered Entities' clause are listed by the Contracting Parties: government procurement; government function;[40] public service; size/scale;[41] and exception to non-conforming measures.[42] Furthermore, in accordance with Art. 1, paragraph 2 of Section II of the CAI, the rules of this section do not apply to audio-visual services, air transport services and auxiliary air services.

It should be noted that, in addition to the above generally applicable exceptions embedded in this section, observation and exceptions made by the Contracting Parties in their respective annexes are also an important basis for understanding the scope of application of the relevant rules on SOEs as well as respective effects. As mentioned above, SOE-specific disciplines in the CAI do not apply to the relevant industries listed by China in Schedule I of the Agreement, and the Parties may also include non-conforming measures in the Schedule II, to exclude the application of non-discriminatory treatment and the obligation of commercial consideration. There are three annexes to relevant sections of the CAI,[43] but none of these incorporate specific exceptions applicable to the SOEs or the 'Covered Entities' clause.

nance standards. See Kajla (2018). Ownership Neutrality describes the avoidance of picking out specific firms such as SOEs in the design and implementation of rules. See Lu (2019).

[40] As defined in Art. 2 Section 1, 'activities performed in the exercise of governmental authority' denotes those performed neither on a commercial basis nor in competition with one or more economic operators.

[41] In Art. 3bis (2) (d), non-discriminatory treatment and commercial considerations, and transparency do not apply to covered entities 'if in any one of the three previous consecutive fiscal years, the annual revenue derived from the commercial activities of such covered entity was less than 200 million Special Drawing Rights.' The threshold for this size exception is consistent with the level of State-Owned Enterprise Chapter of the CPTPP.

[42] This does not apply to the relevant activities of China's Covered Entities in the relevant industries listed in Entries 1.21 to 1.26 of China's schedule in Annex I.

[43] These are Annexes to Section III Subsection II Art. 8 Transparency of Subsidies, Annex I Rules of procedure for state-to-state dispute settlement, and Annex II Code of conduct for members of arbitral tribunals and mediators in state-to-state disputes.

Both China and the EU's schedule of commitments and reservations are absent from exceptions with regard to obligations directly applying to SOEs. It is imperative to note that a limited number of exceptions should be preferred as to the application of SOE disciplines, particularly sector- or entity-specific exceptions. This protect sectors or entities deemed most important to Contracting Parties and also avoids exceptions becoming too wide.[44]

2.4 *Disciplines on SOEs*

The CAI imposes disciplines of non-discriminatory treatment, commercial considerations, and transparency with respect to covered entities.

In general, non-discrimination rules include principles that deal with provisions of the domestic laws of a country discriminating against certain categories of investors. The principle of non-discrimination on the basis of the nationality of the investor is one of the key legal guarantees provided to foreign investors by international investment agreements (IIAs).[45] Two typical non-discriminatory treatment standards (that is, most-favoured-nation treatment and national treatment) are usually embedded in trade, investment and tax treaties, whether bilateral or mega-regional. The non-discriminatory treatment in the CAI requires the Contracting Party to treat investors of the other Party no less favourably than it treats its own investors or the investors of any non-Party, in like situations, with respect to establishment and operation in its territory.[46] However, this non-discriminatory treatment is different from that imposed on 'covered entities', as the former is an obligation on the government while the latter is the rule for SOEs. The specific manifestation of 'covered entities' is that each Party shall ensure that its covered entities, when engaging in commercial activities in their purchases or sales of goods or services, shall treat investors of the other Party no less favourably than they would treat investors of the Party in like situations. However, it is important to note that non-discriminatory treatment, according to footnote 8 of this clause, is only granted to foreign investors who have established and operate a covered investment in the Contracting State.[47] Thus it can be understood that the non-discriminatory discipline is premised on the foreign investor's establishment of a commercial presence in the host State.

[44] It is observed by some scholars that the exceptions applicable to SOEs, in particular sectoral exceptions, do not go beyond China's current market liberalization offers provided by the Negative List for Foreign Investment Access. See Su (2022), p. 555.

[45] These guarantees may directly restrain states' legislative, administrative, or judicial measures taken to implement a host of public policies. See Ortino (2009), p. 344.

[46] CAI, Arts. 4 and 5.

[47] Footnote 8 of Art. 3bis (3) of the CAI states that '[f]or great certainty, it is understood that this does not apply to situations of trade in goods and to supply of services other than through establishment of an enterprise and operation of a covered investment.'

The commercial consideration discipline requires that if a covered entity undertakes commercial activities for commercial purposes, it shall purchase or sell goods or services in accordance with commercial considerations.[48] It also requires that if a 'covered entity' engaged in commercial activities for the purpose of public service, on the basis of not violating the obligation of non-discriminatory treatment, may not comply with the commercial consideration discipline.[49] The obligation imposed on SOEs to act in accordance with commercial considerations can be found not only in CPTPP, but also in CETA and the US-Singapore FTA (although in the US-Singapore FTA, this discipline only applies to Singaporean SOEs, rather than the US ones).

It is important to note that the premise of these two obligations is that they are limited to 'engaging in commercial activities'. The understanding of 'commercial activities' affects the application of the SOE disciplines. However, it is interesting that a clear expression of this term is absent from the CAI. Art. 2 of Section I defines 'economic activities' rather than 'commercial activities'.[50] The 'covered entities' clause does not provide any further footnote clarifying such a term. In CPTPP, in contrast, this term is positively defined in Art. 17.1 as 'activities which an enterprise undertakes with an orientation toward profit-making and which result in the production of a good or supply of a service that will be sold to a consumer in the relevant market in quantities and at prices determined by the enterprise'.[51]

Another core SOE discipline in the 'Covered Entities' clause is transparency. The 'inherent lack of transparency' of SOEs was argued to be an important factor leading to possible distortive practice by SOEs.[52] Under the transparency requirement, the Contracting Party has the right to request disclosure of relevant information if it believes that the commercial activities of covered entities of the other Contracting Party adversely affect its interests. This covers a wide range of information, including the percentage of shares and special shares held by the Contracting Party in the covered entities, the percentage of voting rights and special voting rights, the organisational structure of the enterprise, and annual revenue or total

[48] According to the definition in Section I of the CAI, commercial considerations refer to price, quality, availability, marketability, transportation, and other terms and conditions of purchase or sale, or other factors that would normally be taken into account in the commercial decisions of an enterprise, in the relevant business or industry, that are profit-based, and disciplined by market forces.

[49] Engaging in commercial activities in this Article does not apply to situations of trade in goods and to supply of services other than through establishment of an enterprise and operation of a covered investment. This also makes the model of 'business presence' in GATS relevant here.

[50] Economic activities are defined as including 'activities of an industrial, commercial and professional character and activities of craftsmen, but do not include activities performed in the exercise of governmental authority'.

[51] Footnotes 1 and 2 provide further clarifications. Footnote 1 states that 'activities undertaken by an enterprise which operates on a non-for-profit basis or on a cost-recovery basis are not activities undertaken with an orientation toward profit-making; footnote 2 reads that 'measures of general application to the relevant market shall not be construed as the determination by a Party of pricing, production, or supply decisions of an enterprise'.

[52] Willemyns (2016), p. 676.

assets.[53] If a Contracting Party holds shares or voting rights that differ from ordinary shares, it must disclose its special share or voting status, the organisational structure of the enterprise, the composition of the board of directors or similar bodies exercising control over the enterprise, cross-shareholdings or other legal arrangements. Any immunities, privileges or similar arrangements under the laws of the Contracting Party, the competent authority in the enterprise that exercises the functions of government ownership of the Contracting Party and any other relevant information should be disclosed. Applying this transparency requirement is, however, only possible when the requesting Party can prove that the covered entity is engaged in anti-competitive practices. In addition, it requires compliance with good international practice on corporate governance and transparency, indirectly introducing guidance on SOEs and corporate governance from the OECD and the IWG 'SWF Santiago Principles' into treaty obligations.[54]

Without a corresponding enforcement mechanism, SOE discipline will become a toothless rule. For SOE disciplines to be actionable, it is necessary to having a dispute settlement mechanism for these matters. Currently, a number of existing FTAs with SOE-specific rules do not contain specific provisions regarding the adjudication of relevant disputes. As mentioned, rules concerning enforceability and dispute resolution are regarded as one of the five elements of SOE rules. Although CPTPP does not contain an explicit reference to jurisdiction on disputes regarding SOE rules, it allows for adjudicating SOE rules via a set of options. Breaches of any provision in SOE Chapter of the CPTPP can be brought before a domestic court, ISDS or the dispute settlement mechanism of CPTPP, but the CAI does not set up a special dispute settlement mechanism for 'covered entities' and incorporate ISDS provisions. All disputes are under the scope of Section V, i.e., via State-to-State dispute settlement.

2.5 *Characteristics of SOE Rules in CAI*

The SOE-specific rules in the CAI presents unique characteristics compared to other SOE-specific rules in recent FTAs, in particular those supported, dominated or promoted by the EU and US. These SOE rules in the 'covered entities' clause play a symbolic role. By choosing the term 'covered entities' rather than an SOE-only

---

[53] CAI, Art. 3bis (4) (i) (ii) (iii) (iv).

[54] The OECD Guidelines on Corporate Governance of State-Owned Enterprises are recommendations to governments on ensuring that SOEs operate transparency, efficiently and accountably. These principles were renamed the G20/OECD Principles of Corporate Governance. As outlined in the SOE Guidelines, information disclosure (both financial and non-financial) is essential. See OECD (2015, 2021). The Santiago Principles, or Generally Accepted Principles and Practices of Sovereign Wealth Funds, were drafted by the International Working Group of SWFs and welcomed by the International Monetary Financial Committee in 2008. One of the objectives is to ensure that SWFs comply with all applicable regulatory and disclosure requirements in the countries in which SWFs invest. For more information, please see IWG (2008).

expression, China and the EU maintain a neutral view on establishing and maintaining SOEs and seek to ensure competitive neutrality. The focus is on regulating and limiting governmental intervention of activities of not only SOEs but also other companies having special rights or a high degree of state support or control. The CAI requires Contracting Parties to treat SOEs and other entities equally and to ensure that SOEs compete as market players when engaging in commercial activities. This can also be supported by the regulatory neutrality requirement,[55] as one of the requirements embedded in competitive neutrality, in Art. 3ter of the CAI.[56] Contracting Parties of the CAI are required to treat covered entities and other businesses fairly and equitably, and exclude the adverse effects of covered entities on regulators. This shows that China is willing to put SOEs under the CAI discipline and support SOE reform with the goal of competitive neutrality. CAI can be regarded as an example that integrates both the notion of competitive neutrality and ownership neutrality, which helps to reduce or mitigate the conflict of choosing an economic development model.[57]

Compared with the SOE provisions in the EU-Vietnam FTA, EU-Japan EPA and CPTPP, the 'covered entities' clause adopted in the CAI places more emphasis on ownership neutrality and 'term neutrality'. In terms of the definition of 'SOEs', the CAI seems to cover a wider range of entities than those included in the CPTPP and EU-Vietnam FTA. The definition of SOEs in CPTPP and EU-Vietnam FTA lists three similar criteria to define SOEs, i.e., over 50 percentage of shares, over 50 percentage of voting rights, and power to appoint directors.[58] Apart from these three types of elements, the CAI includes not only SOEs in which the government holds a majority stake in the traditional sense but also include 'control the decisions of the enterprise through any other ownership interest, including minority ownership' and 'has the power to legally direct the actions or otherwise exercise an equivalent level of control in accordance with its laws and regulations'. The definition in the CAI is relatively broad and may lead to the government or political party directives on certain POEs being included in the definition. It should be noted that the CAI does not intend to hinder the State's control or leadership of the enterprise, but requires that the conduct of the enterprise is based on the logic of market forces, which means that inappropriate government intervention in the market needs to be constrained. Similarly, insisting on the separation of government and enterprise, separation of government and capital, separation of ownership and management rights, and ensuring that commercial SOEs realise commercial operation in accordance

[55] Regulatory neutrality requires that a government business is not advantaged by operating in a different regulatory environment to its competitors. See Capobianco and Christiansen (2011), p. 16.

[56] The OECD Competition Committee, throughout the years, has undertaken different initiatives to analyse competitive neutrality in competition policy from different angles. In 2021, the OECD Council adopted the 2021 Recommendation on Competitive Neutrality, which recommends adopting and maintaining neutral market rules and intends to ensure that the legal framework is neutral.

[57] On types of capitalism, see Toplišek (2018), p. 55; Petersmann and Steinbach (2021).

[58] In Art. 11.1 (g) of the EU-Vietnam FTA, SOEs also include an enterprise, in which a Party, directly or indirectly, can 'exercise control over the strategic decisions of the enterprise'.

with market requirements are also important contents of mixed-ownership reform of SOEs in China.[59]

The SOE specific rules in the CAI represent an alternative approach, adopted by both the EU and China, to address issues raised by SOEs under the WTO framework. The SOE disciplines included in the CAI (as well as in the CPTPP) fill the gaps in the SOE rules under the WTO regime. Article XVII of GATT establishes, to a limited extent, non-discrimination and commercial considerations, and transparency obligations for a special category of SOEs, i.e., state trading enterprises. The 'state trading enterprises' under the WTO rules only involve enterprises in the field of trade in goods, and the WTO does not set any special rules for SOEs in the general sense. A state trading enterprise, required by Article XVII of GATT, 'shall…act in a manner consistent with the general principles of non-discriminatory treatment…'. And the non-discriminatory requirement of state trading enterprises is specified to mean that it must act 'solely in accordance with commercial consideration…'. It indicates that non-discriminatory treatment and commercial considerations appear subordinate. The discriminatory behaviour of the enterprise must be judged by commercial considerations to determine whether it is in line with commercial elements. In this regard, commercial considerations are merely a measure attached to the obligation of non-discriminatory treatment. The WTO jurisprudence interpreted these two obligations as illustrative of one another. For example, in the case of *Canada- Measures relating to Exports of Wheat Exports and Treatment of Imported Grain (Canada — Wheat Exports and Grain Imports)*, the Appellate Body contended that non-discriminatory treatment and commercial consideration are 'complementary'.[60] The disciplines set in Article XVII aim at preventing certain types of discriminatory behaviour of state trading enterprises rather than imposing competition-law-type obligations on these entities.[61] The CPTPP puts these two requirements into two separate disciplines with 'no logical link' between them,[62] and the CAI also follows the same approach.

On the other hand, when China joined the WTO, it made commitments to all SOEs on a wider scale through the Protocol on the Accession of China and the Report of the Working Party of the Accession of China. It intends to ensure that all SOEs and state-invested enterprises purchase and sell goods only based on commercial considerations, acknowledging that enterprises of other WTO members will have the opportunity to fully compete with these enterprises on a non-discriminatory basis.[63] It thus is understandable that China's commitment in the CAI is acceptable to China as it is in line with these commitments China made under the WTO regime. However, scholars hold different views on the effect of China's Protocol of

[59] Wang and Cheng-Han (2020); Zhang et al. (2020); Zhang (2019).

[60] Canada – Wheat Exports and Grain Imports, WTO AB Report, WT/DS276/AB/R (30 August 2004), para. 145 (87, 97, 94).

[61] Ibid., para. 145.

[62] Kim (2017), p. 253.

[63] For more information of China's commitment concerning SOEs, please see WTO (2001), p. 9.

Accession or China specific WTO rules governing Chinese SOEs: some argue that problems of Chinese SOEs were not handled or addressed well in the Protocol of Accession;[64] others suggest that China's WTO specific rules on SOEs are broader or stricter than the CPTPP SOE chapter due to the limited coverage of the main obligations and the wide range of exceptions.[65]

In terms of commercial consideration, it was firstly introduced by the US into its FTA practices. It was argued that those treaties inspired by US-led FTAs (e.g., the NAFTA) usually require that SOEs act in accordance with commercial considerations and in a non-discriminatory manner while those treaties inspired by EU-led FTAs require SOEs to be subject to competition laws.[66] It is, however, that the EU's practice demonstrates the convergence of US-led and EU-led FTAs. The US approach is currently adopted by the EU and China. Both the CAI and CPTPP treat the commercial consideration as a separate and independent discipline for SOEs. The CPTPP (and also the USMCA) restricts the notion of 'commercial considerations' that SOEs and designated monopolies need to observe in the purchase and sale of goods and services to other factors that private enterprises in the corresponding industries usually consider in their business decisions. It means that the criteria of 'commercial consideration' should be compared and mirrored with POE's decision making. In *Canada-Wheat Exports and Grain Imports*, the EU suggests that, as the third-party submission, 'the phrase 'commercial considerations' should be interpreted in the light of normal (private) commercial behaviour' and 'the ordinary meaning of this phrase, as well as its context, illustrate that an STE should act just as a private company would react on the market.'[67] The CAI, on the other hand, removes the requirement for the nature of ownership of enterprises, which means that it does not emphasize the 'private enterprises' as the benchmark. It defines 'commercial consideration' at a substantive level as the obligations usually considered in decision-making by entities in the same industry that aim to make profits and are subject to market forces. It abandons the ownership discrimination model, where POE is regarded as the sole comparator, and adopts behaviour-oriented and profit-based requirements. In terms of the application of these SOE rules, as an investment agreement, the CAI only requires the Parties to ensure that the covered entities comply with their obligations regarding commercial considerations and non-discrimination in the course of their domestic operation when purchasing and selling goods and services. The CPTPP, however, extends its coverage to enterprises that provide goods or services to other Contracting Parties in the form of cross-border or overseas investment.

In terms of transparency obligations for SOEs, both the US and EU set standards and specific requirements. The scope of information disclosure covered by the US

[64] Levy (2017), p. 636.

[65] Zhou (2021), p. 589.

[66] Anderson et al. (2018).

[67] Canada – Wheat Exports and Grain Imports, WTO AB Report, WT/DS276/AB/R (30 August 2004), para. 71.

and US treaties is consistent.[68] However, the transparency requirement incorporated in US FTAs focuses more on providing procedural guarantees via dispute settlement mechanisms, while the EU FTAs reflect the connotation of substantive norms of competition law. The CPTPP stipulates that the Contracting Parties are obliged to regularly publish the list of SOEs;[69] and also introduces the adverse inferences method in the WTO dispute settlement mechanism. It means that when the information exchange mechanism fails to operate, the complaint has the right to request the panel to intervene, and if the respondent still does not cooperate, the panel will make adverse inferences against the responding party.[70] CAI, in contrast, does not adopt such an approach.

2.6 *Possible Implications*

In the overall sense, the CAI achieves a breakthrough in the international regulation of SOEs. As mentioned above, the previous treaty practice indicates that China is reluctant to refer to SOEs specifically or directly regulate the conduct of SOEs in FTAs and IIAs (except under the WTO framework). The value of 'covered entities' clause in the CAI is in line with China's domestic reform (in particular SOE reform and investment liberalisation reform) and pre-existing commitments in WTO agreements. Several reasons can be provided as reasonable explanations to answer why the CAI and its positive spill-overs to promote and advance China's domestic reform should not be underestimated. It is consistent with the spirit of SOE reform that China is actively promoting under the principle of competitive neutrality and China's support for the development of enterprises of different ownerships. Since the mid-1990s, the reform of SOEs in China has covered for a long journey and is still in progress. The SOE reform has always been a key link in China's market-oriented reform. The SOE reform has gradually returned to the idea of classification reform (or the mixed ownership reform),[71] after going through reform stages, such as delegating power and transferring profits, contracting and leasing system, shareholding system reform, and piloting the modern enterprise system. The 2015 Guiding Opinions,[72] clearly divides SOEs into commercial and public welfare types,

---

[68] CPTPP Art. 17.10 (3); USMCA Art. 22.10 (3); EU-Vietnam FTA Art. 11.6 (2); CAI Art. 3bis (4).

[69] CPTPP Arts. 17.10 (1) and (2).

[70] CPTPP Annex 17-B Art. 9 states that '[i]n making findings of fact and its initial report, the panel should draw adverse inferences from instances of non-cooperation by a disputing Party in the information-gathering process.'

[71] The Third Plenary Session of the 18th CPC Central Committee set the agenda for reforming SOEs in November 2013. The State Council and CPC Central Committee issued the guidelines on deepening the reform of SOEs in September 2015. Guiding Opinions of the Communist Party of China Central Committee and the State Council on Deepening the Reform of State-Owned Enterprises, Zhong Fa [2015] No.22.

[72] Ibid.

and defined different reform models. Commercial-oriented SOEs are required to implement the reform of corporate governance and shareholding, and state-owned capital can be absolutely or relatively controlled. It is also possible to participate in shares; while public welfare SOEs generally take the form of wholly SOEs, but non-SOEs are also allowed to participate in some fields. Another document released jointly by the State Council and Central Committee of Chinese Communist Party in 2019 also mentioned that "fair competition shall be adhered to, various market participants shall be treated on an equal footing, and a market environment, policy environment, and rule of law environment for fair competition shall be created, so as to ensure equal rights, opportunities, and rules".[73] All of these are in line with the principle of competitive neutrality, which is also a defining part of the CAI.[74]

Investment liberalisation efforts have been adopted by China to ensure the market access of foreign investors and a level playing field between Chinese and foreign investors. The Foreign Investment Law implemented by China and the shortened negative list are welcome attempts to improve the investment treatment and market access in China.[75] And the CAI makes the investment liberalisation efforts binding and promising for EU investors. The Special Administrative Measures (Negative List) for Foreign Investment Access ("National Negative List") and the Special Administrative Measures (Negative List) for Foreign Investment Access in Pilot Free Trade Zones ("FTZ Negative List") play an important role in levelling the playing field for foreign and domestic investors.[76] However, the slow process or pace of reforms, as argued by other economies lead to skeptical view towards China's willingness to truly embrace further reform and market openness. The US and EU current policy and regulatory shift put further pressure on China's reform and the progress achieved so far does not seem to satisfy them.[77]

The CAI provides an alternative model, compared with the CPTPP, for international disciplines on SOEs and also reshapes the existing models of IIAs. The innovative way of treaty drafting and novel issues that are usually not the main focus of IIAs shed some light on further IIA drafting or redrafting. It also implies a trend of the convergence of trade and investment issues rather than maintaining the continued fragmentation of international economic law.[78] It also represents a balanced approach to regulate SOEs compared to CPTPP and other US FTAs. The covered entities clause of the CAI reflects the attempts of China and the EU to construct the

[73] Opinions of the CPC Central Committee and the State Council on Creating a Better Development Environment and Supporting the Reform and Development of Private Enterprises, Zhong Fa (2019) No. 49.

[74] Duan and Song (2021), p. 20.

[75] Garcia-Herrero (2020).

[76] The 2021 National Negative List has removed two restricted items from its 2020 version, cutting it from 33 to 31, while the new 2021 FTZ Negative List removed three items, cutting it from 30 to 27. See Zhou and Zhang (2021).

[77] Yin (2021), p. 17.

[78] For more discussion of the fragmentation of international law and international economic law, see Picker (2017), p. 21; Koskenniemi (2006); Schlemmer-Schulte (2012); van Aaken (2008).

regulation and discipline of SOEs on the basis of non-discrimination of ownership, and reflects the changes in the regulatory logic of SOEs. It exerts sound and important implications for the realisation of economic and trade cooperation between economies with different systems and models, and can be regarded as the application of the 'interface theory' in the new era.[79]

Since the CAI text is still under legal and technical review and needs to go through the EU's procedure, this may constrain the analysis of the implication of SOE rules to a certain extent. In addition, the current murky economic and trade relationship between China and the EU, and disagreements in other areas also cast doubt on the progress of this agreement. But discussions can still be made in combination with the existing practices and measures of China and the EU.

Despite the innovative features of the CAI, there are still concerns with regard to the implementation of relevant provisions and the effectiveness of the CAI *per se*. The wide margin for interpretation and the loose wording for requiring SOEs to 'act according to commercial considerations' leaves much to be resolved.[80] The undefined 'commercial activities' also carry the risk of circumventing the SOE disciplines. Although SOE disciplines incorporated in the CAI imply that EU concerns about fair competition are partly reassured, it is not clear how CAI can help Chinese investors to avoid those regulatory regimes of the EU. Merger control review, FDI screening, and foreign subsidies regulation will continue to apply despite the existence of CAI. It may also trigger further analysis or discussion on whether these new attempts may violate pre-establishment national treatment or raise the issue of indirect expropriation.

The ambiguity of several terms in the 'covered entities' clause makes it difficult to judge whether Contracting Party and/or SOEs violate the disciplines, in particular non-discriminatory treatment and commercial consideration, and what will be the consequences if it is violated. As mentioned before, the existing practice under WTO indicates that disputes involving the understanding or interpreting of relevant SOE rules are addressed via the WTO adjudication. And adequate enforceability is ensured under CPTPP, including not only domestic courts but also international dispute settlement mechanisms. Whether the State-to-State dispute settlement mechanism of the CAI is the optimal choice for dealing with breaches of SOE disciplines is hard to know at this moment. Due to the pervasive role of the SOEs in the Chinese economy, it was argued that an efficient state-to-state dispute resolution mechanism might be necessary.[81] It also provides methods of consultations (Article 3), and mediation (Article 4). This may be understood that as a highly sensitive area, the home state of SOEs may prefer a mechanism that can provide impartial and

---

[79] Ding (2020), pp. 637–663. The interface theory was proposed by John Jackson in the 1970s and 1980s, advocating that economic and trade cooperation between counties with different institutional models should be realized by focusing on trade liberalization and text technology, so as to facilitate the acceptance of the multilateral trading system. See Jackson et al. (1995) pp. 668–672, 1140–1142.

[80] Kassas (2022).

[81] Garcia-Herrero (2020).

reliable adjudication,[82] and can reflect the oriental concept of 'peace is the most precious'. Some scholars, however, argue that the CAI has no real teeth, and remains to be seen whether China can be held to CAI obligation on the behaviour of SOEs.[83]

Both China and the EU made concessions during the negotiation process, in order to reach a consensus, which made the CAI, especially the sensitive 'covered entities' clause adopted certain vague wordings. On the one hand, each Party can interpret relevant terms or provisions based on their own positions; on the other hand, the uncertainty of the clause may bury hidden risks. From China's perspective, although the rules enshrine 'competitive neutrality', the definition in the 'covered entities' clause has the suspicion of broadening its interpretation and leads to more entities being included in the scope of the rules. The initial intention of the CAI is to eliminate the negative impact of SOE activities and governmental intervention on fair competition, but the special regulation for SOEs may have a certain restrictive effect, affecting those SOEs engaging in both commercial activities and public services functions to a certain extent. And it may also limit the positive role of the government in promoting the economy if it is hard to differentiate inappropriate intervention from necessary intervention.[84] It is, of course, worth noting that exceptions embedded in the 'covered entities' clause reserve possible policy space.

The SOE rules introduced by the US into the CPTPP are argued by some scholars as the new model to regulate SOEs and address issues raised by 'state capitalism', in particular Chinese state capitalism.[85] Since among signatories of CPTPP, many economies embrace state capitalism or attach importance to the role of state-owned or controlled entities, the application of SOE disciplines to these countries is reviewed as a test for dealing with China.[86] However, the real and practical effect of the CPTPP SOE rules is still in doubt, especially from the perspective of the EU and US. Both sides have tried to deal with the pervasive role of SOEs without much success while the promising approach so far is the soft regulation of SOEs or guidelines provided by international organisations. In the CPTPP, numerous exceptions and exemptions held by Contracting Parties make the SOE rules less effective. Scholars suggested that it does not provide workable rules but rather has narrower applications and more carve-outs.[87] In CPTPP, certain companies and their activities are exempted from the application of the SOE chapter and each party can claim specific exemptions. Only those SOEs largely at the federal or central government level bear the obligation of these rules. Moreover, the definition of an SOE in the CPTPP SOE chapter is criticised for being too narrow, as it does not cover those enterprises that are effectively controlled, *de facto* or *de jure*, by the government. It is, however,

---

[82] Willemyns (2016), p. 678.

[83] Every (2021).

[84] For discussion of government intervention, please see Rasmussen and Skeel (2016); Knowles and Garces (2000); Belli (1999).

[85] Lefebvre et al. (2021); Nemoto (2019); Kang (2019); see also Matsushita and Lim (2019).

[86] Kawase and Ambashi (2018), p. 2.

[87] Zhou (2021); Willemyns (2016).

worth noting that CPTPP represents the first time those economies, where SOEs play important role in providing vital services, have tried to address anti-competitive challenges arising from SOE conducts, adopting limited steps could be a reasonable and understandable choice.[88]

Similarly, the actual effect of the CAI is also questionable, given the absence of the final version at present and the failure to address the so-called 'public body' issue concerning subsidies.[89] Compared with the CPTPP SOE disciplines, the CAI possesses both merits and disadvantages. Broader definitions and relatively fewer exceptions are the main merits of the CAI. For scholars and relevant literature criticising the effects of the CPTPP SOE disciplines, the CAI's provisions provide a broader scope for disciplining SOEs and their activities. CPTPP incorporates SOE specific obligation, i.e., non-commercial assistance, to address subsidy issues.[90] It extends the obligation of Contracting Party to service subsidies.[91] The CAI, whereas, does not directly address the subsidy rules to be followed by Covered Entities. It was argued by some scholars that the CAI fails to address SOEs' receiving non-commercial assistance either directly or indirectly from the government.[92] This can also be used to explain why the EU continues to adopt a unilateral approach to address the problem of foreign subsidies for acquisition.[93]

It could be argued that the EU will receive economic gains, especially in improving the competitive positions of EU companies as compared to the *status quo*.[94] Some new EU initiatives, as mentioned before, with the intention to tackle Chinese SOEs' overseas investment activities, including EU-level investment screening and moves on foreign subsidies bring about potential risks for Chinese investors. According to the provisional text of the CAI, the concerns of China to ensure the non-discrimination treatment of Chinese SOEs and less cumbersome administrative review have not been addressed. The COVID-19 pandemic and institutional competition caused by geopolitics,[95] have promoted many developed economies, including the EU and its Member States to adopt an even more conservative approach towards foreign investments, especially those from China. It is important to note that at the moment, FDI screening mechanisms have been expanded in all major jurisdictions,

---

[88] Elms (2015).

[89] The legal status of SOEs under the WTO legal regime is usually discussed with regard to the notion of 'public body', which is a subject providing subsidies to other enterprises under the Agreement on Subsidies and Countervailing Measures. See Qin (2004). See also Ding (2014); Wu (2019).

[90] Article 17.6 of the CPTPP.

[91] GATS Article XV targets subsidies in service trades, but does not stipulate any detailed rules. Currently, GATS Article XV only contains guidelines for Members in future negotiations. Limited negotiations on the possible introduction of disciplines on service subsidies took place during the Uruguay Round but have not progressed significantly. See Poretti (2008), p. 466.

[92] Hufbauer (2021); Kassas (2022).

[93] Dominguez-Jimenez and Poitiers (2020).

[94] Every (2021).

[95] Libman (2005); Salleh and Yusoff (2017).

particularly in response to COVID-19 and Chinese SOEs are facing increased scrutiny in the EU and US.

3 Conclusion

As the first mega-regional agreement that China make breakthrough commitments on the operation and management of SOEs and the alternative way the EU trying to address the distortive actions of SOEs outside the WTO framework, the CAI is of milestone significance. It is wise to note that the regulatory model of SOEs in the CAI provides a chance to rethink the international regulation of SOEs and also to find out an optimal approach, among and beyond current ones, e.g., the CPTPP SOE chapter, WTO specific rules and OECD Guidelines, to address issues raised by SOEs and inappropriate governmental intervention. By using the neutral term 'covered entities' rather than sensitive 'SOE Chapter', the CAI demonstrates a good example to reduce the conflict of judging different institutional models. It also indicates the way that seems to be acceptable to China to address concerns of 'state capitalism' raised by several developed economies.

From the surface of the treaty text, there is some overlaps or similarities between the CAI and CPTPP in disciplining SOEs. Both provide definitions for targeted SOEs and incorporate non-discriminatory treatment, commercial considerations, and transparency requirements. However, from the perspective of specific content requirements and expressions, certain differences can be found between these two treaties. The CAI SOE disciplines are drafted with a broader definition and fewer exceptions and exemptions while the CPTPP SOE rules are designed with a narrower definition and various exceptions. The CAI provides only general obligations but the CPTPP includes specific obligations, i.e., non-commercial assistance. It is wise to admit that some requirements in the CAI are in consistent with China's commitment under the WTO framework, which is usually regarded as China's specific WTO obligation. Currently, China has submitted a formal letter of application to join the CPTPP,[96] so that the SOE rules in both CAI and CPTPP attract increasing attention from academia and policy-makers.

The benefits of China to join the CPTPP have been discussed or mentioned in papers and media.[97] But the SOE chapter in the CPTPP is regarded as one of the harsh challenges for China. Further and deepening reform efforts need to be promoted by China to adapt to the relevant requirements of the CPTPP and successfully join the CPTPP. The differences in the intention to draft or design the SOE relevant rules of the CAI and CPTPP show that although the US and EU criticise Chinese investment and China' state capitalism, their approaches in principle, to a certain

[96] Asian Trade Centre (2021).

[97] Petri and Plummer (2019).

extent, are different.[98] The consensus between US and EU chapters on SOEs is not only the pursuit of the free market and free competition but also the intention to use the regulation of SOEs to curb the development of emerging economies or reform some of the institutions in these countries. The differences between the two are manifested in specific rules and paths.

The EU did not implement the anti-subsidy regulation of SOEs, especially Chinese SOEs through its treaty practice, but tried to resort to EU legislation.[99] Excluding the constraints of this rule on its own, in terms of transparency, the EU SOE clause shows greater flexibility, adjusting the intensity and breadth of obligations according to the actual situation of the contracting parties, which is consistent with the EU's complex attitude towards SOEs is not unrelated. Insisting on the 'competitive neutrality' and 'ownership neutrality', maintaining the convergence and reconciling differences in the CAI and CPTPP, may, to a certain extent, help address the negotiation deadlock of the WTO. Further promoting the SOE reform in China could narrow the gap with the CPTPP rules, and the 'covered entities' clause in CAI can serve as the new starting point.

Although CAI is temporarily difficult to take effect, the economic and trade cooperation between China and the EU will not be suspended. The China-EU investment and economic cooperation is an inevitable move for both sides to seek development and a solid foundation for the development and recovery of the global economy. In addition, it is important to notice that SOEs are not a China-only development model or economic phenomenon, they can be found in both developed and developing countries. Any discussion of introducing or updating the international rulebook on SOEs should not merely address concerns from the side of developed countries but must strike a balance between meeting the development needs of developing and less developed countries and reducing market impediments and distortion.[100] As mentioned before, specific exception or exemption is one of the main elements that might be arguably incorporated in any SOE rules. Since some SOEs are given the function of achieving social welfare and policy objectives, providing some limited and well-defined exemptions or exceptions is indispensable. Exceptions regarding SOEs exist not only under the WTO framework but also in bilateral and regional trade and investment agreements.

Fair competition and market integrity are not the core issue limited to SOEs but also issues that can be triggered by POE. Apart from China, some developing countries have signed on to SOE reform rules, e.g., Vietnam, Malaysia, and Brunei (as signatories of recent mega-regional agreements). However, a number of 'carve-out' exceptions in these agreements and the absence of SOE specific rules in many existing FTAs and IIAs imply that developing countries generally do not easily follow the stricter SOE rules and ensuring appropriate policy space is important. Many

[98] Yin (2021), p. 21.

[99] However, the EU has included WTO+ provisions on subsidies in agreements negotiated with several third countries and has various subsidy disciplines set out in these agreements. Borlini (2016), p. 145.

[100] Anuar (2018).

governments are clearly reluctant to be bound by new commitments. But China's commitments in the CAI demonstrate its willingness to address the possible distortive effects of SOEs, upholding the principles of ownership neutrality and competitive neutrality. The CAI indeed provides guidance for China to join the CPTPP and the basis for further multilateral negotiations on addressing market distortion. It also provides an opportunity to rethink international regulation on SOEs, given the entry of China with the largest scale of SOEs. Further discussion on regulating SOEs requires involvement of more economies concerned. Balanced SOE rules bring benefits vis-à-vis development and improved global market.

References

Academy of China Council for the Promotion of International Trade (2021) Business Environment of the European Union 2020/2021. http://www.ccpit-academy.org/v-1-4401.aspx. Accessed 5 Feb 2022

Anderson RD et al (2018) Competition Policy, Trade and the Global Economy: Existing WTO Elements, Commitments in Regional Trade Agreements, Current Challenges and Issues for Reflection. Staff Working Paper ERSE-2018-12. https://www.wto.org/english/res_e/reser_e/ersd201812_e.pdf?msclkid=2930c598ba2611ecbc20955df8235d38. Accessed 1 Feb 2022

Anuar A (2018) Taming Big Brother: G20 Push to Reform SOEs. RSIS Commentaries No. 184. https://dr.ntu.edu.sg/bitstream/10356/80919/1/CO18184.pdf. Accessed 8 Feb 2022

Asian Trade Centre (2021) China Applies to Join the CPTPP. http://asiantradecentre.org/talkingtrade/china-applies-to-join-the-cptpp. Accessed 8 Feb 2022

Baruzzi S (2021) EU, China Reach Agreement on Investments in Principle: What Does it Mean for Businesses. China Briefing. https://www.china-briefing.com/news/eu-china-reach-agreement-on-investments-in-principle-what-does-it-mean-for-businesses/. Accessed 5 Apr 2022

Belli P (1999) The comparative advantage of government: a review. World Bank Policy Research Working Papers. https://elibrary.worldbank.org/doi/epdf/10.1596/1813-9450-1834. Accessed 4 Apr 2022

Borlini L (2016) Subsidies regulation beyond the WTO: substance, procedure and policy space in the 'New Generation' EU Trade Agreements. In: Capaldo GZ (ed) The global community: yearbook of international law and jurisprudence. OUP, Oxford, pp 145–174

Capobianco A, Christiansen H (2011) Competitive neutrality and state-owned enterprises: challenges and policy options. OECD Corp Gov Work Pap 1:16. https://www.oecd-ilibrary.org/docserver/5kg9xfgjdhg6-en.pdf?expires=1644935799&id=id&accname=guest&checksum=BFA99B430487904DDEF78A1968BD6704. Accessed 1 Feb 2022

Clarke L (2021) The EU's crackdown on state-subsidised companies is aimed squarely at China. https://techmonitor.ai/policy/eu-foreign-subsidies-legislation-china#:~:text=The%20European%20Commission%20has%20proposed%20new%20rules%20to,companies%20judged%20to%20unfairly%20benefit%20from%20foreign%20subsidies. Accessed 5 Feb 2022

Delegation of the European Union to the People's Republic of China (2021) Commission Publishes Market Access Offers of the EU-China Investment Agreement. https://www.eeas.europa.eu/delegations/china/commission-publishes-market-access-offers-eu-china-investment-agreement_en. Accessed 3 Sept 2022

Ding R (2014) 'Public Body' or not: Chinese state-owned enterprise. J World Trade 48(1):167–189

Ding R (2020) Interface 2.0 in rules on state-owned enterprises: a comparative institutional approach. J Int Econ Law 23(3):637–663

Dominguez-Jimenez M, Poitiers N (2020) Europe's China problem: investment screening and state aid. https://www.bruegel.org/2020/07/europes-china-problem-investment-screening-and-state-aid/. Accessed 5 Apr 2022

Drake EJ (2013) Trends and implication of Chinese investment in the United States: issues for policymakers. In: Testimony before the US–China Economic and Security Review Commission. https://www.uscc.gov/sites/default/files/USCC%20FDI%20Testimony%20Drake%20May%209%202013.pdf. Accessed 15 Jan 2022

Du M (2021) The status of Chinese state-owned enterprises in international investment arbitration: much ado about nothing. Chinese J Int Law 20(4):785–815

Duan X, Song X (2021) Turning pressure into opportunity: CAI and the future of China's structural reform. Asia Eur J 20:15–20

Elms D (2015) TPP impressions: competition and state owned enterprises (SOEs). http://asiantradecentre.org/talkingtrade/2015/11/17/tpp-impressions-competition-and-state-owned-enterprises-soes. Accessed 5 Apr 2022

European Commission (2016) State-owned enterprises in the EU: lessons learnt and ways forward in a post-crisis context. Institutional Paper 031. https://ec.europa.eu/info/sites/default/files/file_import/ip031_en_2.pdf. Accessed 5 Feb 2022

Every M (2021) Implications of the EU Chins Investment Deal (CAI). https://economics.rabobank.com/publications/2021/january/implications-of-the-eu-china-investment-deal-cai/. Accessed 5 Feb 2022

Garcia-Herrero A (2020) When and how should the European Union conclude an investment agreement with China?' Bruegel Blog. https://www.bruegel.org/2020/12/when-and-how-should-the-european-union-conclude-an-investment-agreement-with-china/. Accessed 5 Feb 2022

Garcia-Herrero A, Wolff GB (2020) China has an unfair advantage in the EU market. What can be done to level the playing field? Bruegel. https://www.bruegel.org/2020/07/china-has-an-unfair-advantage-in-the-eu-market-what-can-be-done-to-level-the-playing-field/. Accessed 7 Apr 2022

García-Herrero A, Xu J (2017) How to handle state-owned enterprises in EU-China investment talks. https://www.bruegel.org/wp-content/uploads/2017/06/PC-18-2017_2.pdf. Accessed 15 Jan 2022

Guluzade A (2019) The role of China's State-owned companies explained. World Economic Forum. https://www.weforum.org/agenda/2019/05/why-chinas-state-owned-companies-still-have-a-key-role-to-play/. Accessed 15 Jan 2022

Hobér K (2008) State responsibility and attribution. In: Muchlinski P et al (eds) The Oxford handbook of international investment law. OUP, Oxford

Hoekman B (2013) Sustaining multilateral trade cooperation in a multipolar world economy. Rev Int Org 9:241–260

Hufbauer GC (2021) EU-China investment accord fails to resolve subsidy disputes. https://www.piie.com/blogs/trade-and-investment-policy-watch/eu-china-investment-accord-fails-resolve-subsidy-disputes. Accessed 5 Apr 2022

IWG (2008) Sovereign wealth funds generally accepted principles and practices. https://www.ifswf.org/sites/default/files/santiagoprinciples_0_0.pdf. Accessed 1 Feb 2022

Jackson J et al (1995) Legal problems of international economic relations: cases, materials and text on the national and international regulation of transnational economic, 3rd edn. West Group, pp 668–672. 1140–1142

Kajla A (2018) Is ownership neutrality a step towards privatisation. CFA Blog. https://www.cenfa.org/finance/is-ownership-neutrality-a-step-towards-privatisation/. Accessed 15 Jan 2022

Kang S (2019) The CPTPP'S competition and SOE chapters: possible impacts for potential new members. TDM. https://www.transnational-dispute-management.com/article.asp?key=2665. Accessed 4 Apr 2022

Kassas R (2022) Does the comprehensive agreement on investment (CAI) level the playing field between the EU and China? Opinio Juris. https://opiniojuris.org/2022/02/01/does-the-comprehensive-agreement-on-investment-cai-level-the-playing-field-between-the-eu-and-china/. Accessed 15 Jan 2022

Kawase T, Ambashi M (2018) Disciplines on state-owned enterprises under the trans-pacific partnership agreement: overview and assessment. ERIA Discussion Paper Series 2017-13: 5. https://www.eria.org/uploads/media/ERIA-DP-2017-13.pdf. Accessed 20 Apr 2022

Kennedy S (2020) The biggest but not the strongest: China's place in the fortune global 500. https://www.csis.org/blogs/trustee-china-hand/biggest-not-strongest-chinas-place-fortune-global-500. Accessed 5 Feb 2022

Kim M (2017) Regulating the visible hands: development of rules on state-owned enterprises in trade agreements. Harv Int Law J 58(1):225–272

Knowles S, Garces A (2000) Measuring government intervention and estimating its effect on output: with reference to the high performing asian economies. CREDIT Research Paper No. 00/14. https://www.nottingham.ac.uk/credit/documents/papers/00-14.pdf. Accessed 4 Apr 2022

Koskenniemi M (2006) Fragmentation of international law: difficulties arising from the diversification and expansion of international law. Report of the Study Group of the International Law Commission. https://legal.un.org/ilc/documentation/english/a_cn4_l682.pdf. Accessed 5 Feb 2022

Kratz A et al (2020) Chinese FDI in Europe: 2019 Update. In: Merics Papers on China. https://merics.org/sites/default/files/2020-05/MERICSRhodium%20GroupCOFDIUpdate2020.pdf. Accessed 5 Jan 2022

Lee J (2015) State responsibility and government-affiliated entities in international economic law: the danger of blurring the Chinese wall between 'State Organ' and 'Non-State Organ' as designed the ILC draft articles. J World Trade 49(1):117–151

Lefebvre K et al (2021) Containing Chinese State-Owned Enterprises? The Role of Deep Trade Agreements. World Bank Group Policy Research Working Paper 9637 https://openknowledge.worldbank.org/bitstream/handle/10986/35516/Containing-Chinese-State-Owned-Enterprises-The-Role-of-Deep-Trade-Agreements.pdf?sequence=1. Accessed 5 Feb 2022

Levy IP (2017) The treatment of Chinese SOEs in China's WTO protocol of accession. World Trade Rev 16(4):635–653

Li S, Xu N (2015) The influences of WTO accession on China's state-owned enterprises. Open J Bus Man 3:192–198

Libman A (2005) Globalization and outcomes of institutional competition. MPRA Paper No. 11779. https://mpra.ub.uni-muenchen.de/11779/1/MPRA_paper_11779.pdf. Accessed 5 Apr 2022

Lu F (2019) Ownership Neutrality vs. Competitive Neutrality: SOE Issue in WTO Reform. https://www.nsd.pku.edu.cn/ccus/news/speakersseries/491143.htm. Accessed 15 Jan 2022

Lyons G (2007) State capitalism: the rise of sovereign wealth funds. J Manage Res 7(3):119–146

Matsushita M, Lim CL (2019) Taming Leviathan as merchant: lingering questions about the practical application of trans-Pacific partnership's state-owned enterprises rules. World Trade Rev 19(3):402–423

McLaughlin M (2020) State-owned enterprises and treats to national security under investment treaties. Chinese J Int Law 19(2):283–327

Morbiato A (2021) CAI: the Comprehensive Agreement on Investments. https://www.invenicement.com/uncategorized/cai-the-comprehensive-agreement-on-investments/. Accessed 15 Jan 2022

Nawawi WK (2021) New rules for state-owned enterprises in the CPTPP. In: Lee C, Bhattacharya P (eds) The comprehensive and progressive agreement for trans-pacific partnership: implications for Southeast Asia. ISEAS–Yusof Ishak Institute, Singapore, pp 138–161

Nemoto T (2019) Could the SOE Rules of the CPTPP Effectively Regulate China's SOEs? TDM. https://www.transnational-dispute-management.com/article.asp?key=2663. Accessed 4 Apr 2022

OECD (2015) G20/OECD Principles of Corporate Governance. https://www.oecd.org/daf/ca/Corporate-Governance-Principles-ENG.pdf. Accessed 1 Feb 2022

OECD (2018) Ownership and governance of state-owned enterprises: a compendium of national practices. https://www.oecd.org/corporate/Ownership-and-Governance-of-State-Owned-Enterprises-A-Compendium-of-National-Practices-2021.pdf. Accessed 5 Feb 2022

OECD (2021) Maintaining Competitive Neutrality: Voluntary Transparency and Disclosure Standard for Internationally-active SOEs and Their Owners. https://www.oecd.org/corporate/Maintaining-Competitive-Neutrality.pdf. Accessed 1 Feb 2022

Omran M (2004) The performance of state-owned enterprises and newly privatized firms: does privatization really matter? World Dev 32(6):1019–1041

Ortino F (2009) Non-discriminatory treatment in investment disputes. In: Dupuy P et al (eds) Human rights in international investment law and arbitration. OUP, Oxford, pp 344–366

Petersmann E, Steinbach A (2021) Neo-liberalism, state-capitalism and Ordo-Liberalism: 'Institutional Economics' and 'Constitutional Choices' in multilevel trade regulation. J World Inv Trade 22(1):1–40

Petri PA, Plummer MG (2019) China Should Join the New Trans-Pacific Partnership. https://www.piie.com/system/files/documents/pb19-1.pdf#:~:text=China%20could%20commit%20to%20CPTPP%20rules%20by%20launching,surprising%20that%20there%20is%20renewed%20interest%20today.2%20Australia%E2%80%99s. Accessed 8 Feb 2022

Picker CB (2017) The coherent fragmentation of international economic law: lessons from trans-pacific partnership agreement. In: Chaisse J et al (eds) Paradigm shift in international economic law rule-making: TPP as a new model for trade agreements? Springer, Singapore, pp 21–44

Poretti P (2008) Waiting for Godot: subsidy disciplines in service trade. In: Panizzon M et al (eds) GATS and the regulation of international trade in services. CUP, Cambridge, pp 466–488

Qin J (2004) WTO regulation of subsidies to state-owned enterprises (SOEs) – a critical appraisal of the China accession protocol. J Int Econ Law 7(4):863–919

Rasmussen RK, Skeel DA Jr (2016) Governmental intervention in an economic crisis. Univ Pa J Bus Law 19(1):7–48

Salleh MFM, Yusoff WS (2017) Institutional geopolitics: a new approach to benchmark the excess value of multinational corporations. In: Kuncoro A et al (eds) Enhancing business stability through collaboration. CRC Press, London, pp 2–10

Schlemmer-Schulte S (2012) Fragmentation of international law: the case of international finance & investment law versus human rights law. Glob Bus Dev Law J 25:409–424

Schonsteiner J (2019) Attribution of state responsibility for actions or omissions of state-owned enterprises in human rights matters. Univ Pa J Int Law 40(4):895–936

Su X (2022) Liberalising the Chinese market: state-owned enterprise disciplines in CAI. J World Invest Trade 23:545–571

Svetlicinii A (2020) Chinese state-owned enterprises and EU merger control. Routledge, London

Svetlicinii A (2021) "Three Great Mountains" for the Chinese State-Owned Investments in the European Union. https://www.lexxion.eu/en/coreblogpost/three-great-mountains-for-the-chinese-state-owned-investments-in-the-european-union/. Accessed 5 Feb 2022

Thatcher M (2012) Western policies towards sovereign wealth fund equity investments: a comparison of the UK, the EU and the US. Policy Brief Number 1: 6. http://eprints.lse.ac.uk/55668/1/__lse.ac.uk_storage_LIBRARY_Secondary_libfile_shared_repository_Content_Kuwait%20Programme_Thatcher_1_2012.pdf. Accessed 3 Feb 2022

Toplišek A (2018) Liberal democracy in crisis: rethinking resistance under neoliberal govern mentality. Palgrave Macmillan, Cham, Switzerland

Van Aaken A (2008) Fragmentation of international law: the case of international investment protection. Finnish Yearb Int Law XVII:91–130

Wang J, Cheng-Han T (2020) Mixed ownership reform and corporate Governance in China's state-owned enterprises. Vanderbilt J Transnatl Law 53(3):1055–1107

Willemyns I (2016) Disciplines on state-owned enterprises in international economic law: are we moving in the right direction? J Int Econ Law 19(3):657–680

WTO (2001) Report of the Working Party on the Accession of China. https://docs.wto.org/dol2fe/Pages/SS/directdoc.aspx?filename=q:/WT/MIN01/3.pdf&Open=True. Accessed 5 Feb 2022
Wu Y (2019) Reforming WTO rules on state-owned enterprises: SOEs and financial advantages. Northwest J Int Law Bus 39(3):275–307
Yin W (2017) The role of state-owned investors and Chinese investments in Europe: the implication of the China-EU BIT. TDM. https://www.transnational-dispute-management.com/article.asp?key=2477. Accessed 4 Apr 2022
Yin W (2018) Challenges, issues in China-EU investment agreement and the implication on China's domestic reform. Asia Pac Law Rev 26(2):170–202
Yin W (2021) A comparison of the US and EU regulatory responses to China's state capitalism: implication, issue and direction. Asia Eur J 19:1–25
Zhang A, Yin W (2020) Chinese State-owned enterprises' investment in Africa: an unequivocal role? Afronomics Law. https://www.afronomicslaw.org/2021/01/07/chinese-state-owned-enterprises-investment-in-africa-an-unequivocal-role/. Accessed 5 Feb 2022
Zhang D, Yin J (2019) China's Belt and Road Initiative, from the inside looking out. The Interpreter. https://www.lowyinstitute.org/the-interpreter/china-s-belt-and-road-initiative-inside-looking-out. Accessed 15 Jan 2022
Zhang X et al (2020) Does mixed-ownership reform improve SOEs' innovation? Evidence from state ownership. China Econ Rev 61:1–22
Zhang ZY (2019) China's SOE reforms: what the latest round of reforms mean for the market. China Briefing. https://www.china-briefing.com/news/chinas-soe-reform-process/. Accessed 1 Feb 2022
Zhou Q, Zhang Z (2021) China's 2021 negative lists widen market access for foreign investment. China Briefing. https://www.china-briefing.com/news/2021-china-negative-lists-update-widen-market-access-for-foreign-investment/. Accessed 5 Feb 2022
Zhou W (2021) Rethinking the (CP)TPP as a model for regulation of Chinese state-owned enterprises. J Int Econ Law 24(3):572–590
Zhou W et al (2019) Building a market economy through WTO-inspired reform of state-owned enterprises in China. Int Comp Law Q 68(4):977–1022

Wei Yin (PhD, LLM, LLB) is an Associate Professor of School of International Law, Southwest University of Political Science and Law. She is also a Research Fellow of China-ASEAN Legal Research Centre. Her research interests include international economic law, international investment law, and international development law. She is currently working on research projects concerning the Belt and Road Initiative and sustainable development, international rules on state-owned enterprises.

The EU-China Comprehensive Agreement on Investment: Disciplining Competition Law Enforcement in China?

Alexandr Svetlicinii

Abstract From the EU perspective, the conclusion of the EU-China Comprehensive Agreement on Investment (CAI) was motivated, among other things, by a wish to ensure a level-playing field for European companies doing business in China. Among the commonly named market access obstacles for EU investors in China were preferential regulatory treatment enjoyed by Chinese state-owned enterprises (SOEs), including being shielded from competition law and occasional instances of discriminatory enforcement of competition rules against foreign companies. The negotiation of the CAI was an opportunity for the EU to address these concerns through legally binding commitments that would be subject to dispute resolution. This chapter analyses the competition-related provisions of the CAI through the lenses of international investment law and competition law. It reviews the current *status quo* of China's competition law enforcement in the light of the binding commitments included in the CAI. This forward-looking assessment attempts to forecast the likely effects of the CAI on the procedural and institutional framework of antitrust enforcement in China, including its treatment of domestic SOEs and foreign companies.

1 Introduction: Competition Rules on the Global Agenda

Multilateral attempts to address anti-competitive practices employed by companies in domestic and international trading alike were initially incorporated in the trade liberalization agenda of the World Trade Organization (WTO). The 1996 Singapore Ministerial Conference of the WTO established the Working Group on the Interaction between Trade and Competition Policy with the aim of identifying

A. Svetlicinii (✉)
University of Macau, Faculty of Law, Macao, SAR, China
e-mail: alexandrs@um.edu.mo

© The Author(s), under exclusive license to Springer Nature Switzerland AG 2024

A. Svetlicinii, I.-J. Chen (eds.), *The EU-China Comprehensive Agreement on Investment*, European Yearbook of International Economic Law,
https://doi.org/10.1007/978-3-031-66862-3_7

issues that could be addressed in the WTO framework.[1] The 2001 Doha Ministerial Conference re-affirmed the mandate of the Working Group and advised it to focus on the core principles, hardcore cartels, modalities for cross-border enforcement cooperation, and capacity-building of competition authorities in developing countries.[2] However, no consensus on competition policy agenda was achieved at the 2003 Cancun Ministerial Conference due to opposition from the US (unwilling to accept the lowest common standard and relying on the success of the ongoing convergence of competition laws and international cooperation) and developing countries (favoring stronger industrial policies and fearful of the consequences of their low levels of technical capacity and how this might prevent effective enforcement of competition laws).[3] As a result, in 2004 the WTO General Council concluded that competition issues "will not form part of the Work Programme set out in that Declaration and therefore no work towards negotiations on any of these issues will take place within the WTO during the Doha Round".[4] Unable to reach consensus at the multilateral level, the WTO members continued to pursue trade and competition agenda at the regional and bilateral levels by inserting competition provisions into the preferential trade agreements (PTAs) and pushing for convergence of the national competition laws through the Organisation for Economic Co-operation and Development (OECD),[5] the United Nations Conference on Trade and Development (UNCTAD),[6] the International Competition Network (ICN)[7] and other multilateral networks and fora.[8]

To provide a better understanding of this extra-WTO cooperation, Horn, Mavroidis, and Sapir proposed a categorization of the PTA provisions based on their relationship to existing WTO agreements.[9] They distinguish between the WTO-plus (WTO+) and WTO-extra (WTO-X) provisions. The WTO+ provisions address issues already covered in WTO agreements but go further, while WTO-X provisions cover a range of areas not addressed by WTO agreements. Following this categorization, competition provisions in the PTAs belong to the category of

[1] See Singapore Ministerial Declaration, WT/MIN(96)/DEC, 18 December 1996, para 20.

[2] See Doha Ministerial Declaration, WT/MIN(01)/DEC/1, 20 November 2001, paras 23–25.

[3] See Demedts (2015), pp. 414–415. See also Hufbauer and Kim (2008) International Competition Policy and the WTO (Peterson Institute for International Economics, https://www.piie.com/commentary/speeches-papers/international-competition-policy-and-wto; Bradford (2007), pp. 410–413.

[4] WTO (2004) WT/L/579, https://www.wto.org/english/tratop_e/dda_e/draft_text_gc_dg_31july04_e.htm.

[5] See OECD, Directorate for Financial and Enterprise Affairs, Competition, https://www.oecd.org/daf/competition/.

[6] See UNCTAD, Competition and Consumer Protection, https://unctad.org/Topic/Competition-and-Consumer-Protection.

[7] See ICN, International Cooperation, https://www.internationalcompetitionnetwork.org/working-groups/icn-operations/cooperation/.

[8] See Singh (2014), pp. 261–268.

[9] See Horn et al. (2010), p. 1567.

WTO-X provisions. A study of 596 PTAs signed between 1945 and 2010 concluded that roughly 51% included some antitrust-related provisions.[10] By 2012, about 80% of PTAs notified to the WTO contained competition provisions.[11] By 2015, the share of PTAs with competition-specific provisions had risen to 88%.[12] In 2017, competition policies were included in more than 200 PTAs and were enforceable in 185.[13] According to the OECD data, in 2019, 90% of all the trade agreements included competition-specific provisions or chapters.[14] The OECD has also proposed the following categorization of the competition provisions in PTAs: (1) adopting, maintaining and applying competition measures; (2) coordination and cooperation provisions (notifications, exchange of information, consultations, negative and positive comity); (3) provisions addressing anti-competitive behavior (anti-competitive agreements, abuse of dominance, state aid, merger control, SOEs and monopolies); (4) competition-specific provisions concerning non-discrimination, due process, transparency; (5) exclusion of antidumping; (6) recourse to trade measures; and (7) dispute settlement (exclusion of competition matters from dispute settlement, consultations, arbitration).[15]

To clarify the inclusion of certain competition-related provisions in the PTAs, Bradford and Büthe advanced two hypotheses: (1) the parties attempt to restrain each other's protectionist actions through enforcing national competition laws; (2) the parties attempt to solidify their cooperation in terms of competition law enforcement to address anti-competitive actions by companies that affect cross-border trade. Referring to the first hypothesis, the authors suggested that "[t]o the extent that trade agreements contain competition provisions, they should reflect concern about selective enforcement and contain measures to prevent or discipline such enforcement against firms from the other Parties".[16] Their study seems to disprove the first hypothesis since the obligation to notify another party before taking enforcement measures against its persons/entities is contained in 22% of PTAs, while negative comity provisions can be found in only 5%.[17] The second hypothesis also lacks definitive confirmation as the authors observe that only 8% of PTAs containing competition provisions included commitments to competition policy cooperation.[18] Negative comity obligations would require a party undertaking enforcement action under competition law to consider important interests of another party (often combined with an obligation to notify such enforcement actions and conduct

[10] See Bradford and Chilton (2021), p. 112.

[11] Demedts (2015), p. 416.

[12] Laprévote et al. (2015), p. 2.

[13] See Hoffman et al. (2017), p. 11.

[14] OECD (2021a), p. 2.

[15] See Solano and Sennekamp (2005), pp. 7–9. See also Evenett (2005), p. 39.

[16] Bradford and Büthe (2015), p. 262.

[17] See Bradford and Büthe (2015), p. 267.

[18] See Bradford and Büthe (2015), p. 269.

consultations with another party when requested).[19] These provisions where identified by Bradford and Chilton in 4% of PTAs signed between 1945 and 2010.[20] Positive comity, which allows a party to a PTA to request another party undertake certain competition law enforcement actions,[21] was observed in 25% of the respective PTAs.[22]

PTAs frequently require their signatories to maintain a competition law system to which importers or foreign investors could resort for protection of their businesses from anti-competitive practices in the domestic markets of the host states. To that end, the competition chapters contain "substantive provisions such as the requirement to maintain competition laws and a(n efficient) competition authority, rules on state monopolies, state enterprises and enterprises entrusted with special rights, have complemented cooperation provisions".[23] For example, the recently concluded Comprehensive and Progressive Agreement for Trans-Pacific Partnership (CPTPP) features a competition chapter requiring the parties to maintain effective competition laws, to adhere to the principles of procedural fairness, cooperation and transparency in their enforcement, and to allow for private right of action and access to independent court or tribunal in matters related to competition law enforcement.[24] In relation to the EU's earlier PTAs, legal scholars noted "their focus on mutual recognition and cooperation, rather than substantive issues, and that mergers are consistently excluded".[25] Similarly, an empirical study of the competition chapters in the PTAs of the Latin American countries concluded that "unlike other areas of law covered by international trade agreements, antitrust chapters are non binding, specifically in relation to the traditional core of antitrust activities such as mergers, monopolization/dominance, and cartels."[26] An OECD study from 2019 suggested that competition chapters were subject to dispute settlement procedures only in 34% of the studied PTAs.[27] In 2021, Bradford and Chilton found that 71% of PTAs containing antitrust provisions extend dispute settlement mechanism to these provisions.[28]

The EU's approach to competition chapters in PTAs was characterized by the lack of an articulated strategy, absence of clear choice and lack of determination.[29]

[19] See examples of negative comity provisions in OECD (2021b).

[20] See Bradford and Chilton (2021), p.117.

[21] See e.g. Decision of the Council and of the Commission of 29 May 1998 concerning the conclusion of the Agreement between the European Communities and the Government of the United States of America on the application of positive comity principles in the enforcement of their competition laws, OJ L 173, 18 June 1998.

[22] See Bradford and Chilton (2021), p. 117.

[23] Demedts (2015), p. 425.

[24] See Abrenica and Bernabe (2017), pp. 175–178.

[25] Demedts (2015), p. 421.

[26] Sokol (2008), p. 282.

[27] See Anderson et al. (2019), p. 29.

[28] See Bradford and Chilton (2021), p. 119.

[29] See Demedts (2015), p. 435.

The European Commission has admitted that the "EU approach on competition provisions in trade agreements is not a 'one-size fits all approach'".[30] For example, the Commission explained the EU's approach to the dispute settlement and competition chapters as follows: "the EU generally excludes the provisions on anticompetitive conduct and merger control from dispute settlement, since the EU does not consider dispute settlement to be an appropriate mechanism to deal with competition cases".[31] As a result, the competition chapters in EU PTAs range from close approximation with the EU competition law *acquis* (pre-accession agreements, European Neighborhood Policy countries, certain Euro-Mediterranean partners, etc.) to a lack of specific provisions within PTAs with countries with limited trade flows, to the second generation PTAs where the EU experimented with WTO+ and WTO-X obligations in relation to its trading partners such as Korea, Singapore, and Vietnam.[32]

China has not been an active promoter of global competition policy. Its participation in the work of the WTO Working Group on the Interaction between Trade and Competition Policy was limited as it joined the WTO in 2001 and did not have its own competition legislation until 2008.[33] China's competition authorities also did not participate in the ICN.[34] Although it engaged in far-reaching reforms to transform its own economy from centrally managed by the government to a more market-oriented, China remained suspicious of outside attempts to discipline its competition policy and direct it at the anti-competitive practices of state-owned enterprises (SOEs). In its 2019 proposal for WTO reform, China regarded SOEs as "equal players in the market as other types of enterprises" and opposed "differentiated rules on the basis of ownership of enterprises" adopted by some WTO members.[35] As a result, China consistently proposed dropping SOE-specific provisions from the subsidy disciplines and ensuring non-discrimination in the conduct of foreign investment security reviews.[36] While calling upon the WTO membership to uphold the principle of fair competition for all enterprises, China's proposal stopped short of calling for a resumption of WTO's competition policy agenda. This approach echoes an earlier position paper, where China suggested that the WTO reform should "pro-

[30] OECD (2019) Competition Provisions in Trade Agreements – Contribution from the European Union, DAF/COMP/GF/WD(2019)7, https://one.oecd.org/document/DAF/COMP/GF/WD(2019)7/en/pdf, p. 2.

[31] DAF/COMP/GF/WD(2019)7, p. 3.

[32] See Borlini and Dordi (2017), pp. 577–578.

[33] Hong Kong SAR, as a distinct WTO member using the designation "Hong Kong, China" participated in the work of the WTO Working Group on the Interaction between Trade and Competition Policy during 1997–2003. Hong Kong SAR did not have competition law until the adoption of the Competition Ordinance in 2012.

[34] See ICN, Members, https://www.internationalcompetitionnetwork.org/members/?location=asia. Among the current ICN members are the Hong Kong Competition Commission and the Taiwan Fair Trade Commission.

[35] China's Proposal on WTO Reform (2019) WT/GC/W/773, para 2.35.

[36] WT/GC/W/773, para 2.37.

Preferential Trade Agreement	Year (of conclusion)	Obligation to maintain competition law and authorities	Principles of enforcement (non-discrimination, fairness, due process rights)	Transparency specific to competition enforcement (publication of laws, regulations, decisions)	Exchange of information on competition law enforcement	Institutional cooperation (voluntary)	Dispute settlement
Regional Comprehensive Economic Partnership	2020	☑ (13.3)	☑ (13.3)	☑ (13.3)	☑ (13.4, 13.6)	☑ (13.4, 13.6)	☒ (13.9)
Cambodia	2020	☒	☒	☒	☒	☒	☒
Mauritius	2019	☑ (9.2)	☑ (9.3)	☑ (9.4)	☑ (9.5)	☑ (9.5)	☒ (9.8)
Georgia	2017	☑ (10.3)	☑ (10.4)	☑ (10.5)	☑ (10.7)	☑ (10.6)	☒ (10.10)
Australia	2015	☒	☒	☒	☑ (16.7)	☑ (16.7)	☑
Korea	2015	☑ (14.2)	☑ (14.3)	☑ (14.4)	☑ (14.9)	☑ (14.6)	☒ (14.12)
Switzerland	2013	☑ (10.10)	☒	☒	☒	☑ (10.10)	☒ (10.10)
Iceland	2013	☑ (5.62)	☒	☒	☑ (5.62)	☑ (5.62)	☒ (5.62)
Costa Rica	2010	☒	☒	☒	☑ (11.126)	☑ (11.126,)	☒ (11.118)
Peru	2009	☑ (12.159)	☒	☒	☑ (12.159)	☑ (12.159)	☒ (12.166)
Singapore	2008	☑ (16.3)	☑ (16.4)	☑ (16.5)	☑ (16.6)	☑ (16.6)	☒ (16.10)
New Zealand	2008	☑ (21.3)	☑ (21.4)	☑ (21.5)	☑ (21.6)	☑ (21.6)	☒ (21.11)
Chile	2005	☑ (5.61)	☑ (5.62)	☑ (5.63)	☑ (5.64)	☑ (5.64)	☒ (5.68)
Pakistan	2006	☒	☒	☒	☒	☒	☒
Association of Southeast Asian Nations	2002	☒	☒	☒	☒	☒	☒
Hong Kong SAR (Closer Economic Partnership Arrangement)	2003	☒	☒	☒	☒	☒	☒
Macao SAR (Closer Economic Partnership Arrangement)	2005	☒	☒	☒	☒	☒	☒

Fig. 1 Competition chapters in China's preferential trade agreements

hibit discrimination against enterprises of certain members in investment security review and anti-trust investigations".[37] In relation to China's opposition to the SOE-specific disciplines, it was noted that "China is reluctant to accept specific SOE disciplines before it has carried out adequate domestic reforms and formed corresponding institutions, which could effectively respond to the adverse effects of SOE disciplines".[38]

With the progress of SOE reform and against a background of the above-mentioned PTA trends, China has gradually become more open to the incorporation of competition chapters in its trade agreements as shown in the Fig. 1. For example, the China-Korea FTA, labelled "one of China's deepest FTAs"[39] contains a detailed competition chapter. It includes a general obligation to maintain competition laws

[37] China's Position Paper on WTO Reform (2018) 20 December 2018, http://kw2.mofcom.gov.cn/article/chinanews/201812/20181202818679.shtml.

[38] Ying (2020), pp. 109–146.

[39] Wang (2017), p. 304.

and competition enforcement authorities as well as to abide by the principles of transparency (publication of laws, regulations, decisions), non-discrimination, and procedural fairness (rights of defense and appeal) in competition law enforcement.[40] More specifically, in relation to SOEs (public enterprises) the parties agreed that the former should be subject to competition law "in so far as the application of these principles and competition laws does not obstruct the performance, in law or in fact, of the particular tasks assigned to them".[41] While competition-related obligations are not subject to dispute settlement,[42] the PTA provides a consultation mechanism requiring "full and sympathetic consideration to the concerns raised by the other Party".[43]

2 The EU-China Comprehensive Agreement on Investment: Competition-Related Concerns and Proposed Solutions

Public consultation on the future of EU-China investment relationship conducted in 2011 did not present competition law enforcement in China as a major concern for European investors.[44] Nevertheless, it was noted that the "merger review procedures are equally an area of concern for EU investors in China, with only 12% of respondents considering that those procedures are followed in a fair, reasonable, predictable and non-discriminatory way".[45] The stakeholders' concerns related "mostly to the lack of transparency and predictability that surrounds the mergers review procedures, which, in addition to being long, also entail undue delays".[46] These delays were the result of the apparent lack of clarity as to what documents and information constitute a complete notification of economic concentration, which triggers the commencement of the review period.[47] For example, in several mergers involving foreign companies, the Ministry of Commerce (MOFCOM) strategically used pre-notification periods to await clearance decisions in other jurisdictions and then used these as a baseline for its own decisions, requesting more substantial conditions to

[40] Free Trade Agreement between the Government of the People's Republic of China and the Government of the Republic of Korea, 1 June 2015, http://fta.mofcom.gov.cn/korea/annex/xdzw_en.pdf, Art. 14.3.

[41] PRC-ROK FTA, Art. 14.5.

[42] PRC-ROK FTA, Art. 14.12.

[43] PRC-ROK FTA, Art. 14.8.

[44] European Commission, Public consultation on the future investment relationship between the EU and China, http://trade.ec.europa.eu/consultations/?consul_id=153.

[45] European Commission (2013) Staff Working Document "Impact Assessment Report on the EU-China Investment Relations" SWD (2013) 185 final, https://ec.europa.eu/smart-regulation/impact/ia_carried_out/docs/ia_2013/swd_2013_0185_en.pdf, p. 90.

[46] Impact Assessment Report on the EU-China Investment Relations, p. 100.

[47] See Goldstein (2011), p. 233.

be met by the merging parties.[48] Consideration of various non-competition interests in merger control appraisals under the Anti-Monopoly Law (AML) allowed the MOFCOM to block or impose conditions on transnational mergers that were cleared in other merger control jurisdictions, such as the EU and US.[49]

At the same time, one of the major concerns of European investors was the fact that China has agreed to open some of its markets only after they were fully saturated by domestic companies, especially SOEs benefitting from various forms of state support due to their role in industrial policy. This state of affairs was vividly characterized by the European Union Chamber of Commerce in China (EUCCC): "the fact that the reform took place so late in the game made it more akin to letting foreign investors onto a railway platform only after the train had long since departed".[50] The EUCCC claimed that China is decisively moving towards a "one economy, two systems" model, where only certain sectors are open to foreign investors, while others are reserved for SOEs and protected from outside competition.[51] So, until "true competitive neutrality comes into practice, China's SOE-dominated sectors will remain yet another major barrier to meaningful market opening and sustainable development".[52] Due to their monopolistic or protected market positions and soft budget constraints, Chinese SOEs have been reportedly engaging in predatory pricing, raising rivals' costs, excessive pricing, tying, price discrimination, refusing to inter-connect and cross-subsidization.[53]

SOEs are featured in the CAI as "covered entities", organized into the four categories: (1) enterprises where the state owns more than a 50% share of capital, exercises more than 50% of voting rights, appoints the majority of members of the board of directors or management, or controls the decision of the enterprise through any other ownership interest, including minority shareholding; (2) enterprises where the state has the power to legally direct actions or exercise an equivalent level of control; (3) any public or private entity authorised by the state as the sole supplier or purchaser of goods or services; and (4) a small number of enterprises, public or private, designated by the state as the only suppliers or purchasers of a particular good or service in a relevant market.[54] The above definitions essentially covered the SOEs and state-granted monopolies regardless of ownership. In relation to potential anti-competitive practices of SOEs, the CAI attempts to discipline them not through AML enforcement but through direct obligations of the state as owner/controlling shareholder of "covered entities" to ensure they act in accordance with commercial

[48] See US Chamber of Commerce (2014), p. 52.

[49] See Hamp-Lyons (2009), pp. 1599–1602.

[50] European Union Chamber of Commerce in China, European Business in China Position Paper 2020/2021, p. 5.

[51] European Business in China Position Paper 2020/2021, p. 22.

[52] European Business in China Position Paper 2020/2021, p. 25.

[53] See Cheng (2014), p. 178.

[54] CAI, Art. 3bis(1).

considerations.[55] As a result, the competition-related provisions of the CAI when addressing non-discrimination against foreign investors frequently refer to "covered entities" and their relationship with regulatory authorities. The potentially discriminatory application of the AML by Chinese enforcement authorities was addressed in the CAI by the requirements of impartiality, non-discrimination and independence of the regulatory authorities.[56] The CAI requires *inter alia* that regulatory authorities act "impartially in like circumstances with respect to all enterprises that it regulates, including the covered entities".[57] The parties have also committed to apply their laws and regulations "in a consistent and non-discriminatory manner, including on the covered entities".[58]

The CAI attempts to discipline the application of the AML through general obligations of transparency in administrative proceedings by requiring that "laws, regulations, administrative guidelines, procedures, judicial decisions and administrative rulings of general application" should be publicly available.[59] The above requirement covers administrative regulations and by-laws issued by the competition enforcement authorities but does not extend to individual enforcement decisions or judicial decisions in specific cases.[60] When it comes to the conduct of competition enforcement proceedings, the CAI aims at ensuring non-discrimination between "covered entities" and foreign investors. The relevant provisions require *inter alia* that: (1) prohibitions, penalties and other remedies must be based on a formally adopted decision, a non-confidential version of which must be published; (2) prior to the adoption of the decision, the person concerned must be informed of the evidence on which the decision will be based; (3) the person concerned shall have the right to submit written comments to the competition authority; (4) the person concerned shall have a right to legal representative of its choice; and (5) the addressees of competition law decisions shall have a right to appeal the final decision before a court of law.[61] In relation to judicial review of competition law decisions, the CAI requires such courts or quasi-judicial tribunals to be impartial and independent and allow the review of substantive or procedural errors that have occurred through imposition of sanctions or remedies for violations of competition law.[62]

When placed in the context of the typical competition chapters as categorized by the OECD and discussed above, the CAI contains a very limited set of competition-related obligations, which are essentially reduced to the protection of foreign investors as potential targets of competition law enforcement in the host state. For instance, it does not require the parties to maintain any specific competition

[55] See Dadush and Sapir (2021), pp. 7–8.

[56] CAI, Sect. II, Art. 3ter.

[57] CAI, Sect. II, Art. 3ter(1).

[58] CAI, Sect. II, Art. 3ter(2).

[59] CAI, Sect. II, Art. 2(1).

[60] CAI, Sect. III, Art. 2(2).

[61] CAI, Sect. III, Art. 5.

[62] CAI, Sect. III, Art. 6.

legislation, as long as such legislation is published according to the applicable transparency obligations. The CAI also does not provide for any cooperation concerning competition law enforcement such as negative or positive comity provisions, which are frequently inserted in the PTA competition chapters. At the same time, the limited competition-related provisions of the CAI are not exempt from the dispute settlement mechanism. For better understanding of the CAI's potential impact on the AML enforcement in China, the next section will discuss the *status quo* of China's legislation and enforcement record in this domain.

3 Competition Law Enforcement in China

Although the enforcement of the AML does not play a primary role in China's legal toolbox of market regulation, the authorities continuously reiterate their intention to ensure "fair competition" and constrain monopolistic behavior. In 2021, China's Premier Li Keqiang pledged that authorities "will promote fair competition between domestic and foreign companies and protect the lawful rights and interests of foreign-invested enterprises".[63] This excerpt from the National Development and Reform Commission's (NDRC) 2021 plan of actions is also telling:

> [w]e will improve the competition policy framework and the fair competition review mechanism, strengthen law enforcement in relation to monopolies and unfair competition, guard against disordered capital expansion, and strive to create a fair and impartial environment in which all market entities are treated as equals and engage in fair competition.[64]

While declaring an impartial attitude to all market entities, the above statement indicates that undistorted market competition has never been the sole objective of market regulators. Multiple objectives are embedded in the text of the AML, which was adopted for the purpose of "preventing and restraining monopolistic conducts, protecting fair market competition, enhancing economic efficiency, safeguarding the interests of consumers and the interests of the society as a whole, and promoting the healthy development of [a] socialist market economy".[65] The legislative history of the AML indicates that, from the very outset of the drafting process, legislators attempted to reconcile multiple interests: to promote market competition, to curb abuses of market power, to protect national economic interests, to narrow income disparity, etc.[66] Chinese scholars issued early warnings about the controversial

[63] Li (2021), p. 27.

[64] National Development and Reform Commission (2021), 'Report on the implementation of the 2020 Plan for national economic and social development and on the 2021 Draft Plan for national economic and social development', delivered at the Fourth Session of the 13th National People's Congress of the People's Republic of China, p. 40.

[65] AML, Art. 1.

[66] See Huang (2008), pp. 121–124.

nature of the public interest concept embedded in the AML.[67] Case studies on AML enforcement generally conclude that the public interest concept, which in practice is equalized with the state's industrial policies, supersedes the objectives of competition law enforcement such as prohibition of anti-competitive practices, promotion of market efficiency and protection of consumer interests.[68] Analysis of the IP-related cases concerning patent licensing and FRAND terms pursued by the Chinese competition authorities and courts prompted the conclusions that "it appears that China increasingly will use its AML to help its indigenous companies gain favorable access to IPR held by foreign companies".[69] The suppression of patent licensing fees paid by domestic companies using the AML prohibition on abuse of dominance have been labelled as enforcement abuses, along with administrative intimidation and restrictions on the legal counsel that could be used by foreign parties.[70] These examples demonstrate that multiple objectives embedded in the AML enforcement can create a *de facto* discrimination against foreign investors due to the peculiar roles accorded to them in the industrial policies shaping the development trajectories of particular markets in China. As noted by Fox, "[t]o the Western world, the most obvious special characteristic of the Chinese competition system is its mixture of antitrust with ad-hoc, non-transparent strategic industrial policy".[71]

Another major issue addressed by the CAI competition-related provisions is AML enforcement in relation to the Chinese SOEs. Despite ongoing reform, which aims to "transform the management mechanism of state-owned enterprises, and to establish a modern enterprise system which meets the requirements of the market economy",[72] the SOEs are expected to remain the backbone of the "socialist market economy" where they should be "closely centering around the missions of serving national strategies, and enforcing State industrial policies and the general requirements of adjusting the layout of key industries".[73] The AML's multiple goals and the special importance of the SOEs in China's economic development are reflected in the AML's enforcement. Initial doubts as to the formal exemption of SOEs from the enforcement of competition rules with reference to Article 7 AML have been largely settled with emerging enforcement actions against SOEs. At the same time, one observes that "[ne]arly all these investigations and decisions have involved SOEs owned and controlled by local governments".[74] Earlier attempts of the NDRC to subject the SOEs to antitrust enforcement have been thwarted, often through the

[67] See Wang (2008), p. 142.

[68] See Cahill and Wang (2021), p. 652.

[69] Horton (2016), p. 137. See also Svetlicinii (2017), pp. 163–206.

[70] See Epstein (2014), p. 7.

[71] Fox (2020), p. 1432.

[72] Decision of the CPC Central Committee on Some Issues Concerning the Establishment of a Socialist Market Economic Structure, 22 November 1993, para 2.

[73] Guiding Opinions of the CPC Central Committee and the State Council on Deepening the Reform of State-Owned Enterprises, 24 August 2015, para 14. See also Svetlicinii (2021), pp. 29–51.

[74] Ng (2017), p. 278.

intervention of other government departments or sectoral regulators. For example, the *China Telecom/China Unicom* case is routinely cited as an occasion on which the NDRC has prepared to fine the two SOEs for abuse of dominance, but due to strong opposition from other government entities, particularly the Ministry of Industry and Information Technology, the case was closed.[75] In another case, the *TravelSky* cartel formed by state-owned airlines saw the intervention of the Civil Aviation Authority of China, which defended the pricing practices of the airlines under its supervision.

While the large SOEs are notably absent from antitrust enforcement records, the secondary competition legislation is drafted in a way that suggests non-discriminatory treatment of all undertakings under the AML. For example, the Provisions prohibiting abuse of dominant positions require the competition authority to "treat all operators equally when investigating into and handling abuse of dominant market positions".[76] A similar obligation is included in the Provisions on anti-competitive agreements.[77] While the above provisions formally uphold the principle of equality before the law of all undertakings concerned, when it comes to the substantive appraisal of unilateral practices, the State Administration for Market Regulation (SAMR) considers a wide range of factors that could *de facto* place the SOEs in a privileged position due to their special importance to the national economy. For example, when assessing the "unfairness" of prices and justifications of the dominant companies under investigation, the SAMR considers factors such as the impact of the relevant acts on social and public interests, economic operational efficiency, and economic development.[78]

In terms of procedural requirements, the SAMR regulations governing investigations and penalties for competition law infringements are already in line with the provisions of the CAI. For example, when investigating alleged abuses of dominant positions, the SAMR is required to adopt written decisions substantiating administrative penalties or acceptance of commitments and suspension of the investigation.[79] The SAMR regulations also specify the mandatory contents of the infringement decisions including facts and evidence, objections, justification of penalties and/or remedies imposed, and ways to appeal the decision.[80] The results of

[75] See Ng (2017), pp. 254–256.

[76] SAMR, Order No 11 of 26 June 2019, Interim Provisions on Prohibiting Abuse of Dominant Market Positions, Art. 4.

[77] SAMR, Order No. 10 of 26 June 2019, Interim Provisions on Prohibiting Monopoly Agreements, Art. 4.

[78] SAMR, Order No 11 of 26 June 2019, Interim Provisions on Prohibiting Abuse of Dominant Market Positions, Art. 20.

[79] SAMR, Order No 11 of 26 June 2019, Interim Provisions on Prohibiting Abuse of Dominant Market Positions, Arts. 28-31.

[80] SAMR, Order No. 10 of 26 June 2019, Interim Provisions on Prohibiting Monopoly Agreements, Art. 20.

SAMR investigations also have to be publicly announced with the registration of penalties in the National Enterprise Credit Information Publication System.[81]

When it comes to merger control regulations, they provide for a fixed 30-day review period, which can be extended by 90 days if a case merits further investigation. At the same time, the SAMR has preserved the possibility to reject an application as incomplete unless the parties provide all "other documents and materials required by the Anti-monopoly Bureau of the SAMR".[82] This allows the SAMR to consult relevant government departments to decide which competition-related and other concerns would be addressed in the eventual decision concerning the notified concentration. Such practice was commonly applied by the MOFCOM "to build consensus to support a merger outcome. Sometimes the MOFCOM's merger enforcement powers are partially shared with the consulted government departments".[83] In addition to merger control under the AML, the acquisition of domestic companies by foreign investors may be subjected to national security screening, which does not apply to domestic mergers and acquisitions.[84]

The relevant AML provisions stipulate that Chinese competition authorities consider multiple factors when carrying out merger assessment of the notified concentrations: market shares of the merging parties, level of market concentration, effect of the merger on market entry and technological progress, effect of the merger on the development of national economy, as well as "other factors".[85] These legal provisions were labelled "a blend of competition and non-competition mandates, which sow the seeds of tension for future regulations and enforcement".[86] As a result, although the merger control rules do not contain any formally discriminatory provisions, their *de facto* application presents more substantial hurdles for foreign investors as opposed to the "covered entities", because the latter play a more important role in China's "socialist market economy" and their mergers are largely conditioned by the implementation of the state industrial policies.[87]

When assessing the application of merger control rules to the SOEs in China, one observes an inconsistency between the number of SOE-related mergers and acquisitions reported by the business intelligence sources and those notified to the MOFCOM for clearance. For example, Cheng pointed out that allegations of the selective enforcement of the AML by the Chinese authorities were partly based on examples of SOE-to-SOE mergers that were not notified to the MOFCOM despite meeting notification thresholds.[88] As noted by Ng, "the MOFCOM's merger

[81] SAMR, Order No 11 of 26 June 2019, Interim Provisions on Prohibiting Abuse of Dominant Market Positions, Arts. 35.

[82] SAMR, Guidelines for the Anti-Monopoly Review for Concentration of Business Operators, 29 September 2018.

[83] Ng (2017), p. 250.

[84] AML, Art. 31.

[85] AML, Art. 27.

[86] Gu and Foster (2015), p. i34.

[87] See Svetlicinii (2022b), pp. 17–28.

[88] Cheng (2015), p. 8.

enforcement statistics do not appear to reflect the actual level of SOE-related merger activity"[89] and "investigation into an SOE for failing to notify a merger might be perceived as an unwelcome intrusion on regulatory turf by industry regulators".[90] Reluctance to notify their concentrations does not apply only to SOEs. For instance, during 2008–2013, out of 750 merger notifications, only 57 or 8% were transactions involving only domestic companies.[91] In that regard, Su and Wang suggested that "it is rumoured that Chinese lawyers advising on merger transactions normally advise that purely domestic transactions do not need to be notified".[92]

The above review of the AML provisions and their application in the antitrust and merger control practices of the competition authorities in China identified the following major challenges to implementing the competition-related provisions of the CAI. First, the multiple objectives embedded in China's competition legislation have an inevitable impact on how it is enforced by the competition authorities. The role of industrial policies and SOEs as pillars of China's economic statecraft will channel AML enforcement in a way that may appear *de facto* discriminatory against foreign investors for the reason that they play a distinct role in the China's state-guided economy (compared to SOEs and domestic companies). Second, due to the availability of additional political and ownership-based channels of exercising control over market conduct of the SOEs and other domestic enterprises, it is inevitable that the AML will be enforced more assertively in relation to foreign enterprises where such supplementary channels of control are absent. Third, the procedural rules for AML enforcement are already largely aligned with the due process requirements included in the CAI. As a result, it is unlikely that the CAI provisions will motivate the Chinese authorities to reform the current institutional and/or procedural framework for the AML enforcement, which (without formally discriminating among different enterprises), provides competition authorities with sufficient discretion to pursue various policy objectives in their enforcement activities. Nevertheless, the competition-related provisions of the CAI will supplement existing channels for cooperation between the EU and China in the field of competition law and policy. The following section provides a brief overview of such cooperation.

4 Looking Beyond the CAI: Institutional Cooperation of the Antitrust Authorities

As noted by Frédéric Jenny, the Chairman of the WTO Working Group on the Interaction between Trade and Competition Policy, international cooperation among competition authorities remains "largely an informal process initiated on a selective

[89] Ng (2017), p. 283.

[90] Ng (2017), p. 285.

[91] See Sobel (2014), p. 4. See also Svetlicinii (2022a), pp. 37–72.

[92] Su and Wang (2013), p. 222.

basis by a small group of competition authorities for their own benefit or for the benefit of firms in their jurisdiction".[93] This description is equally applicable to the state of affairs in the institutional cooperation between the European Commission and China's competition authorities.

The EU-China Competition Policy Dialogue was established in 2004, prior to China's adoption of the AML, between the MOFCOM, then headed by Bo Xilai, and the Directorate General (DG) Competition of the European Commission, then headed by Mario Monti.[94] The terms of reference provided for "exchange of views", "exchange of experiences" and capacity-building activities. The dialogue was shaped by the early stage of competition law development in China and included the following basic questions: How to regulate company mergers? How to set up a competition authority? How to liberalise public utility sectors and limit state intervention in market processes? How to raise companies' and public's awareness of competition law and policy?

In 2012, following the entry into force of the AML, the DG Competition and China's antitrust enforcers, the NDRC and the State Administration for Industry and Commerce (SAIC), have signed a memorandum of understanding on the matters of competition law containing similar provisions concerning regular exchanges and capacity-building.[95] Although the memorandum acknowledges that "competition legislation is an important factor in ensuring consumer welfare and in providing a level playing field as well as legal certainty for the business community in the market",[96] it does not provide for any commitments to enforce competition legislation in a particular manner or to coordinate enforcement activities with the other party.

In 2017, the Competition Commissioner Vestager and the NDRC Chairman He Lifeng signed another memorandum, with specific focus on state aid and the Fair Competition Review System (FCRS) in China.[97] Generally, the EU state aid control and China's FCRS have a common objective "to prevent public policies from distorting and restricting competition while maintaining fair market competition and

---

[93] Jenny (2003), p. 1002.

[94] Terms of Reference of the EU-China Competition Policy Dialogue, 6 May 2004, https://ec.europa.eu/competition/international/bilateral/china_tor_en.pdf.

[95] Memorandum of Understanding on Cooperation in the area of anti-monopoly law between the European Commission (Directorate-General for Competition) and the National Development and Reform Commission (NDRC) and the State Administration of Industry and Commerce (SAIC) of the People's Republic of China, 20 September 2012, https://ec.europa.eu/competition/international/bilateral/mou_china_en.pdf.

[96] Memorandum of Understanding on Cooperation in the area of anti-monopoly law, para 1.1.

[97] Memorandum of Understanding on a dialogue in the area of the State aid control regime and the Fair Competition Review System between the Directorate-General for Competition of the European Commission and the National Development and Reform Commission of the People's Republic of China, 2 June 2017, https://ec.europa.eu/competition/international/bilateral/mou_china_2017.pdf.

promoting a unified market".[98] At the same time, while the EU state aid regime applies to the advantages given by the State to the selected undertakings, the FCRS is much broader and encompasses all kinds of legislation and policies that may restrict market competition.[99] After its commencement in 2016, the implementation of the FCRS in China has encountered a number of problems including lack of effective judicial review of the FCRS decisions taken by the local authorities.[100] Due to the substantial differences between the two systems, the parties have limited their cooperation to the exchange of views and experiences related to implementation of FCRS and state aid control, operation of the relevant authorities, advocacy activities, and technical cooperation.[101] This dialogue was carried out through the contact points established within the NDRC Bureau of Price Supervision and Anti-Monopoly and the DG Competition's Directorate for Policy and Strategy.[102]

Following the consolidation of the AML enforcement powers in the SAMR, the parties renewed their terms of reference in 2019, which now pledged "to enhance an effective, transparent and non-discriminatory enforcement of the competition rules in both jurisdictions" and "providing a level playing field as well as in furthering legal certainty for the business community in the market".[103] The new terms envisaged "formulation of practical guidance documents to facilitate cooperation with respect to the concrete enforcement of their respective competition laws".[104] The parties agreed that if one party believes that anti-competitive activities are taking place on the territory of the other party and negatively affect competition in its territory, it can request the other party to initiate appropriate enforcement activities in accordance with applicable laws.[105] Although such a request would not limit the discretion of the requested party, the requesting party should be duly informed about the outcome of the requested party's consideration on the matter.[106]

According to SAMR's director general Wu Zhenguo, the "Chinese antitrust enforcers attach great importance to international exchanges and cooperation on competition policies and anti-monopoly work and have built all-aspect, multi-level,

---

[98] Memorandum of Understanding on a dialogue in the area of the State aid control regime and the Fair Competition Review System, preamble.

[99] See Lyu et al. (2019), p. 43.

[100] See Lyu et al. (2020), pp. 605–609; Lyu et al. (2022), pp. 123–156.

[101] See Memorandum of Understanding on a dialogue in the area of the State aid control regime and the Fair Competition Review System, para 3.1.

[102] See Memorandum of Understanding on a dialogue in the area of the State aid control regime and the Fair Competition Review System, para 2.2.

[103] Terms of Reference of the EU-China Competition Policy Dialogue between the Directorate-General for Competition of the European Commission and the State Administration for Market Regulation of the People's Republic of China, 9 April 2019, https://ec.europa.eu/competition/international/bilateral/agreement_tor_china_2019.pdf.

[104] 2019 ToR, para 3.1(f).

[105] 2019 ToR, para 4.1.

[106] 2019 ToR, para 4.2.

and extensive anti-monopoly cooperation with their counterparts globally".[107] In 2019, DG Competition, represented by the Deputy Director General Carles Esteva Mosso, and the SAMR, represented by the Vice Minister Gan Lin, adopted joint practical guidance on investigating anti-monopoly cases. It focuses exclusively on cases investigated by both sides and provides for a limited exchange of information subject to confidentiality waivers and the possibility of coordinating the outcomes of such investigations without limiting the discretion of the respective competition authorities.[108] In such cases, the parties have agreed to communicate on issues of procedure and substance such as timing of the review, definition of the relevant market, theory of harm, remedies, etc.[109] A similar piece of guidance concerning merger cases was limited to economic concentrations assessed by both parties.[110]

The institutional cooperation arrangements between the EU and China in the field of competition law enforcement contain no positive comity obligations, no criteria for accommodating positive comity requests, so that any coordinated enforcement activity relies on the discretion of each party.[111] For example, in relation to the investigation the global LCD cartel in 2010–2013, which involved competition authorities from the EU, US, and China, it was noted that the information sharing between the respective authorities was limited due to the "lack of trust between the US and the EU on the one hand and China, on the other".[112]

This brief overview of the EU-China Competition Policy Dialogue demonstrates that it offers no immediate relief to the European investors in China affected by the AML enforcement (or lack thereof). Despite the assumption that Chinese competition authorities "are changing quickly and appear to be genuinely intent on cooperating with other nation's enforcement agencies, both on a bilateral and multilateral basis",[113] the current institutional arrangements continue to rely on the goodwill of the parties, which is subject to change depending on the prevailing geo-political environment.

---

[107] Interview with Wu Zhenguo, Director General, Anti-Monopoly Bureau of the State Administration for Market Regulation (SAMR), People's Republic of China, The Antitrust Source, June 2021, 1–22, https://www.samr.gov.cn/xw/zj/202107/P020210707589294998827.pdf, p. 18.

[108] Practical Guidance for Cooperation on Investigating Anti-Monopoly Cases between the Directorate-General for Competition of European Commission and the State Administration for Market Regulation of People's Republic of China, 7 May 2019, https://ec.europa.eu/competition/international/bilateral/practical_guidance_antimonopoly.pdf.

[109] See Practical Guidance for Cooperation on Investigating Anti-Monopoly Cases, para 5.

[110] Practical Guidance for Cooperation on Reviewing Merger Cases between the Directorate-General for Competition of European Commission and the State Administration for Market Regulation of People's Republic of China, 7 May 2019, https://ec.europa.eu/competition/international/bilateral/practical_guidance_merger.pdf.

[111] See Wu and Wang (2022), p. 60.

[112] Wu and Wang (2022), p. 69.

[113] Federal Trade Commission (2013), p. 10.

5 Conclusion: China's Competition Law Enforcement After CAI

As the preceding discussion has shown, the inability of WTO members to reach a consensus on the issue of binding international rules for the protection of market competition has brought this issue within the ambit of numerous PTAs incorporating competition chapters. The motivation of the signatories to undertake these WTO-X obligations ranged between an intention to discipline each other's competition law enforcement and a wish to promote enforcement cooperation in cross-border cases. Neither the EU nor China are strangers to competition chapters, which have been routinely included by both parties in bilateral and multilateral PTAs. In this context, the CAI provisions related to competition law and its enforcement do not go beyond the competition-related commitments already undertaken by the parties in other PTAs and are essentially limited to non-discrimination and transparency obligations in the enforcement of domestic competition legislation.

In 2012, Bradford anticipated a global "Brussels effect" of EU competition rules: "[b]y the time China might be able to overtake the EU, the EU might already have entrenched its norms in other jurisdictions and institutions by changing the way business is conducted in a lasting way".[114] While the "Brussels effect" was clearly manifested in the China's substantive and procedural standards of competition law already prior to the negotiation of the CAI, the agreement added a binding commitment to abide by the due process, non-discrimination and transparency principles in their enforcement. However, the "Brussels effect" has been less pronounced in terms of enforcing the AML. An overview of the AML provisions and secondary legislation regulating its enforcement indicates that China's competition law already largely corresponds to the requirements of the CAI and does not require substantial changes. When it comes to the actual enforcement of the AML in China, its multiple goals, ambiguous assessment standards and significant discretion exercised by the SAMR may lead to situations in which foreign investors experience a different degree of antitrust scrutiny or merger review compared to their domestic counterparts, especially SOEs.

While the EU and China are expected to continue negotiations on the investment protection and investment dispute settlement, the provisions of the CAI on regulatory framework including competition law enforcement and special obligations of "covered entities" will remain subject to state-to-state dispute settlement. The enforcement of competition law is highly case-specific and dependent on variables such as definitions of the relevant market, the market power of the undertakings concerned, alleged theory of harm, proposed remedies and the companies' willingness to offer commitments, competition authority's discretion in determining the amount of fine, etc. As a result, the factual differences between the cases will make it difficult to support a claim of systemic non-compliance with the competition-related provisions of the CAI. The existing institutional channels for competition

[114] Bradford (2012), p. 49.

law enforcement cooperation between the EU and Chinese competition authorities are limited to the general experience sharing and possible coordination of enforcement in the cases that are investigated by the competition authorities of both parties. As a result, until the introduction of the investor-state dispute settlement mechanism, the CAI will have a limited effect on competition law enforcement in China. Or, as summarized by Foster, "it seems prudent to prepare for a regime that remains discerning and selective in choosing which parts of traditional global practice to adopt wholesale and which to adapt to the unique characteristics of China".[115]

References

Abrenica MJV, Bernabe J (2017) Competition chapter in the trans-Pacific partnership agreement: developing a template for a multilateral framework. In: Chaisse J, Gao H, Lo C (eds) Paradigm shift in international economic law rule making: TPP as a new model for trade agreements? Springer, Singapore, pp 165–186

Anderson RD, Kovacic WE, Müller AC, Sporysheva N (2019) Competition Policy, Trade and the Global Economy: An Overview of Existing WTO Elements, Commitments in Regional Trade Agreements, Some Current Challenges and Issues for Reflection, DAF/COMP/GF(2019)11, 5 November 2019. https://one.oecd.org/document/DAF/COMP/GF(2019)11/en/pdf

Borlini L, Dordi C (2017) Deepening international systems of subsidy control: the (different) legal regimes of subsidies in the EU bilateral preferential trade agreements. CJEL 23(3):551–606

Bradford A (2007) International antitrust negotiations and the false hope of the WTO. Harv Int Law J 48(2):383–439

Bradford A (2012) The Brussels effect. Northwest Univ Law Rev 107(1):1–68

Bradford A, Büthe T (2015) Competition policy and free trade: antitrust provisions in PTAs. In: Dür A, Elsig M (eds) Trade cooperation: the purpose, design and effects of preferential trade agreements. Cambridge University Press, Cambridge, pp 246–274

Bradford A, Chilton AS (2021) Regulating antitrust through trade agreements. Antitrust Law J 84:103–125

Cahill D, Wang J (2021) How competition ideals are emasculated in China, and pathways for reform. Fordham Int Law J 44(3):609–670

Cheng TK (2014) Competition and the State in China. In: Cheng TK, Lianos I, Sokol DD (eds) Competition and the State. Stanford University Press, Stanford, pp 170–186

Cheng TK (2015) Competitive neutrality from an Asian perspective, DAF/COMP/WD(2015)49, 11 June 2015

China's Position Paper on WTO Reform, 20 December 2018., http://kw2.mofcom.gov.cn/article/chinanews/201812/20181202818679.shtml

Dadush U, Sapir A (2021) Is the European Union's Investment Agreement with China Underrated? Bruegel Policy Contribution 09/2021, https://www.bruegel.org/2021/04/is-the-european-unions-investment-agreement-with-china-underrated/

Decision of the Council and of the Commission of 29 May 1998 concerning the conclusion of the Agreement between the European Communities and the Government of the United States of America on the application of positive comity principles in the enforcement of their competition laws, OJ L 173, 18 June 1998

Decision of the CPC Central Committee on Some Issues Concerning the Establishment of a Socialist Market Economic Structure, 22 November 1993

[115] Foster (2017), p. 84.

Demedts V (2015) Which future for competition in the global trade system: competition chapters in FTA. J World Trade 49(3):407–436
Doha Ministerial Declaration (2001) WT/MIN(01)/DEC/1, 20 November 2001
Epstein RA (2014) Curbing the abuses of China's anti-monopoly law: an indictment and reform agenda, George Mason University School of Law, Center for the Protection of Intellectual Property, https://cpip.gmu.edu/2014/12/01/curbing-the-abuses-of-chinas-anti-monopoly-law-an-indictment-and-reform-agenda/
European Commission (2013) Staff Working Document "Impact Assessment Report on the EU-China Investment Relations" SWD(2013) 185 final, 23 May 2013, https://ec.europa.eu/smart-regulation/impact/ia_carried_out/docs/ia_2013/swd_2013_0185_en.pdf
European Commission, Public consultation on the future investment relationship between the EU and China, http://trade.ec.europa.eu/consultations/?consul_id=153
European Union Chamber of Commerce in China, European Business in China Position Paper 2020/2021
Evenett SJ (2005) What can we really learn from the competition provisions of regional trade agreements? In: Brusick P, Alvarez AM, Cernat L (eds) Competition provisions in regional trade agreements: how to assure development gains. United Nations
Federal Trade Commission (2013) Taking notes: observations on first five years of the Chinese anti-monopoly law, remarks of Commissioner Maureen K. Ohlhausen at the Competition Committee Meeting, US Council for International Business, Washington DC, 9 May 2013, https://www.ftc.gov/sites/default/files/documents/public_statements/taking-notes-observations-first-five-years-chinese-anti-monopoly-law/130509uscib.pdf
Foster AL (2017) Navigating the unique features of China's competition landscape. Antitrust Law J 31(2):79–86
Fox EM (2020) Should China's competition model be exported: a reply to Wendy Ng. Eur J Int Law 30(4):1431–1440
Free Trade Agreement between the Government of the People's Republic of China and the Government of the Republic of Korea (PRC-ROK FTA), 1 June 2015. http://fta.mofcom.gov.cn/korea/annex/xdzw_en.pdf
Goldstein KB (2011) Reviewing cross-border mergers and acquisitions for competition and national security: a comparative look at how the United States, Europe, and China separate security concerns from competition concerns in reviewing acquisitions by foreign entities. Tsinghua China Law Rev 3:215–256
Gu H, Foster AL (2015) Substantive analysis in China's horizontal merger control: a six-year review and beyond. Antitrust Law J 3(S1):i26–i48
Guiding Opinions of the CPC Central Committee and the State Council on Deepening the Reform of State-Owned Enterprises, 24 August 2015
Hamp-Lyons C (2009) The dragon in the room: China's anti-monopoly law and international merger review. Vanderbilt Law Rev 62(5):1577–1621
Hoffman C, Osnago A, Ruta M (2017) Horizontal Depth: A New Database on the Content of Preferential Trade Agreements, Policy Research Working Paper 7981. World Bank Group
Horn H, Mavroidis PC, Sapir A (2010) Beyond the WTO? An anatomy of EU and US preferential trade agreements. World Econ 33(11):1565–1588
Horton TJ (2016) Antitrust or industrial protectionism?: emerging international issues in China's anti-monopoly law enforcement efforts. Santa Clara J Int Law 14(1):109–142
Huang Y (2008) Pursuing the second best: the history, momentum, and remaining issues of China's anti-monopoly law. Antitrust Law J 75(1):117–132
Hufbauer GC, Kim J (2008) International Competition Policy and the WTO. Peterson Institute for International Economics, 11 April 2008, https://www.piie.com/commentary/speeches-papers/international-competition-policy-and-wto
ICN, International Cooperation, https://www.internationalcompetitionnetwork.org/working-groups/icn-operations/cooperation/
ICN, Members, https://www.internationalcompetitionnetwork.org/members/?location=asia

Interview with Wu Zhenguo, Director General, Anti-Monopoly Bureau of the State Administration for Market Regulation (SAMR), People's Republic of China, The Antitrust Source, June 2021. 1–22, https://www.samr.gov.cn/xw/zj/202107/P020210707589294998827.pdf
Jenny F (2003) International cooperation on competition: myth, reality and perspective. Antitrust Bull 48(4):973–1004
Laprévote F, Frisch S, Can B (2015) Competition policy within the context of free trade agreements. International Centre for Trade and Sustainable Development, World Economic Forum
Li K (2021) Report on the Work of the Government, delivered at the Fourth Session of the 13th National People's Congress of the People's Republic of China, 5 March 2021
Lyu S, Buts C, Jegers M (2019) Comparing China's fair competition review system to EU state aid control. Eur St Aid Law Q 1:37–60
Lyu S, Buts C, Jegers M (2020) China's fair competition review system and market access: the case of Shenzhen THSware Technology. J Eur Comp Law Pract 11(10):605–609
Lyu S, Buts C, Jegers M (2022) China's fair competition review system: a single case study. World Comp Law Econ Rev 45(1):123–156
Memorandum of Understanding on a dialogue in the area of the State aid control regime and the Fair Competition Review System between the Directorate-General for Competition of the European Commission and the National Development and Reform Commission of the People's Republic of China, 2 June 2017. https://ec.europa.eu/competition/international/bilateral/mou_china_2017.pdf
Memorandum of Understanding on Cooperation in the area of anti-monopoly law between the European Commission (Directorate-General for Competition) and the National Development and Reform Commission (NDRC) and the State Administration of Industry and Commerce (SAIC) of the People's Republic of China, 20 September 2012. https://ec.europa.eu/competition/international/bilateral/mou_china_en.pdf
National Development and Reform Commission (2021) Report on the implementation of the 2020 Plan for national economic and social development and on the 2021 Draft Plan for national economic and social development, delivered at the Fourth Session of the 13th National People's Congress of the People's Republic of China, 5 March 2021
OECD (2019) Competition Provisions in Trade Agreements – Contribution from the European Union, DAF/COMP/GF/WD(2019)7, 30 October 2019, https://one.oecd.org/document/DAF/COMP/GF/WD(2019)7/en/pdf
OECD (2021a) Competition Provisions in Trade Agreements – Executive Summary, DAF/COMP/GF(2019)18, 5 February 2021, https://one.oecd.org/document/DAF/COMP/GF(2019)18/en/pdf
OECD (2021b) Competition cooperation and enforcement inventory of cooperation agreements, Provisions on negative comity, https://www.oecd.org/daf/competition/competition-inventory-provisions-negative-comity.pdf
OECD, Directorate for Financial and Enterprise Affairs, Competition, https://www.oecd.org/daf/competition/
Practical Guidance for Cooperation on Investigating Anti-Monopoly Cases between the Directorate-General for Competition of European Commission and the State Administration for Market Regulation of People's Republic of China, 7 May 2019. https://ec.europa.eu/competition/international/bilateral/practical_guidance_antimonopoly.pdf
SAMR, Guidelines for the Anti-Monopoly Review for Concentration of Business Operators, 29 September 2018
SAMR, Order No 11 of 26 June 2019, Interim Provisions on Prohibiting Abuse of Dominant Market Positions
SAMR, Order No. 10 of 26 June 2019, Interim Provisions on Prohibiting Monopoly Agreements
Singapore Ministerial Declaration (1996) WT/MIN(96)/DEC, 18 December 1996
Singh VK (2014) Failed WTO platform for competition law convergence: evolving alternate regime of MoUs on internationalization of competition law. Ind J Int Law 54:247–272
Sobel YY (2014) Domestic-to-domestic transactions—a gap in China's merger control regime? Antitrust Source:1–12

Sokol DD (2008) Order without (enforceable) law: why countries enter into non-enforceable competition policy chapters in free trade agreements. Chi.-Kent Law Rev 83(1):231–292
Solano O, Sennekamp A (2005) Competition provisions in regional trade agreements, OECD Trade Policy Working Paper No. 31 COM/DAF/TD(2005)3/FINAL
Su J, Wang X (2013) China: the competition law system and the Country's norms. In: Fox EM, Trebilcock MJ (eds) The design of competition law institutions: global norms, local choices, OUP, pp 194–231
Svetlicinii A (2017) Private litigation under China's anti-monopoly law: empirical evidence and procedural developments. KLRI J Law Legisl 7(1):163–206
Svetlicinii A (2021) Chinese state owned enterprises and EU merger control. Routledge
Svetlicinii A (2022a) China's merger control: competition assessment or foreign investment screening? KLRI J Law Legisl 12(1):37–72
Svetlicinii A (2022b) Consolidation of the state-owned enterprises in China: a missed opportunity for the EU merger control? J Eur Compet Law Pract 13(1):17–28
Terms of Reference of the EU-China Competition Policy Dialogue, 6 May 2004. https://ec.europa.eu/competition/international/bilateral/china_tor_en.pdf
Terms of Reference of the EU-China Competition Policy Dialogue between the Directorate-General for Competition of the European Commission and the State Administration for Market Regulation of the People's Republic of China, 9 April 2019. https://ec.europa.eu/competition/international/bilateral/agreement_tor_china_2019.pdf
UNCTAD, Competition and consumer protection, https://unctad.org/Topic/Competition-and-Consumer-Protection
US Chamber of Commerce (2014) Competing Interests in China's Competition Law Enforcement
Wang H (2017) The differences between China's recent FTA and the TPP: a case study of the China-Korea FTA. In: Chaisse J, Gao H, Lo C (eds) Paradigm shift in international economic law rule making: TPP as a new model for trade agreements? Springer, Singapore, pp 293–305
Wang X (2008) Highlights of China's new anti-monopoly law. Antitrust Law J 75(1):133–150
WTO (2004) WT/L/579, 2 August 2004, https://www.wto.org/english/tratop_e/dda_e/draft_text_gc_dg_31july04_e.htm
Wu Q, Wang X (2022) Two steps forward and one step back? – US, EU and China's bilateral antitrust cooperation and international trade. World Comp Law Econ Rev 45(1):53–74
Ying P (2020) Taming SOEs within a redefined competition policy framework: an alternative approach for consensus. China WTO Rev 1:109–146
Ng W (2017) The Political Economy of Competition Law in China. Cambridge

Alexandr Svetlicinii is Associate Professor of Global Legal Studies at the University of Macau, Faculty of Law, where he also serves as Programme Coordinator of the Master of International Business Law in English Language. Prior to joining the University of Macau, Svetlicinii was a senior researcher at the Jean Monnet Chair of European Law at the Tallinn Law School, Tallinn University of Technology, in Estonia. Svetlicinii has published extensively on the subjects of international economic law, competition law, and commercial dispute settlement. In addition to his academic work, Prof. Svetlicinii served as the Co-Director of the Academic Society for Competition Law in South-East Europe, member of the International Advisory Board of the Institute for Consumer Antitrust Studies at the Loyola University Chicago, Ambassador of the Value of Competition initiative at the University of Oxford, Centre for Competition Law and Policy, and the Non-Governmental Advisor to the International Competition Network. He has recently published the monograph *Chinese State Owned Enterprises and EU Merger Control* (Routledge, 2021).

Intellectual Property Dimension of the EU-China Comprehensive Agreement on Investment: The EU Approach Against Non-Market-Mediated International Technology Transfer

Danny Friedmann

Abstract To compete economically and geopolitically, a country needs to have access to cutting-edge technology, which is often proprietary, protected by intellectual property rights (IPRs) including patents or trade secrets. Before countries can innovate indigenously, they need to catch up. One can distinguish between market-mediated and non-market-mediated methods of international technology transfer. This chapter explores the EU approach to China's non-market-mediated international technology transfer.

Two USTR 301 Reports and an EU request for consultation with China at the WTO, provided incentives for China to include prohibitions of technology transfer in both the Foreign Investment Law and Administrative License Law. Nevertheless, after the promulgation of these laws, prohibitions against forced technology transfer were included in first the US-China Economic and Trade Agreement ("Phase One"), and then in the EU-China Comprehensive Agreement on Investment (CAI). At different moments in its history, China has relied on non-market-mediated technology transfer. As a truly developing country that was opening up in 1978, this was justified and effective. *Anno* 2022, just one year short of the World Bank prediction that China will become a high-income country, non-market-mediated international technology transfer might be counterproductive to China's ability to indigenously innovate.

1 Introduction

The United Nations Conference on Trade And Development (UNCTAD) draft on the International Code on the Transfer of Technology defined "technology" as 'systematic knowledge for the manufacture of a product, for the application of a process

D. Friedmann (✉)
Peking University, School of Transnational Law, Shenzhen, People's Republic of China

© The Author(s), under exclusive license to Springer Nature Switzerland AG 2024

A. Svetlicinii, I.-J. Chen (eds.), *The EU-China Comprehensive Agreement on Investment*, European Yearbook of International Economic Law,
https://doi.org/10.1007/978-3-031-66862-3_8

or for the rendering of a service', which does not extend to 'transactions involving the mere sale or mere lease of goods.'[1] Access to cutting-edge, often proprietary technology is imperative if a country aspires to compete economically and geopolitically. Proprietary technology is protected by intellectual property rights (IPRs), such as patents and trade secrets, which also make it possible to monetize this technology. IPRs are private property and not public goods. From an economic liberal paradigm, private property owners should have full control and freedom of contract over their property, unlike public goods that are for all free to use. The idea is that Adam Smith's 'invisible hand'[2] can guide these market parties to contracts that generate the greatest value for society.

Before countries can innovate indigenously, they need to catch up via technology transfer and diffusion. One can distinguish between the market-mediated and non-market-mediated methods of international technology transfer.

1.1 'Invisible Hand'

Market-mediated international technology transfer is when the private owners of IPRs with superior technology voluntarily transfer their technology to a company in a country that aspires to use that technology. Because of the potentiality of market power between the owner and recipient of the technology, multilateral agreements such as the Agreement on Trade-Related Aspects of Intellectual Property Rights (TRIPs)[3] that promote market-mediated international technology transfer have built in guarantees against abuse of market power by IPRs.[4] In general, this method aims to create market conditions conducive to increased investment, which may then lead to increased technology transfer and diffusion. An example of this method can be found in the preamble to the China-Netherlands Bilateral Investment Treaty (BIT) 2001:

> Recognising that agreement upon the treatment to be accorded to such investments will stimulate the flow of capital and technology and the economic development of the Contracting Parties and that fair and equitable treatment of investment is desirable.[5]

---

[1] Draft International Code of Conduct on The Transfer of Technology [1985 version] Chapter 1, para. 1.2, p. 174. International Investment Instruments: A Compendium, three volumes (Geneva: United Nations), United Nations publications, Sales Nos. E.96.II.A.9; E.96.II.A.10; and E.96.II.A.11.

[2] Smith (1759), para. 10.

[3] TRIPs, signed on 15 April 1994, which came into effect 1 January 1995.

[4] Technology Transfer, UNCTAD Series on issues in international investment agreements, UNCTAD/ITE/IIT/28, Geneva, October 2001, p. 44. Available at: https://unctad.org/system/files/official-document/psiteiitd28.en.pdf.

[5] Agreement on encouragement and reciprocal protection of investments between the Government of the PRC and the Government of the Kingdom of the Netherlands, signed 26 November 2001, and came into effect 1 August 2004. Available at: https://investmentpolicy.unctad.org/international-investment-agreements/treaty-files/763/download.

1.2 Market-Intervention

Non-market-mediated international technology transfer is also called the regulatory approach to international technology transfer. The relation between companies with technology (source countries) and the recipients of that technology (host countries) is potentially unequal, using internal transfer via Foreign Direct Investment (FDI) or external transfer via licensing. A host country's regulations on technology transfer, promoting non-market-mediated international technology transfer, prohibits certain terms in technology transfer that are detrimental to development goals, and are used to overcome potentially adverse economic consequences.[6]

Jurisdictions such as the EU, US, Japan and Taiwan, have argued that China has selected certain strategic emerging industries in which it wants to compete, and that within these industries it has exerted its bargaining power in regard of FDIs and licensing, to pressure foreign companies to transfer technology. Dan Prud'homme et al. distinguish between three kinds of technology transfer:

- Undermine market policies (including market access preconditioned on meeting technology transfer requirements);
- Violate the law policies (including provisions in technology import export regulations; and certain policies related to the intersection of anti-trust and IP, and IP and technical standards);
- "No choice policies" (including unfair court rulings in IP civil litigation).[7]

Prud'homme et al. consider only the last of these three to be 'forced technology transfer'.[8] Foreign companies that want to enter the Chinese market, where they have to transfer certain technology or agree with certain licensing terms for their IP, can also decide not to do so. Jyh-An Lee rightly argues that this does not mean they are not forced to transfer the technology.[9] A company from a WTO member with IPRs can have a justified expectation that it can enter the market of another WTO member; that there is a level-playing field where it can use its IPRs in the way it chooses to and compete without being forced to tie one hand behind its back.

Non-market-mediated technology transfer is not unique to China. The governments of Brazil, Japan and South Korea[10] were also engaged in this strategy.[11] Between 1976 and 1985, countries negotiated and drafted, under the auspices of the

[6] Technology Transfer, UNCTAD Series on issues in international investment agreements, UNCTAD/ITE/IIT/28, Geneva, October 2001, p. 44.

[7] Prud'homme et al. (2018), p. 152.

[8] Ibid.

[9] Lee (2020a), p. 348.

[10] Omer (2001), pp. 301–303.

[11] Lee (2020a), p. 341.

UNCTAD, the International Code of Conduct on the Transfer of Technology.[12] The draft Code has not been adopted by the United Nations General Assembly.[13]

The phenomenon of non-market-mediated international technology transfer has been recurring and receding in China. China has used a 'market-for-technology strategy'[14] since Deng Xiaoping, when China started its opening up policy from 1978 onwards.[15] The US-China Memorandum of Understanding of 1992 stated that China, pursuant to its policy of bringing its trade regime into line with international standards, 'will not condition issuance of import licenses upon transfer of technology or meeting requirements related to investment in China'.[16]

In the WTO Protocol on the Accession of the PRC (Accession Protocol), China committed to ensuring that any government approval of foreign investment is not conditioned on 'performance requirements of any kind, such as local content, offsets, the transfer of technology, export performance or the conduct of research and development in China.'[17] In order to fully overcome the asymmetry of information and create a competitive level-playing field in the selected industries, China has drafted legislation that should stimulate the international transfer of advanced or cutting-edge technology. In other words, China is supplementing its market-mediated international technology transfer with state intervention. This has recently led to a crescendo of complaints against China's non-market-mediated international technology transfer by the US and EU, followed by China's accommodations to these complaints: two USTR 301 Reports[18] and an EU request for consultation with China at the WTO[19] provided incentives for China to include prohibitions of

---

[12] Draft International Code of Conduct on The Transfer of Technology [1985 version] Chapter 1, para. 1.2, p. 174.

[13] International Investment Instruments: A Compendium, three volumes (Geneva: UN), UN publications, Sales Nos. E.96.II.A.9; E.96.II.A.10; and E.96.II.A.11, Chapter 1, 172.

[14] Qin (2019), p. 749.

[15] Lee (2020a), p. 341.

[16] Art. II (iv) Quantitative Restrictions on Import Memorandum of Understanding between the Government of the United States of America and the Government of the People's Republic of China Concerning Market Access, 31 I.L.M. 1275, 1277 (1992).

[17] Para 7.3 Part I Protocol on the Accession of the PRC, WT/L/432, 23 November 2001: '[w]ithout prejudice to the relevant provisions of this Protocol, China shall ensure that the distribution of import licences, quotas, tariff rate quotas, or any other means of approval for importation, the right of importation or investment by national and sub national authorities, is not conditioned on: whether competing domestic suppliers of such products exist; or performance requirements of any kind, such as local content, offsets, the transfer of technology, export performance or the conduct of research and development in China.' Report of the Working Party on the Accession of the PRC to the WTO, WT/ACC/CHN/49, 1 October 2001.

[18] 2018 Special 301 Report, USTR, 27 March 2018. Available at: https://ustr.gov/sites/default/files/files/Press/Reports/2018%20Special%20301.pdf.

Update Concerning China's Acts, Policies and Practices Related to Technology Transfer, Intellectual Property, and Innovation, 20 November 2018. Available at: https://ustr.gov/sites/default/files/enforcement/301Investigations/301%20Report%20Update.pdf.

[19] DS549: China – Certain Measures on the Transfer of Technology, WTO 1 June 2018.

technology transfers in both the Foreign Investment Law[20] and Administrative License Law.[21] Nevertheless, after the promulgation of the respective law, and amendments to it, prohibitions against forced technology transfer were included in first the US-China Economic and Trade Agreement ("Phase One"),[22] and then in the EU-China Comprehensive Agreement on Investment (CAI).[23]

As pointed out, China has at different moments in its history relied on non-market-mediated international technology transfer. As a truly developing country that was opening up in 1978, this was justified and effective. China has transformed itself in four decades into a superpower with concomitant aspirations, competing to become a global technology leader in several fields of industry. Especially in first tier and "new first tier" cities in China, replete with science parks, there is sophisticated infrastructure, conducive to research and technology. One can also argue that the IP protection on the books is one of the highest in the world, encouraging foreign companies to license their technology to Chinese companies. This confidence is tempered by the uneven enforcement of IP on the ground. One can argue that non-market-mediated international technology transfer is counterproductive to China's capacity to indigenously innovate. This chapter addresses the two dimensions of technology transfer: IP and investment (Sect. 2); the EU's approach against China's non-market-mediated international technology transfer (Sect. 3); followed by the conclusions (Sect. 4).

2 Two Dimensions of Technology Transfer: IP and Investment

There is an intimate relation between IP and investment. One the one hand, standards of IP protection and enforcement influence the attractiveness of the investment climate. On the other hand, IPRs are intangible assets that are often explicitly protected in international investment agreements (IIAs), including bilateral investment treaties (BITs). Intangible assets have become (and will become more) important in the total profile of investments for the US and EU on the one hand and China on the other hand. In March 2021, China's 14th Five Year Plan (2021–2025) made clear that it is aiming for leadership in the following R&D fields: aerospace,

[20] The Foreign Investment Law of the PRC, adopted 15 March 2019, and came into effect 1 January 2020. Available at: https://en.ndrc.gov.cn/policies/202105/t20210527_1281403.html.

[21] Amendment to the Administrative License Law of the PRC, adopted 23 April 2019, and effective on the same date. Available at: http://www.npc.gov.cn/npc/c30834/201905/64f52a065d3142ae92d95fa860e2f0e0.shtml.

[22] Economic And Trade Agreement Between The Government Of The USA And The Government Of The PRC (Phase One), concluded 15 January 2020, and came into effect 14 February 2020.

[23] EU-China Comprehensive Agreement on Investment (CAI) in principle was concluded in principle 30 January 2020.

biotech, neuroscience, artificial intelligence, quantum computing, and semiconductors.[24]

The encouragement of technology transfer is closely related to the broader treatment of proprietary knowledge through IP laws.[25] An internalized mode of technology transfer can occur when there is direct investment, which by definition remains in the sphere of influence of transnational companies. This mode of technology transfer is preferred over licensing, in case of weak IP property protection and enforcement. In this scenario, transnational companies may hold back deeper learning processes, which might not induce spill-over effects into the local economy.[26] Weak IPRs might reduce formal inward technology transfer, but might increase informal inward technology transfer, via imitation and reverse engineering as pointed out above. But for many a foreign company it might still be wise to register its IPRs, because otherwise there is no possibility to stop the production and sales of counterfeit and pirated versions of its products in the developing country, which in turn could lead to a stream of counterfeit and pirated goods exported back into the home market of the foreign company. The attractiveness of a country for inward FDIs is complex,[27] but it seems that a relatively high standard of protection and enforcement of IPRs is a minimum requirement to motivate investment.

Susy Frankel points to the need for investment in development opportunities at the place where relevant IPRs are exploited.[28] There is no adequate empirical support for the idea that a strong IPR regime could enable countries to access new technologies.[29] Therefore, it is hard to determine the "Goldilocks zone" of IP protection to promote optimal international technology transfer. When there is more confidence in the IP regime of the host state, externalized modes of technology transfer by transnational companies include minority joint ventures, franchising, capital goods sales, licences, technical assistance, subcontracting or original equipment manufacturing arrangements,[30] to capitalize on their market power embodied in their IPRs.

[24] The 14th Five-Year Plan (2021–2025) for National Economic and Social Development of the PRC was approved by the 13th National People's Congress on March 2021. The 14th Five-Year Plan of the PRC — Fostering High-Quality Development, Asian Development Bank, NO. 2021-01, para 7.

[25] Technology Transfer, UNCTAD Series on issues in international investment agreements, UNCTAD/ITE/IIT/28, Geneva, October 2001, p. 1.

[26] Ibid., pp. 14–15.

[27] Drahos and Braithwaite (2002), p. 451.

[28] Frankel (2019), p. 52.

[29] Dhar and Joseph (2012), p. 17.

[30] Technology Transfer, UNCTAD Series on issues in international investment agreements, UNCTAD/ITE/IIT/28, Geneva, October 2001, p. 15.

2.1 *IPRs Under Investment Law*

IPRs are private rights and investment laws that fall under public (international) law designed to protect against state interference, based on customary international law to protect the property of aliens.[31] IPR can also recognise an investment made by a foreign inventor that deserves protection under investment law.[32] Thus an IIA adds a layer to IPR protection.[33] The IPR dimension is protected by a specific standard of IP law and compensation in case of a breach; while the investment dimension of the IPR asset is protected by the IIA, imposing sanctions in case of discriminatory, expropriatory or otherwise unfair or arbitrary behavior of the host state.[34]

IIAs often include an Investor State Dispute System (ISDS). This enables an IPR owner to directly initiate ISDS proceedings against the host state.[35] Under the CAI, the EU and China need to further negotiate a possible dispute settlement system. In a press conference, the European Commission stated that 'China agrees to an enforcement mechanism (state-to-state dispute settlement), as in our trade agreements.'[36]

IIAs include bilateral investment agreements (BITs). China has concluded over 20 BITs with EU member states that are in force.[37] These BITs between China and EU member states each comprise a provision that provides the categories of investment assets including IPRs.[38] The CAI has made it clear that this agreement is not a replacement for these BITs.[39] But it seems the pendulum is swinging away from the fragmentation caused by BITs towards harmonization via the CAI and a future Trade and Economic Cooperation Agreement, or a future Framework Agreement, or perhaps an investment agreement under a reformed WTO.

---

[31] Grosse Ruse-Khan (2019).

[32] Correa and Viñuales (2016), p. 91.

[33] Grosse Ruse-Khan (2019), p. 8.

[34] Ibid.

[35] Ibid., p. 10.

[36] Key elements of the EU-China Comprehensive Agreement on Investment, European Commission, Press Release, 30 December 2020. Available at: https://ec.europa.eu/commission/presscorner/detail/es/ip_20_2542.

[37] International Investment Agreements Navigator, UNCTAD, China. Available at: https://investmentpolicy.unctad.org/international-investment-agreements/countries/42/china.

[38] China-Germany BIT, Art. 1(1)(d): intellectual property rights, in particular copyrights, patents and industrial designs, trade-marks, trade-names, technical processes, trade and business secrets, know-how and good-will. Available at: https://investmentpolicy.unctad.org/international-investment-agreements/treaty-files/736/download.

[39] Comprehensive Agreement on Investment (CAI) Agreement in Principle, 30 January 2020. Available at: https://trade.ec.europa.eu/doclib/press/index.cfm?id=2237. Art. 15.1 Sub-section 2 Section VI.

2.2 *IP and Market-Mediated International Technology Transfer*

Art. 66.2 TRIPs instructs developed country members to provide incentives to enterprises and institutions in their territories to encourage technology transfer to least-developed country members to enable them to create a sound and viable technological base. It seems reasonable to apply this also to a scenario where developing countries acquire technology from developed countries. China has been self-identifying as a developing country and received developing country status within the WTO, but its GDP per capita has risen meteorically to over US$10,000 in 2020, which qualifies China as an upper middle-income country.[40] It is arguable that China is both a developing and developed country at the same time, depending on the location, rural or urban, within its vast territory. China is on course to become a developed country by 2023, when it is expected to surpass the high income country threshold of US$12,536 set by the World Bank.[41] Keith Maskus points to empirical evidence, which suggests that enforceable patents can increase inward flows of international technology transfer in middle-income and large developing countries.[42] But Art. 7 TRIPs assumes that the international technology transfer is market-mediated through 'trade, foreign direct investment, licensing, and personnel movements, along with informal means through imitation, reverse engineering, and spillovers.'[43] It is not clear whether Art. 7 TRIPs justifies public intervention other than IP if the market fails to cause sufficient international technology transfer or when the tempo is considered too low.

Art. 8 TRIPs is relevant too. Art. 8(1) TRIPs states that members may, in formulating or amending their laws and regulations, adopt measures necessary to protect public health and nutrition, and to promote the public interest in sectors of vital importance to their socio-economic and technological development, provided that such measures are consistent with the provisions of this Agreement. China could argue that its technological transfer measures promote the public interests in sectors of vital importance to their socio-economic and technological development (the strategic emerging industries).

Art. 8(2) TRIPs states that appropriate measures, if they are consistent with the provisions of this Agreement, may be needed to prevent the abuse of IPRs by right holders or the resort to practices which unreasonably restrain trade or adversely affect the international transfer of technology. The remaining open question is, relevant to Art. 8(1) and (2) TRIPs, whether non-market-mediated international technology transfer is consistent with TRIPs.

---

[40] The World by Income and Region 1987–2020, World Bank. Available at: https://datatopics.worldbank.org/world-development-indicators/the-world-by-income-and-region.html.

[41] *Ibid.*

[42] Maskus (2004), p. 22, V.

[43] Ibid.

In the EU and US, China has been perceived as a country with good IP laws on the books but insufficiently enforced IP on the ground. This has led foreign firms to assess the risk of losing control over their information and appropriability challenges, which could lead to a decreased appetite for them to transfer technology, or alternatively, to transfer older generation technologies.

3 EU's Approach Against China's Technology Transfer

In 2018, the EU first requested consultation with China at the WTO to stop it from using non-market-mediated international technology transfer. Pressured by the EU and US, China explicitly prohibited forced technology transfer in its Foreign Investment Law and Administrative License Law in 2019. Nevertheless, the EU insisted on including provisions against non-market-mediated international technology transfer in the CAI in 2020, an agreement divided into several Sections but lacking one dedicated to IP.

3.1 WTO Case and Relevant Regulations

On 1 June 2018, the EU delegation requested consultation with the government of China regarding the transfer of foreign technology into China. According to the EU, Chinese measures adversely affect the protection of the IPRs of foreign companies transferring technology to China.[44] The EU asserted that:

> China imposes a different set of rules on the import of technology, including industrial property rights, other IPRs and undisclosed Information than the rules which are applicable to technology transfers occurring between Chinese companies.[45]

These measures appear to discriminate against foreign holders of IPRs, and restrict the foreign right holders' ability to protect certain IPRs in China, contrary to China's WTO obligations.[46]

On 20 December 2018, the EU revised its request of 6 June 2018 for consultation with more sources.[47] In both its communications, the EU points to China's domestic regulation that allegedly violates national treatment of EU companies and restricts the EU companies' ability to protect their IPRs.[48] It uses four regulations as case studies: Regulations on the Administration of the Import and Export of Technologies

[44] China – Certain Measures on The Transfer of Technology, Request for consultations by the European Union, WT/DS549/1, 6 June 2018.

[45] Ibid.

[46] Ibid.

[47] Ibid., Rev.1, 8 January 2019.

[48] Ibid.

(TIER) 2011;[49] Regulations for the Implementation of the Law on Chinese-Foreign Equity Joint Ventures (JV Regulation) 2014;[50] New Energy Vehicle Production Enterprises and Product Admissions Regulations (NEV Regulation) 2017;[51] and Administration of the Examination Approval and Registration of Foreign-invested Crop Seed Enterprises Provisions (Seed FIE Approval Provisions) 1997.[52]

3.1.1 TIER

Arts. 18–21 TIER create administrative burdens on foreign importers of technology: all technology import contracts must be notified to and registered by the Chinese authorities and copies of the contracts must be provided, even if the contract is subsequently amended or terminated.[53] Art. 24 TIER requires that licensors of imported technology indemnify licensees for all liabilities for infringement resulting from the use of the transferred technology.[54] In general, to make licensors of technology responsible in the case that this technology infringes someone else's IPRs seems reasonable. However, it is not reasonable if the licensee uses the technology beyond the scope of the license. Art. 353 Contract Law of the PRC, which governs the contracts between Chinese parties, allocates the liability to the licensor, but leaves open the possibility that the parties stipulate otherwise, based on the freedom of contract.[55]

Art. 27 TIER requires that any improvements to imported technology belong to the party making the improvement.[56] In patent law, the question is whether the

[49] Regulations of the PRC on the Administration of the Import and Export of Technologies (Order of the State Council No. 331, issued 10 December 2001, effective 1 January 2002, amended 8 January 2011, in Order of the State Council No. 588).

[50] Regulations for the Implementation of the Law of the PRC on Chinese-Foreign Equity Joint Ventures (State Council, Guo Fa [1983] No. 148, issued September 20, 1983, effective September 20, 1983, amended 15 January 1986, in Guo Fa [1986] No. 6, further amended 21 December 1987, in Guo Fa [1987] No. 110, 22 July 2001, in Order of the State Council No. 311, 8 January 2011, in Order of the State Council No. 588, and 19 February 2014, in Order of the State Council No. 648).

[51] New Energy Vehicle Production Enterprises and Product Admissions Regulations (including Annex 1 on Review Requirements for Access of New Energy Vehicle Manufacturers), (Decree of the Ministry of Industry and Information Technology No. 39 6 January 2017, reviewed and passed at the 26th Ministerial Meeting of the Ministry of Industry and Information Technology of the People's Republic of China 20 October 2016, adopted 6 January 2017, effective 1 July 2017).

[52] Administration of the Examination, Approval and Registration of Foreign-invested Crop Seed Enterprises Provisions (promulgated by the Ministry of Agriculture, State Planning Commission, MOFTEC and State Administration for Industry and Commerce, effective 8 September 1997).

[53] Regulations of the PRC on the Administration of the Import and Export of Technologies.

[54] Ibid.

[55] Contract Law of the PRC, adopted at the Second Session of the Ninth National People's Congress 15 March 1999 and promulgated by Order No. 15 of the President of the PRC on the same day. Available at: http://www.lawinfochina.com/display.aspx?lib=law&id=6145&CGid=&EncodingName=big5.

[56] Regulations of the PRC on the Administration of the Import and Export of Technologies.

improvement is a substitution or whether it builds upon an existing invention (follow-on invention). Cross-licenses are often used to allow the original and follow-on inventors to use each other's patent.

In case of domestic technology transfer or licensing contract, Art. 354 Contract Law of the PRC makes it possible to share any subsequently improved technological result obtained from patent exploitation or utilization of the technical know-how, between the exporter and importer of the technology.[57] Art. 355 Contract Law of the PRC clarifies that specific laws can deviate from this principle.[58] TIER is such a specific law.

Art. 29 TIER appears to restrict the terms of import technology contracts by prohibiting a number of clauses in import technology transfer contracts.[59] In particular, Art. 29(3) TIER provides that a technology import contract cannot contain clauses restricting the transferee from improving the technology supplied by the supplying party, or restricting the receiving party from using the improved technology.[60] For the sake of innovation, it seems desirable that a receiving party can improve upon existing technology. However, confirming the distinction made above between prior patents and improvement patents that build upon the prior patent, the prior patent holder retains the negative rights to exclude others from making, using, selling the prior patent. So here the EU has a point, that this provision is in violation of Art. 3 TRIPs national treatment. The EU also argues that China appears to limit the exclusive rights of non-Chinese patent holders, contrary to Art. 28.1(a) and (b) TRIPs and appears to limit their rights to assign or transfer by succession patents and to conclude licensing contracts, contrary to Art. 28.2 TRIPs. If these restrictions are the case, then China cannot ensure effective protection for foreign holders of undisclosed information under Arts. 39.1 and 39.2 TRIPs.

3.1.2 JV Regulation

The EU points also to the JV Regulation, which seems inconsistent with China's commitments under Para 7.3 Part I Accession Protocol[61] and Para 1.2 Part I Accession Protocol, which incorporates the commitments under Para 49 and Para

[57] Contract Law of the PRC, adopted at the Second Session of the Ninth National People's Congress.

[58] Ibid.

[59] Regulations of the PRC on the Administration of the Import and Export of Technologies.

[60] Ibid.

[61] Para 7.3 Part I Protocol on the Accession of the PRC, WT/L/432, 23 November 2001: '[w]ithout prejudice to the relevant provisions of this Protocol, China shall ensure that the distribution of import licences, quotas, tariff rate quotas, or any other means of approval for importation, the right of importation or investment by national and sub national authorities, is not conditioned on: whether competing domestic suppliers of such products exist; or performance requirements of any kind, such as local content, offsets, the transfer of technology, export performance or the conduct of research and development in China.'

203 of the Report of the Working Party on the Accession of the PRC to the WTO (Working Party Report).[62] In Para 49 Working Party Report the representative of the PRC 'confirmed that the terms and conditions of technology transfer, production processes or other proprietary knowledge particularly in the context of an investment, would only require agreement between the parties to the investment.'[63] Para 203 Working Party Report states China's commitment in regard of

> The allocation, permission or rights for importation and investment would not be conditional upon performance requirements set by national or sub-national authorities, or subject to secondary conditions covering, for example, the conduct of research, the provision of offsets or other forms of industrial compensation including specified types or volumes of business opportunities, the use of local inputs or the transfer of technology. Permission to invest, import licences, quotas and tariff rate quotas would be granted without regard to the existence of competing Chinese domestic suppliers. Consistent with its obligations under the WTO Agreement and the Draft Protocol, the freedom of contract of enterprises would be respected by China.

Art. 5 JV Regulation requires that the technology and equipment contributed by a foreign partner to a JV be advanced and suitable to the needs of China.[64] With this law and Art. 41 JV Regulation,[65] the Chinese government signals the ambition that Chinese companies upgrade their technologies to advanced levels to compete both domestically and internationally. Art. 4(3) JV Regulation precludes approval of a JV if the project is not in conformity with the development of China's national economy.[66] Art. 5 JV Law also requires the foreign partner to the JV to pay compensation if losses occur due to the intentional supply of outdated technology or equipment.[67] A foreign partner of a JV, which has access to a significantly more advanced version of a technology, is often willing to contribute a more advanced version of the technology relative to the Chinese partner's level of technology. But such a foreign partner is not willing to contribute its latest cutting-edge version of technology to the Chinese company, because it does not want to create a future competitor. This law could lead to conflicts over whether the foreign partner supplied outdated technology or equipment, and goes against the freedom to contract between foreign and Chinese parties. The technology transferred to the JV by the foreign partner needs to be submitted to the Chinese authorities, who will examine and approve whether the technology is sufficiently advanced.[68] This appears to be inconsistent with Art.

[62] Report of the Working Party on the Accession of the PRC to the WTO, WT/ACC/CHN/49, 1 October 2001.

[63] Ibid.

[64] Regulations for the Implementation of the Law of the PRC on Chinese-Foreign Equity Joint Ventures.

[65] Ibid.

[66] Ibid.

[67] Regulations for the Implementation of the Law of the PRC on Chinese-Foreign Equity Joint Ventures.

[68] Arts. 7, 11, 26 and 27 Regulations for the Implementation of the Law of the PRC on Chinese-Foreign Equity Joint Ventures.

3 TRIPs (National Treatment), Art. 28.1(a) (exclusive rights for a product patent) and (b) TRIPs (exclusive rights for a process patent), Art. 28.2 TRIPs (right to assign, transfer by succession, conclude licensing contracts), Art. 33 (term of protection of 20 years) and Arts. 39.1 (undisclosed information shall be protected) and 39.2 TRIPs (everyone can protect undisclosed information for commercial purposes), because China allegedly 'imposes restrictions on the rights of foreign intellectual property right holders, notably, on their right to freely negotiate and agree on market-based contractual terms in licensing and other technology-related contracts concerning the import of technology to China.'

Article 43(1) JV Regulation provides a general examination and approval requirement for any technology transfer agreements entered into by a joint venture.[69] Point 3 of Art. 43(2) JV Regulation provides that the duration of a technology transfer agreement is generally no longer than 10 years.[70] Point 4 of Art. 43(2) JV Regulation provides that the technology importing party retains the right to use the transferred technology continuously, after the expiration of the technology transfer agreement.[71] This provision might be based on the premise that technology transfer means that technology is not just made accessible during the duration of the technology transfer agreement, but is being irreversibly transferred. However, even if a technology transfer agreement has expired after 10 years, the patent holder has the exclusive right over it for another 10 years, in conformity with Art. 28 TRIPs *juncto* Art. 33 TRIPs.

Logically, if the patent holder has lost control over his or her patent after the technology transfer agreement, this will limit the exclusive rights of foreign patent holders, contrary to Art. 28.1(a) and (b) TRIPs and limits their rights to assign or transfer by succession patents and to conclude licensing contracts, contrary to Art. 28.2 TRIPs. As a result of these restrictions China also appears not to ensure effective protection for foreign holders of undisclosed information contrary to its obligations under Art. 39.1 and 39.2 TRIPs. Finally, the EU makes the point that this technology transfer is in violation of China's obligations under Art. X.3(a) GATT 1994 and Paragraph 2(A)2 Accession Protocol, which both oblige China to administer in a uniform, impartial and reasonable manner all its laws, regulations, decisions and rulings pertaining to or affecting GATT 1994, trade in goods, services, TRIPs and foreign exchanges.[72]

---

[69] Regulations for the Implementation of the Law of the PRC on Chinese-Foreign Equity Joint Ventures.

[70] Ibid.

[71] Ibid.

[72] General Agreement on Tariffs and Trade 1994 is contained in Annex 1A of the WTO Agreement. It incorporates by reference the provisions of the GATT 1947. Available at: https://www.wto.org/english/res_e/publications_e/ai17_e/gatt1994_e.htm.

3.1.3 NEV Regulation

The EU also points to some problematic provisions of the New Energy Vehicle Production Enterprises and Product Admissions Regulations (NEV Regulation),[73] where China imposes performance requirements on foreign car manufacturers as conditions for foreign investors to access and operate in the New Energy Vehicle (NEV) market in China: mandatory requirements to 'understand and master' relevant technologies, and to possess specific tools, equipment, software, facilities, production capacity and other capabilities. For example, 'enterprises applying for access to the plug-in hybrid electric vehicle (PHEV) market are required to also understand and master technologies of the control systems for engine and electromechanical coupling devices.'[74]

3.1.4 Seed FIE Approval Provisions

The Administration of the Examination, Approval and Registration of Foreign-invested Crop Seed Enterprises Provisions (Seed FIE Approval Provisions) imposes requirements that relate to the transfer of technology, genetic material and biotechnology to China as conditions for the approval of foreign-invested crop seed enterprises. A foreign party to a foreign-invested crop seed enterprise shall be an enterprise that possesses a high level of scientific seed breeding, and seed production technology and enterprise management.[75] This requirement does not apply to the Chinese party of the foreign-invested crop seed enterprise. Moreover, the foreign-invested crop seed enterprise should be capable of introducing or adopting superior varieties (germplasm resources), advanced seed technology and equipment from abroad.[76] In addition, granting the necessary licenses on the conduct of R&D in China is conditional on meeting specific targets, for example percentages of the company's income or in absolute financial terms.[77] The application requirements include a detailed documentation of the company's R&D activities.[78]

---

[73] China – Certain Measures on The Transfer of Technology, Request for consultations by the European Union, WT/DS549/1/Rev.1, 8 January 2019, pp. 6–7.

[74] Item I(2), point (5) of Annex 1 NEV Regulation.

[75] Administration of the Examination, Approval and Registration of Foreign-invested Crop Seed Enterprises Provisions, Art. 4(1).

[76] Ibid., Art. 4(2).

[77] Ibid., Art. 9(4).

[78] Ibid., Art. 12.

3.1.5 Foreign Investment Law

China drafted a version of the Foreign Investment Law (FIL) in 2015. Due to disagreements between policy-makers, the law that was to promote China as a destination of FDIs was put on ice.[79] After criticisms of the US and EU, a draft which included the prohibitions on forced technology transfer was approved on 15 March 2019.[80] Art. 22(2) FIL states that:

> During the process of foreign investment, the State shall encourage technology cooperation on the basis of free will and business rules. Conditions for technology cooperation shall be determined by all investment parties upon negotiation under the principle of equity. No administrative department or its staff member shall force any transfer of technology by administrative means.[81]

This provision does not explain the scope of 'administrative means', which would have led to greater legal certainty and predictability for foreign investors and staff members at administrative departments.[82] Art. 23 FIL prohibits that government officials divulge trade secrets of foreign investors. In case of a violation of Arts. 22 or 23 FIL, Art. 39 FIL will provide administrative liability. If the conduct constitutes a crime, the government official will be criminally liable.

3.1.6 Amendment to the Administrative License Law

The amendment to the Administrative License Law in 2019 also includes a provision dedicated to the protection of trade secrets. Art. 5(2) Administrative License Law states:

> Without the consent of the applicant, an administrative agency, its functionaries, or an expert on a panel shall not disclose any trade secret, undisclosed information, or confidential business information submitted by the applicant, unless the law provides otherwise, or national security or the material social and public interest is involved; and if the administrative agency discloses such information of the applicant to the public according to the law, the applicant shall be allowed to file an objection within a reasonable period of time.[83]

---

[79] Qian (2019).

[80] It replaced the Law on Sino-Foreign Equity Joint Ventures, the Law on Sino-Foreign Contractual Joint Ven-tures, and the Law on Foreign-Capital Enterprises—enacted between 1979 and 1990. Lee (2020b), pp. 167–168.

[81] Foreign Investment Law of the PRC, order of the President of the PRC No. 26, adopted at the Second Session of the 13th National People's Congress on 15 March 2019, and came into force on 1 January 2020. Available at: https://en.ndrc.gov.cn/policies/202105/t20210527_1281403.html.

[82] Qian (2019).

[83] Administrative License Law of the PRC (adopted at the 4th session of the Standing Committee of the 10th National People's Congress of the PRC 27 August 2003, and amended in accordance with the Decision to Amend Eight Laws Including the Construction Law of the PRC adopted at the 10th Session of the Standing Committee of the Thirteenth National People's Congress of the PRC of China 23 April 2019). Available at: http://www.lawinfochina.com/display.aspx?id=30314&lib=law.

3.2 *CAI and Technology Transfer*

After the USTR 301 Reports and the EU request for consultations at the WTO in 2018, China agreed to explicitly prohibit 'forced technology transfer' in the enactment of the Foreign Investment Law 2019 and amendment to the Administrative License Law 2019. Despite these domestic laws, the EU insisted on (and China agreed to) prohibitions against non-market-mediated international technology transfer in the CAI, an 'agreement in principle'.[84]

3.2.1 Rise and Fall of the CAI

In 2003, the EU and China established the first Comprehensive Strategic Partnership. Both sides expressed a determination to fully exploit the opportunities brought about by China's Twelfth Five-Year Plan and the Europe 2020 Strategy[85] to foster synergies and promote cooperation in all fields. In 2012, at the 15th EU-China Summit, both countries agreed to make joint efforts to conclude an ambitious bilateral agreement on the protection of geographical indications (GI),[86] and called for intensification of joint efforts on IPR border enforcement.[87] The investments in GIs, products that link to a certain place and that are made according to certain specifications, can be harnessed by IP.[88] This summit was followed by the EU-China Innovation Cooperation Seminar in November 2012.[89] The objective of IP is incentivizing innovation and providing opportunities for the monetization of innovation. In 2013, the EU-China 2020 Strategic Agenda for Cooperation was set up.[90] José Manuel Barroso, the former president of the European Commission, described the rationale for this cooperation: 'We have decided to fully tap the potential of investment by launching negotiations for an ambitious investment agreement, covering

---

[84] CAI Agreement in Principle, 30 January 2020. Available at: https://trade.ec.europa.eu/doclib/press/index.cfm?id=2237.

[85] Europe 2020, Communication from The Commission, COM (2010) 2020 final Brussels, 3 March 2010. Available at: https://eur-lex.europa.eu/LexUriServ/LexUriServ.do?uri=COM:2010:2020:FIN:EN:PDF.

A strategy for smart, sustainable and inclusive growth. [this addition is relevant, because it is not clear from the title].

[86] Joint Press Communiqué 15th EU-China Summit, Towards a stronger EU-China Comprehensive Strategic Partnership, 20 September 2012, para 17. Available at: https://www.consilium.europa.eu/media/26292/132507.pdf.

[87] Ibid., para 19.

[88] Friedmann (2020), pp. 311–345.

[89] Joint Press Communiqué 15th EU-China Summit, Towards a stronger EU-China Comprehensive Strategic Partnership, 20 September 2012, para 21.

[90] EU-China 2020 Strategic Agenda for Cooperation, Delegation of the EU to China, 23 November 2013. Available at: https://eeas.europa.eu/sites/default/files/20131123.pdf.

both investment protection and market access.'[91] The EU and China viewed the ongoing investment agreement negotiations as one of the most important issues in EU-China bilateral economic and trade relations: 'While welcoming the progress made so far, the two sides are determined to intensify their efforts aiming at the expeditious conclusion of an ambitious and comprehensive Investment Agreement,'[92] which would include investment protection, market access and other elements further facilitating investment. The negotiation teams of both jurisdictions tried to establish the text of the agreement by the end of 2015. Both parties were sanguine that the CAI was only a first step towards a deep and comprehensive FTA.[93] Both parties welcomed the signing of a Memorandum of Understanding on Reinforcing the EU-China IP Dialogue Mechanism,[94] which upgraded the IP Dialogue Mechanism to vice-ministerial level, requested the Dialogue Mechanism to report progress to the EU-China High Level Economic and Trade Dialogue, and set combating online counterfeiting and piracy as a priority.[95]

Signs of disagreements between both parties started to simmer in 2016: at the 18th EU-China summit, Donald Tusk, former President of the European Council, expressed the need to openly discuss the differences between the jurisdictions.[96] In 2017, the European Commission published a sustainability impact assessment of the planned investment agreement.[97] This paper criticized among other things, the level of IP enforcement, forced technology transfer and lack of market access.[98]

---

[91] Statement by President Barroso at the press conference of the EU-China Summit, European Commission, 21 November 2013. Available at: https://ec.europa.eu/commission/presscorner/detail/en/speech_13_959.

[92] EU-China Summit joint statement, The way forward after forty years of EU-China cooperation, 29 June 2015. Available at: https://www.consilium.europa.eu/media/23732/150629-eu-china-summit-joint-statement-final.pdf; China-EU Summit Joint Statement, The way forward after forty years of China-EU cooperation, Mission of the PRC to the EU, 30 June 2015. Available at: https://www.mfa.gov.cn/ce/cebe//eng/zywj/zywd/t1277314.htm.

[93] Ibid., p. 10.

[94] Memorandum of Understanding on reinforcing the EU-China IP Dialogue Mechanism, 29 June 2015. Available at: https://trade.ec.europa.eu/doclib/docs/2015/july/tradoc_153588.pdf.

[95] EU-China Summit joint statement, The way forward after forty years of EU-China cooperation, 29 June 2015, p. 13.

[96] Remarks by President Donald Tusk at the EU-China summit in Beijing, European Council, 12 July 2016. Available at: https://www.consilium.europa.eu/en/press/press-releases/2016/07/12/tusk-opening-remarks-eu-china.

[97] Sustainability Impact Assessment (SIA) in support of an Investment Agreement between the EU and the PRC, Final report, European Commission, November 2017. Available at: https://trade.ec.europa.eu/doclib/docs/2018/may/tradoc_156862.pdf.

[98] Ibid.

Since 11 December 2019, appointments to the Appellate Body of the WTO were blocked,[99] which incapacitated the WTO dispute settlement mechanism.[100] This was probably another incentive for the EU to include provisions in the CAI to address non-market-mediated international technology transfer. In its 2020 resolution on the EU-China GIs Agreement,[101] the European Parliament called for the creation of a parliamentary dimension for the CAI's implementation.[102] The CAI "in principle" was concluded by leaders of the European Council on 30 December 2020. The European Commission qualified it in regard to investments, as the most ambitious agreement that China has ever concluded with a third party.[103] On 23 March 2021, the EU imposed sanctions on four Chinese officials related to alleged human rights violations in Xinjiang province, followed by counter-sanctions from China,[104] which affected Members of the European Parliament, scholars and entities of the EU Political and Security Committee, the European Parliament Subcommittee on Human Rights, as well as two national foundations. The High Representative of the EU for Foreign Affairs and Security Policy, Josep Borell, found this unacceptable.[105] In September 2021, the European Parliament expressed

> concern about the increasing incidence of hybrid attacks, Chinese industrial espionage and cyber theft against European companies; stresses the importance of strengthening private and public cyber capabilities; calls for stronger cooperation and the establishment of a system aimed at ending malicious acts in cyber space on the part of China, including cyber-attacks, forced technology transfers, cyber-espionage and cyber-enabled intellectual property theft.[106]

The European Parliament repeated its deep concern about the many barriers that European businesses face when accessing and operating on the Chinese market,

---

[99] This blockage, when the Appellate Body has been composed of fewer than three members, started on 11 December 2019 and continues (as of 1 December 2021); Report on the Appellate Body of the World Trade Organization, USTR (February 2020). Available at: https://ustr.gov/sites/default/files/Report_on_the_Appellate_Body_of_the_World_Trade_Organization.pdf; Starshinova (2021), p. 787.

[100] Anonymous (2019), pp. 822–831.

[101] Friedmann (2023), pp. 19–20.

[102] Jochheim (2022).

[103] Key elements of the EU-China Comprehensive Agreement on Investment, European Commission, 30 December 2020. Available at: https://ec.europa.eu/commission/presscorner/detail/en/ip_20_2542.

[104] EU sanctions to four Chinese individuals and a Chinese entity on human rights violations; Counter-sanctions by the PRC Statement by the Chair of the Delegation for relations with the PRC, 23 March 2021. Available at: https://www.europarl.europa.eu/cmsdata/231386/03_23_D-CN_Chair's%20statement_Chinese%20counter-sanctions_Uyghurs.pdf. Lau (2021).

[105] Foreign Affairs Council: Remarks by High Representative/Vice-President Josep Borrell at the press conference, EEAS, UNIQUE ID: 210322_20, 22 March 2021. Available at: https://eeas.europa.eu/headquarters/headquarters-homepage/95458/foreign-affairs-council-remarks-high-representativevice-president-josep-borrell-press_en.

[106] European Parliament resolution of 16 September 2021 on a new EU-China strategy (2021/2037(INI)), p. 27. Available at: https://www.europarl.europa.eu/doceo/document/TA-9-2021-0382_EN.html.

declaring that it was 'worried that China's "dual circulation strategy" referred to in its 14th Five-Year Plan will further deteriorate the business environment for EU companies; highlights, once again, its particular concern about the market distorting practices such as, but not limited to, industrial subsidies, the beneficial treatment of Chinese state-owned enterprises, intellectual property theft, forced technology transfers and data localisation, industrial overcapacity in sectors such as steel and the related dumping of exports, other unfair trading practices and the overall increasing political interference in the business environment, including the private sector.'[107]

In September 2021, Minister of Foreign Affairs of the PRC Wang Yi argued that 'bilateral exchanges should be based on mutual respect, seeking common ground while shelving differences, expanding cooperation and reducing antagonism.'[108] Due to the non-ratification of the CAI, its entry into force is delayed indefinitely.

3.2.2 Restrictions for Foreign Patent Holders

Foreign investors in China may not invest in the development and application of human stem cells, or the development and application of genetic diagnosis or treatment technology.[109] China requires approval of the R&D activities conducted by foreign-invested enterprises utilizing biological resources (including human, animal, plant and microbe resources) originated from and protected by China. China also requires the foreign-invested enterprises to conduct the aforesaid activities in the form of cooperation with Chinese institutions, and to share with Chinese partners the benefits generated from such R&D as well as subsequent applications and commercialization. This performance requirement can be considered technology transfer,[110] which, since it concerns biological resources indigenous to China, could be justified if it would allow benefit-sharing with indigenous or local communities (which is not happening in practice).[111] Nevertheless, the European Commission describes China's position in regard to R&D in biological resources optimistically: 'China has not previously committed openness to foreign investment in R&D in biological resources. China has agreed not to introduce new restrictions and to give

[107] Ibid., p. 49.

[108] Wang Yi Co-chairs the 11th Round of China-EU High-level Strategic Dialogue with EU High Representative for Foreign Affairs and Security Policy Josep Borrell Fontelles, Ministry of Foreign Affairs of the PRC, 28 September 2021. Available at: https://www.fmprc.gov.cn/mfa_eng/topics_665678/kjgzbdfyyq/202109/t20210929_9591823.html.

[109] Annex I CAI Entry 18 – Medicine.

[110] Annex I CAI Entry 19 – Protection of Biological Resources.

[111] Nagoya Protocol on Access to Genetic Resources and The Fair and Equitable Sharing of Benefits Arising from Their Utilization to The Convention on Biological Diversity, signed 29 October 2010, and entered into force 12 October 2014. China acceded to it 8 June 2016, and went into effect 6 September 2016. Available at: https://www.cbd.int/abs/doc/protocol/nagoya-protocol-en.pdf.

to the EU any lifting of current restrictions in this area that may happen in the future.'[112]

3.3 *"Imposed" Technology Transfer*

Section II CAI dealing with investment liberalization, and Section III CAI, dealing with the regulatory framework of the CAI, try to level the playing field with the prohibition of forced technology transfers.

3.3.1 Prohibition Against Several Types of Investment Requirements

Art. 3(1)(f) Section II CAI deals with performance requirements: neither Party may, in connection with the establishment or the operation of all enterprises in its territory, impose or enforce any requirement or enforce any commitment or undertaking to transfer technology, a production process, or other proprietary knowledge to a natural person or an enterprise in its territory.[113] A production process can be either protected by a patent[114] or a trade secret, just as proprietary knowledge can be protected as a trade secret. Art. 3(1)(f) and (2)(f) Section II CAI each both refer to footnote 9*bis*, which makes clear that "to transfer" includes to license. However, the requirement is allowed if it is imposed by a court or administrative tribunal or a competition authority to prevent or remedy a restriction or a distortion of competition; or a Party authorizes a compulsory license according to Art. 31 TRIPs, when the Party has the capacity to manufacture the patented good, or if it has not the capacity to manufacture it, to import it, according to Art. 31*bis* TRIPs;[115] or adopts or maintains measures requiring the disclosure of data or proprietary information that falls within the scope of, and is consistent with Art. 39(3) TRIPs.[116] The possibility of using the data or proprietary information of originators' trials to gain approval of bio-equivalent drugs avoids redundant research into safety, quality and efficacy.[117]

---

[112] Key elements of the EU-China Comprehensive Agreement on Investment, European Commission, Press Release, 30 December 2020. Available at: https://ec.europa.eu/commission/presscorner/detail/en/ip_20_2542.

[113] This article is a bit more detailed than Art. 2.3.1 ETA: 'Neither Party shall adopt or maintain administrative and licensing requirements and processes that require or pressure technology transfer from persons of the other Party to its persons.'

[114] Article 2 Patent Law of the PRC (2021) defines "Invention patent" as any new technical solution proposed for a product, a process or the improvement thereof. Article 64(2) European Patent Convention also allows the protection of process patents.

[115] Art. 3(5) Section II CAI.

[116] Spina Ali' (2017).

[117] Spina Ali' (2017), p. 14.

3.3.2 Directly or Indirectly Interfere in Contractual Freedom in Technology Licensing

Actions that interfere in contractual freedom in technology licensing include Art. 3(1)(i) Section II CAI, which prohibits requirements for a given percentage or value of R&D in a Party's territory; and (j) to use or favour technology that is owned by or licensed to a natural person or an enterprise of the Party. Art. 3(2) Section II CAI states that neither Party may condition the receipt or continued receipt of an advantage, in connection with the establishment or operation of all enterprises in its territory, on compliance with any requirement: (e) to use or favour technology that is owned by or licensed to a natural person or an enterprise of the Party; or (f) to transfer technology, a production process or other proprietary knowledge to a natural person or an enterprise in its territory. However, it is permitted to receive such an advantage in connection with the establishment or operation of an enterprise if the requirement is to provide a service, train or employ workers or carry out R&D.[118]

Art. 3(3) Section II CAI asserts that neither Party 'shall directly or indirectly require, force, pressure or otherwise interfere with the transfer or licensing of technology between natural persons and enterprises of a Party and those of the other Party. Such transfer or licencing of technology shall be based on market terms that are voluntary and reflect mutual agreement.'

"Directly or indirectly" goes further than "formal or informally" in ETA.[119] Indirect pressure, is, for example, when it is suggested that a seemingly unrelated business license that has become an insurmountable barrier can be overcome if the foreign partner transfers its technology. "Formal or informal" seems limited to the chosen communication channels.[120]

Art. 3(8) Section II CAI clarifies that the Article is without prejudice to the obligations of a Party under the WTO Agreement, thus including TRIPs and Trade-Related Investment Measures (TRIMs). TRIMs does not cover specifically export performance and transfer of technology requirements that were discussed in the Uruguay Round negotiations. However, since forced technology transfer is inconsistent with the obligation of national treatment provided in Art. III GATT 1994, it is also a prohibited trade-related investment measure.[121] If an investor is required to provide undisclosed information, which is one of the categories of IPRs that need to be protected under Section 7 Part II TRIPs,[122] it would constitute non-market-mediated international technology transfer.

[118] Art. 3(4) Section II CAI.

[119] Art. 2.3(2) ETA.

[120] Ibid.

[121] Art. 2(1) TRIMs. On technology transfer-related performance requirement prohibitions rules under international investment agreements, see Qian (2022), pp. 117–118.

[122] *Supra* n. 85.

3.3.3 Disclosure of Confidential Business Information Collected by Administrative Bodies from Unauthorised Disclosure

Art. 1 Sub-section 1 (Transparency) Section III CAI states no party shall be required to disclose confidential information that would 'impede law enforcement or otherwise be contrary to the public interest, or which would prejudice the legitimate commercial interests of particular enterprises, public or private.' Confidential information includes trade secrets[123] that are not protected via patents, such as early-stage inventions, manufacturing processes and lists of suppliers and clients. Art. 1 Sub-section 2 (Transparency) Section III CAI prohibits the forced disclosure of confidential information, which would prejudice the legitimate commercial interests of particular enterprises, public or private. According to economic liberalism, since trade secrets are private rights, it is up to the owner of trade secrets to decide whether to divulge them or not. If that decision is positive, it is between the private parties to decide a price and the terms of the deal. Thus, the CAI instructs its parties to let the market decide in case of confidential information.

Art. 5(1)(3) Sub-section 2 (Transparency) Section III CAI stresses the need for administrative proceedings to be in conformance to domestic law in respect of the protection of confidential business information. Art. 5(1)(2) Sub-section 2 (Transparency) Section III CAI states that the confidentiality of information obtained during the administrative proceeding, needs to be respected. Art. 5(2) Sub-section 2 (Transparency) Section III CAI makes clear that

> [a] Party shall not require disclosure of confidential business information in authorisation and administrative proceedings, unless such information is necessary to show conformity with the administrative or regulatory requirements governing those proceedings. A Party shall protect the confidentiality of such information.

This provision seems to leave much discretionary room for non-market-mediated international technology transfer, because it does not make clear when an administrative or regulatory requirement is justified.

Art. 2(3) Sub-section 3 (Financial Services) Section III CAI states that no party shall be required to disclose information relating to the affairs and accounts of individual consumers or any confidential or proprietary information in the possession of public entities.

[123] Articles 9, 15, 17, 21, 30 and 31 Anti-Unfair Competition Law of the PRC (2019), protect trade secrets. The EU provides a directive on the topic: Art. 2 Directive (EU) 2016/943 of the European Parliament and of the Council of 8 June 2016 on the protection of undisclosed know-how and business information (trade secrets) against their unlawful acquisition, use and disclosure. OJ L 157, 15.6.2016, pp. 1–18.

3.3.4 Critique of the CAI

Although the prohibition of non-market-mediated international technology transfer is welcome, these provisions lack a monitoring and enforcement system.[124] *A fortiori*, a CAI without an IP section makes the interpretation of the IP-relevant investments more unpredictable. There are several investment agreements that dedicate a specific chapter to IP. For example, the Trilateral Investment Agreement signed by China, Japan, and Korea in 2012,[125] which was the first legal framework between the three East Asian nations aiming to enhance and protect investments between the parties, whilst also paving the way for a potential FTA. The Trilateral Investment Agreement's rules are more ambitious than previous BITs signed by China, as it includes not only commitments on transparency regarding IPRs, but also the protection of these rights. This Agreement also identifies international arbitration as 'the key dispute resolution mechanism for foreign investors.'[126]

4 Conclusion

Since the opening up policy of Deng Xiaoping, a policy of non-market-mediated international technology transfer has waxed and waned. However, in the last forty years, China has transformed itself from developing country to a technology-driven superpower. Therefore, the tipping point might have already occurred when technology transfer becomes an obstacle for indigenous innovation.

In its Accession Protocol, China accepted to not condition any government approval of foreign investment on performance requirements, which includes non-market-mediated technology transfer. Nevertheless, China has turned several times to non-market-mediated international technology transfer, selecting technologies and companies that should excel in these fields; and restricting the access and operation of foreign investment in its territory, by conditioning the approval of foreign investments upon performance requirements, including requirements related to the transfer of technology and the conduct of R&D in China, which is discriminatory and in violation of the National Treatment requirement of Article 3 TRIPs. In addition, China imposed measures that adversely affect the protection of IPRs of foreign companies, which transfer technology into China, including in the context of joint ventures with Chinese companies.

Despite the explicit implementation of prohibition against "forced technology transfer" in both the Foreign Investment Law and amendments to the Administrative

[124] Lee found this to be also the case for the ETA. Lee (2020a), p. 351.

[125] Trilateral Investment Agreement for the Promotion, Facilitation and Protection of Investment, signed by China, Japan and South Korea on 13 May 2012, which entered into force in May 2014 (day unknown).

[126] Sustainability Impact Assessment (SIA) in support of an Investment Agreement between the EU and the PRC, Final report, European Commission, November 2017, p. 26.

License Law, the EU has followed in the footsteps of the ETA, with relevant CAI provisions that are a bit more detailed. The CAI distinguishes three kinds of prohibitions: several types of investment requirements that compel transfer of technology; directly or indirectly interfere in contractual freedom in technology licencing; and disclosure of confidential business information collected by administrative bodies from unauthorised disclosure. However, CAI lacks a monitoring and enforcement system. In addition, the CAI lacks a dedicated Section on the protection and enforcement of IP, unlike ETA, which would help in the interpretation of the scope of the IPRs and enforcement procedures relevant in technology transfer.

There is no adequate empirical support for the idea that a strong IPR regime could enable countries to get access to new technologies. Therefore, it is hard to determine the "Goldilocks zone" of IP protection to promote optimal market-mediated international technology transfer.

References

Anonymous (2019) United States continues to block new appellate body members for the World Trade Organization, risking the collapse of the appellate process. AJIL 113(4):822–831

Correa C, Viñuales JE (2016) Intellectual property rights as protected investments: how open are the gates? J Int Econ Law 19:91–120

Dhar B, Joseph R (2012) foreign direct investment, intellectual rights and technology transfer, the north-south and the south-south dimension, the rise of the south and new paths of development in the 21st century. UNCTAD Background Paper No. 6, 17

Drahos P, Braithwaite J (2002) Intellectual property, corporate strategy, globalisation: TRIPS in context. Wisconsin Int Law J 20:451–480

Frankel S (2019) The object and purpose of mingling intellectual property, trade and investment. In: Geiger C (ed) Research handbook on intellectual property and investment law. Edward Elgar Publishing, Cheltenham UK/Northampton, MA, pp 48–62

Friedmann D (2020) Grafting the old and new world: towards a universal trademark register that cancels generic IGO terms. In: Chaisse J, Dias Simões F, Friedmann D (eds) Wine law and policy: from national terroirs to a global market. Brill Nijhoff, Boston, pp 311–345

Friedmann D (2023) Revitalizing TRIPs as global norm-setter for geographical indications. In: Chaisse J, Rodriguez-Chiffelle CH (eds), The Elgar companion to the World Trade Organization. Cheltenham, Edward Elgar Publishing, Cheltenham, pp 377–396

Grosse Ruse-Khan H (2019) Protecting intellectual property through trade and investment agreements: concepts, norm-setting, and dispute settlement. In: Geiger C (ed) Research handbook on intellectual property and investment law. Edward Elgar Publishing, (Cheltenham (UK)/ Northampton MA, pp 11–47

Jochheim U (20 January 2022) Legislative train schedule, a balanced and progressive trade policy to harness globalisation. European Parliament Research Service. Available at: https://www.europarl.europa.eu/legislative-train/theme-a-balanced-and-progressive-trade-policy-to-harness-globalisation/file-eu-china-investment-agreement

Lau S (22 March 2021) China throws EU trade deal to the wolf warriors, EU-China relations have nose-dived in a showdown over sanctions. Politico. Available at: https://www.politico.eu/article/china-throws-eu-trade-deal-to-the-wolf-warriors-sanctions-investment-pact

Lee J-A (2020a) Forced technology transfer in the case of China. Boston J Sci Technol Law 26(2):324–352

Lee J-A (2020b) Shifting IP battlegrounds in the US–China trade war. Colum J Law Arts 43:147–195

Maskus K (2004) Encouraging international technology transfer, UNCTAD-ICTSD Project on IPRs and Sustainable Development. Issue Paper No. 7

Omer A (2001) An overview of legislative changes. In: Patel SJ, Roffe P, Yusuf A (eds) International technology transfer: the origins and aftermath of the united nations negotiations on a draft code of conduct. London, The Hague and Boston, Kluwer Law International, pp 295–312

Prud'homme D, von Zedtwitz M, Thraen JJ, Bader M (2018) "Forced Technology Transfer" policies: workings in China and strategic implications. Technol Forecast Soc Change 134:150–168

Qian Y (2022) Forced technology transfer performance requirement in international investment agreements—a Chinese perspective. JIPLP 17(2):114–131

QianZ(17October2019)China'snewforeigninvestmentlaw:abackgrounder.ChinaBriefing.Available at: https://www.china-briefing.com/news/china-new-foreign-investment-law-backgrounder

Qin JY (2019) Forced technology transfer and the US-China trade war: implications for international economic law. Int Econ Law 22:743–762

Smith A (1759) The Theory of Moral Sentiments. Available at: https://en.wikisource.org/wiki/The_Theory_of_Moral_Sentiments/Part_IV

Spina Ali' G (November 2017) Article 39(3) TRIPS: understanding the obligations, exploiting the flexibilities. PhD thesis, HKU

Starshinova O (2021) Is the MPIA a solution to the WTO appellate body crisis? J World Trade 55(5):787–803

Danny Friedmann is Associate Professor at Peking University School of Transnational Law in Shenzhen. Friedmann has a PhD in Laws from the Chinese University of Hong Kong; a *Meester in de rechten* (equivalent to LLM including LLB) from the University of Amsterdam; and a BBA from the Nyenrode Business University in Breukelen, the Netherlands. In 2021, he wrote the chapter on Trademark Law and Related Rights (GIs, enterprise and trade names, and domain names) for the 2nd edition of 'Intellectual Property Law in China' edited by Christopher Heath; and co-edited/co-authored the book 'Wine Law and Policy, From National Terroirs to a Global Market, with Julien Chaisse and Fernando Dias Simões in 2020. The book was awarded the OIV prize in 2021. In 2015 Friedmann wrote a monograph called 'Trademarks and Social Media, Towards Algorithmic Justice'. His peer-reviewed articles are published by Asia Pacific Law Review, Journal of Intellectual Property Law and Practice (Oxford University Press), European Intellectual Property Review, Journal of World Intellectual Property, Benelux Trade Marks and Design Rights (BMM) Bulletin and GRUR International. His book chapter on Google and China was quoted by the Advocate General of the Court of Justice of the European Union in *Google Spain* (C-131/12) in 2013. Friedmann researches the intersection between AI and copyright law, trademark law, domain names and GIs, patent law, and ethics and innovative food.

Regulating Subsidies in the EU-China Comprehensive Agreement on Investment: Implications for Global Subsidies Reform

Ben Czapnik

Abstract The use of subsidies is a major irritant in multilateral trade relations and a source of tension between China and its main trade partners. Even though subsidies can be a useful tool in response to major policy concerns, such as the Covid-19 pandemic or climate change, their use can also lead to trade conflicts when they distort trade or negatively affect foreign producers. The EU is at the forefront of efforts to reform global subsidies rules at the WTO, including in ways that directly target Chinese practices, but there are few signs of progress in the multilateral context. This chapter assesses the extent to which the EU-China Comprehensive Agreement on Investment (EU-CAI) contributes to the EU's objectives on subsidies reform. In addition to summarising the EU-CAI agreement's substantive content on subsidies, it inquires whether the agreement effectively addresses the EU's concerns. These concerns relate to the extensive use of subsidies in trade-distorting ways, the lack of transparency about subsidies and the burden on governments seeking to challenge subsidies through WTO litigation or through the imposition of countervailing measures. The EU-CAI negotiations make a marginal contribution to the EU's pursuit of its objectives for global subsidies regulation, but this low-ambition outcome is not surprising in the context of a bilateral agreement focused on investment. While there currently appears to be no realistic pathway for the entry into force of the EU-CAI, the agreement may nonetheless provide some hints about the future direction of global subsidies reform, including at the multilateral level.

B. Czapnik (✉)
National University of Singapore, Faculty of Law, Queenstown, Singapore
e-mail: bczapnik@nus.edu.sg

© The Author(s), under exclusive license to Springer Nature Switzerland AG 2024

A. Svetlicinii, I.-J. Chen (eds.), *The EU-China Comprehensive Agreement on Investment*, European Yearbook of International Economic Law,
https://doi.org/10.1007/978-3-031-66862-3_9

1 Introduction

This chapter assesses the outcome of the EU-China Comprehensive Agreement on Investment (EU-CAI) negotiations with respect to subsidies regulation. It describes the main content of the Agreement and notes some of the key areas of unfinished business. While the EU-CAI could potentially contribute to the investment relationship between the EU and China on some of the topics addressed elsewhere in this volume, this chapter suggests that it represents a low ambition outcome relative to current debates about global subsidies reform. It further explains why this low-ambition outcome is not surprising for a bilateral investment agreement, especially considering the current geopolitical context. Finally, this chapter considers the implications of the EU-CAI Agreement for further subsidies reform in other fora, especially the WTO, but suggests it is difficult to draw too many lessons from the content of this Agreement.

The EU announced that agreement was reached on the EU-CAI in December 2020 and it made the draft text publicly available on its official website.[1] Due to broader political tensions between the EU and China, the Agreement has not been signed and there is little prospect of it being ratified or entering into force in the near future.[2] The Agreement was finalised at a highly unstable time in global politics and trade as the world was coming to terms with the Covid-19 pandemic and the US-China trade war was still simmering (despite agreement on a Phase One deal). To understand the EU-CAI Article on the Transparency of Subsidies, it is important to recognise that, in its relationship with China, the EU is the demandeur for stronger disciplines on subsidies, transparency and, of course, the transparency of subsidies. This is part of a broader trend in global trade regulation, especially at the WTO, where certain leading economies have been pressing for stricter disciplines on the use of subsidies that have harmful trade effects.[3] While subsidies regulation is more than just a Chinese issue, it is clear that China is the 'implied target' of current reform efforts, the reason for the current urgency in global subsidies discussions, and the main party resisting reform.[4]

Since the EU is the demandeur for both subsidy disciplines and greater transparency, this chapter seeks to: (i) assess how successful the EU has been at achieving its objectives; and (ii) identify the implications of the EU-CAI disciplines for global

---

[1] EU-China agreement in principle; https://policy.trade.ec.europa.eu/eu-trade-relationships-country-and-region/countries-and-regions/china/eu-china-agreement/eu-china-agreement-principle_en.

[2] In theory, the EU-CAI could have been the first major step on the road towards establishing a free trade agreement between the EU and China, but this now seems highly implausible.

[3] While the current tensions at the WTO (including on subsidies) are often framed in terms of China versus "the West" or "capitalist countries", it is important to note that concerns about China's conduct also include non-Western and developing countries, as well as countries that support the WTO as a bastion for the rules-based system, regardless of their particular view of free market principles. This chapter seeks to avoid framing the debate as a China v West issue.

[4] Chi (2022), p. 1.

subsidies regulation going forwards. This chapter therefore considers the EU-CAI outcomes from the EU's perspective.[5] It identifies the EU's main concerns with respect to Chinese subsidies, including by reference to its trilateral statements (alongside the US and Japan), its WTO proposals, its general approach to FTAs and the broader literature. While it is not realistic to expect the EU to achieve all or even most of its subsidies-related objectives in EU-CAI negotiations, it is still useful to set out what these goals are. These objectives will serve as a benchmark to show that the EU made little progress towards its broader strategic objectives in EU-CAI negotiations.

2 Global Subsidies Regulation

In recent years, subsidies regulation has become increasingly controversial and politically sensitive at the WTO.[6] Crafting global rules is difficult because, unlike tariffs, which are widely seen as a protective instrument, subsidies can be a first best policy response to certain key policy problems. Over the last 15 years, there have arguably been compelling reasons for widespread government subsidisation in response to world events such as the global financial crisis and Covid-19, or to address pressing global problems such as climate change.[7] This leads to difficult debates about how to draw the line between "good" and "bad" subsidies, especially when programs which pursue legitimate policy goals can be designed in ways which lead to abuse and protectionism.[8] Indeed, it is important to note that many countries which criticise China's subsidy practices are also, themselves, major subsidisers.[9] In order to assess the validity of these complaints, it is therefore necessary to understand how WTO rules regulate subsidies and the implicit value judgments which underpin this regulatory approach.

The basic framework of global subsidies regulation is established under the WTO's Agreement on Subsidies and Countervailing Measures ("Subsidies Agreement" or "SCM Agreement"), although disciplines can also be found in other related Agreements, including GATT, GATS and the Agreement on Agriculture

[5] By contrast, from China's perspective, the lack of new disciplines in the EU-CAI Agreement could be perceived as a successful outcome insofar as it is defensive on subsidies and transparency.

[6] Evenett and Fritz (2021, p. 5) note that the number of subsidies disputes and countervailing investigations has 'increased sharply since 2010'.

[7] In all of these cases, subsidies to services firms were a critical part of the solution, such as the bank bailouts following the global financial crisis.

[8] See, for example, the *Canada FIT* litigation in which Canada's green energy goals were laudable, but the use of local content requirements was highly protectionist without making a valid contribution to Canada's environmental objectives. *Canada – Feed-In Tariff Program* (DS426).

[9] See Evenett and Fritz (2021). This includes major subsidies to their services sectors and through their sub-national levels of government.

(AoA).[10] The AoA regulates subsidies to agricultural products, and the recent Agreement on Fisheries Subsidies (FSA), once it enters into force, will impose new disciplines on subsidies to the fisheries sector that lead to overcapacity and overfishing.[11]

Many key elements of global subsidies regulation were established, albeit with modest disciplines, under the GATT 1947, including transparency, mechanisms for consultation on trade-distorting subsidies, disciplines on export subsidies and rules governing the application of countervailing duties.[12] The framework was further developed under the Tokyo Subsidies Code, but the nuts and bolts of subsidies regulation and the application of countervailing measures were fully developed in the far more detailed and prescriptive SCM Agreement. Art. 1.1 defines a subsidy as a 'financial contribution'[13] from 'a government or any public body'[14] which confers a 'benefit'.[15] With the exception of prohibited subsidies (discussed further below), a Member seeking to challenge a subsidy, in WTO litigation or through a countervailing duty investigation, must also show that the subsidy is "specific" within the meaning of Art. 2.[16]

2.1 Prohibited and Actionable Subsidies

The SCM Agreement draws a distinction between prohibited subsidies and actionable subsidies. The strictest level of discipline applies to prohibited subsidies as regulated under Part II of the Agreement.[17] The prohibited subsidy category, which

[10] See Lester et al. (2018).

[11] The trade-distorting effects of subsidies to the fisheries sector are also covered under the SCM Agreement.

[12] These rules are primarily captured in Arts. VI and XVI of GATT 1947. Subsidies could also be challenged through non-violation complaints where the effect of a subsidy was to nullify the benefit of a negotiated concession. See 1992 GATT Panel—*EEC – Payments and Subsidies to Processors and Producers of Oilseeds* [37/S, 86].

[13] This means that regulatory measures are not covered by the SCM Agreement, even though they may sometimes produce similar effects to a subsidy.

[14] The question of whether state-owned enterprises qualify as public bodies, and under which circumstances, has been a major source of tension between China and those WTO Members that frequently countervail Chinese subsidies, especially the US and EU. This was addressed in the highly controversial *US – AD/CVD (China)* decision (discussed further below); *US – AD/CVD (China) (DS379).*

[15] The question of "benefit" often requires an assessment of whether the government act, such as a loan or purchase, is based on market terms. Art. 14 establishes market benchmarks for different acts, including equity infusions, loans, loan guarantees, purchases of goods or the provision of goods/services.

[16] In essence, the subsidy must be 'specific to an enterprise or industry or group of enterprises or industries' (Art. 2.1). Art. 2.2 further addresses certain types of regional specificity.

[17] SCM Agreement, Part II.

was further elucidated and applied multilaterally to all Members in the Uruguay Round, focuses on subsidies contingent on export[18] or on the use of local content.[19] WTO law requires that Members refrain from granting such subsidies or, where programs have been found to be prohibited in WTO dispute settlement, to withdraw such subsidies without delay.[20] Lester argues that these types of subsidies are prohibited because they are protectionist insofar as they discriminate in favour of domestic producers at the expense of foreign producers.[21] These protectionist subsidies can be distinguished from those subsidies that pursue legitimate social policy goals, but nonetheless raise concerns where they produce trade-distorting effects.

Unlike prohibited subsidies, actionable subsidies are not disciplined based on their design/nature, but rather on the effects they cause.[22] WTO law is essentially concerned with trade-distorting effects on global markets, including any impact on imports/exports, prices or sales for those firms affected by subsidised competitors.[23]

There are two mechanisms in WTO law for challenging actionable subsidies. First, Members can challenge such subsidies through WTO dispute settlement, under the Dispute Settlement Understanding (DSU) as qualified by the specific rules in Art. 7 of the SCM Agreement. If a subsidy is found to cause adverse effects, the subsidising Member is required to either amend its program to remove the adverse effects caused by the subsidy or to withdraw the subsidy altogether. Second, where a subsidy causes injury to a Member's domestic industry, it can seek to impose countervailing duties on subsidised imports in accordance with Part V of the SCM Agreement. This means that Members can take unilateral action, and avoid the need for WTO dispute settlement, provided they comply with the highly prescriptive rules established by the SCM Agreement for the conduct of countervailing investigations and the imposition of countervailing measures. While seemingly less complicated than WTO litigation, countervailing duty investigations are still time-consuming and resource-intensive.[24] WTO law contains highly prescriptive rules

[18] See for example Australian Automotive Leather II (DS126).

[19] See for example Canada FIT.

[20] Art. 4.7. Art. 4 further establishes certain expedited dispute settlement provisions in the case of prohibited subsidies, although these timeframes have proved untenable in certain complex disputes, including the *Airbus* dispute (DS316).

[21] Lester (2011). According to this definition, export subsidies qualify as protectionist if they have a mercantilist or beggar-thy-neighbour character even if, strictly speaking, they do not protect the subsidised firm in its home market.

[22] In simple terms, it may be possible to identify certain types of prohibited subsidy merely by looking to the design of the program. For other types of disciplines, it is usually necessary to observe the real-world effects of the subsidy to know if it is actionable (although some subsidies are deemed to cause adverse effects which shifts the onus onto the subsidising Member to disprove the presence of such effects).

[23] See for example, SCM Agreement, Art. 6.3.

[24] This may explain why many countries do not use trade remedies, although most of the major economies, including the EU and China, have devoted significant government resources to establishing investigating authorities and actively using these types of measures.

that govern the work of investigating authorities and their decisions and processes can be challenged before a WTO tribunal if investigating authorities fail to comply with the SCM Agreement.[25]

Review by WTO tribunals is not limited to procedural questions. They can also question the investigating authorities' methodologies, as famously occurred in *US – AD/CVD (China)* where the Appellate Body ruled that the American method for defining and identifying "public bodies" was inconsistent with WTO law and that it had therefore failed to establish the existence of subsidies in accordance with Art. 1.1 of the SCM Agreement.

2.2 Other Tools in Subsidies Regulation

There are some other useful tools that subsidies negotiators can access when crafting rules. It is possible to create a category of "green light" or desirable subsidies that are excluded from the rules because they have positive externalities or otherwise promote important social policy goals.[26] While the WTO rulebook has adopted certain green light exceptions in the case of agricultural subsidies, it does not contain explicit carve-outs under the SCM Agreement (with the minor exception of "public infrastructure", which is excluded from the definition of a subsidy).[27]

The SCM Agreement originally permitted the provisional application of certain positive exceptions for a variety of reasons (research and development, regional development and environmental protection), but these exceptions automatically lapsed five years after entry into force when they were not renewed by consensus.[28] This means there is no category of *a priori* permitted subsidies under the SCM Agreement, although it is possible to identify permitted subsidies by a process of exclusion if they are neither prohibited nor actionable, for example if they are not specific or do not demonstrably produce adverse effects.[29]

The EU has proactively pushed for the reintroduction of green light subsidies. In its Doha Round proposals it sought to reinvigorate the lapsed Art. 8 green light subsidies and has actively promoted similar exceptions in the subsidies provisions of its FTAs.[30] There is also a scholarly movement pressing for explicit carve-outs under the SCM Agreement, perhaps in the form of GATT-style general exceptions (Art. XX), especially for those subsidies targeting climate change and the environ-

[25] Since the investigating authorities qualify as administrative agencies, these processes and decisions are also frequently challenged in domestic courts.

[26] Of course, Members also negotiate exceptions in the absence of compelling economic or policy reasons in cases where the removal of subsidies programs is simply too politically difficult.

[27] SCM Agreement, Art 1.1.

[28] SCM Agreement, Ar.e 8.

[29] Programs that cause adverse effects may also be tolerated in some cases if there is no constituency pressing for those subsidies to be countervailed or otherwise challenged.

[30] This is discussed by Sekine (2020).

ment, but this has gained little traction among Members.[31] Despite the EU's proactive attempts to reintroduce a greenlight category into the regulation of industrial subsidies, this idea was not pursued in its recent concept paper on WTO reform or in the trilateral statement.[32]

In some cases, rather than requiring empirical proof of the actual effects of a measure, WTO law creates a rebuttable presumption of adverse effects which switches the onus of proof onto the subsidising Member. These types of deeming mechanisms reduce the burden on complaining Members seeking to prove an effects-based claim and thus make it easier to challenge actionable subsidies. Finally, WTO law creates transparency obligations requiring Members to notify their subsidies. It is important to note that WTO obligations on subsidies apply to *Members*, not just to the national government. Subsidy programs managed at the sub-national level, such as by state/provincial governments, are also subject to WTO disciplines and can have significant trade effects.[33]

2.3 Services Subsidies

Historically, the main progress on global subsidies regulation (and trade regulation more broadly) has occurred in the goods space. Subsidies affecting trade in goods have been part of the rulebook since the inception of the GATT. Subsidies rules were relatively modest under GATT 1947 before being fleshed out in the Tokyo Subsidies Code. The crowning achievement in the regulation of industrial subsidies was the SCM Agreement, which introduced detailed, meaningful new disciplines—on both the use of subsidies and the application of countervailing measures—and applied them multilaterally to all WTO Members.[34]

The SCM Agreement does not seek to regulate subsidies to services firms, but the Agreement does mention services. Negotiators were concerned that governments might subsidise their goods-producing firms through the provision of cheap government-supplied services on terms that ultimately gave their firms a competitive edge. This type of subsidy—by the government, through the provision of cheap services, to goods-producing firms—was therefore included within the definition of a subsidy.[35] That said, the rules did not seek to regulate the provision of subsidies to services firms, even if those subsidies had the potential to distort services markets.

[31] See for example Rubini (2012).

[32] Sekine (2020), p. 21. Since the inclusion of a new green light category does not form a pillar of the EU's engagement with China on subsidies, I do not address it in this chapter.

[33] For example Canada—Feed-In Tariff where the subsidy program was maintained by the Province of Ontario.

[34] While some progress has also been made on subsidies affecting trade in agricultural goods, this has generally been a more sensitive topic with weaker disciplines and greater flexibility.

[35] Art 1.1(a)(1)(iii).

When the WTO did finally get around to regulating trade in services in the 1990s as part of the Uruguay Round negotiations that established the WTO, subsidies to services were ultimately placed in the too-hard basket. This issue is addressed under GATS Art. XV, which contains a high-level statement that 'subsidies may have distortive effects on trade in services' but does little on substantive regulation apart from mandating a work program for further negotiations.[36] The GATS does contain some rules affecting subsidies to the services sector, such as transparency obligations and the application of MFN and national treatment rules.[37] However, with respect to substantive disciplines, the WTO has made little progress from the "place holder" arrangements put in place in the 1990s.[38] Members have failed to establish any meaningful rules regarding prohibited or actionable subsidies. Indeed, they have even failed to define what subsidies are in the context of services trade, even though many people tend to rely on the approach in the SCM Agreement as a de facto definition.

3 EU Concerns and Objectives

The frontline in the debate on global subsidies reform is the substantive disciplines, especially those targeting subsidies that produce the greatest trade-distorting effects on global markets. The current debate is largely a response to China's state capitalism model, which supports its state-owned and private firms in ways that were not envisaged when the SCM Agreement was finalised.[39] As Wu observes, the "China Inc" model 'raises a series of new legal questions not found in other economic systems that the WTO has yet to confront'.[40] Leading economies have also been seeking stronger transparency disciplines, largely as a response to China's poor record on notifying subsidies, especially those at the sub-national level, and to the general opaqueness of its regime.[41] This section seeks to describe the EU's overall concerns about Chinese subsidy practices and its main objectives for subsidy reform.

[36] The GATS disciplines on subsidies are discussed in further detail in Part V below.

[37] The precise application to services of GATS non-discrimination rules may vary depending on a Member's scheduled commitments, including sectoral coverage and any limitations which have been inscribed. For a general discussion of how GATS regulates services subsidies, and subsequent discussions in the Working Party on GATS Rules, see e.g., Sauvé and Soprana (2018).

[38] Ibid., p. 600.

[39] Perhaps it would be more accurate to say that it was not envisaged that a party to the GATT/WTO system, which embraced the system's implicit norms about market orientation, would resort to such mechanisms.

[40] Wu (2016), p. 300.

[41] In recent years, the EU, US and others have become increasingly vocal about China's poor notification record, although China is certainly not the only culprit. They have consistently raised this in relevant WTO committees and even by counter-notifying certain Chinese programs. At China's recent TPR, the US expressed concerns about the lack of transparency in China's subsidy programs 'particularly related to aluminum [sic], electric vehicles, glass,

Part of the subsidies-related tension between China and its trade partners relates to broader philosophical differences about the role of government in the market, including China's state capitalism model. The EU and other longstanding WTO Members have both ideological and commercial concerns about how the Chinese government uses subsidies, especially the size and scale of subsidisation practices that seek to foster national champions[42] or promote strategic industries.[43] Indeed, this concern over Chinese subsidies has unified countries who have historically been at loggerheads—in both negotiations and WTO dispute settlement—over how subsidies should be regulated and used in practice.

While some observers suggest that the problem of Chinese subsidies can and should be resolved through WTO dispute settlement,[44] others suggest that the current rulebook is inadequate.[45] There are many gaps in the SCM Agreement: some caused by the difficulties of achieving consensus among heterogenous Members; others caused by the fact that certain underlying assumptions about market orientation were simply taken-for-granted as tacit norms. This leads to a difficult question about whether China's approach to subsidies violates the actual rules of the SCM Agreement or whether it merely violates some sort of amorphous spirit of the Agreement. The answer very much depends on whether the observer believes that Members' obligations derive exclusively from the literal text of the Agreement or whether it is reasonable to adopt interpretative approaches that complement the text by reference to implicit assumptions and tacit norms that promote market orientation.

In Art. XX cases involving moral, health and environmental regulation, the disputes record this century suggests that tribunals do not read market orientation into the WTO Agreements. Decisions in right to regulate cases have become increasingly deferential to regulators in a way that suggests that non-trade values can take priority over the impetus towards greater liberalisation. However, in trade remedies cases, there is a perception that the Appellate Body considers these types of measures protectionist and that it sometimes takes an "activist" approach to promote market orientation by narrowing the scope of their use.[46]

---

shipbuilding, semiconductors or steel'. Bloomberg News (5 November 2021), "China Is Open to Talks on Industrial Subsidies, Xi Says" available at https://www.bloomberg.com/news/articles/2021-11-04/xi-says-china-open-to-talks-on-industrial-subsidies-state-firms

[42] For example, the China World Top Brand Programme and Chinese Famous Export Brand Programme, which were the subject of consultations in China—Grants, Loans and Other Incentives (DS387).

[43] For example, the Made in China 2025 program.

[44] Zhou et al. (2019) argue that the West's objectives can be achieved by litigating under current rules.

[45] See for example Wu (2016), p. 265 where he argues that the unique characteristics of China Inc 'make it difficult to determine certain legal issues under WTO rules—such as whether an entity is associated with the state'.

[46] This is a major concern of the US, including in the highly emblematic series of "zeroing" disputes.

Leaving aside the fierce debate over whether the AB should engage in this type of ideological activism, there is a further technical complication under the SCM Agreement about which interpretative approach actually promotes market orientation. This is because of the difficulty in determining whether it is the act of the subsidising government or of the countervailing government which is the source of "protectionist" mischief. On one hand, the countervailing Member may be perceived as protectionist insofar as its measure restricts the import of foreign products. However, when applied in accordance with the rules, countervailing measures can just as equally be perceived as a legitimate response to a protectionist act by the subsidising government through the granting of an illegal or trade-distorting subsidy.

While this chapter does not have space to enter into the broader debate and jurisprudence, it is worth noting that if the AB's approach is activist and ideological, it appears to perceive countervailing measures as a greater threat to market orientation than the use of subsidies. It has adopted interpretations that increase the burden on investigating authorities and make it harder to establish the existence of a subsidy, most notably in the *US - AD/CVD (China)* dispute, but it does not appear to be taking any activist interpretative steps to promote market orientation by strengthening the substantive disciplines on those Members looking to grant subsidies. In essence, this means that WTO dispute settlement is not really a plausible option for the EU and likeminded countries who wish to challenge China's model by having tacit norms about the use of subsidies affirmed by the AB, or by having vague subsidies disciplines interpreted in a way that promotes market orientation. Even before the AB ceased to be operational, the only plausible pathway for those Members seriously concerned by the effect of subsidies on the multilateral trading system was to pursue a political solution through negotiations, rather than relying on market-friendly interpretations to fill in gaps in the current rules.[47]

The EU is concerned by subsidies that distort capacity in key sectors, including steel, aluminium and solar panels.[48] It is further concerned with the methods that China uses to subsidise its firms, including so-called "foreign subsidies" disbursed outside its territory[49] and subsidies channelled through its state-owned enterprises (SOEs) and state-owned commercial banks (SOCBs) providing cheap inputs—finance, energy, steel—to certain enterprises and industries seemingly based on government policy objectives rather than commercial considerations. This chapter synthesises the EU's demands into four key objectives for subsidy reform, primarily by reference to the Trilateral Statement.

[47] It is worth noting that the EU has recently been taking advantage of some of the ambiguity in the SCM Agreement to take a harder line with China. For example, on the issue of "foreign subsidies" whose legal status is unclear, the EU has interpreted the SCM Agreement to treat such subsidies as covered by the Agreement and therefore countervailable.

[48] Bown and Hillman (2019).

[49] See for example Crochet and Hegde (2020).

First, the EU seeks to impose new substantive disciplines on subsidy practices, including through four new types of unconditionally prohibited subsidy[50] and through an expanded definition of "serious prejudice" to incorporate subsidies that distort global capacity in a given market. Second, the EU seeks to reduce the time and resource burden for Members seeking to challenge actionable subsidies either through WTO litigation or countervailing investigations. It suggests that harmful effects should be deemed in a wide range of new cases, thus shifting the burden onto the subsidising Member to prove that its subsidies do not cause such effects. It further seeks greater flexibility in countervailing investigations to make it easier for investigators to reject in-country prices and rely on third country benchmarks. Third, due to China's practice of using SOEs and SOCBs as providers of subsidised inputs and finance to other firms throughout the economy,[51] the EU seeks to expand the definition of subsidies, specifically by addressing the question of which actors qualify as "public bodies" under the SCM Agreement. This would require Members to negotiate to overturn the outcome of the highly controversial Appellate Body ruling in *US—AD/CVD (China)*, which proposed a narrow definition of public body based on 'government authority' (the exercise of a governmental function) rather than mere 'government control' (through ownership and board positions).[52]

It is worth noting that the regulation of SOEs in WTO law is relatively weak even when dealing with the classic problem of SOEs receiving significant subsidies or other competitive benefits from their home government while competing on global markets. While Chinese SOEs certainly raise these types of issues (addressed in Chapter 5 in this volume), they also raise a unique issue where these firms act to implement the government's strategic objectives, by subsidising other firms rather than seeking to maximise profits. Following the *US—AD/CVD (China)* decision, it has become increasingly difficult for trading partners to use subsidies disciplines to challenge this usage of SOEs which, out of the world's large trading nations, seems unique to China.

Finally, due to China's history of failing to notify subsidies, especially those managed by sub-national branches of government, the EU is a demandeur for stricter transparency disciplines, including real-world consequences for the failure to notify, for example by deeming non-notified subsidies as prohibited.[53] While the

---

[50] These proposed prohibitions relate to both the nature of the subsidy (unlimited guarantees, direct forgiveness of debt) or the nature of the firm/sector where the subsidy is being directed (firms which are not commercially viable in the long term, sectors which suffer from overcapacity).

[51] See Wu (2016, p. 276), who notes state control over pricing of inputs, including electricity, oil, natural gas and water as one key features of China Inc. He further notes that China's Commercial Banking Law requires banks to 'carry out their loan business upon the needs of [the] national economy and the social development and under the guidance of State industrial policies' (p. 303).

[52] This reversed the panel's preferred "government control" standard, which would have made it easier for investigating authorities—in terms of both the legal standard and evidence-gathering workload—by allowing them to rely on indicators such as majority ownership, majority voting shares or majority control of Board appointments.

[53] This would occur where another Member counter-notifies the subsidy. This type of proposal may be hard to implement in practice, especially if there is disagreement about whether a particular

failure to notify does count as a substantive violation in WTO law, Members have little incentive to seek enforcement through formal dispute settlement due to the absence of any meaningful remedies or other consequences which flow from a breach.

4 Content and Gaps

The EU-CAI arguably makes progress, albeit modestly, with respect to both the transparency of subsidies and their substantive regulation. It introduces an obligation for Members to publish the subsidies they provide to a number of key service sectors, including business services, communications, construction, distribution, environmental services, financial services, health, tourism and transport.[54] These transparency obligations are implemented on a most-favoured nation (MFN) basis in that parties must make this information publicly available, thus rendering it accessible to interested non-parties, rather than merely notifying the information privately among themselves. The information to be notified includes the objective of the subsidy, legal basis, form, amount and recipients.[55] This increased transparency may assist the EU or other countries seeking to use their WTO law rights to challenge Chinese subsidies through anti-subsidy investigations or dispute settlement.[56]

The EU-CAI arguably contributes to the substantive regulation of subsidies by further placing new disciplines on subsidies that have or could have 'a negative effect' on the 'investment interests' of the other party. This provision potentially represents a substantive new discipline on subsidies for services firms, but it is unlikely to have much practical legal impact for two key reasons. First, as far as the remedy is concerned, this provision fundamentally lacks teeth. The affected party has procedural rights to 'request consultations' as well as 'additional information', but the Agreement provides little by way of substantive rights. Following these 'consultations, if the affected party 'considers that the subsidy concerned has or could have a significant negative effect', the Agreement merely encourages the subsidising party to use its 'best endeavours to find a solution'. This 'best endeavours' obligation is further weakened by the qualification that the solution must be

---

program meets the WTO definition of a subsidy and is therefore subject to the transparency obligations.

[54] These sectors are "scheduled" as a positive list contained in the Annex to Section III Subsection II Art. 8 (Transparency of Subsidies).

[55] Art. 8(5).

[56] Hufbauer (2021) EU-China investment accord fails to resolve subsidy disputes. https://www.piie.com/blogs/trade-and-investment-policy-watch/eu-china-investment-accord-fails-resolve-subsidy-disputes. Accessed 2 March 2023. Members can only take advantage of this increased transparency if the notified subsidy is of the sort that can be challenged under the current SCM Agreement, i.e. industrial subsidies affecting goods markets.

'considered feasible and acceptable by both Parties' and, importantly, these "negative effects" rules are explicitly excluded from the Agreement's dispute settlement mechanism. Unlike the SCM Agreement's approach to adverse effects, there are no remedies requiring the subsidising party to withdraw the subsidy or remove its "negative effects" nor is there anything which would permit the EU to investigate such subsidies for the purpose of using countervailing duties to remedy any injurious effects.

Second, the content of the provision is defined in an extremely vague manner that will likely ensure that any gains for the EU will ultimately come from using the EU-CAI as a hook for diplomatic engagement. These types of diplomatic mechanisms can be highly effective in some cases, especially in relationships where the EU has significant leverage, but there is a growing perception that extracting value from Agreements with China depends on the presence of clear and enforceable obligations. The concept of negative effects is not defined in the Agreement; while it may share some similarities with the concept of "adverse effects", including "serious prejudice" and "injury", the parties evidently elected to avoid using these predefined terms. This may suggest that the usual indicators and standards within the SCM Agreement do not apply to "negative effects" claims, but it is unclear where else interpreters of the provision (in reality, the parties themselves) could look for guidance on the meaning of this term. If the EU ever sought to take advantage of this mechanism to address the effects of harmful subsidies, it could easily become embroiled in circular debates about the meaning of negative effects, which would only serve to delay any benefit it might obtain from pragmatic negotiations aimed at finding a politically palatable solution.

While the Agreement arguably makes some modest progress in terms of both transparency and substantive disciplines, it contains many gaps relative to the EU's broader strategic objectives on global subsidies reform. Apart from extending the scope of subsidies disciplines to certain services sectors, in a limited way, the EU-CAI does not actually make any meaningful changes to the definition of what a subsidy is.[57] Most importantly, it does not address the meaning of "public body", one of the major subsidies-related irritants between China and its main trading partners. This is in contrast to the EU-CAI's provisions on the liberalisation of investment, which provide a relatively broad definition of state-owned enterprises (referred to as "covered entities" in Section II), including those entities where the government has majority ownership, voting right or board positions.[58] These entities are required to operate on the basis of "commercial considerations", including when selling inputs, and must comply with national treatment obligations with respect to European investors. However, it is important to note that this expansive definition of SOEs has no implications for the operation of the EU-CAI's subsidies provisions or

[57] It is common for the EU to extend the SCM Agreement's definition of subsidies to services in its FTAs, even if it does not extend the substantive disciplines. Sekine (2020), p. 1. This represents some progress compared to the Working Party on GATS Rules which has yet to develop a definition of subsidies in the services context. Sauvé and Soprana (2018), p. 610.

[58] Section II, Art. 3bis (Covered Entities).

for the operation of the SCM Agreement where the definition of public body remains relatively narrow.

Further, the EU-CAI does not produce any meaningful substantive disciplines on the use of subsidies.[59] While it does create a new mechanism for consultation on subsidies that cause negative effects, it does not introduce any new categories of prohibited or actionable subsidies. It therefore fails to reduce the burden on Members seeking to challenge such subsidies either through dispute settlement or countervailing investigations. Although the Agreement creates some explicit transparency obligations with respect to services subsidies, it does not introduce any consequences for non-compliance or incomplete compliance.[60] There are no incentives for the parties to comprehensively provide details of their subsidies to the services sector nor are there any adverse consequences for the failure to do so.

Finally, it is worth noting that the coverage of the Agreement is modest. While it is promising that the parties have started to discuss services subsidies, the exclusion of fisheries subsidies from the Agreement is questionable. After all, fisheries subsidies are normally regulated as industrial (rather than agricultural) subsidies and are therefore covered by the SCM Agreement.[61] It is unclear why EU-CAI treats fisheries subsidies less ambitiously than other types of industrial subsidies, especially when China is such a major subsidiser in the fisheries sector.[62]

5 Explaining the CAI's Low Ambition

The key gaps in the EU-CAI's subsidies provisions, described in the previous section, are not at all surprising. This is primarily because bilateral investment treaties are not a fruitful arena for politically sensitive subsidies reform. This was exacerbated by two other key variables: the fact that subsidies reform (or indeed any meaningful reform to the WTO system) seems highly implausible in the current geopolitical climate[63] and the fact that the Agreement had the somewhat modest

[59] Importantly, the Agreement explicitly excludes the application of MFN and national treatment obligations to subsidies (Section II, Art. 1.4).

[60] Hufbauer (2021) remains sceptical that the EU-CAI's transparency provisions would actually lead to compliance in the form of timely and comprehensive notifications by China.

[61] Indeed, once the FSA enters into force, a case could be made that fisheries subsidies are the most strictly regulated sector at the multilateral level as they are subject to the full force of the SCM Agreement plus additional disciplines (including additional prohibitions) under the FSA.

[62] See for example Hopewell (2020), Chapter 3.

[63] See for example Gulotty (2022). For a broader discussion of the challenge China poses to the WTO as a rules-based system, not merely to its free market principles, see Czapnik and Mercurio (2023).

goal of addressing transparency for services subsidies rather than substantive new disciplines.[64]

The pursuit of these negotiations in a bilateral format between the EU and China was unlikely to lead to meaningful subsidies reform. FTAs are not a particularly fruitful forum for seeking to introduce new, politically difficult disciplines that constrain Members' policy space to grant subsidies. Historically, the EU's early agreements were relatively low-ambition, merely reinforcing the SCM Agreement or creating transparency obligations, but it has recently become more active in pursuing subsidies reform in FTAs.[65] While many FTAs do not necessarily pursue WTO+ obligations, some Members have managed to make modest progress by promoting stricter disciplines on issues such as 'export subsidies, agricultural support, and CVDs.'[66] Indeed, the EU has introduced new prohibitions in its recent agreements with Japan, Singapore and Korea, on issues such as unlimited guarantees and bailouts for insolvent enterprises which lack a 'credible restructuring plan'.[67] This suggests there is some scope to achieve subsidies reform in bilateral agreements, but there are also serious limits on what can be achieved outside of the WTO. The key problem outside multilateral negotiations is that trade-distorting subsidies generally have diffuse global effects and are not limited to a specific bilateral relationship. Unlike tariffs, subsidies cannot be reformed in a targeted and transactional way that only produces benefits among the parties to the Agreement. This is particularly true when new rules will require parties to undertake politically sensitive reforms such as the removal or amendment of existing programs, although agreement can also be difficult for provisions that merely restrict policy space without requiring any immediate implementation. In theory, the parties could negotiate new disciplines that oblige China to withdraw certain trade-distorting programs, but the rest of the world would benefit from these Chinese concession as "free-riders" without having to make any concessions of their own in return. The EU would be the only country "paying" for Chinese reform, but other countries would share equally in the benefits.[68] This difficulty is compounded by the fact that EU-CAI is a mere investment agreement. The EU has been most successful at raising the ambition on subsidies disciplines in FTAs that cover goods trade and therefore build on the robust approach in the SCM Agreement. In the EU-CAI, the focus was on subsidies to services firms

[64] The provision in the final Agreement is titled "Transparency of Subsidies" even if, somewhat confusingly, it also contains some substantive disciplines through the rules on "negative effects".

[65] Sekine (2020). Rubini (2020, p. 458) notes that 'the most developed subsidy and state aid disciplines can be found in the PTAs signed by the EU'. This is in contrast to the US which has generally taken a 'minimal approach to subsidy regulation' (ibid.). It is worth noting that Rubini's survey of FTAs ends in February 2016 and therefore does not capture the US's recent increased aggressiveness on subsidies.

[66] Rubini (2020), p. 458.

[67] Sekine (2020), pp. 18–19. Sekine notes that the EU was unable to achieve the same level of ambition in its FTA with Vietnam.

[68] As Hufbauer (2021) states: 'Taken together, Trump's failed US-China phase one agreement and the CAI show that neither the United States nor the European Union alone has sufficient leverage to sway Beijing to accept effective discipline on subsidies'.

affecting the other party's investment interests. To the extent that this issue still has not been effectively regulated at the WTO, it is not surprising that EU-CAI fails to break any meaningful new ground.

If the EU wishes to change China's approach to subsidies, a more effective method would be to negotiate multilaterally where others, including the US and Japan, would contribute to the heavy lifting by making their own concessions as part of the overall offer to China. This may explain why the trilateral requests from the US, EU and Japan are far more ambitious than the subsidies content of the EU-CAI.

6 CAI and Prospects for Future Subsidies Reform

What does EU-CAI portend for the future of subsidies regulation? It is clear that the Agreement makes little substantive progress on subsidies regulation. This could be interpreted as an indicator that China is not ready to enter into serious negotiations on subsidies. However, since expectations for the EU-CAI were modest, and it was never likely to be the forum where China would seek to make meaningful concessions, this interpretation might be excessive. While bilateral agreements can sometimes serve as "building blocks" for multilateral reform in trade regulation, subsidisation is not the type of issue where progress is typically made by multilateralising preferential arrangements. There appears to be significant fragmentation—perhaps better viewed as bifurcation—in the approach to rule-making outside the WTO. The China agreements—the CAI Agreement and the Phase One deal between the US and China—make little substantive progress on subsidies. By contrast, there are a number of non-China agreements that have started making creative changes to the subsidies rulebook, including the EU-Japan EPA as well as the Comprehensive and Progressive Agreement for Trans-Pacific Partnership (CP-TPP) and United States-Mexico-Canada Agreement (USMCA).

It is hard to tell what the future holds for the new rules being experimented with in non-China agreements. In some cases, the rules seem somewhat "expressive" in nature as, even though they represent the parties' normative views on how subsidies should be used, they require little implementation by parties to the agreement.[69] Sauvé suggests that 'one can only bemoan that such discussions do not engage the countries, chief among them China and other major emerging trade and FDI powers, at which these disciplines appear primarily aimed'.[70] While the EU-CAI barely moves the needle, perhaps some of the other agreements provide better hints regarding the future of subsidies reform, especially the CP-TPP. This is because Vietnam, a country whose economic approach has important similarities with China's state capitalism model, has signed onto the agreement's new subsidies rules. Further,

[69] This is not to suggest they have no effect. After all, legal rules have the effect of constraining policy space even in cases where no implementation is required upon entry into force.

[70] Sauvé and Soprana (2018), p. 618.

China has officially expressed interest in acceding to this agreement, which means it could provide an opportunity to test whether it will be willing to make concessions by accepting new disciplines specifically designed to constrain its current practices.[71] In its statement following the conclusion of EU-CAI negotiations, the EU publicly 'reiterated its expectation that China will engage in negotiations on industrial subsidies in the WTO'.[72] In November 2021, Xi made public statements suggesting that China 'is open to negotiations on subsidies to its industrial firms as well as state-owned companies'.[73] That said, China has failed to take any substantive steps that would suggest that global subsidies reform is realistic in the near term and observers remain highly sceptical.[74]

While the CP-TPP theoretically creates an opportunity for progress on subsidies among a critical mass of key WTO Members, its progress may also be thwarted by American introduction of a "poison pill" into the USMCA that deters parties from entering into negotiations with a 'non-market country'.[75] It is unclear whether Canada and Mexico will be able to engage in meaningful discussions with China, while also seeking to retain USMCA as the basic framework for trade relations with their most important partner. The US/EU/Japan trilateral proposal represents an ambitious opening bid for subsidy reform. So far, it has made little progress, but this is not surprising. Bilateral fora, such as EU-CAI are poorly placed for discussions about these types of systemic reforms. The WTO is the best-suited forum, but it has been hamstrung in recent years by a distinct lack of political will, largely connected to the philosophical differences between China and its main negotiating partners at the WTO.

Meaningful progress will only occur when all these countries are in the room with China in a context where there is political will and a general preparedness by all to make compromises and trade-offs. There are no indications that this will occur in the near future. In the meantime, perhaps the EU-CAI is actually a good indicator about the future of subsidies reform: small, symbolic wins may be achievable, but it looks like all the major issues will continue to get kicked down the road in the near term.

---

[71] That said, due to the complex geo-politics at the moment, it is unclear if China's request will actually lead to meaningful negotiations or accession.

[72] EU Statement Following EU-CAI Signature: https://ec.europa.eu/commission/presscorner/detail/en/statement_20_2546.

[73] Bloomberg News (5 November 2021), "China Is Open to Talks on Industrial Subsidies, Xi Says" available at https://www.bloomberg.com/news/articles/2021-11-04/xi-says-china-open-to-talks-on-industrial-subsidies-state-firms.

[74] Hufbauer (2021, p. 3) states that 'it seems unlikely that China will accept even modest WTO reforms to the SCM'.

[75] Chi (2022), p. 7.

References

Bown CP, Hillman JA (2019) WTO'ing a resolution to the China subsidy problem. J Int Econ Law 22:557–578

Chi M (2022) International regulation of industrial subsidy. J Int Econ Law 26(1):146–153. https://doi.org/10.1093/jiel/jgac052

Crochet V, Hegde V (2020) China's 'Going Global' policy: transnational production subsidies under the WTO SCM agreement. J Int Econ Law 23:841–863

Czapnik B, Mercurio B (2023) The use of trade coercion and China's model of 'passive-aggressive legalism'. J Int Econ Law. https://doi.org/10.1093/jiel/jgac055

Evenett S, Fritz J (2021) Subsidies and market access: Towards an inventory of corporate subsidies by China, the EU and the US. Available at https://www.hinrichfoundation.com/research/wp/trade-distortion-and-protectionism/gta-28-report-subsidies-marketaccess-corporate-subsidies-by-china-eu-us/

Gulotty R (2022) WTO subsidy disciplines. World Trade Rev 21:330–341

Hopewell K (2020) Clash of powers: US-China rivalry in global trade governance. CUP, Cambridge

Lester S (2011) The problem of subsidies as a means of protectionism: Lessons from the WTO EC – 'Aircraft case'. Melbourne J Int Law 12:97–124

Lester S, Mercurio B, Davies A (2018) World trade law: text, materials and commentary. Hart Publishing, London

Rubini L (2012) Ain't Wastin' time no more: subsidies for renewable energy, the SCM agreement, policy space, and law reform. J Int Econ Law 15:525–579

Rubini L (2020) Subsidies. In: Matto A, Rocha N, Ruta M (eds) Handbook of deep trade agreements. The World Bank, Washington DC, pp 427–462

Sauvé P, Soprana M (2018) Disciplining service sector subsidies: where do we stand and where can we (realistically) go? J Int Econ Law 21:599–619

Sekine T (2020) Possibility of developing and expanding the regulation of subsidies through free trade agreements (FTAs): analysis focusing on a trend in FTAs concluded by the EU. Public Policy Rev 16:1–33

Wu M (2016) The 'China, Inc.' challenge to global trade governance. Harv Int Law J 57(2):261–324

Zhou W, Gao H, Bai X (2019) Building a market economy through WTO-inspired reform of state-owned enterprises in China. Int Comp Law Q 68:977–1022

Ben Czapnik is a Postdoctoral Fellow at the National University of Singapore (NUS) where he researches international economic law with a focus on the interaction between WTO law and non-trade policy objectives such as public morals and the environment. He previously worked as a postdoctoral fellow at the Chinese University of Hong Kong (CUHK) on a project addressing China's trade relations including its trade tensions with the US, Australia and others. He was awarded a PhD from the University of Birmingham and has published his research in leading international law journals. He previously served with the Australian government as a trade diplomat and lawyer, including in Doha Round negotiations on subsidies, fisheries subsidies, trade remedies and other rules issues. He has provided legal and policy advice to dozens of countries as a trade policy adviser serving with the United Nations and Pacific Islands Forum. He is admitted to practice as a Barrister and Solicitor in Australia.

Disputing Personal Data in the EU-China Comprehensive Agreement on Investment

Mark McLaughlin

Abstract This chapter analyses the emerging data realms in China and the European Union against the backdrop of the Comprehensive Agreement on Investment (CAI). It examines the link between data protection and investment flows and undertakes a comparative analysis of the PIPL and GDPR. Moreover, this chapter will also analyse the Digital Silk Road in promoting China's model of data sovereignty. While early trade and investment agreements did not consider data relevant for the regulation of cross-border commerce, modern treaties are increasingly cognisant of rules for data protection. As such, the data-related provisions of the CAI will be placed in the context of other international investment treaties that seek to address the regulation of data flows.

1 Introduction

On November 1st 2021, the Personal Information Protection Law (PIPL) of the People's Republic of China entered into force.[1] It is the third pillar of China's emerging data regime, comprising the 2017 Cybersecurity Law, the 2021 Data Security Law, and the 2021 Personal Information Protection Law.[2] The PIPL establishes new rules for the processing of the personal information of Chinese residents, regardless of whether the data processor has a business presence in China. Like the EU's General Data Protection Regulation (GDPR), the PIPL addresses the role of

[1] Personal Information Protection Law adopted by the 30th meeting of the Standing Committee of the 13th National People's Congress of the People's Republic of China on August 20, 2021, full English translation at Briefing (2021).

[2] Cai and Chen (2022).

M. McLaughlin (✉)
Singapore Management University, Yong Pung How School of Law, Singapore, Singapore
e-mail: mmclaughlin@smu.edu.sg

© The Author(s), under exclusive license to Springer Nature Switzerland AG 2024

A. Svetlicinii, I.-J. Chen (eds.), *The EU-China Comprehensive Agreement on Investment*, European Yearbook of International Economic Law,
https://doi.org/10.1007/978-3-031-66862-3_10

data localization, mutual recognition of data protection standards, and the status of individual consent to data processing. Despite these points of confluence, divergences remain in the data regimes of the EU and China that reflect competing and conflicting definitions of sovereignty and security.[3] As the regulation of data, broadly understood, engages matters of free speech, national security, economic development, and technological innovation, this divergence is perhaps inevitable; navigating the data-driven future involves a plethora of value-laden judgements.

Against the background of these emerging data realms, the status of data in international economic law is the subject of renewed scrutiny. Divergent approaches to the regulation of cross-border data flows have implications for the World Trade Organisation and international trade law.[4] Indeed, reformed WTO rules that take account of the privacy, cybersecurity, consumer protection, and services-related policy implications of data flows can contribute to the global regulation of the digital economy. The growing frequency with which data-related provisions are included within investment treaties demands greater attention and is the focus of this chapter.

This chapter examines the nascent data realms in China and the European Union in the context of the Comprehensive Agreement on Investment (CAI). Part 1 examines the link between data protection and investment flows and undertakes a comparative analysis of the PIPL and GDPR. Part 2 offers an account of how the Digital Silk Road may facilitate the development of data sovereignty in recipient host countries. Given its potential to affect investment flows, Part 3 analyses the role of data protection in the CAI. While early trade and investment agreements did not consider data relevant for the regulation of cross-border commerce, the CAI is one of the first to reference data protection. Part 4 will examine how the substantive investment protections of the CAI might interact with data protection regulations. Finally, Part 5 considers whether the exceptions in the CAI are sufficient to address data-related issues.

2 Data Protection, Investment Flows and EU-China Data Regimes

In an increasingly data-driven global economy, the collection, storage, and processing of data generates billions of dollars in cross-border economic activity.[5] For companies like Facebook and Google, data is a source of new growth and the bedrock of their commercial value. Indeed, the business model of many social media companies is to offer data as ‘the product’ to advertisers. Disruptive technologies such as artificial intelligence (AI) also rely upon datasets to train new models, and the applications of AI are proliferating as systems become more advanced. Given the strate-

[3] Tan and Zhang (2021).

[4] Aaronson and Leblond (2018); Mitchell and Mishra (2019); Sen (2018).

[5] Meltzer and Lovelock (2018).

gic importance of high-tech industries, it is perhaps unsurprising that data and data flows are gradually being treated by states as a strategic asset.[6] However, there are also several non-protectionist public policy reasons to restrict the transfer or storage of data. Two are particularly important: privacy and national security.[7]

There is no international consensus on how to protect the online privacy of individuals, nor how to categorise different types of data. Some governments have focused regulatory measures on data held within sectors deemed "sensitive" or "confidential", with health and financial information typically afforded the highest level of protection.[8] A growing number of data protection regimes refer to 'personal data' held by institutions or companies and prevent unauthorised disclosure or place conditions upon transfer. Indeed, data protection as been described as an 'expression of the right to privacy'.[9] Subject to lawful exceptions, these regimes limit the scope of data collection, data storage, and commercial or government surveillance. Concerns have also been raised about the status of ostensibly de-identified metadata that can be reverse engineered to target individuals.[10] The consequences range from the trivial (being targeted by advertising agencies) to the life-threatening (being identified as a dissident in an authoritarian regime).

National security is also cited by governments as a legitimate justification for limiting the cross-border transfer of data or mandating data localization.[11] Disclosures by Edward Snowden about the extent of the surveillance programs operated by the National Security Agency in the US sparked a wave of data protection regimes.[12] To prevent foreign surveillance and protect defence- or military-related sensitive information, states have required that data be stored on local servers within the territory, and prohibited cross-border transfer of data except if strict conditions are satisfied. In theory, these measures prevent unauthorised access or disclosure of information that could compromise national security. As with privacy, there is no common understanding of data that falls within the ambit of national security, nor the most proportionate measures to address these security concerns.

Is this relevant to the investment regime? Does data impact upon cross-border economic activity? In March 2016, consulting firm McKinsey estimated that cross-border data flows generated $2.8 trillion in value in the global economy.[13] According to this evaluation, 'soaring cross-border data flows now generate more economic value than traditional flows of traded goods'.[14] It can be inferred from the value-

[6] Choer Moraes (2019).

[7] Ferracane (2017).

[8] Murdoch (2021).

[9] Bygrave (2014).

[10] Rubinstein (2013).

[11] Giles (2016).

[12] Force Hill (2014).

[13] Digital globalization: The new era of global flows. https://www.mckinsey.com/capabilities/mckinsey-digital/our-insights/digital-globalization-the-new-era-of-global-flows. Accessed 1 February 2023.

[14] Ibid.

generating nature of data flows that these positive economic spill over effects will be absent where such data flows are constrained or throttled by regulation. To that end, data protection regulations may engage the provisions of the CAI, to the extent that that they are designed to reduce or eliminate the barriers to mutual investment.

However, designing data protection regulations involves balancing a diverse and eclectic array of value-laden judgements about fundamental societal questions. That different states hold dissimilar political and social values is not a new challenge in international economic law; modern international instruments are often infused with policy flexibility on moral or security issues. But the emerging data-driven economy poses a challenge to a legal system built to facilitate the cross-border flow of goods. Data flows raise public policy concerns that are more complex than those associated with most traditional traded goods. There is no international consensus on how privacy might be defined or regulated, no international consensus on the legitimacy of state surveillance, no international consensus on the use of AI for public service provision, nor how to detect and prevent algorithmic discrimination in a private setting. To the extent that international law arises from a set of common values, such values remain half-formed and in their infancy in a data context.

The divergent approaches of China and the EU exemplify the distinct yet related ways in which states are constructing data realms consistent with their values.

2.1 The Rights-Based Approach in the European Union's General Data Protection Regulation

The General Data Protection Regulation (GDPR) entered into force in the European Union on May 25th 2018.[15] It was intended to harmonise approaches to data protection among the Member States. Underpinning the logic of the GDPR is the notion that the protection of personal data is a fundamental right of persons. Indeed, the GDPR dovetails with Art. 8(1) of the Charter of Fundamental Rights of the EU and Art. 16(1) of the Treaty on the Functioning of the EU in addressing personal data in the context of fundamental rights. Expressing data protection is such terms is consistent with the rights-based approach contained in the EU's founding documents, and is also consistent with the unique approach to protecting human rights in the European Convention on Human Rights. While the European Court of Human Rights is not an EU institution, they have significant overlapping membership, and the ECHR can therefore serve as an expression of values for those EU Member States who hold dual membership. GDPR regulates the processing of personal data in EU states.[16] It establishes principles for the processing of personal data and rights

---

[15] The General Data Protection Regulation (GDPR) Regulation (EU) 2016/679 on the protection of natural persons with regard to the processing of personal data and on the free movement of such data.

[16] GDPR, Art. 1.

for data subjects, imposes obligations on data controllers and processes, and establishes a framework for the transfer of personal data to third countries. Compliance with the provisions in the GDPR has required investment by local and international firms. Accountancy firm Ernst and Young estimated that the world's 500 biggest corporations are likely to spend a combined total of $7.8 billion to comply with GDPR.[17] Data subjects are afforded the right to know how and when their personal information is collected, what it will be used for, and are empowered to request access to this information.[18] They may insist that their information is corrected or erased and have the right to object to their personal data being used or collected, including as part of automated decision-making.[19]

In addition, GDPR distinguishes between data controllers and data processors, imposing obligations for each. The controller determines the purposes and means of the processing, while the processor implements this processing as determined by the controller.[20] Both the controller and processor are obliged to ensure the security of data, including pseudonymisation, being prepared for a physical or technical incident, and regularly testing security measures.[21] Organisations are obligated to notify authorities and data subjects of potential data breaches, appoint a data protection officer, and ensure compliance with a code of conduct for this officer.[22]

With respect to cross-border data transfer, at the core of the GDPR provisions are two central concepts: adequate protection and consent. Transfer to a third country is only permitted when the Commission has decreed that the level of data protection in the recipient country is adequate.[23] In assessing adequacy, the commission considers: the rule of law, respect for human rights, and relevant legislation; the existence of a functioning supervisory authority to enforce compliance with data protection rules; and international commitments of the third country relating to data protection.[24]

GDPR requires equivalence in national data protection regulation of regular data transfers.[25] Moreover, assessing equivalence in national data protection regulation has proven complex and contentious. For example, the EU approach is focused on the human right to privacy, whereas the US considers privacy a consumer right.[26] In

[17] Ersnt and Young (2021).

[18] GDPR, Section 2.

[19] GDPR, Sections 3 and 4.

[20] GDPR, Art. 4.

[21] GDPR, Art. 32.

[22] GDPR, Arts. 37–39.

[23] GDPR, Art. 45.

[24] Ibid.

[25] Regulation (EU) 2016/679 of the European Parliament and of the Council of 27 April 2016 On the Protection of Natural Persons with Regard to the Processing of Personal Data and on the Free Movement of Such Data, and Repealing Directive 95/46/EC (General Data Protection Regulation), 2016 OJ (L 119) 1 [hereinafter GDPR], Arts. 7 & 44–50; Ryngaert and Taylor (2020).

[26] Aaronson and Leblond, *supra* note, p. 256.

two landmark rulings, *Schrems* and *Schrems II*,[27] the European Court of Justice has found that the "Safe Harbor" agreement between the EU and US and the "EU-US Privacy Shield", each of which asserted equivalent data protection standards, did not provide adequate protection for the fundamental right to respect for private life and GDPR, respectively.[28] In response, the EU and US have since devised a US-EU Trans-Atlantic Privacy Framework to affirm the 'adequacy' of the US system of data protection in respect of GDPR.[29] By contrast to the EU human-rights based approach, China's approach is based upon security considerations.

2.2 China's Securitised Data Protection Regime

Unlike in the EU, personal data protection is not considered a component of fundamental rights discourse in China. The pillars of China's approach to data governance are three distinct but interoperable pieces of legislation: the 2017 Cybersecurity Law, Data Security Law, and the 2021 Personal Information Protection Law. Data governance in China is a multi-ministerial affair. The most important ministries to oversee the process are the Ministry of Public Security, Ministry of Industry and Information Technology, and Cyberspace Administration of China.[30] Collectively, these stage agencies are responsible for ensuring that the relevant rules and regulations are implemented.

The Cybersecurity Law was promulgated in 2017.[31] It requires 'territorial data localization': companies operating in China must store data collected in China on local servers. Firms that store or process "personal information", including financial and health information relating to a natural person, and "important data", broadly defined as relating to national security, economic security, or social stability, must store the data on servers located in mainland China. In particular, companies deemed to be "critical information infrastructure" that operate in certain sensitive sectors must store data on local servers.

In addition to data localization requirements, the Cybersecurity Law imposes strict conditions for the transfer of data outside mainland China. It must be 'necessary for business needs' and undergo a system of official approval after a security assessment. While Chinese officials have explained that the system is to determine

---

[27] Case C-362/14 Maximillian Schrems v. Data Protection Commissioner [2015]; Case C-311/18 Data Protection Commissioner v. Facebook Ireland Ltd and Maximillian Schrems [2020].

[28] Tracol (2020).

[29] United States and European Commission Announce Trans-Atlantic Data Privacy Framework. https://www.whitehouse.gov/briefing-room/statements-releases/2022/03/25/fact-sheet-united-states-and-european-commission-announce-trans-atlantic-data-privacy-framework/.

[30] Gao (2021).

[31] Standing Committee of the National People's Congress, 2016 Cybersecurity Law (7 November 2016).

whether data 'endanger[s] national security or social and public interests', its precise scope is not provided within the legal framework. Draft guidelines refer to relevant factors within the process of security review as: the type and sensitivity of data, the system of data protection operated by the recipient, and the legal environment of the country in which the recipient is domiciled.

This preference for guidelines and clarifications reflects a broader ambiguity about the scope of caught entities under China's data governance framework. Firms deemed part of the "critical information infrastructure" cover broad swathes of the economy, including finance, transport, internet service provision, energy, and telecommunications networks. Each government department has the discretion to identify further firms or industries deemed to be involved in critical information infrastructure.

Just as important as the fact that firms must store data locally is the prescription of who they must store it with. Servers located in China must be controlled by Chinese entities. It is prohibited for foreign investors to own and operate cloud computing services without a local partner owning at least 50% of the venture.

Alongside the Cybersecurity Law, the PIPL came into force in 2017, which introduces provisions consistent with existing legislation, while adding some GDPR-like elements. Since the PIPL entered into force, data localization remains a central aspect of data governance in China. Unlike the GDPR, the PIPL does not distinguish between data controllers and data processors. The term of art used in the PIPL is 'personal information handlers',[32] which refers to those that decide on the 'collection, storage, use, processing, transmission, provision, disclosure, [and] deletion'.[33] The processing or storage of personal information must be consistent with regulations promulgated by the Cyberspace Administration of China (CAC). The PIPL dovetails with the Cybersecurity Law in imposing duties on 'critical information infrastructure operators' to seek approval before transferring data outside China, after which the request will undergo a safety assessment.[34] However, this may be foregone if there is a relevant exemption in domestic law and/or the business has utilized a standard contract (formulated by the CAC) underpinning the data transfer arrangements.

Indeed, when a business must regularly utilize cross-border data transfer as part of their ordinary activities, they may seek to obtain a personal information protection certificate from a specialized body according to the regulations of the CAC.[35] This process, whereby Chinese authorities vet the standards of data protection in recipient countries is akin to the EU "adequacy decision" in the GDPR. Even in such cases whereby a foreign judicial or law enforcement entity submits a request

[32] PIPL, Art. 51.

[33] PIPL, Art. 4.

[34] PIPL, Art. 40.

[35] PIPL, Art. 38.

pertaining to personal data, the relevant local authorities will decide in accordance with the principles of equality and mutual benefit.[36]

If stringent data localization measures become a fixture of legislative frameworks around the world, populous nations may view restrictions on cross-border data transfer as vehicles through which to advantage their comparative advantage. The challenge has been described as one of 'geoeconomics', whereby data is controlled as a strategic asset.[37] Requiring data localization and imposing conditions on data transfer are the primary instruments of Chinese data sovereignty. Indeed, China has assumed an increasingly influential role in the formation of transnational data governance standards through engagement with international organizations and the Digital Silk Road.[38]

3 The Digital Silk Road and Chinese Digital Infrastructure as a Route to Chinese Data Sovereignty

Unlike the treaty-centric approaches of the US and EU, China's approach focuses on internet governance institutions.[39] At the forefront of these efforts are participation specialized institutions such as the Internet Engineering Task Force, the International Telecommunication Union, and more general institutions like the Asian Infrastructure Investment Bank and the UN.[40] At each level, Chinese representatives promote the concept of data sovereignty and cyber sovereignty. Indeed, in late 2020, China promoted the Global Initiative on Data Security, which includes an undertaking to 'respect the sovereignty, jurisdiction and governance of data of other States, and shall not obtain data located in other States through companies or individuals without other States' permission'.[41] The Digital Silk Road is an important pillar of the effort to further the concept of data sovereignty. Erie and Streinz have highlighted three interrelated ways in which the Digital Silk Road supports Chinese influence in molding data governance standards in recipient countries: provision of digital infrastructure components, Chinese companies acting as 'infrastructural agents', and the DSR's legal and governance framework.[42] Each of these will be addressed in turn.

---

[36] PIPL, Art. 41.

[37] Roberts et al. (2019).

[38] Erie and Streinz (2021).

[39] Tao (2019).

[40] Erie and Streinz (2021).

[41] Ministry of Foreign Affairs of the People's Republic of China, 'Global Initiative on Data Security', https://www.fmprc.gov.cn/mfa_eng/zxxx_662805/t1812951.shtml (visited 20 July 2021).

[42] Erie and Streinz (2021).

To fulfil the promise of "connectivity" and the "information Silk Road", China is the primary supplier of physical components of digital infrastructure for BRI projects. This includes cross-border optical cables, sea cable infrastructure, terrestrial cables, internet satellites, and internet exchange points.[43] Numerous projects have been initiated to integrate these physical components into host state infrastructure across Africa, Asia, and the Middle East. As a consequence, the platforms that comprise that digital domain in countries involved in the DSR are Chinese-designed and Chinese-built.[44] The accompanying default protocols are set by the companies that install and maintain them. As such, the influence of China's standards that are set domestically can extend beyond Chinese borders.

Unlike the more traditional forms of infrastructure like ports and airports, DSR projects are implemented by enterprises that are not always owned by the state. The leading companies in the furtherance of the DSR are Huawei, Alibaba, Tencent, and ZTE.[45] As the foremost providers of telecommunication networks within China, state-owned enterprises China Unicom, China Mobile and China Telecom also have an increasing number of branches along the BRI. However, it can be difficult to disentangle public and private enterprises in the Chinese context.[46] Indeed, under the State-Owned Assets Law, it is the function of the state to participate in major decision-making and contribute to the selection of management.[47] Even with privately-owned companies, it has been suggested that analysis of state control must move "beyond ownership", and that we must instead examine the extent of "state capture" of enterprises.[48] In a DSR context, Alibaba has been involved in launching the Malaysian Digital Free Trade Zone;[49] Hauwei is one of the world's leading suppliers of surveillance equipment; and ZTE has a presence in over 53 BRI states.[50] The export of Chinese technology that is maintained by Chinese companies along the DSR helps to align approaches to data governance.

Finally, mechanisms of cooperation have been embedded within the legal and governance framework of the DSR that will help to further the reach of data sovereignty. Perhaps the most prominent is the Belt and Road Digital Economy International Cooperation Initiative, which, alongside moves to improve broadband and further digital transformation, includes commitments on respect for cyber sovereignty and security concerns.[51] Memoranda of Understanding have been concluded

---

[43] Kelkar (2018).

[44] He (2022).

[45] Triolo (2020).

[46] McLaughlin (2019).

[47] Art. 12, Law of the People's Republic of China on the State-owned Assets of Enterprises (promulgated by the Standing Comm. National People's Congress, October 28, 2008, effective May 1, 2009), http://www.lawinfochina.com/Display.aspx?lib=law&Cgid=109891.

[48] Milhaupt and Zheng (2015).

[49] Neilson (2022).

[50] Feldstein (2019).

[51] State Council Information Office, 'Initiative on Belt and Road digital economy cooperation launched', http://english.scio.gov.cn/beltandroad/2017-12/04/content_50084315.htm.

between China's Ministry of Industry and Information Technology and equivalent government agencies Cambodia, Iran, Bangladesh, and Afghanistan, and China has concluded a further agreement with ASEAN on Cooperation in Information and Communications Technology.[52] Many of the existing projects relating to the construction of digital infrastructure have such agreements as their foundation. As with other areas of the BRI, the mechanisms and relationships established through these documents are explicitly cooperative and non-binding.[53] They provide the conditions for equivalent approaches to data governance without mandating harmonization.

In light of these three features of the DSR, there is considerable potential for the growth of China's model of data sovereignty as a prominent method of data governance. As such, it is pertinent to examine the extent to which data localization measures and restrictions on cross-border data transfer are compatible with investment obligations with agreements in host countries. To the extent that such regulations in the EU and China affect foreign investors, they do not exist in a regulatory vacuum. Measures should be viewed in the context of the investment and trade obligations to which all parties have acceded. To that end, the Comprehensive Agreement on Investment has several provisions that take into account data-related measures.

4 Data-Related Provision in the CAI

Traditionally, investment treaties did not address data, nor explicitly consider data protection as an element of any obligations to investors. As the first BIT was concluded in 1959, its absence in BITs that precede the digital age is unsurprising. However, one might have expected the regimes of international economic law to be more explicit in constructing data regimes in light of the value-generating effects of cross-border data flows. The investment regime has been slow to accommodate or address data within international instruments. More recent treaties suggest an emerging trend towards recognising the role of data as an element of investment protection. The CAI is part of this trend. Two elements of the CAI directly reference data protection: the treaty objectives and the exceptions clause.

[52] 'MoU Between The Association Of Southeast Asian Nations And The People's Republic Of China On Cooperation In Information And Communications Technology', https://asean.org/?static_post=memorandum-of-understanding-between-the-association-of-southeast-asian-nations-and-the-people-s-republic-of-china-on-cooperation-in-information-and-communications--technology. Accessed 19 July 2021.

[53] Wang (2019).

4.1 Data Protection as Expressly within a State's 'Right to Regulate'

Within Section 1 on the 'Objectives and Definitions' of the CAI, Art. 1 expressly provides the objectives of the agreement. It provides that

> [t]he Parties reaffirm the right to regulate within their territories to achieve legitimate policy objectives, such as the protection of public health, social services, public education, safety, the environment, including the fight against climate change, public morals, social security or consumer protection, ***privacy and data protection*** or the promotion and protection of cultural diversity.[54] *(emphasis added)*

While this provision does not impose positive obligations on either state, nor create additional rights for investors, it does demonstrate that privacy and data protection were expressly considered by Contracting Parties when crafting the CAI. Most notably, however, it will be relevant for interpreting otherwise ambiguous treaty provisions. The Vienna Convention on the Law of Treaties (VCLT) provides customary rules of interpretation for public international law.[55] Art. 31 provides that a treaty shall be interpreted in good faith in accordance with its ordinary meaning 'in their context and in the light of its object and purpose'.[56] Crucially, the object and purpose is to be determined by considering its context, comprising its texts and preamble.[57] In this regard, reference to data may be prove influential if and when adjudicators consider whether data and data flows are protected investments under the CAI.

4.2 Data Protection Regulations as Exceptions from Investment Treaties

Secondly, Section VI of the CAI contains the 'Institutional and Final Provisions', within which are explicit exceptions. Alongside orthodox provisions on measures necessary for the maintenance of public order or the protection of human animal and plant life, Art. 4 notes that

> [N]othing in [the CAI] shall be construed to prevent the adoption or enforcement by either Party of measures…necessary to secure compliance with laws or regulations which are not inconsistent with the provisions of this Agreement including those relating to… ***the protection of the privacy of individuals in relation to the processing and dissemination of personal data and the protection of confidentiality of individual records and accounts.***[58] *(emphasis added)*

---

[54] CAI, Section 1 'Objective and Definitions', Art. 1.

[55] Vienna Convention on the Law of Treaties (1969), Art. 31.

[56] Ibid., Art. 31(1).

[57] Ibid., Art. 31(2).

[58] CAI, Section VI, Institutional and Final Provisions, Art. 4.

As with their inclusion in the preamble, privacy and data protection are referenced again in the section of the CAI dealing with general exceptions. As such, this may be another element in favour of concluding that data is protected under the CAI, and forming part of the 'context' crucial to treaty interpretation under the VCLT. However, the practical effect of this provision is blunted by the qualifier that it shall only apply to measures that are 'not inconsistent with the provisions of this agreement'. It is unlikely that this drafting creates more regulatory space for states than would exist in its absence. Nevertheless, it does affirm that regulations directed at the protection of data or privacy are not *prime facie* violations of the CAI. This may be relevant in the context of claims of potential breach.

4.3 Could EU or Chinese Data Protection Regulations Breach CAI Provisions?

Assessing the extent to which the data regimes of China and the EU comply with the CAI requires three steps: to establish data as a protected investment under investment treaties, to apply substantive investment protection standards to the respective data protection regulations, and then consider whether such measures fall within the scope of elaborated general exceptions or excluded sectors. There is no mechanism for investor-state dispute settlement in the CAI. Section V provides the rules of procedure and code of conduct for arbitrators and mediators which will be applicable in the case of a state-state dispute.[59]

4.4 Is Data an Investment Under the CAI?

As a first step, the CAI does not expressly mention data within a definition of investment. If the data flows or digital infrastructure include a physical component, such as a data storage center in the territory of a host state or fiberoptic cables, this comfortably falls with the scope of the CAI.[60] Indeed, the tribunals in *PSEG Global v Turkey*[61] and *MCI Power Group LC v Ecuador*[62] did not consider it necessary to engage in a comprehensive analysis of investment activity where the investment

[59] CAI, Section V 'Dispute Settlement', Art. 6.

[60] Gordon and Pohl (2015).

[61] PSEG Global Inc., The North American Coal Corporation, and Konya Ilgin Elektrik Üretimve Ticaret Limited Sirketi v. Republic of Turkey, ICSID Case No. ARB/02/5 Decision on Jurisdiction, 4 June 2004 para 114.

[62] MCI Power Group L.C. and New Turbine, Inc. v. Republic of Ecuador, ICSID Case No. ARB/03/6, Award, 31 July 2007 para 165.

was 'readily recognizable'.[63] On this basis, the straightforward case of a data storage center is likely to be considered a protected investment. However, the status of data itself is uncertain.

The role of data in international economic law is contested. This is reflective of a broader ambiguity about the classification of data within legal systems and economic theory.[64] Regulatory structures are not keeping pace with technological advancements, and the value being ascribed to assets is failing to take account of data-intensive economic activity. The legal status of data in domestic legal systems remains fluid.[65] There are at least two cases in which 'Big Data' will be subject to property rights: the Shenzhen SEZ Data Regulation and the Shanghai Data Regulation.[66] In criminal trials in the Netherlands and Germany, courts have found that data can be 'stolen' suggesting property-like rights.[67] And yet, in most jurisdictions, data subjects are the only beneficiary of legal protections in data, but these protections stop short of ownership. They include rights of access, deletion, and correction.

The definition of investment within investment treaties typically requires the existence of 'every kind of asset'. The phrase 'every kind of asset' is followed by a non-exhaustive list of covered assets that includes intellectual property and other intangibles, such as concessions and mortgages, liens and pledges. It is unlikely that data alone will qualify as protected intellectual property as it lacks the human creativity or intellectual effort required for copyright or patent. Similarly, to meet the characteristics of an investment, there are additional criteria that must be satisfied. Commonly referred to as the "Salini criteria", these involve a contribution of money or assets, over a certain duration, and assumption of risk.[68]

The application of these tests will be highly context specific but may be difficult to meet for data-only disputes that do not involve accompanying infrastructure. For example, it is difficult to establish a contribution of capital and assumption of risk if data is merely collected in the territory from a third territory. Moreover, datasets are rarely owned by the companies that use them but merely controlled. With respect to the GDPR and PIPL, they are designated "data controllers" or "data processors" respectively. As most of the case law that interprets the phrase "owned or controlled" in investment treaties relates to shareholder claims for reflective loss, it is unclear if the tests of "legal capacity to control" data will be sufficient to meet the gateway provisions of investment agreements, including the CAI.[69]

[63] OECD, *Definition of Investor and Investment in International Investment Agreements*, 17 March 2008.

[64] Ritter and Mayer (2018); Drexl (2016).

[65] Ritter and Mayer (2018).

[66] See Huang (2022).

[67] van Erp (2017); Hoeren (2014).

[68] Salini et al. v. Morocco, ICSID Case No. ARB/00/4, Decision on Jurisdiction, 152 (Jul. 23, 2001), 42 I.L.M. 609 (2003) para 52.

[69] Aguas del Tunari v. Bolivia ICSID, Decision on Respondent's Objections to Jurisdiction para 264.

Passing through this gateway will be more straightforward when the data has accompanying physical infrastructure or tangible investment. For example, if a social media company establishes sales offices in a new jurisdiction, engages in a marketing campaign, and invests in translation services to ready their platforms for a new jurisdiction, this data-adjacent investment may be sufficient for the purposes of *ratione materiae*.[70] Most notably, in the case of the CAI, privacy and data protection are expressly referenced in both the 'objectives' of the CAI and in the sections relating to general exceptions. In accordance with VCLT Art. 31, these provide persuasive context for interpreting "investment" as including data. Therefore, data and data flows would be included within the ambit of protection in the CAI and thus subject to the same substantive protections as other assets. One such substantive protection is the prohibition on performance requirements.

4.5 Data Restrictions and CAI Article 3: Performance Requirements

A performance requirement is the obligation upon an investor to purchase a certain percentage of content locally, hire a certain percentage of local workers, or transfer intellectual property into the territory as a prerequisite of admission to a host state.[71] At the heart of classical economic theory lies the idea that market forces reigned supreme; government measures that interfered with commercial decision-making by requiring a company to transfer their technology would undermine each states' comparative advantage. As such, performance requirements became regarded as barriers to foreign investment and were prohibited in IIAs, the Agreement on Trade-Related Aspects of Intellectual Property Rights (TRIPs), and Agreement on Trade-Related Investment Measures (TRIMs).[72] These regulations are often a point of contention between developing and developed states, with the former arguing that they are necessary to maximize the economic benefit of foreign investment, and the latter claiming that such measures design out the international comparative advantage at the core of economic liberalism. CAI prohibits performance requirements in Art. 3:

> Neither Party may, in connection with the establishment or the operation of all enterprises in its territory, impose or enforce any requirement or enforce any commitment or undertaking:
>
> …(c) to purchase, use or accord a preference to goods produced or services provided in its territory, or to purchase goods or services from natural persons or enterprises in its territory;

[70] Horváth and Klinkmüller (2019), p. 613.

[71] See Genest (2019), p. 52.

[72] Ibid., pp. 16–29.

> …(f) to transfer technology, a production process, or other proprietary knowledge to a natural person or an enterprise in its territory.

Data localization measures, such as those contained in China's Cybersecurity Law or Personal Information Protection Law may represent a prohibited local content requirement, as it requires the foreign investor to use a local server. However, there is a significant difference between the EU and China in this regard. The EU does not require data localization, whereas China's data regime does (this may be prohibited by sections (c) and (f) of the CAI as highlighted above). To constitute a requirement, the tribunal in *Mobil & Murphy v Canada.* ruled that the measures had to demonstrate a 'degree of legal obligation' and a 'degree of compulsion'.[73] If storing data locally is presented as a condition of entry or expansion, the absence of which would result in civil or criminal penalties, this would constitute the legal compulsion envisioned in *Mobil* and other cases. The extensive series of penalties contained in the CSL and PIPL would likely be sufficient to establish the necessary degree of compulsion. Therefore, data localization requirements consistent with the Chinese model may breach the provision.

4.6 Data Restrictions and CAI Art. 4: National Treatment

European or Chinese investors may also seek to challenge the data restrictions or regulations as discriminatory measures. Art. 4 of the CAI embeds the principle of non-discrimination in a national treatment provision:

> Each Party shall accord to investors of the other Party and to covered enterprises treatment no less favourable than the treatment it accords, in like situations,* to its own investors and to their enterprises, with respect to establishment and operation in its territory.
>
> *For greater certainty, whether the treatment is accorded in 'like situations' requires a case-by-case, fact-based analysis.

Several investment tribunals have adopted a three-stage test for assessing compliance with national treatment obligations: identifying the appropriate comparator, examining whether the challenged measure constitutes treatment less favorable, and considering if the measure can be justified by non-protectionist public policy.[74] However, the application of these tests is neither consistent nor predictable across investment jurisprudence. Most of the cases involving national treatment obligations occur in the particular context of NAFTA Chapter 11 claims, and each case requires individualized assessment.

---

[73] Mobil Investments v Canada (I), ICSID Case No. ARB(AF)/07/4, Decision on Liability, (22 May 2012) para. 233–234.

[74] Mitchell et al. (2016).

Identifying the appropriate comparator, or an investor in 'like circumstances/situations', is a central issue in many national treatment cases.[75] The CAI provides that tribunals should proceed via 'case-by-case, fact-based analysis'. This is consistent with the approach of many tribunals, which have insisted that they are 'context dependent and have no unalterable meaning across the spectrum of fact situations'.[76] This enquiry necessitates consideration of the regulatory context in which the foreign investor and purported comparator operate. In *SD Myers v Canada*, the tribunal adopted a sector-based approach in finding that an appropriate comparator for SD Myers was the Canadian waste disposal industry. The existence of a competitive relationship was central to the decision. Similarly, the tribunal in *UPS v Canada* found that Canada's Publications Assistance Program, which subsidises Canada Post, did not violate national treatment obligations as Canada Post could deliver to any address in Canada, while UPS could not.[77] Therefore, they were not in like circumstances. Identification of the appropriate comparator is not isolated from the alleged violative treatment; they are inherently intertwined. For example, the tribunal in *Champion Trading Co v Egypt* denied that local cotton producers were an appropriate comparator for cotton-producing Champion Trading, because the local cotton producers had sold their product in government-owned collection centers at a fixed price, whereas Champion trading had not.[78] Economic sector is a guiding but not a determinative factor.

For claims involving data regulations in China and the EU, the appropriate comparator would be determined in accordance with other investors operating in the sector and the regulatory context of the measure. Claimants must be able to identify local investors with whom they are competing that are treated differently due to the impugned measure. As currently drafted, neither GDPR nor China's triumvirate of data protection regulations *de jure* distinguish between data controllers and data processors in order to establish data sovereignty.

The second phase of the analysis of a national treatment claim under CAI is assessing whether the regulations constitute treatment less favorable than the domestic investor. Tribunals have taken different approaches to whether the national treatment obligation prohibits only nationality-based discrimination, or whether a differential impact will be sufficient to establish a breach. The tribunal in Siemans v Argentina, for example, adopted the latter approach in concluding that 'the impact of the measure on the investment would be the determining factor'.[79]

---

[75] Nykomb Synergetics Technology Holding AB v. Latvia,Stockholm Chamber of Commerce, Award, December 16, 2003, 34; Consortium RFCC v. Morocco, ICSID Case No. ARB/00/6, Award, December 22, 2003, para. 53.

[76] Pope & Talbot Inc. v. Canada, UNCITRAL, Award on the Merits of Phase 2, April 10, 2001, para. 75.

[77] United Parcel Service of America, Inc. v. Canada, UNCITRAL, Award, May 24, 2007, para. 99.

[78] Champion Trading Co. et al. v. Arab Republic of Egypt, ICSID Case No. ARB/02/9 (Award) (Oct. 23, 2006), paras. 131, 155–156.

[79] *Siemens AG v The Argentine Republic* [2007] ICSID ARB/02/8, Award [321].

If a tribunal applied a simple test of disparate impact to the EU and Chinese data regulations, there are circumstances in which there may be a breach of national treatment. The costs of compliance with data localization requirements for data storage or cloud services may incur additional costs by being obligated to construct or rent space on local servers that would not otherwise be required due to their existing capacity in other jurisdictions. By contrast, local providers of such services may have the infrastructure in place and not incur additional costs. This analysis may equally be applied to the requirement of an adequacy decision (EU) or security review (China) before transferring data overseas. If the personnel that manage and analyze the data are based overseas, the absence of an adequacy decision or approval for transfer may have a disparate impact on foreign firms than domestic firms.

However, much of the literature argues against the test of disparate impact in favor of an approach that requires some protectionist intent.[80] Consistent with the historical development of national treatment obligations, this finds some support in case law. The tribunal in *GAMI* concluded that '[i]t is not conceivable that a Mexican corporation becomes entitled to the anti-discrimination protections of international law by virtue of the sole fact that a foreigner buys a share of it.'[81] Differential impact alone was insufficient. The position was made explicit in the *Loewen* award, stating that national treatment 'proscribes only demonstrable and significant indications of bias and prejudice on the basis of national origin'.[82] By this standard, claimants would have to prove that the data protection regulations target their investments on the basis of their nationality. As drafted, neither the Chinese nor EU regulations distinguish between local data processors or foreign data processors. Investors would be unable to rely on *de jure* discrimination to advance their claim. In certain circumstances, it may be possible that the specific, *de facto* implementation of the GDPR, Cybersecurity Law, Data Security Law, or Personal Information Protection Law was violative, but this would be highly context-specific.

The final stage of analysis is to consider whether the data protection regulations can be justified by reference to non-protectionist public policy. This is by no means a universal approach within arbitral awards. Older generations of IIAs make no exceptions for public policy, and thus some arbitrators have considered public purpose at point of obligation.[83] In *Feldman v Mexico*, the tribunal considered whether rational public policy could justify different treatment for foreign and domestic investors.[84] Data protection measures in the Chinese model vary according to the stated importance to national security. In fact, the security-focused orientation of the Chinese model is apparent throughout the legislation. National security is a well-established public policy exception within non-precluded measures provisions.

[80] Kurtz (2015).

[81] GAMI Investments Inc. v. Mexico, UNCITRAL, Final Award, November 15, 2004, para. 115.

[82] The Loewen Group Inc. & Raymond L. Loewen v. United States, ICSID Case No. ARB(AF)/98/3, Award, June 26, 2003, para. 139.

[83] Weiler (2004).

[84] Marvin Roy Feldman Karpa v. United Mexican States, ICSID Case No. ARB(AF)/99/1, Award, 16 December 2002, para. 170.

By contrast, measures adopted to protect the privacy of data subjects have not yet been adjudicated in investment jurisprudence. An EU state justifying the need for an 'adequacy decision' would have to invoke privacy or human rights arguments to justify potentially discriminatory measures. The tribunal's analysis would likely pay close attention to the risks involved in the data and how far the impugned measure addressed that risk.

However, the third 'justification' stage of analysis is by no means a universal approach. From the preceding analysis, it is clear that there are circumstances in which there may be investment disputes over data between Chinese or European investors and their host countries. In that context, it is necessary to examine the scope of exceptions in the CAI.

5 Are CAI Exceptions Sufficient to Address Data-related Public Policy Concerns?

General exceptions clauses elevate areas of public policy above investment protection in the hierarchy of norms in certain circumstances.[85] Permissible objectives in IIAs typically include the protection of human, animal or plant life, public health, public morality, national or artistic treasures, and the conservation of exhaustible national resources. In combination with dedicated exceptions for security, these provisions attempt to ensure that a state can regulate in cases of emergency or in relation to public policy.

In the CAI, Section VI contains the general exceptions that apply to the chapter on investment liberalization. Art. 10 provides that:

> Nothing in this Agreement should be construed:
>
> (a) To require a Party to furnish or allow access to any information the disclosure of which it considers contrary to its essential security interests; or
> (b) To prevent a Party from taking an action which it considers necessary for the protection of its essential security interests…

The operative aspect of this provision is the term "essential security interests". Is it broad enough to encompass the objectives sought by data protection regulations? "Essential security interests" has been interpreted narrowly to encompass merely instances of armed attacked and military activities.[86] The security-related issues raised by data would not fall within this narrow interpretation. Only data relating to the military or defensive capabilities would be non-precluded. However, the security exception in the CAI includes an explanatory list of the scope of "essential security interests". Interests that fall within its purview include those 'connected to the production of or traffic in arms… and to economic activities, carried out directly

[85] Pathirana and McLaughlin (2020).

[86] Moon (2012).

or indirectly for the purpose of supplying a military establishment'.[87] The inclusion of 'economic activities' is a notable expansion. Given their potential to generate cross-border economic value, data flows may constitute economic activities for the purposes of the provision. For example, datasets used to train targeting software for automated weapons would fall under the exceptions clause, as would data relating to nuclear power.

By contrast, privacy is rarely referenced as a permissible objective within investment treaties. Non-security public policy exceptions remain rare in the context of IIAs overall, and public policy exceptions that reference data or privacy are even rarer. CAI is one of the rare treaties to reference privacy and data protection within expressly enumerated general exceptions. Art. 4 provides:

> [N]othing in [the CAI] shall be construed to prevent the adoption or enforcement by either Party of measures…necessary to secure compliance with laws or regulations which are not inconsistent with the provisions of this Agreement including those relating to… ***the protection of the privacy of individuals in relation to the processing and dissemination of personal data and the protection of confidentiality of individual records and accounts'*** *(emphasis added)*

In the CAI, the exception is limited to those measures which are 'not inconsistent with the provisions' and so does not create a positive right. However, it affirms that regulations for privacy and data protection are *prime facie* within a state's right to regulate and firmly establishes privacy as a legitimate policy objective in international investment law. While by no means unique—recent treaty practice in Singapore and Japan also references data and privacy issues—its inclusion the CAI emphasis the shared importance of data protection regulations in China and the European Union. It is part of a broader trend of incorporating digital economy issues in international economic agreements. While this is far more developed in the trade law sphere, CAI could be a model for the inclusion of data in investment agreements in the future.

6 Conclusion: The Future of Data Protection in Investment Treatise: Limited to the CAI Model?

The growing prominence of cross-border data flows in international trade and investment requires appropriate regulatory frameworks as part of global economic governance. While the trade regime is increasingly cognisant of data-related issues, drafters of investment treaties have, thus far, been more reluctant to establishing a relationship between data protection and investment flows. A new generation of investment treaties, of which CAI is a part, envisage data protection measures as relevant to the investment regime. It is unclear whether this will become the dominant view in the decades ahead. Nevertheless, the question must not merely be *if*

[87] CAI, Art. 10 (b)(i).

investment treaties should reference data as a protected investment, but also *how* distinctive policy preferences can be reflected within the investment framework.

The CAI model of incorporating data into the investment regime is limited in scope. There is no express reference to data with a definition of investment. Those sections of the CAI that refer to investment will be relevant primarily for guiding the interpretation of arbitrators, adjudicators and states against the background of a growing number of restrictions on cross-border data transfer. In particular, the inclusion of privacy and data protection in the clause on general exceptions is limited by its soft language; inclusion within the list of permissible objectives would be a clearer signal to arbitrators not to limit the regulatory scope of states with respect to data protection.

Given the lack of consensus on how data should be regulated across jurisdictions, the CAI represents the most high-profile example of influential states slowly cementing the role of data flows in cross-border trade as a form of investment. If more crystallised principles begin to emerge with broad consensus, these may enter investment treaties in a more concrete way. As it stands, the EU and China have drafted the CAI so as to acknowledge the relevance of data flows without imposing prescriptive solutions as to how it should be regulated. It remains to be seen whether adventurous investors or states attempt to firm up the limits of legitimate data protection through applying traditional standards of investment protection. For now, it is sufficient to observe the gradual embedding of data-related issues within investment law.

Mark McLaughlin is the Global Visiting Assistant Professor at the Yong Pung How School of Law, Singapore Management University and Singapore International Dispute Resolution Academy (SIDRA). Mark has been a trainer for government officials around the world in managing their investment treaty commitments and navigating investor-state disputes. In 2022, he became of a member of the ISDS Academic Forum. His research areas are international economic law and dispute resolution, particularly arbitration and mediation. He has published in leading international journals on novel areas of law, such as investor-state mediation, state-owned enterprises, and emerging technologies.

References

Aaronson SA, Leblond P (2018) Another digital divide: the rise of data realms and its implications for the WTO. J Int Econ Law 21:245–272

Briefing C (2021) The PRC personal information protection law (final): a full translation. China Briefing News. https://www.china-briefing.com/news/the-prc-personal-information-protection-law-final-a-full-translation/. Accessed 24 June 2022

Bygrave LA (2014) Data privacy law: an international perspective. OUP, Oxford

Cai P, Chen L (2022) Demystifying data law in China: a unified regime of tomorrow. Int Data Priv Law 12:75–92

Choer Moraes H (2019) The geoeconomic challenge to international economic law: lessons from the regulation of data in China. SSRN. https://doi.org/10.2139/ssrn.3479504

Drexl J (2016) Designing competitive markets for industrial data – between propertisation and access. SSRN. https://doi.org/10.2139/ssrn.2862975
Erie MS, Streinz T (2021) The Beijing effect: China's digital silk road as transnational data governance. New York Univ J Int Law Policy 54:1–92
Ersnt and Young (2021) How to prepare for global data compliance. https://www.ey.com/en_sg/consulting/how-to-prepare-for-global-data-compliance. Accessed 24 June 2022
Feldstein S (2019) The global expansion of AI surveillance. Carnegie Endowment for International Peace
Ferracane MF (2017) Restrictions to cross-border data flows: a taxonomy. European Centre for International Political Economy Working Paper No 1/2017
Force Hill J (2014) The growth of data localization post-Snowden. Harvard Kennedy School, Belfer Center for Science and International Affairs
Gao HS (2021) Data regulation with Chinese characteristics. In: Burri M (ed) Big data and global trade law. CUP, Cambridge, pp 245–267
Genest A (2019) Performance requirement prohibitions in international investment law. Brill
Giles K (2016) The next phase of Russian information warfare
Gordon K, Pohl J (2015) Investment treaties over time – treaty practice and interpretation in a changing world. OECD Working Paper on International Investment 2015/02
He A (2022) The Digital Silk Road and China's influence on standard setting. Centre for International Governance Innovation
Hoeren DT (2014) Big data and the ownership in data: recent developments in Europe. Eur Intel Prop Rev 12:751–754
Horváth E, Klinkmüller S (2019) The concept of 'Investment' in the digital economy: the case of social media companies. J World Invest Trade 20:577–617
Huang J (2022) Digitalization of special economic zones in China. In: The Elgar companion to the WTO
Kelkar K (2018) From silk threads to fiber optics: the rise of China's digital silk road. ORF. https://www.orfonline.org/expert-speak/43102-from-silk-threads-to-fiber-optics-the-rise-of-chinas-digital-silk-road/. Accessed 1 Feb 2023
Kurtz J (2015) Balancing investor protection and regulatory freedom in international investment law: the necessary, complex, and vital search for state purpose'. In: Bjorklund AK (ed) Yearbook on international investment law and policy 2013–2014. OUP, Oxford, pp 251–304
McLaughlin M (2019) Defining a state-owned enterprise in international investment agreements. ICSID Rev – Foreign Invest Law J 34:595–625
Meltzer JP, Lovelock P (2018) Regulating for a digital economy: understanding the importance of cross-border data flows in Asia. In: Brookings. https://www.brookings.edu/research/regulating-for-a-digital-economy-understanding-the-importance-of-cross-border-data-flows-in-asia/. Accessed 1 Feb 2023
Milhaupt CJ, Zheng W (2015) Beyond ownership: state capitalism and the Chinese firm. The Georgetown Law J 103:665–722
Mitchell AD, Mishra N (2019) Regulating cross-border data flows in a data-driven world: how WTO law can contribute. J Int Econ Law 22:389–416
Mitchell AD, Heaton D, Henckels C (2016) Non-discrimination and the role of regulatory purpose in international trade and investment law. Edward Elgar Publishing
Moon WJ (2012) Essential security interests in international investment agreements. J Int Econ Law 15:481–502
Murdoch B (2021) Privacy and artificial intelligence: challenges for protecting health information in a new era. BMC Med Ethics 22(122):1–5
Neilson B (2022) Working the digital silk road: Alibaba's digital free trade zone in Malaysia. In: Graham M, Ferrari F (eds) Digital work in the planetary market. MIT Press
Pathirana D, McLaughlin M (2020) Non-precluded measures clauses: regime, trends, and practice. In: Chaisse J, Choukroune L, Jusoh S (eds) Handbook of international investment law and policy. Springer, Singapore, pp 1–23

Ritter J, Mayer A (2018) Regulating data as property: a new construct for moving forward. Duke Law Technol Rev 16:220–277
Roberts A, Choer Moraes H, Ferguson V (2019) Toward a geoeconomic order in international trade and investment. J Int Econ Law 22:655–676
Rubinstein IS (2013) Big data: the end of privacy or a new beginning? Int Data Priv Law 3:74–87
Ryngaert C, Taylor M (2020) The GDPR as global data protection regulation? AJIL Unbound 114:5–9
Sen N (2018) Understanding the role of the WTO in international data flows: taking the liberalization or the regulatory autonomy path? J Int Econ Law 21:323–348
Tan Z, Zhang C (2021) China's PIPL and DSL: is China following the EU's approach to data protection? J Data Protect Priv 5:7–25
Tao J (2019) TPP and China: a tale of two economic orderings? In: Kingsbury B, Malone DM, Mertenskötter P et al (eds) Megaregulation contested: global economic ordering after TPP. OUP, Oxford, pp 79–100
Tracol X (2020) "Schrems II": the return of the privacy shield. Comput Law Secur Rev 39(105484):1–11
Triolo P (2020) The digital silk road and the evolving role of Chinese technology companies. Adelphi Ser 60:65–88
van Erp S (2017) Ownership of digital assets and the numerus clausus of legal objects. Brigham-Kanner Prop Rights Conf J 6:235–257
Wang J (2019) China's governance approach to the belt and road initiative (BRI): relations, partnership, and law. Glob Trade Cust J 14:222–228
Weiler T (2004) Prohibitions Against Discrimination in Nafta Chapter 11. Brill

Part III
EU-China Comprehensive Agreement on Investment: Procedural Issues

The Future of Investor-State Dispute Settlement in the EU-China Comprehensive Agreement on Investment

Ming Du

Abstract This chapter intends to explore the future of the ISDS provisions in the CAI. Contrary to the dominant view that it is unlikely for China to be a supporter of the EU's ISDS reform proposal, this chapter argue that such a conclusion may be premature. After a careful analysis of China's submission to the UNITRAL Working Group III, the key feature of EU's ICS, and a systemic evaluation of pertinent factors that are most relevant to China's approach to ISDS reform, it is submitted that the divergence between the approaches to ISDS reform of the EU and China may not be unbridgeable. It is possible for China to agree to a two-tier ICS in the CAI, as the EU has concluded with other countries. Similarly, there are no strong reasons for China to oppose the EU's MIC proposal, in particular after the EU indicated that the MIC proposal could take an open architecture.

1 Introduction

On 30 December 2020, the EU and China reached an agreement in principle on EU-China Comprehensive Agreement on Investment (CAI), after thirty-five rounds of intense negotiations which lasted seven years. The EU's general objective for the CAI was to use the exclusive competence for foreign direct investment it gained after the Lisbon Treaty to modernize and replace the bilateral investment treaties (BITs) all EU Member States except Ireland concluded with China with a single EU-China CAI. The EU's specific objectives, among others, were to provide for new opportunities and improved conditions for access to the Chinese markets for EU investors; establish guarantees regarding the treatment of EU investors in China; support sustainable development initiatives by encouraging responsible investment and promoting core environmental and labour standards, and allow for the effective

M. Du (✉)
Durham University Law School, Durham, UK
e-mail: ming.du@durham.ac.uk

© The Author(s), under exclusive license to Springer Nature Switzerland AG 2024

A. Svetlicinii, I.-J. Chen (eds.), *The EU-China Comprehensive Agreement on Investment*, European Yearbook of International Economic Law,
https://doi.org/10.1007/978-3-031-66862-3_11

enforcement of commitments through investment dispute settlement mechanisms.[1] To what extent the EU's strategic interests were served in the CAI was hotly debated.[2]

The originally envisaged 'comprehensive' China-EU BIT has not been fully completed since the CAI does not cover substantive standards of investment protection, nor does it include any investor-state dispute settlement (ISDS) clauses. Instead, China and the EU agreed to a detailed state-to-state dispute settlement system, coupled with a monitoring mechanism at the pre-litigation phase established at a political level to ensure effective monitoring of the implementation of the CAI. Moreover, both sides are committed to pursue the negotiations on investment protection and investment dispute settlement within two years of the signature of the CAI. The common objective is to work towards modernized investment protection standards and a dispute settlement that takes into account the work undertaken in the context of the United Nations Commission on International Trade Law (UNCITRAL) Working Group III (WGIII) on a permanent multilateral investment court (MIC) advocated by the EU.[3]

In view of the EU's long-held position that the traditional ISDS should be replaced by the two-tier International Investment Court System (ICS) in EU free trade agreements (FTAs), it is reasonable to assume that the EU tabled its ICS proposal to China during the CAI negotiations. After all, the EU has successfully negotiated this reformed ISDS mechanism in its FTAs with Canada, Singapore, Vietnam, and Mexico. The fact that there is no ISDS provision in the CAI is a strong signal that China is not yet ready to endorse the EU's ICS proposal in either bilateral or multilateral negotiations.[4] It is also reasonable to expect that the EU will continue to push for the ICS model in future CAI negotiations on ISDS with China as the EU vowed that 'there can be no return to the old-style ISDS'.[5] Then, is there any likelihood that China may sign up to the EU's ICS proposal in future CAI negotiations and ultimately support the EU's MIC proposal? For good reasons, both Chinese and Western observers of the CAI are pessimistic about this prospect.[6]

This chapter intends to explore the future of the ISDS provisions in the CAI. Contrary to the dominant view that it is unlikely for China to be a supporter of the EU's ISDS reform proposal, this chapter argues that such a conclusion may be premature. After a careful analysis of China's submission to the UNITRAL Working Group III, the key feature of EU's ICS, and a systemic evaluation of pertinent factors that are most relevant to China's approach to ISDS reform, it is submitted that the divergence between the approaches to ISDS reform of the EU and China may not be unbridgeable. It is possible for China to agree to a two-tier ICS in the CAI as

[1] European Parliament (2022).

[2] Hu (2021), pp. 23–24.

[3] European Commission (2020).

[4] GÓMEZ (2021), pp. 54–61.

[5] European Commission (2018).

[6] Chaisse and Ji (2022), pp. 123–124; Li and Wu (2020), pp. 52–53.

the EU has concluded with other countries. Similarly, there are no strong reasons for China to oppose the EU's MIC proposal, particularly after the EU indicated that the MIC proposal could take an "open architecture".

The chapter proceeds as follows. Section 2 provides an overview of China's UNITRAL submission, situating China's approach to ISDS reform in the context of global dialogue of ISDS regime and competing reform proposals. Section 3 analyses a range of contextual factors which contribute to shape China's approach to ISDS reform. Section 4 seeks to show that China's approach to ISDS reform shares more similarities with the EU than are commonly acknowledged and explains why China should consider adopting the EU's two-tier ICS in the CAI. Section 5 concludes the chapter.

2 An Analysis of China's UNCITRAL Submission on ISDS Reform

2.1 Overview of China's UNITRAL Submission

The UNCITRAL WGIII has been mandated to deliberate possible multilateral reform of the ISDS system since 2017, with the ultimate objective of formulating a multilateral instrument that allows each state the choice of whether and to what extent it wishes to adopt the relevant reforms in 2026.[7] On 19 July 2019, the Government of China submitted the first proposal on ISDS reform to UNCITRAL WGIII. In the proposal, China reaffirms its commitment to ISDS as an important mechanism for resolving investor-state disputes, outlines its concerns about the current ISDS regime, and suggests several priority areas for reform.[8] However, the content of China's proposal on ISDS reform has received only scant analysis in the literature to date.[9]

In recent years, the ISDS system has been frequently criticized as suffering a 'legitimacy crisis'.[10] China concurs with many criticisms levelled at the current *ad hoc* ISDS system: lack of an appropriate error-correcting mechanism; lack of stability and predictability in arbitral awards; arbitrator's professionalism and independence have been put into question; a small club of lawyers and arbitrators that lack gender and geographical diversity; the risks that third-party funding in ISDS pose to the public and to the investment regime itself; and length and cost of ISDS proceedings.[11] In this respect, it is notable that China has not openly criticized aspects of the

[7] Report of the Working Group III on the Work of its Resumed Fortieth Session (2021).

[8] Note by the Secretariat, 'Possible Reform of Investor-State Dispute Settlement: Submission from the Government of China' (8 July 2019), A/CN.9/WG.III/WP.177.

[9] Roberts and John (2019).

[10] Langford and Behn (2018), pp. 554–558; Dietz et al. (2019), pp. 750–751.

[11] Puig and Shaffer (2018), p. 366.

current ISDS system that many other states find problematic: the pro-investor interpretation of substantive treaty protections, chilling effects on state regulatory powers, and bypassing national judicial systems that might provide appropriate legal protection.[12]

Despite China's criticisms of the current ISDS system, China makes it clear that it supports the maintenance of the ISDS system in its UNCITRAL submission. China views the present ISDS system as playing an important role in protecting the rights and interests of foreign investors, promoting cross-border investment, and avoiding the politicization of investment disputes between foreign investors and host states.[13] China's overall positive attitude towards ISDS distances it from other emerging powers such as Brazil and India, which advocate either a return to state-to-state arbitration or local remedies.[14] Moreover, rather than being a norm entrepreneur as the EU is in FTAs, China supports a multilateral approach to reforming ISDS rules and mechanisms since 'some of the institutional issues tend not to lend themselves to resolution through BITs between member states'.[15] China's preference for a multilateral approach to ISDS reform echoes Chinese President Xi Jinping's call for multilateralism in global governance in many international fora.[16]

China has made five specific recommendations on ISDS reform. First, China supports the study of establishing a permanent appellate mechanism with fixed procedures, institutions, and staff. China views the creation of an ISDS appellate mechanism important in ensuring procedural and substantive correctness of decisions and in rectifying errors in decisions by ISDS tribunals. China further indicated that an appellate mechanism would serve to improve consistency, coherence and predictability in ISDS decisions. Therefore, an appellate mechanism would narrow the legitimacy gap of the ISDS system. Institutionally, China prefers to establish a permanent multilateral appeal mechanism modelled on the WTO dispute settlement system over doing so through BITs, viewing the former approach as highly efficient and minimizing institutional costs.[17] This proposal is of course not surprising as China has long held a favourable view of the WTO dispute settlement system.[18] However, China has not elaborated on specific institutional form that ISDS reform shall be carried out. For example, it is not clear whether China supports a standalone multilateral appellate body complementing the current ISDS system, such as a possible appeals facility under the ICSID framework, or an appellate mechanism as a second tier in a MIC.[19]

---

[12] EFILA (2015), pp. 26–33.

[13] Submission from China (2019), p. 2.

[14] Schill and Vidigal (2018), pp. 15–17.

[15] Submission from China (2019), p. 5.

[16] Xi (2021).

[17] Submission from China (2019), p. 5.

[18] Shaffer and Gao (2018), pp. 134–137.

[19] Note by the Secretariat, 'Possible Reform of Investor-State Dispute Settlement: Submission from the Government of China' (8 July 2019), A/CN.9/WG.III/WP.177, p. 10.

Second, China states that the right of the parties to appoint arbitrators is the core and most attractive feature of international arbitration. China is therefore leaning towards retaining the right of the parties to appoint arbitrators at the first-instance stage of arbitral proceedings. At first sight, China's position is contrary to what the EU submitted to UNCITRAL. According to the EU, since the choice of arbitrator is made after a dispute has arisen, investors and state respondents tend to appoint arbitrators to the dispute primarily in their capacity as disputing parties, with a view to best serving their interests in a particular case. This leads them to appoint arbitrators predisposed to one side or the other. However, the long-term interests of the ISDS system lie in providing for adjudicative bodies that faithfully interpret and apply the underlying substantive provisions.[20] Therefore, the EU advocates moving away from appointment of arbitrators by the disputing parties to a two-tier court system of full time adjudicators on long, non-renewable terms.[21]

Third, China submits that it is necessary to improve the rules governing arbitrators' qualifications, conflicts of interest, selection and disqualification procedures. Specifically, China notes that arbitrators should have professional knowledge in the fields of public international law and international economic law.[22] In addition, China wants to have rules that avoid potential conflicts of interest and prevent inequities that may be caused by arbitrators improperly practicing as legal counsel in other arbitral proceedings. The double-hatting problem may give arbitrators improper incentives to decide cases in a manner that favours the party that appointed them so as to assure a flow of future client instructions, calling into question their independence and impartiality.[23]

Fourth, China reaffirms its commitment to alternative means of dispute settlement, including a mandatory three-to-six-month pre-arbitration consultation procedure between investor and the central government of the host country, and a more effective investment conciliation mechanism.[24] The integration of mediation or conciliation into ISDS system has become more frequent in IIAs. For example, out of 2,572 BITs, 624 provide for mediation or conciliation procedures, accounting for 24% of all BITs.[25] In China's view, these procedures can help the parties to achieve mutually beneficial results and avoid lengthy arbitration proceedings and high litigation costs. Compared with investment arbitration, alternative dispute settlement methods can provide host states and investors with a high degree of flexibility and autonomy, allow the parties to adopt creative and forward-looking methods to promote the settlement of investment disputes while maintaining long-term cooperative relationships.[26]

---

[20] Submission from the European Union (2017), p. 10.

[21] Ibid.

[22] Ibid., p. 11.

[23] Langford, Behn and Lie (2017), p. 328.

[24] Submission from China (2019), p. 5.

[25] Fan (2020), p. 331.

[26] Coe (2015), pp. 21–23.

Fifth, China supports the stipulation of transparency disciplines for third-party funding. Recent years have seen significant increases in the number of third party funded ISDS cases. In such cases, investors turned to third-party funders who would pay the expenses incurred in pursuing the claim and enforcing the arbitral award in exchange for a share of the eventual financial award and influence over case management.[27] There are serious concerns about the impact of third-party funding on the arbitral proceedings, on investors' incentives, on respondent states' exposure, liability, responses to ISDS claims, and on the investment law system itself.[28] However, in many cases third-party funding of ISDS cases remains largely unregulated both in the IIAs and under applicable arbitration rules.[29] China supports the regulation of third-party funding in ISDS by imposing transparency obligations on the parties. In China's view, the parties involved in ISDS should disclose related funding on a continuous basis, including the content of the funding contract or arrangement, and avoid direct or indirect conflicts of interests between arbitrators and third-party funders. The legal consequences of the relevant parties for failure to fulfil their disclosure obligations should also be clarified.[30]

China's approach to ISDS reform is mostly uncontroversial. Almost all states agree that issues such as the regulation of arbitrators, third-party funding, and alternative means of dispute settlement should be incorporated into BITs. For instance, general support was expressed for developing a code of conduct for ISDS tribunal members at UNCITRAL WGIII. For this purpose, the ICSID and UNCITRAL have prepared jointly a draft code of conduct.[31] The more controversial parts in China's proposal are the establishment of appellate system and China's insistence on the right of the parties to appoint arbitrators at the first-instance stage of arbitral proceedings. Therefore, my analysis will focus on these two issues when reflecting on China's attitude towards the EU's ICS in future CAI negotiations.

2.2 *Comparing China's Position with Competing ISDS Reform Proposals*

To better understand China's position on ISDS reform, it is useful to provide a brief overview of competing ISDS reform proposals made by other states and situate the Chinese submission in this broader context. Roberts has identified three main camps that have emerged with distinct proposals at UNCITRAL: incrementalists, systemic

---

[27] Third Party Funding in Investor-State Dispute Settlement Round Table Discussion of the ICCA-Queen Mary Task Force Draft Report (October 17, 2017), p. 2.

[28] Guven and Johnson (2019), p. 1.

[29] Brabandere (2017), pp. 127–128.

[30] Submission from China (2019), p. 5.

[31] Note by the Secretariat, 'Possible Reform of ISDS: Draft Code of Conduct', A/CN.9/WG.III/WP.209 (15 September 2021), p. 2.

reformers and paradigm shifters.[32] The main supporters of an incremental reform favour retaining the ISDS system and downplay the criticisms levelled at it as perceptions rather than reality.[33] Even though they recognize that there are some outstanding problems to be addressed, they prefer to adopt small-to-moderate adjustments and more targeted reforms as opposed to systematic reforms. For example, incrementalists view the problem of inconsistent awards from *ad hoc* tribunals either as a natural and positive consequence of the bilateral nature of BITs or something to be rectified by adopting more precise and detailed treaty language or authoritative interpretations.[34] The typical example of an incremental approach to ISDS reform is the Comprehensive and Progressive Agreement for Trans-Pacific Partnership (CPTPP).

The CPTPP allows investors to resort to ISDS without prior recourse to domestic courts.[35] However, the CPTPP defines more precisely the contours of contracting parties' obligations, such as fair and equitable treatment and indirect expropriation, towards foreign investors and investments, in an attempt to eliminate the likelihood of successful challenges to non-discriminatory public welfare measures.[36] The CPTPP also restricts the types of claims that can be submitted to ISDS. These exceptions cover important policy areas such as tobacco control measures, authorization of foreign investment, and restructuring of public debt to ensure that these sensitive issues are not subject to review by arbitral tribunals. Moreover, the CPTPP addresses the double-hatting problem of arbitrators by establishing the Code of Conduct for ISDS Proceedings, requiring *inter alia* that an arbitrator, upon selection, shall refrain for the duration of the proceedings from acting as counsel or party-appointed expert or witness in any pending or new investment dispute.[37] In short, the CPTPP has addressed current concerns about the ISDS in an 'evolutionary' rather than 'revolutionary' manner.[38] Largely operating under the traditional ISDS framework, the CPTPP does not even pursue the creation of an appeals facility and only contains an 'opening clause' that requires the contracting parties to consider opting into a future appellate mechanism.[39] This stands in stark contrast to the EU's efforts to replace the current ISDS system with a novel MIC.

Systemic reformers move further compared to incrementalists. They see merit in retaining the ISDS based on its oft-repeated advantages. However, they view the current ISDS as seriously flawed and push for systematic and structural reforms.[40]

[32] Roberts (2018), p. 410.

[33] Roberts and Bouraoui (2018).

[34] Ibid.

[35] CPTPP, Art. 9.19 (1).

[36] CPTPP, Art. 9.6 and Annex 9-B; Henckels (2016), pp. 33–43.

[37] Art. 3 (d), Code of Conduct for Investor-State Dispute Settlement under Chapter 9 Section B of the CPTPP.

[38] Markert et al. (2020).

[39] CPTPP, Art. 9.23 (11).

[40] Submission from the European Union (2019, para 2.4).

The most vocal advocate for this camp is the EU. In 2015, the European Commission proposed the establishment of an ICS to replace the traditional ISDS system within the context of the negotiations of the free trade agreements with the US. The novel ICS retains the standing of private investors to file claims directly against states, but it effectively creates a permanent tribunal of first instance and an appellate tribunal mirroring the WTO Appellate Body, with the full-time adjudicators having fixed terms, a regular salary, and being selected on a random basis from a roster designated by states.[41] The new model was designed to respond to the criticisms that party-appointed, *ad hoc* arbitrators make investment arbitration insufficiently accountable to democratic institutions by moving away from appointment by the disputing parties to ensure independence and impartiality of arbitrators. Viewing a standing two-tier mechanism as the only available option that effectively responds to all the concerns about the traditional ISDS model, the EU later effectively incorporated the ICS in recent free trade agreements concluded with Canada, Singapore, Vietnam and Mexico, and described it as an important first step towards the EU's ultimate goal of a MIC.[42]

Paradigm shifters hold the most critical view of ISDS system, dismissing the current system as irrevocably flawed and arguing for a fundamental overhaul, returning to a time before the existence of ISDS.[43] As discussed above, China distances itself from countries such as Brazil and South Africa that call for a paradigm shift in ISDS reform. However, it is challenging to put China in either the incrementalist or systemic reform camps in the UNCITRAL process.[44] On the one hand, China has identified some structural problems of the current *ad hoc* ISDS system and supported institutional reforms, such as the establishment of an appellate mechanism modelled on the WTO dispute settlement system.[45] In comparison, the CPTPP does not pursue the creation of an appeal facility.[46] On the other, China does not explicitly endorse the EU's permanent MIC proposal and prefers to retain the right of the parties to appoint arbitrators.[47] Consequently, China's approach to ISDS reform is widely perceived as ambiguous.[48]

The ensuing developments after China's UNCITRAL submission have further deepened the ambiguity of China's approach to ISDS reform. On the one hand, China formally submitted a request to accede to the CPTPP in September 2021.[49] On the other, the EU and China have agreed to take into account the work undertaken in the context of UNCITRAL WGIII deliberations on the EU's MIC

[41] Brown (2017), pp. 682–684.

[42] European Commission (2016).

[43] Vidigal and Stevens (2018), pp. 487–489.

[44] Du and Shen (2021), p. 23.

[45] Submission from China (2019), p. 4.

[46] CPTPP, Art. 9.23 (11).

[47] Submission from China (2019), p. 4.

[48] Roberts and John (2019); McLaughlin (2018), p. 97.

[49] Olcott (2021).

proposal.[50] China's mixed signals are confusing precisely because the ISDS mechanism in the CPTPP could not be more different from the systemic MIC reform proposal advocated by the EU.[51] As will be further elaborated in part 4 below, the ambiguity of China's approach to ISDS reform has created some space to discuss why China might accept the EU's ICS proposal in future CAI negotiations.

3 Exploring the Underlying Factors Affecting China's Approach to ISDS Reform

3.1 ISDS Clauses in Three Generations of Chinese BITs

Based on the scope of consent to ISDS provisions, Chinese BITs may be categorized into three generations. Signed from the early 1980s to the late 1990s, China's first-generation BITs provide either no ISDS provisions at all or a narrowly constructed ISDS clause that only admits "the amount of compensation for expropriation" to arbitration. Two factors may explain China's conservative attitude towards ISDS during the period. First, sceptical of international dispute resolution mechanisms as Western-biased after long isolation from the international community, China perceived accepting the jurisdiction of international arbitral tribunals as inconsistent with the sacred notion of sovereign independence.[52] Second, being a capital-importing country with scarce overseas foreign investment at the time, it would be in China's interest to retain the adjudicative prerogatives within Chinese domestic courts in settling disputes with foreign investors.[53]

China deposited its instruments of ratification of the Convention for the Settlement of Investment Disputes Between States and Nationals of Other States (ICSID Convention) on 7 January 1993. The accession to the ICSID Convention was hailed as one of the milestones in China's engagement with mechanisms of international adjudication as China for the first time accepted the possibility of submitting disputes over its sovereign actions to the jurisdiction of a third-party arbitration system.[54] Nevertheless, as a reflection of China's wary approach to ISDS, China limited the scope of its consent to ICSID's jurisdiction with a declaration under Art. 25 (4) of the ICSID Convention that 'the Chinese Government would only consider submitting to the jurisdiction of the ICSID disputes over compensation resulting from expropriation and nationalization'.[55]

---

[50] European Commission (2020).

[51] Schacherer (2016), p. 629.

[52] Kong (1999), p. 105.

[53] Chi and Wang (2015), p. 874.

[54] Ku (2013), p. 34.

[55] Notifications Concerning Classes of Disputes Considered Suitable or Unsuitable for Submission to the Centre (7 January 1993).

The second generation of Chinese BITs (1998 to 2011) are characterized by unobstructed access to ISDS clauses.[56] In contrast to the narrowly constructed ISDS clauses in the first generation BITs, ISDS provisions in second generation Chinese BITs adopted extended and liberal access to international arbitration, which usually stipulated that '*any dispute* concerning an investment between an investor of one Contracting Party and the other Contracting Party can be submitted unconditionally at the request of the investor concerned either to the ICISD or an ad hoc arbitral tribunal'.[57] This drastic policy shift towards liberal ISDS provisions is explained by China's changed status to become a capital-exporting country, particularly in developing countries.[58] Deeply integrated into the global economy, China is no longer a mere capital-importing country and the protection of its overseas investment against risks through BITs has become an important policy prerogative. It is no coincidence that out of the 46 second generation Chinese BITs, 37 signatory states are developing countries located in Africa, South-East Asia and Latin America, which are commonly considered as capital importing countries.[59]

The emergence of China's second-generation BITs with liberal ISDS clauses raises the question of the legal effects of China's declaration concerning classes of disputes when acceding to the ICSID in 1993. Would the declaration that China would only consider submitting to the ICSID disputes over compensation resulting from expropriation and nationalization mean that the unconditional consent given in the second generation BITs is only valid to the extent that it does not conflict with China's ICSID declaration? Some commentators believe so, arguing that China's declaration constitutes a reservation and that China's acceptance of the ICSID jurisdiction is limited to investment disputes over compensation resulting from expropriation and nationalization.[60] The prevailing view, however, is that the legal nature of China's ICSID declaration is not a reservation but for information purposes only.[61] Art. 25(4) of the ICSID Convention allows that 'any Contracting State may, at the time of ratification, acceptance of approval of this Convention or at any time thereafter, notify the Centre of the class or classes of disputes which it would or would not consider submitting to the jurisdiction of the Centre'. At the same time, Art. 25 (4) makes it clear that 'such notification shall not constitute the consent required by Article 25 (1)'. Since a state's consent to jurisdiction under the ICSID Convention Art. 25 (1), in addition to the ratification of the ICSID Convention, is a condition for an ISCID arbitral to have personal jurisdiction over the State, any declarations the state makes under Art. 25(4) has no direct legal consequences. An ISCID contracting state is free at any moment to accept the jurisdiction of the ICSID

[56] Gallagher and Shan (2009), pp. 41–42.

[57] For example, Art. 10 (3) of China-Germany BIT (2003) and Art. 10(3) of China-Netherlands BIT (2001).

[58] Cai (2006), p. 646.

[59] Li and Cheng (2020), p. 516.

[60] Cymrot (2006), p. 82.

[61] Heymann (2008), pp. 517–518.

for all investment disputes.[62] This is exactly what China has done in its second and third generations of BITs.

As part of a move in the international investment regime to reformulate IIAs aiming to recalibrate the relationship between the level of protection for foreign investors and the policy space of host states, China has begun to conclude the third generation BITs since China-Canada BIT in 2012.[63] In comparison with the unobstructed access to ISDS in second generation BITs, the third generation BITs have adopted a more balanced approach: procedural pre-requisites are added that aim to discourage abuse of rights by foreign investors; exceptions and a variety of exclusions are stipulated to constrain the arbitral tribunal's jurisdictional outreach and to ensure that it is not unlimited or overly expansive.[64] For example, in the China-Canada BIT, only breaches of specific provisions that cause a loss or damage to investors are admissible to arbitration.[65] At the same time, specific provisions in the BIT such as prudential measures in the financial sector, approval of foreign investment project and taxation measures are explicitly excluded from the application of ISDS clauses.

The developmental trajectory of China's approach to ISDS system makes it plain that allowing foreign investors access to ISDS has been a standard feature of Chinese BITs for two decades by now. China is now deeply engaged and intertwined with ICSID and other mechanisms of investment protection and investor-state arbitration. China views ISDS as an important mechanism to promote cross-border investment flows and the rule of law in international investment governance.[66]

3.2 China's (Limited) Experience with ISDS

For some time, international investment lawyers have been debating the puzzle of so-called 'China disequilibrium' in international investment arbitration. Despite the fact that China is a signatory of almost 150 IIAs in which comprehensive ISDS procedures are a common feature, there are only few investor-state investment disputes involving the Chinese government, Chinese investors or Chinese BITs.[67] According to public records, the Chinese government is the respondent in nine reported cases by December 2022 (of which three were discontinued by the claimant investors). Similarly, Chinese investors were claimants in 19 cases before the

[62] Ibid.

[63] Berger (2015), p. 850.

[64] Li and Cheng (2020), p. 522.

[65] For example, Art. 20.1 of the China-Canada BIT provides *inter alia*, that an investor may submit a claim to arbitration when the investor or its investment has incurred loss or damage by reason of, or arising out of breaches of obligations under Arts, 2 to 7(2), 9, 10-13, 14 (4) or 16 of the BIT.

[66] Wang (2009), p. 584.

[67] Shen (2021), p. 240.

ICSID and other international arbitration forums by December2022. Excluding Hong Kong and Macau investors, the number would be reduced to 11.

Several reasons were offered to explain the China's absence from investment arbitration. One explanation is that the Chinese government has always appreciated the important role of foreign investment in Chinese economic development and offered sufficient investment protection to foreign investors.[68] For example, China used to accord foreign investors superior national treatment in the sense that they enjoy more favourable treatment in terms of tax rate and other conditions of competition.[69] Next, China's emphasis on the rule of law has afforded foreign investors protection close to the Western practice. The risk of the Chinese government violating BIT obligations is very low. This point is best illustrated through China's position on expropriation in its BIT practice. After amendment of Chinese constitutional law in 2004 and passing of the Chinese Property Rights Law in 2007, illegal expropriation is unlikely in contemporary China.[70]

Opposite to this optimistic explanation, a competing argument holds essentially that a dearth of ISDS claims against China is precisely due to the lack of the rule of law in China. Foreign investors may fear that their ISDS claim could jeopardize their relationship with the Chinese government and in turn put their business dealings in China at risk. By contrast, foreign investors may gain more from non-adversarial means such as negotiation and mediation to resolve their disputes with the Chinese government in view of its preference for settling disputes informally. Initiating arbitration against China is therefore likely to be a last resort.[71] Yet another school of thought attributes the low utility rate of Chinese BITs to the fact that the early-generation Chinese BITs often incorporate restrictive terms of investor, investment, dispute, fork-in-the road, among others with the practical effect of discouraging foreign investors to initiate ISDS against China.[72] A typical example is that early Chinese BITs provide only disputes involving the amount of compensation for expropriation may be submitted for arbitration.

Careful analysis of China-related ISDS arbitral awards up to date shows that most of the arbitral awards ruled in China's favour. First, it is confirmed that Chinese state-owned enterprises (SOEs) are qualifying 'investors' capable of initiating ISDS proceedings against a host state under BITs. In *Beijing Urban Construction Group Co., Ltd. (BUCG) v. Republic of Yemen,* one of the jurisdictional objections raised by Yemen was that BUCG, as a Chinese SOE, should not be regarded as a 'national of another Contracting State' as required by Art. 25(1) of the ICSID Convention because 'it was under the direction and control of the Chinese government in carrying out its activities, and that it was empowered to exercise elements of

[68] Zhang (2008), p. 159.

[69] For example, until 2007 when the new Income Tax Law was enacted, Chinese enterprises had been taxed at up to 33 percent while foreign enterprises were subject to as little as 15 percent. See Shan, Gallagher and Zhang (2012), pp. 125–130.

[70] Shen (2015), pp. 600–601.

[71] Trakman (2015), p. 279.

[72] Schill (2007), p. 118.

governmental authority in China'.[73] The tribunal held that, notwithstanding the fact that BUCG was an SOE, the evidence demonstrated that the claimant was acting as a commercial contractor in carrying out the work and was neither an agent of the Chinese government nor fulfilling governmental functions.[74] The tribunal further found that the assertion that the Chinese State is the ultimate decision maker' for BUCG 'too remote to be relevant'.[75] Given that Chinese SOEs have played a significant role in China's overseas FDI[76] the Chinese government welcomed this decision as it would afford Chinese SOEs direct access to ISDS to protect their interests rather than having to recourse to traditional diplomatic protection. In *Ansung Housing Co., Ltd. v. China*, the tribunal found that the Korean investor Ansung's claim was time-barred and, as such, manifestly without legal merit since Ansung submitted its arbitration request to ICSID more than three years after acquiring knowledge of the investment loss.[77]

Second, the arbitral tribunals in disputes related to Chinese BITs have ruled consistently against the extension of the most-favoured nation (MFN) clause to procedural rights in ISDS. In *Ansung Housing Co., Ltd. v. China*, Ansung sought to invoke the MFN clause to save its claim from being time-barred as other Chinese BITs do not prescribe a three-year limitation period within which an investor is required to initiate an arbitration claim against the host state. Relying upon a plain reading of the MFN clause, the tribunal held that the MFN clause did not extend to a state's consent to arbitrate with investors nor to the temporal limitation period for investor-state arbitration.[78] Again, this ruling is consistent with China's preference. Recent Chinese BITs have eliminated potential controversies over the scope of the MFN clause by making clear that the MFN treatment does not cover the procedural rights to dispute settlement.[79]

Granted, China has not always been content with investment arbitral tribunals' awards. For example, a recurrent issue in China-related investment disputes is whether individuals or companies from Hong Kong and Macau qualify as "Chinese investors" protected by Chinese BITs under the "one country, two systems" policy. Two arbitral tribunals of *Tza Yap Shum v. Peru* and *Sanum v. Lao Republic* answered this question in the affirmative. The UNCITRAL award of *Sanum v. Lao Republic* was later annulled by the Singapore High Court, holding that Macau investors could not avail themselves of the China-Lao BIT because the BIT does not apply to Macau. But Sanum later prevailed in its appeal against the Singapore High Court's

[73] *Beijing Urban Construction Group Co., Ltd. (BUCG) v Republic of Yemen*, ICSID Case NO. ARB/14/3, Decision on Jurisdiction (31 May 2017), para 29.

[74] Ibid., para. 39.

[75] Ibid., para. 43.

[76] Michaels (2020).

[77] *Ansung Housing Co., Ltd. v. People's Republic of China*, ICSID Case No. ARB/14/25, para 115.

[78] Ibid., paras 140–141.

[79] For example, Art. 139 (2) of New Zealand–China Free Trade Agreement (2008).

decision before Court of Appeal of Singapore (SGCA), Singapore's highest court.[80] Notably, even though the Lao Government produced formal diplomatic correspondence between itself and China in 2014 and 2015 expressing both governments' view that the China-Laos BIT is not applicable to Macau, the SGCA declined to place any weight on such evidence as it was adduced only after Sanum's commencement of the arbitration proceedings. The Chinese Ministry of Foreign Affairs reacted to the SGCA ruling by issuing a statement criticizing the judgment and reiterating its position that only mainland Chinese investors are entitled to treaty protection of Chinese BITs and that Hong Kong and Macau investors should not be allowed to claim Chinese nationality for such purposes.[81]

On balance, different from other developing countries which are more likely to suffer net losses when getting involved in ISDS proceedings,[82] China has to date rarely been a respondent in ISDS proceedings and China has never lost in ISDS proceedings. China's limited but triumphant exposure to ISDS partially explains China's overall positive attitude towards ISDS.

3.3 *China's 'Go Global' Strategy and the Belt & Road Initiative*

As an essential part of its government-directed development model, China has adopted a government-mandated 'Go Global' policy since 2000. The essence of this policy is to promote the international operations of capable Chinese firms through outbound direct investment (ODI) with a view to enhancing international competitiveness.[83] This policy has been very successful, with a dramatic increase in Chinese ODI and an even larger potential for growth. UNCTAD ranked China third in the world in term of ODI in 2019, after the US and Japan.[84] In 2020, global FDI fell by 42% whilst China's ODI posted a year-on-year increase of 3.3 percent, reaching US$130 billion.[85]

With the introduction of China's ambitious Belt and Road Initiative (BRI), Chinese OFDI has reached a new level. As one of the most ambitious infrastructure projects ever conceived, the BRI includes a vast network of railways, energy pipelines, highways and streamlined border crossings both westward and southward, as well as investment in port development along the Indian Ocean, from Southeast Asia all the way to East Africa.[86] In 2020, Chinese ODI in 58 BRI countries stood at

[80] *Laos v Sanum* [2016] SGCA 100–121.

[81] Sun (2018), p. 104.

[82] Samples (2019), p. 163.

[83] Morrison (2019), pp. 17–18.

[84] UNCTAD (2020), p. 15.

[85] Chinese Ministry of Commerce (2021).

[86] Chatzky and McBride (2019).

US$17.8 billion, rising 18.3% compared to 2019.[87] The BRI has resulted in US$117.3 billion worth of ODI in total from its inception in 2013 to 2019.[88]

Despite all the rhetoric, however, China's BRI represents an inherently risky endeavour given the severe political instability and the lack of rule of law in many countries expected to participate in the BRI.[89] Many BRI countries perform poorly in the World Bank's Doing Business and Rule of Law rankings.[90] Some of these, such as Czechia, Poland, Egypt, and Russia, are among the most frequent respondents in ISDS proceedings.[91] Consequently, the protection of China's ODI from investment risks in BRI countries figures prominently in Chinese government's approach to BIT negotiations. In particular, Chinese investors may increasingly fall back on ISDS mechanisms in Chinese BITs, which promise to provide an enforceable procedural remedy against infringing host states.[92] Indeed, five mainland China investors have brought ISDS claims against host states in which they have invested since 2020. The advantages of ISDS in 'delocalizing' investment disputes by affording foreign investors an alternative to domestic courts, and in 'depoliticizing' investment disputes by removing them from the realm of diplomatic protection, have long been acknowledged.[93] For decades, ISDS has been the preferred means for capital exporting countries to protect the interests of their investors and to enforce the terms of investment agreements. Likewise, strong ISDS clauses have had positive effects on capital importing countries to attract inbound FDI flows.[94] Therefore, having fair, efficient and transparent ISDS mechanisms at either global, regional or bilateral level is in China's interest as both a major capital exporting and capital importing country in the world.

In summary, ISDS has been a standard feature of Chinese BITs. China's limited and triumphant experience with ISDS makes China more receptive to this dispute settlement mechanism. With increasing ODI after the launch of BRI, China now views ISDS as an important mechanism to promote cross-border investment flows and the rule of law in international investment governance.

---

[87] Ministry of Commerce of the PRC (2021).

[88] Ministry of Commerce of the PRC (2020), p. 17.

[89] Li and Zeng (2019).

[90] Davis et al. (2012).

[91] UNCTAD Investment Policy Hub (2021), https://investmentpolicy.unctad.org/investment-dispute-settlement.

[92] Pathirana (2017), p. 422.

[93] Kaufmann-Kohler and Potesta (2020), pp. 17–21.

[94] Asian Development Bank (2016), p. 163; Yackee (2008), pp. 827–828.

4 The Future of ISDS in the CAI

The conventional wisdom is that it is unlikely China will accept ICS in future CAI negotiations.[95] To begin with, China has made it clear in its UNCITRAL submission that China favours a *multilateral* instead of a bilateral approach to ISDS reform.[96] This is reflected in the commitment expressed in the CAI that both sides should continue to pursue the negotiations on ISDS, taking into account the work undertaken in the context of the UNCITRAL WGIII deliberations on the EU's MIC proposal. Second, China is not yet convinced that the EU's ICS proposal is the best path to reform ISDS. For instance, critics argued that the clamour for radical ISDS reform is a populist trend inspired by irrational fear, repeated by left-wing intellectuals and allied non-governmental organizations long on inflammatory rhetoric and emotion and very short on established facts and substance.[97] Questions were also raised on whether judges appointed only by states would not be biased in favour of states; the impact of an international investment court on the well-functioning ICSID, and substantial problems of coherence, rationalization, negotiation, ratification, establishment, functioning, staffing and financing that the new international investment court would face.[98] Indeed, many other states are lukewarm about the idea of moving ISDS forward to ICS.[99]

I argue that, while it is true that China is ambivalent about the EU's ICS proposal, there are really no strong reasons for China to oppose it either. In other words, China's approach to ISDS reform and the EU's ICS proposal are not inherently in conflict. There are good reasons for China to agree to a two-tier ICS in the CAI, as the EU has concluded with Canada, Singapore and other countries. To begin with, it is clear from China's UNCITRAL submission that China shares with the EU many concerns about the traditional ISDS model, in particular the lack of error-correcting mechanism and the lack of consistency and predictability of investment arbitral awards. Therefore, China supports the idea of an appeal body within the wider ISDS mechanism. An appeal mechanism was envisaged in China-Australia FTA in 2015, even though no substantial outcome emerged from the negotiations.[100]

Furthermore, one may argue that China's support for an appellate mechanism does not necessarily lead to its support for the EU's idea of a two-tier ICS. For example, when it comes to the appointment of the investment tribunal, the EU advocates a standing mechanism with the same body of adjudicators appointed for long and staggered terms who will form panels for individual cases on a randomised basis. China, by contrast, emphasizes party autonomy in selecting and nominating arbitrators, at least at the first instance level. But even though this argument may be

[95] Bickenbach and Liu (2018), pp. 15, 21.

[96] Submission from China (2019), p. 4.

[97] Brower and Ahmad (2018), pp. 1139, 1157.

[98] Van den Berg (2019), pp. 169–174.

[99] Brower and Ahmad (2018), p. 1155.

[100] China-Australia Free Trade Agreement (CHAFTA), Art. 9.23.

relevant to explaining China's reticence about the EU's MIC proposal at multilateral forums, to be discussed below, it is less relevant to a BIT such as the CAI. This is because, for the purpose of the CAI, China's preference for party autonomy in appointing adjudicators in the first instance could largely be accommodated by the EU's two-tier ICS. This can be illustrated by the ISDS clauses in the EU-Canada Comprehensive Economic and Trade Agreement (CETA) if they provide some guidance to the CAI. Among fifteen members of the tribunal, five of the members shall be nationals of a member state of the EU, five shall be nationals of China, and the remaining five are nationals of third countries. The tribunal shall hear investment disputes in divisions consisting of three members of the tribunal, of whom one shall be a national of a member state of the EU, one a national of China and one a national of a third country. The division shall be chaired by the member of the tribunal who is a national of a third country.[101] Therefore, China retains the right to appoint an arbitrator of Chinese national at the first-instance stage of arbitration proceeding. Moreover, while the ICS differs from traditional ISDS in some respects, notably regarding the existence of a permanent adjudicatory body and an appeal mechanism, in many other respects the ICS merely accommodates to trends already developed under IIAs and case law.[102] Both China and the EU have already expressed support for these trends, including strengthening ethical rules to avoid conflicts of interest for arbitrators and inclusion of alternative dispute resolution provisions in ISDS clauses.

It is a slightly different question whether China will support the EU's permanent MIC proposal at UNITRAL WGIII. China has so far not commented on the MIC proposal for several reasons. For one thing, different from the CAI, China's preference to retain the right to appoint arbitrators at the first-instance stage of arbitration proceeding cannot be accommodated in a multilateral treaty. But this concern may be mitigated because the EU has recently suggested an "open architecture", i.e., building a certain level of flexibility into its MIC proposal. For example, some countries may like to stick to *ad hoc* arbitral tribunals and utilize only the appeal mechanism of the two-tier MIC; or some might want to use the standing mechanism for state-to-state dispute settlement, but do not use ISDS in their agreements.[103] This flexibility enhances the appeal of the MIC for countries like China that may want an appeal mechanism only. In addition, the EU's proposal to establish a standing MIC is institutionally modelled after the WTO dispute settlement system.[104] As an active player and staunch defender of the WTO dispute settlement system, China may find the EU's MIC proposal familiar and is willing to support it. This is particularly true if other initiatives such as an appeal facility in lieu of ICSID annulment under the ICSID framework does not gain much traction.

101 CETA Art. 8.27 (3) and (6).

102 Alvarez (2020), p. 2.

103 Submission from the European Union (2019), para 3.16.

104 European Commission (2015), p. 9.

Finally, China's preference for multilateralism does not necessarily prevent China from agreeing to the ICS in the CAI. For one thing, given the diversified preferences to ISDS reform, current ISDS reform efforts are likely to produce an ever-more complex regime, governed by more diverse substantive rules interpreted by more complex options for dispute resolution.[105] It is unlikely that China will see a multilateral agreement on dispute settlement. Indeed, at UNCITRAL WGIII, the work plan proceeds on the assumption that these reforms will be brought together in a multilateral instrument that gives states the choice of which reforms to accept and with respect to which treaties, modelled on the Mauritius Convention.[106] China must choose accordingly. For instance, China's recent bid to join the CPTPP implicitly accepted that it can accept an incremental improvement over the traditional ISDS model without an appellate facility for some IIAs. For another, given that China's preferences can be accommodated in the ICS, there are no strong reason for China to be against the ICS in future CAI negotiations. It is entirely possible for China to embrace both incremental reforms embodied in the CPTPP and the ICS in the CAI. It should also be highlighted that China is not alone in adopting such an open and flexible approach to ISDS reform. Similar positions are taken by other countries such as Canada, Mexico and Japan.[107]

5 Conclusion

This chapter explores the future of the ISDS provisions in the CAI. Challenging the mainstream view that it is unlikely for China to be a supporter of the EU's ICS proposal in CAI negotiation, this chapter argues that such a conclusion may be premature. To support this claim, this chapter analyses China's approach to ISDS reform, explains how this approach is shaped by the underlying political and economic forces, and argues that the divergence between the approaches to ISDS reform of the EU and China may not be unbridgeable. For the purpose of the CAI, it is entirely possible for China to agree to a two-tier ICS as the EU has concluded with other countries because China's preferences in ISDS reform could be accommodated in the EU's proposal. Similarly, there are no strong reasons for China to oppose the EU's MIC proposal, particularly after the EU indicated that the MIC proposal could take an "open architecture".

[105] Alvarez (2020), p. 23.

[106] Note by the Secretariat, 'Possible Reforms of ISDS: Multilateral Instrument on ISDS Reform', A/CN.9/WG.III/WP.194 (16 January 2020).

[107] For example, these three countries have signed with the EU FTAs which provide two-tier ICS, but also members of CPTPP with traditional ISDS clauses.

References

Alvarez JM (2020) How Innovative is the EU's Proposal for an Investment Court System: A Comparison between ICS and Traditional Investor-State Dispute Settlement. Stanford-Vienna Transatlantic Technology Law Forum European Union Law Working Papers No. 43. https://law.stanford.edu/publications/no-43-how-innovative-is-the-eus-proposal-for-an-investment-court-system-a-comparison-between-ics-and-traditional-investor-state-dispute-settlement/. Accessed 20 Jan 2023

Asian Development Bank (2016) ASEAN Economic Integration Report 2016: What Drives Foreign Direct Investment in Asia and the Pacific. https://www.adb.org/sites/default/files/publication/214136/aeir-2016.pdf. Accessed 22 Jan 2023

Berger A (2015) Hesitant embrace: China's recent approach to international investment rulemaking. J Int Invest Trade 16:843–868

Bickenbach F, Liu WH (2018) Chinese direct investment in Europe - challenges for EU FDI policy. CESIFO Forum 19(4):15–22

Brabandere ED (2017) Mercantile adventurers? The disclosure of third-party funding in investment treaty arbitration. In: van Boom WH (ed) Litigation, costs, funding and behavior: implications for the law. Routledge, Abingdon, pp 105–128

Brower CN, Ahmad J (2018) Why the "Demolition Derby" that seeks to destroy investor-state arbitration? Southern Calif Law Rev 91:1139–1196

Brown CM (2017) A multilateral mechanism for the settlement of investment dispute: some preliminary sketches. ICSID Rev 32:673–690

Cai CY (2006) Outward foreign direct investment protection and the effectiveness of Chinese BIT practice. J World Inv Trade 7:621–652

Chaisse J, Ji XL (2022) Stress test for EU's investment court system: how will investments be protected in the comprehensive agreement on investment? Legal Issues Econ Integr 49(1):101–124

Chatzky A, McBride J (2019) China's massive belt and road initiative backgrounder. Council on Foreign Relations Report. https://www.cfr.org/backgrounder/chinas-massive-belt-and-road-initiative. Accessed 23 Jan 2023

Chi MJ, Wang X (2015) The evolution of ISA clauses in Chinese IIAs and its practical implications: the admissibility of disputes for investor-state arbitration. J World Invest Trade 16:869–898

Coe JC (2015) Toward a complementary use of conciliation in investor-state disputes - a preliminary sketch. U.C. Davis J Int Law Policy 12:7–46

Cymrot MA (2006) Investment disputes with China. Disp Resol J 61(3):80–87

Davis K et al (2012) Governance by indicators: global power through quantification and rankings. OUP, Oxford

Dietz T et al (2019) The legitimacy crisis of investor-state arbitration and the new EU investment court system. Rev Int Polit Econ 26(4):749–772

Du M, Shen W (2021) The future of investor-state dispute settlement: exploring China's changing attitude. In: Chaisse J et al (eds) Handbook of international investment law and policy. Springer, Heidelberg, pp 2483–2506

European Commission (2016) European Commission Proposes Signature and Conclusion of EU-Canada Trade Deal Press Release. https://ec.europa.eu/commission/presscorner/detail/en/IP_16_2371. Accessed 23 Jan 2023

European Commission (2018) Key Elements of the EU-Japan Economic partnership Agreement. https://ec.europa.eu/commission/presscorner/detail/en/MEMO_18_6784. Accessed 23 Jan 2023

European Commission (2020) EU-China Comprehensive Agreement on Investment: The Agreement in Principle. https://trade.ec.europa.eu/doclib/docs/2020/december/tradoc_159242.pdf. Accessed 23 Jan 2023

European Commission Concept Paper (2015) Investment in TTIP and Beyond-the Path for Reform. https://trade.ec.europa.eu/doclib/docs/2015/may/tradoc_153408.PDF. Accessed 23 Jan 2023

European Federation for Investment Law and Arbitration (EFILA) (2015) A Response to the Criticism against ISDS. https://files.core.ac.uk/pdf/1/83952088.pdf. Accessed 23 Jan 2023

European Parliament (2022) Legislative Train: EU-China CAI. https://www.europarl.europa.eu/legislative-train/theme-a-balanced-and-progressive-trade-policy-to-harness-globalisation/file-eu-china-investment-agreement. Accessed 23 Jan 2023

Fan K (2020) Mediation of investor-state disputes: a treaty survey. J Disp Resol 2:327–341

Gallagher N, Shan WH (2009) Chinese investment treaties: policies and practice. OUP, Oxford

Gómez KF (2021) EU-China negotiations on investor state dispute settlement within the CAI framework: are we on the right track. Revista General de Derecho Europeo 55:47–75

Guven B, Johnson L (2019) The policy implications of third-party funding in investor-state dispute settlement. Columbia Centre on Sustainable Investment Working Paper. https://scholarship.law.columbia.edu/cgi/viewcontent.cgi?article=1007&context=sustainable_investment_staff-pubs. Accessed 22 Jan 2023

Henckels C (2016) Protecting regulatory autonomy through greater precision in investment treaties: the TPP, CETA and TTIP. J Int Econ Law 19:27–50

Heymann MCE (2008) International law and the settlement of investment disputes relating to China. J Int Econ Law 11(3):507–526

Hu WN (2021) The EU-China comprehensive agreement on investment: an in-depth reading. CEPS Policy Insights No PI2021-07. https://www.ceps.eu/ceps-publications/the-eu-china-comprehensive-agreement-on-investment/. Accessed 21 Jan 2023

Kaufmann-Kohler G, Potesta M (2020) Investor-state dispute settlement and national courts: current framework and reform options. Springer, Heidelberg

Kong QJ (1999) Bilateral investment treaties: the Chinese approach and practice. Asian Yearb Int Law 8:105–136

Ku JG (2013) Enforcement of ICSID awards in the People's Republic of China. Contemp Asia Arbitr J 6:31–48

Langford M, Behn D (2018) Managing backlash: the evolving investment treaty arbitrator? Eur J Int Law 29(2):551–580

Langford M, Behn D, Lie RH (2017) The revolving door in international investment arbitration. J Int Econ Law 20:301–332

Li J, Wu SL (2020) From bilateral to multilateral: EU's reform of investment dispute settlement mechanism and China's choice. Int Trade 9:46–54

Li XJ, Zeng K (2019) Beijing is counting on its massive belt and road initiative, but are Chinese firms on board? Washington Post. https://www.washingtonpost.com/politics/2019/05/14/beijing-is-counting-its-massive-bridge-road-initiative-are-chinese-firms-board/. Accessed 23 Jan 2023

Li YW, Cheng B (2020) China's stance on investor-state dispute settlement: evolution, challenges, and reform options. Netherlands Int Law Rev 67:503–551

Markert L et al (2020) The investment treaty arbitration review: the comprehensive and progressive agreement for trans-pacific partnership. https://thelawreviews.co.uk/title/the-investment-treaty-arbitration-review/the-comprehensive-and-progressive-agreement-for-trans-pacific-partnership. Accessed 23 Jan 2023

McLaughlin M (2018) Global reform of investor-state arbitration: a tentative roadmap of China's emergent equilibrium. Chinese J Com Law 6(1):73–102

Michaels D (2020) Behind China's decade of European deals, state investors evade notice. Wall Street Journal. https://www.wsj.com/articles/behind-chinas-decade-of-european-deals-state-investors-evade-notice-11601458202. Accessed 23 Jan 2023

Ministry of Commerce of the PRC, National Bureau of Statistics and State Administration of Foreign Exchange (2020) 2019 Statistical Bulletin of China's Outward Foreign Direct Investment. China Commerce and Trade Press, Beijing.

Ministry of Commerce of the PRC, Regular Press Conference (January 24, 2021). http://www.mofcom.gov.cn/xwfbh/20210121.shtml. Accessed 23 Jan 2023

Morrison WM (2019) China's economic rise: history, trends, challenges, and implications for the United States. Congressional Research Service. https://crsreports.congress.gov/product/pdf/RL/RL33534. Accessed 23 Jan 2023
Olcott E (2021) China seeks to join transpacific trade pact. Financial Times. https://www.ft.com/content/df94b345-8fb9-473f-8e58-0cb230c0a1fa. Accessed 22 Jan 2023
Pathirana D (2017) Making an arbitration claim under Chinese BITs: some inferences from recent ISDS cases. Chinese J Comput Law 5(2):420–432
Puig S, Shaffer G (2018) Imperfect alternatives: institutional choice and the reform of investment law. Am J Int Law 112:361–409
Roberts A (2018) Incremental, systemic, and paradigmatic reform of investor-state arbitration. Am J Int Law 112:410–432
Roberts A, Bouraoui Z (2018) UNCTIRAL and ISDS Reform: What are States' concerns? https://www.ejiltalk.org/uncitral-and-isds-reforms-what-are-states-concerns/. Accessed 23 Jan 2023
Roberts A, John TS (2019) UNCITRAL and ISDS Reform: China's Proposal. https://www.ejiltalk.org/uncitral-and-isds-reform-chinas-proposal/. Accessed 23 Jan 2023
Samples TR (2019) Winning and losing in investor-state dispute settlement. Am Bus Law Rev 56(1):115–175
Schacherer S (2016) TPP, CETA and TTIP between innovation and consolidation-resolving investor-state disputes under mega-regionals. J Int Dispute Settlement 7:628–653
Schill SW (2007) Tearing down the great wall: the new generation investment treaties of the People's Republic of China. Cardozo J Int Comp Law 15:73–118
Schill SW, Vidigal G (2018) Cutting the Gordian Knot: Investment Dispute Settlement a la carte. RTA Exchange, International Centre for Trade and Sustainable Development (ICTSD) and the Inter-American Development Bank (IDB). https://uncitral.un.org/sites/uncitral.un.org/files/rta_exchange_-_investment_dispute_settlement_-_schill_and_vidigal.pdf. Accessed 23 Jan 2023
Shaffer G, Gao H (2018) China's rise: how it took on the U.S. at the WTO. Illinois Law Rev 2018(1):115–184
Shan WH, Gallagher N, Zhang S (2012) National treatment for foreign investment in China: a changing landscape. ICSID Rev 27:120–144
Shen W (2015) Expropriation in transition: evolving Chinese investment treaty practices in local and global contexts. Leiden J Int Law 28(3):579–604
Shen W (2021) Guarding the great wall? Jurisprudential review of treaty interpretative tools in Chinese BIT-based arbitration cases. Arbitr Int 37(1):239–286
Sun HW (2018) Emerging investment treaty arbitration practice in China. Proc ASIL Annual Meeting 112:103–105
Trakman LE (2015) Geopolitics, China, and investor-state arbitration. In: Toohey L, Picker CB, Greenacre J (eds) China in the international economic order. CUP, Cambridge, pp 268–292
UNCTAD (2020) World Investment Report 2020: International Production beyond the Pandemic https://unctad.org/system/files/official-document/wir2020_en.pdf. Accessed 23 Jan 2023
Van den Berg AJ (2019) Appeal mechanism for ISDS awards: interaction with the New York and ICSID conventions. ICSID Rev 34(1):156–189
Vidigal G, Stevens B (2018) Brazil's new model of dispute settlement for investment: return to the past or alternative for the future? J World Inv Trade 19:475–512
Wang GG (2009) China's practice in international investment law: from participation to leadership in the world economy. Yale J Int Law 34:575–587
Xi JP (2021) Let the torch of multilateralism light up humanity's way forward. Special Address at the World Economic Forum. https://www.fmprc.gov.cn/mfa_eng/wjdt_665385/zyjh_665391/202101/t20210125_678968.html. Accessed 23 Jan 2023
Yackee J (2008) Bilateral investment treaties, credible commitment, and the rule of (international) law: do BITs promote foreign direct investment. Law Soc Rev 42(4):805–832
Zhang YQ (2008) The case of China. In: Moser M (ed) Investor-state arbitration – lessons for Asia. Juris Publishing, Beijing, pp 159–167

Ming Du is Professor and Co-Director of Global Policy Institute at Durham University. He was raised in China and completed his Chinese law training at Tsinghua University School of Law in Beijing. He holds an LLM from Harvard Law School, where he was a Victor and William Fung Fellow and a DPhil from University of Oxford (Brasenose College) where he was a Clarendon Scholar. His current research focuses on the theoretical and structural issues of global economic governance (trade, investment and finance), China's approach to international law, and the development of the rule of law in contemporary China. His recent publications have appeared in Vanderbilt Journal of Transnational Law, Yearbook of European Law, European Law Journal, Georgetown JIL, Washington ILJ, and many other leading journals. He is the co-editor of Elgar Chinese Law and Policy Series and he sits on editorial boards of Chinese Journal of International Law, The Journal of World Investment & Trade, Chinese Journal of Transnational Law and Asia Pacific Law Review. He was a recipient of British Academy Senior Research Fellowship in 2024.

A New Dish of "CAI" for State-to-State Dispute Settlement in the EU-China Comprehensive Agreement on Investment

Anran Zhang

Abstract A new treaty dish of *Cai* (literally "cuisine") concerning investment access and protection was prepared by the European Union (EU) and China at the end of 2020. The EU-China Comprehensive Agreement on Investment (CAI) contain a settlement section for resolving disputes arising between the EU and China, which also includes a chapter on the State-to-State Dispute Settlement (SSDS). SSDS in CAI establishes a comprehensive and step-by-step arbitration mechanism for resolving disputes between the Parties compared with other investment treaties signed between China and EU member states. This chapter is an exhaustive study on the SSDS in the CAI. It argues that SSDS designed with political expectations shows joint effort from both the EU and China towards a reformative mechanism to resolve disputes arising from the investment treaty.

1 Introduction

The end of the year 2020 is to be remembered and celebrated by all businessmen and industrial players from the European Union (EU) and China. The same feelings have also been experienced by scholars and analysts specialising in international investment and trade (law) between the EU and China. On 30 December 2020, the negotiation of the EU-China Comprehensive Agreement on Investment (CAI) was finally concluded with an agreement in principle. Leaders of both the EU and China joined the signing ceremony virtually. However, the honeymoon period did not last long, and the European Commission voted to freeze the ratification of the CAI on 4 May 2021. How and when the two sides will iron out the differences and push the ratification process forward is yet to be determined.

CAI contains a dispute settlement section for resolving disputes arising between the EU and China (collectively the "Parties"). The State-to-State dispute settlement

A. Zhang (✉)
International Chamber of Commerce (ICC) Dispute Resolution Services, Shanghai, China

© The Author(s), under exclusive license to Springer Nature Switzerland AG 2024

A. Svetlicinii, I.-J. Chen (eds.), *The EU-China Comprehensive Agreement on Investment*, European Yearbook of International Economic Law,
https://doi.org/10.1007/978-3-031-66862-3_12

(SSDS) provisions contained in the CAI establish a comprehensive and step-by-step dispute settlement mechanism for resolving disputes between the Parties. However, CAI remains silent on investment dispute settlement, traditionally the investor-State dispute settlement (ISDS). Once the political tension between the Parties is looser, the Parties will finally get back to the table to ratify the treaty and move forward to negotiate the ISDS provisions.

After giving a brief introduction, this chapter will provide an overview of the SSDS mechanism adopted in the CAI. CAI creates a toolkit for the Parties to choose from, including consultation, mediation, and arbitration for resolving disputes by reaching a mutual agreement. Successful conclusion of the principal treaty provisions is a remarkable achievement for the Parties and more broadly for the world. The rationale of including the SSDS in the CAI will be analysed to foresee the tendency of the Parties to make use of the dispute settlement mechanism (DSM) in negotiations. This chapter argues that CAI has signalled a new era, demonstrating joint efforts from both the EU and China. The CAI is expected to make a new dish of *Cai* for resolving investment disputes.

2 Dispute Settlement Mechanism in CAI

Section V of the CAI establishes a comprehensive DSM for resolving disputes arising from the CAI. DSM only covers disputes concerning the interpretation and application of the provisions in the CAI.[1] This implies that SSDS is the exclusive DSM until ISDS is negotiated within two years of signing the CAI.[2] However, it remains unknown whether this estimated timeline will be met, because the EU has frozen its internal process of moving the CAI forward. The Parties also agreed to establish an investment committee at the level of Vice Premier for China and of Executive Vice President of the European Commission for the EU (the "Investment Committee"). The Parties intend to set up the Investment Committee at a higher governmental level to implement and monitor the CAI. This internal committee intends to comment on urgent matters with institutional oversight.[3] The SSDS mechanism contained in the CAI gives the most detailed and step-by-step provisions compared with other bilateral investment treaties (BITs) signed by the EU member states and China.[4]

[1] CAI, Section V Dispute Settlement, Art. 2 (Scope of Application).

[2] Answer given by Executive Vice-President Dombrovskis on behalf of the European Commission, press release (26 April 2021) https://www.europarl.europa.eu/doceo/document/E-9-2021-000926-ASW_EN.html.

[3] The EU, 'The EU-China Comprehensive Agreement on Investment-The Agreement in Principle' (30 December 2020) https://trade.ec.europa.eu/doclib/docs/2020/december/tradoc_159242.pdf.

[4] The China-Austria BIT (1985); The China-Belgium Luxembourg Economic Union BIT (2005); The China-Bulgaria BIT (1989); The China-Croatia BIT(1993); The China-Cyprus BIT (2001); The China-Czech Republic BIT (1991); The China-Demark BIT (1985); The China-Estonia BIT

The typical SSDS provisions in the BITs usually have the same scope of application as the CAI, covering the application and interpretation of the agreements.[5] Investment treaties usually set up a cooling-off period for disputant parties to conduct internal consultations and negotiations with each other before submitting their disputes to an ad hoc tribunal.[6] Some treaties may explicitly request consultation and/or negotiation via existing diplomatic channels between the parties.[7] When parties decide to pursue arbitration for dispute settlement, treaties may further ask how an ad hoc tribunal should be constituted and if one cannot be convened, the

(1993); The China-Finland BIT (2004); The China-France BIT (2007); The China- Germany BIT (2003); The China-Greece BIT (1992); The China-Hungary BIT (1991); The China-Italy BIT (1985); The China-Latvia BIT (2004); The China-Lithuania BIT (1993); The China-Malta BIT (2009); The China-the Netherlands BIT (2001); The China-Poland BIT (1988); The China-Portugal BIT (2005); The China-Romania BIT (1994); The China-Slovakia BIT (1991); The China-Slovenia BIT (1993); The China-Spain BIT (2005); The China-Sweden BIT (1982). This is based on UNCTAD, "Investment Policy Hub Database' http://investmentpolicyhub.unctad.org/IIA/CountryBits/42#iiaInnerMenu.

[5]According to the UNCTAD International Investment Agreements Navigator, 2556 out of 2574 mapped treaties include SSDS provisions. See https://investmentpolicy.unctad.org/international-investment-agreements/iia-mapping. Accessed 27 March 2022. This research takes the BITs signed between China and the EU Member States as examples, finding that SSDS provisions in the following treaties cover the application and/or interpretation of the treaties: China-Austria BIT (1985), Art. 10.1; China-Belgium Luxembourg Economic Union BIT (2005), Art. 9.1; China-Bulgaria BIT (1989), Art. 8.1; China-Croatia BIT(1993), Art. 7.1; China-Cyprus BIT (2001), Art. 8.1; China-Czech Republic BIT (1991), Art. 8.1; China-Demark BIT (1985), Art. 9.1; China-Estonia BIT (1993), Art. 7.1; China-Finland BIT (2004), Art. 8.1; China-France BIT (2007), Art. 10.1; China-Germany BIT (2003), Art. 8.1; China-Greece BIT (1992), Art. 9.1; China-Hungary BIT (1991), Art. 9.1; China-Italy BIT (1985), Art. 11.1; China-Latvia BIT (2004), Art. 8.1; China-Lithuania BIT (1993), Art 7.1; China-Malta BIT (2009), Art. 8.1; China-the Netherlands BIT (2001), Art. 9.1; China-Poland BIT (1988), Art. 9.1; China-Portugal BIT (2005), Art. 8.1; China-Romania BIT (1994), Art. 8.1; China-Slovakia BIT (1991), Art. 8.1; China-Slovenia BIT (1993), Art. 7.1; China-Spain BIT (2005), Art. 8.1; and China-Sweden BIT (1982), Art. 6.1.

[6]China-Austria BIT (1985), Art. 10.2; China-Belgium Luxembourg Economic Union BIT (2005), Art. 9.3; China-Croatia BIT(1993), Art. 7.2; China-Cyprus BIT (2001), Art. 8.2; China-Czech Republic BIT (1991), Art. 8.2; China-Demark BIT (1985), Art. 9.1; China-Estonia BIT (1993), Art. 7.2; China-Finland BIT (2004), Art. 8.2; China-France BIT (2007), Art. 10.2; China-Germany BIT (2003), Art. 8.2; China-Greece BIT (1992), Art. 9.2; China-Hungary BIT (1991), Art. 9.2; China-Italy BIT (1985), Art. 11.2; China-Latvia BIT (2004), Art. 8.2; China-Lithuania BIT (1993), Art. 7.2; China-Malta BIT (2009), Art. 8.2; China-the Netherlands BIT (2001), Art. 9.2; China-Poland BIT (1988), Art. 9.2; China-Portugal BIT (2005), Art. 8.2; China-Romania BIT (1994), Art. 8.2; China-Slovakia BIT (1991), Art. 8.2; China-Slovenia BIT (1993), Art. 7.2; China-Spain BIT (2005), Art. 8.2.

[7]China-Belgium Luxembourg Economic Union BIT (2005), Art. 9.1; China-Croatia BIT(1993), Art. 7.1; China-Cyprus BIT (2001), Art. 8.1; China-Czech Republic BIT (1991), Art. 8.1; China-Estonia BIT (1993), Art. 7.1; China-Finland BIT (2004), Art. 8.1; China-France BIT (2007), Art. 10.1; China- Germany BIT (2003), Art. 8.1; China-Greece BIT (1992), Art. 9.1; China-Hungary BIT (1991), Art. 9.1; China-Italy BIT (1985), Art. 11.1; China-Latvia BIT (2004), Art. 8.1; China-Lithuania BIT (1993), Art. 7.1; China-Malta BIT (2009), Art. 8.1; China-the Netherlands BIT (2001), Art. 9.1; China-Poland BIT (1988), Art. 9.1; China-Portugal BIT (2005), Art. 8.1; China-Romania BIT (1994), Art. 8.1; China-Slovakia BIT (1991), Art. 8.1; China-Slovenia BIT (1993), Art. 7.1; China-Spain BIT (2005), Art. 8.1.

International Court of Justice (ICJ) could appoint the chairperson of an ad hoc tribunal, at the request of either disputant party.[8]

However, the SSDS in the EU-China CAI is different from the SSDS provisions within other traditional investment treaties. The CAI consists of 22 articles in Section V (subject to any further modification made in the legal and technical revision process). Two annexes are also included, one establishing the rules of procedure for SSDS (the "Rules of Procedure") and the other covering the code of conduct for members of arbitral panellists and mediators in State-to-State disputes (the "Code of Conduct"). The Rules of Procedure set up procedural regulations for conducting SSDS under the CAI. SSDS mechanism in the CAI adopt three options for resolving disputes between the two Parties, including consultation as a primer and compulsory DSM, mediation as a voluntary and optional DSM and arbitration as the core and essential DSM.

The objective of SSDS in the CAI is to establish an effective and efficient mechanism for the Parties to reach a mutual agreement on dispute resolution.[9] To achieve this goal, mutual agreement between the Parties should be sufficiently respected and can be made at any time, regardless of whether the parties are in the midst of proceedings.[10] Once a mutual agreement is achieved, disputant Parties shall abide by the agreement with no delay and in good faith and take any necessary measure to implement the solution within the agreed period of time.[11] The Party taking the implementation measures shall notify the other Party within the agreed time.[12] As a guiding principle, transparency should always be guaranteed, including requests for consultations and statements to the arbitration proceedings, and hearings should be open to the public unless otherwise provided in the Rules of Procedures.[13] Moreover, natural persons from one Party or legal persons established in one Party are able to recommend *amicus curiae* briefs to the arbitration panel by following the Rules of Procedure.[14]

---

[8] China-Austria BIT (1985), Art. 10.4; China-Belgium Luxembourg Economic Union BIT (2005), Art. 9.3; China-Croatia BIT (1993), Art. 7.4; China-Cyprus BIT (2001), Art. 8.4; China-Czech Republic BIT (1991), Art. 8.4; China-Demark BIT (1985), Art. 9.2; China-Estonia BIT (1993), Art. 7.4; China-Finland BIT (2004), Art. 8.4; China- Germany BIT (2003), Art. 8.4; China-Greece BIT (1992), Art. 9.4; China-Hungary BIT (1991), Art. 9.4; China-Italy BIT (1985), Art. 11.4; China-Latvia BIT (2004), Art. 8.4; China-Lithuania BIT (1993), Art. 7.4; China-Malta BIT (2009), Art. 8.4; China-the Netherlands BIT (2001), Art. 9.4; China-Poland BIT (1988), Art. 9.4; China-Portugal BIT (2005), Art. 8.4; China-Romania BIT (1994), Art. 8.4; China-Slovakia BIT (1991), Art. 8.4; China-Slovenia BIT (1993), Art. 7.4; China-Spain BIT (2005), Art. 8.4. In addition, Article 10.4 of the China-France BIT (2007) and Article 6.4 of the China-Sweden BIT (1982) request the Secretary General of the UN as the appointing authority.

[9] CAI, Section V Dispute Settlement, Art. 1.

[10] CAI, Art. 5.1.

[11] CAI, Art. 5.4.

[12] CAI, Art. 5.5.

[13] CAI, Arts. 19.1 & 19.2; Annex I Rules of Procedure for State-to-State Dispute Settlement, Art. X.

[14] CAI, Art. 19.3; Annex I Rules of Procedure for State-to-State Dispute Settlement, Art. XIII regulates how *amicus curiae* submissions should be made under the CAI.

2.1 Primer and Compulsory Consultation

In the first stage, the disputant parties are obligated to pursue consultations in good faith to reach an agreement.[15] Using the word "shall" in the provision, Article 3.1 explicitly sets up the legal obligation on the parties to start a formal DSM to discuss the disputed matter and find a satisfactory resolution. The form of the consultation request is also specified by the CAI: it should be in writing and set out the reasons, including (1) identifying the measure at issue; (2) the legal basis for the complaint; (3) specifying the terms of reference and the scope of application of the CAI.[16]

After the complaining party sends the request for consultation, the other party shall replay within 10 days.[17] Parties are free to choose the date of the consultation and the date to conclude. With no parties' agreement, consultation processes shall start within 30 days by default and be concluded within 30 days of receipt of the request.[18] In principle, consultations take place in the territory of the Party complained against unless the parties agree on another location.[19] During the consultation, both parties are obligated to give sufficient factual information for a full examination of the disputed matters.[20] However, all information disclosed and arguments made by the parties during the consultations are strictly bound by confidentiality, and thus cannot prejudice the parties' rights in any further DSM. Mutual agreements reached between the parties during the negotiation process is an ideal circumstance that will subsequently bar the disputant parties to submit another claim to arbitration.[21] In the other words, mutual agreements made through negotiation are final and binding to the parties.

Only when consultation fails may the complaining party make a request in writing to establish a panel for arbitration.[22] The failure of consultation can occur in many circumstances, including (1) where the party complained against fails to respond to the request within 10 days; (2) where consultations are not held within the timeframes required by the CAI; and (3) where concluded consultations do not reach any mutual agreement.[23]

Exhausting consultation before submitting disputes to arbitration was not initiated in the BITs between China and EU Member States. However, the existing BITs do not provide a comprehensive procedure related to consultation. One exception is

---

[15] CAI, Art. 3.1.

[16] CAI, Art. 3.2.

[17] CAI, Art. 3.3 defines the Parties involved in the dispute as the complaining Party and the Party complained against. Art. 22 of Section V further defines that all time periods shall be counted in calendar days from the day following the act to which they refer, unless otherwise specified.

[18] CAI, Art. 3.3.

[19] CAI, Art. 3.5.

[20] CAI, Art. 3.6.

[21] CAI, Art. 5.2.

[22] CAI, Art. 6.1.

[23] CAI, Art. 3.4.

the China-Belgium Luxembourg Economic Union BIT (2005), Articles 9.2 and 9.3 of which request a joint commission consisting of representatives of the Contracting Parties to convene and settle disputes. If the joint commission fails, the Contracting Party can submit the claim to an arbitration panel.

2.2 *Voluntarily and Optional Mediation*

Compared with consultation, mediation is a voluntary DSM that parties are free to choose at any time pursuant to the CAI.[24] This may imply that even when parties have an ongoing negotiation or formal arbitration process, they still have the liberty to continue or switch to mediation to reach a mutual agreement. When parties agree to start the mediation process, they shall also agree on the selection, tasks, and powers of the mediator, selecting the rules governing the procedure, and indicating the procedural matters of mediation such as timeframe, termination and costs.[25] However, no particular mediation rule is selected in the CAI, so parties shall choose either an institutional mediation rule or specify their procedural rules on an ad hoc basis, depending on the follow-up approach, which may be concluded three years after the entry into force of the CAI.[26] CAI respects the nature of mediation, which is confidential. As a consequence, the parties may disclose to the public the fact that mediation is taking place, but no information or content obtained from the mediation proceeding may be disclosed. In principle, mediation under the CAI shall be confidential, in particular the terms of parties' legal positions, evidence obtained by the parties, and any advice or solution proposed by the mediator.[27] Similar to consultation proceedings, mediation proceedings do not prejudice the rights of either party in any further DSM proceedings, such as arbitration.[28]

2.3 *Core and Customised Arbitration*

Arbitration is the most comprehensive DSM adopted by the CAI. CAI provides a step-by-step arbitration mechanism, from the establishment of an arbitration panel to the implementation of the panel report, for disputant parties to avail themselves of if consultation fails. When the complaining party seeks arbitration for dispute settlement, an arbitration panel should be established first, by delivering the request

---

[24] CAI, Art. 4.1.

[25] CAI, Art. 4.2.

[26] CAI, Art. 4.4.

[27] CAI, Art. 4.3.

[28] Ibid.

in writing from the complaining party to the party complained against.[29] Once the request is successfully delivered, an arbitration panel will be established. The request shall indicate the exhaustion of consultation, identify the specific measure at issue, and give a brief explanation of how the measure breaches the provisions of the CAI, to grant a sufficient legal basis for the complaints.[30]

Within 10 days of delivering the request for arbitration, parties shall consult to agree on the composition of a three-person tribunal.[31] However, it may be practically difficult for parties to agree on the composition of all panellists within the time. In this case, parties can appoint their arbitrators from the panellists of the CAI (the "List"), which will be finalized within six months after the entry into force of the CAI. CAI requests the Investment Committee to establish a list of at least twelve individuals in three sub-lists, each including at least four individuals.[32] Both the EU and China will propose individuals who are willing and able to serve as the panellists in their sub-lists.[33] The third sub-list consists of nationals who should be neither from the EU nor China for the maintenance of neutrality and will serve as the chair for the arbitration process (the "Chairperson List"). All those on the lists and sub-lists shall be professionals with leading expertise in law and international trade or investment.[34] The Investment Committee may propose additional people with knowledge and expertise in specific sectors under the CAI to join the arbitration panel.[35] All panellists shall follow the Code of Conduct under the CAI, being independent of other external instructions and without any affiliation to the government of any Party.[36]

With a textual understanding of the CAI, parties may not be obligated to choose their panellists from the List with a condition of reaching a mutual agreement on all the panellists within the time limits, 10 days from the delivery of the arbitration request. Only when the parties fail to agree on all names may each party appoint panellists from the List. Each party appoints one panellist from their respective sub-lists within 5 days from the expiry of the time limit. Collectively, each party can only start their appointment processes a minimum of 15 days from the delivery of the request. When one party fails to appoint its panellist arbitrator, the other party shall select another panellist arbitrator from the sub-list of that party. For the chair of the arbitration panel, if parties can not reach an agreement, the complaining party shall select a chair from the chairperson list. Once all three arbitrators are selected or agreed upon by the parties, the date of composition of the panel is the date when all arbitrators accepted their appointment according to the Rules of Procedure where

[29] CAI, Art. 6.1.

[30] CAI, Art. 6.2.

[31] CAI, Arts. 7.1 & 7.2.

[32] CAI, Art. 8.2.

[33] CAI, Art. 8.1.

[34] CAI, Art. 8.3.

[35] CAI, Art. 8.4.

[36] CAI, Art. 8.3.

applicable.[37] Both parties shall subsequently make the constitution of the arbitration public without delay.

CAI further specifies the functions of the arbitration panel and its standard terms of reference. Concerning the functions, the arbitration panel shall "a) make an objective assessment of the matter before it, including an objective assessment of the facts of the case and the applicability of the conformity with the covered provisions; b) consult regularly with the parties and provide adequate opportunities for the development of a mutually agreed solution."[38] The arbitration panel has full power to start, suspend, terminate and end the proceedings. To obtain adequate information and technical advice, the arbitration panel may, on request of a party or its own initiative, seek assistance or opinions from any sources.[39] When the arbitration panel considers inviting experts' witnesses, it shall consult with the parties.[40] All the information and technical advice received by the arbitration panel should be disclosed to the parties for comment.[41]

The panel may suspend the proceeding for a maximum 12 months after receiving the request from the complaining party or at the request of both parties to give the party complained against a chance to comment.[42] During the suspension period, the periods under the CAI will be extended by the same time as the suspension.[43] The arbitration panel shall recommence the proceeding at the request of the complaining party or both parties, depending on who requested the suspension. If the party does not request a resumption at the expiry of the suspension period, the arbitration panel will lose authority and the arbitration procedure is terminated.[44] Arbitration can also be terminated if parties notify the arbitration panel accordingly.[45]

While the proceeding continues, the arbitration panel shall examine and decide the disputed matters following the CAI. Concerning the scope of SSDS, disputes usually relate to the interpretation of the relevant provisions, so customary rules on the interpretation of public international law, as coded in the Vienna Convention of the Law of Treaties, shall be followed.[46] Innovatively, CAI allows for the arbitration panel to additionally consider related interpretations in reports of the World Trade Organization (WTO) panels and the Appellate Body, which may serve as a reference to the arbitration procedure under the CAI. The domestic law of the party

[37] CAI, Art. 7.5.

[38] CAI, Art. 9.1.

[39] CAI, Art. 20.1.

[40] CAI, Art. 20.2.

[41] CAI, Art. 20.3.

[42] CAI, Art. 10.1.

[43] CAI, Art. 10.2.

[44] Ibid.

[45] CAI, Art. 10.3.

[46] CAI, Art. 11.1.

complained against may also be considered as a matter of fact without any prejudice if the law is relevant to the claim.[47]

CAI determines the outcomes of arbitration proceedings, a panel report rather than an arbitral award published. Instead of issuing the interim/final award, the arbitration panel is required to draft two reports. The interim report shall be delivered within 120 days after the composition of the panel and the final report shall be delivered within 150 days.[48] Reports are final and binding to the Parties on the matter to which reports refer and the Parties shall unconditionally accept any decisions and reports made by the panel.[49] Reports and decisions, excluding confidential information, should be made public and overt within 15 days after the issuance to the Parties.[50]

Concerning the interim report, if the time cannot be met, the chairperson of the panel shall notify the parties in writing and explain the consequences of the delay and the planned date for delivering the report. However, in any case, the interim report should be delivered no later than 150 days after the composition of the arbitration panel.[51] After receiving the interim report, each party has 10 days to review the interim report and deliver a written response, if any.[52] One party has 6 days to respond to the comments of the other after receiving their comments.[53]

Similarly, any delay of the final report should also be notified to the parties and the final report should be delivered no later than 180 days after the composition of the arbitration panel.[54] However, compared with the interim report, CAI gives more weight to the content of the final report, which shall include a discussion of the parties' written comments on the interim report and "set out the findings of the facts, the applicability of the covered provisions and the basic rationale behind any findings and conclusions."[55] For effective decision-making, the arbitration panel shall in principle reach a consensus, but if this is not possible, decisions shall be made by a majority vote with no dissenting opinion on either the issue or the disagreeing parties disclosed.[56] The Rules of Procedures give more detail on how the arbitration panel should be constituted in terms of the appointment and replacement of panellists and how the panel should operate in terms of written submissions, organizational meetings, hearings, and questions to the parties for resolving disputes.

If the arbitration panel supports the complaining party and concludes that the party complained against has acted inconsistently with the legal obligations of the

---

[47] CAI, Art. 11.2.

[48] CAI, Art. 12.1.

[49] CAI, Art. 12.6.

[50] CAI, Art. 12.7.

[51] CAI, Art. 12.1.

[52] CAI, Art. 12.2.

[53] Ibid.

[54] CAI, Art. 12.3.

[55] CAI, Art. 12.4.

[56] CAI, Art. 12.5.

CAI, then the arbitration panel shall request the party complained against to correct the inconsistency and conform with the CAI. CAI is silent on what will happen if the arbitration panel does not find any inconsistency in the behaviour of the party complained against, but it may be conjectured that the arbitration panel will dismiss the claims of the complaining party. Implementation of the report then becomes key for the objectives of the SSDS to be achieved. The party failing to comply with its obligations under the CAI should take necessary measures to promptly comply with the final report.[57] That party shall, within 30 days of receipt of the final report or a date agreed by both parties, inform the other party of its intentions in respect of compliance.[58] Although the party is supposed to undertake prompt measures to implement the panel report, immediate compliance may not possible. The party complained against is required to set out a reasonable timeframe for compliance for the other party to agree.[59] If the other party disagrees, the party complained against shall request the arbitration panel to decide on a reasonable period.[60]

Prior to the date of expiry of the reasonable period, the party complained against shall notify the complaining party about what measures have been taken to comply with the report. The complaining party reserves the right to review the compliance measures. If the measures taken do not adhere to the CAI provisions established by the panel report, the complaining party may request the arbitration panel to make a further determination.[61]

Mutually acceptable compensation between the party complained against and the complaining party should be negotiated by following the steps provided by the CAI.[62] To implement the panel report, temporary remedies may be adopted if the Parties do not reach a compensation agreement or the party complained against notifies the complaining party that it is not able to comply with the report. The party complained against shall notify the complaining party if it fails to make effective and practical compensation within a reasonable time. The complaining party may notify its intention to suspend the application of concessions and obligations under the CAI to the party complained against, and such a suspension would come into effect 10 days after notification.[63] In the notification, the complaining party should indicate the level and scope of suspension, which is not unlimited.[64] The complaining parties "should first seek to suspend obligation in the same sector(s) as that affected by the measure that the arbitration panel has found to be inconsistent with the obligations under this Treaty; and if the complaining party considers that it is not

[57] CAI, Art. 13.1.

[58] CAI, Art. 13.2.

[59] CAI, Art. 14.1.

[60] CAI, Arts.14.4 & 14.5. The maximum period is 15 months from the issuance of the panel report unless both Parties extend this limit.

[61] CAI, Art. 15.2 & 15.2. The arbitration panel must deliver its further report within 50 days after the date of the receipt of the request for further determination.

[62] CAI, Art. 16.

[63] CAI, Art. 16.2 & 16.3.

[64] CAI, Art. 16.1.

practical nor effective in inducing compliance to suspend obligations in the same sector(s), it may suspend obligations in other sectors."[65]

The party complained against has the right to assess the suspension measures. Wherein it considers the level and scope exceed the nullification and impairment caused by the violation of the CAI, the party complained against can ask the arbitration panel to gauge the measures; during the examination period, the suspension continues until the arbitration panel decides. Suspension is temporary until the suspending circumstances disappear, including mutual agreement of a solution, compliance measures being undertaken, or the arbitration panel withdrawing or amending the existing measures.[66]

After temporary remedies are adopted, the parties need to agree the amended measures. The party complained against shall notify the complaining party of the measures that have been undertaken to comply following the suspension of obligation or application of temporary compensation.[67] The notification should also describe how non-conformity has been removed in its measures. If the notified measures are accepted by the complaining party, the suspension and compensation (where applicable) shall be completed no later than 30 days after the delivery of the notification. If the notified measures are not accepted and the parties do not agree, the arbitration panel may decide the matter.[68] As can be seen, the arbitration panel exercises wide and full authority according to the CAI. Their authority covers not only its decisions in the form of reports but also temporary remedies for the effective implementation of its reports.

The CAI pays great attention to bilateral dialogue between the two parties. CAI mentions that, when a dispute arises from a particular measure in alleged breach of an obligation under the treaty, the parties should select the forum for dispute settlement.[69] Fora include State-to-State arbitration under the CAI, WTO disputes with a panel established under the WTO Rules (Article 6 of the Understanding on Rules and Procedures Governing the Settlement of Disputes of the WTO) and other disputes under other treaties shall follow the applicable treaty provisions.[70] The selection of each forum mentioned above is made by one party and has a duration of exclusivity in the sense that the selected forum will be adopted until no findings can be discovered for procedural or jurisdictional reasons.[71] However, CAI does not preclude any party from suspending obligations authorized in the WTO proceedings or other DSM of any other treaty involved by the parties. Conversely, the WTO

[65] CAI, Art. 16.4.

[66] CAI, Art. 16.6.

[67] CAI, Art. 17.1.

[68] CAI, Art. 17.2. Article 17.4 rules how the arbitration panel should decide the matter.

[69] CAI, Art. 21.1.

[70] CAI, Art. 21.3.

[71] CAI, Art. 21.1.

Agreement and other treaties do not preclude a party from suspending obligations under the CAI.[72]

3 SSDS: Political-Driven and Joint Design

CAI is a political target set by both the EU and China and its necessity and importance were confirmed in many political dialogues. Since the first treaty negotiation in 2013 during the EU-China Summit, the EU and China have concluded 35 rounds of negotiation. Both sides sped up, with 10 intensive rounds of negotiation with a commitment to finalize the principal provisions within the year 2020. The CAI was finally signed at the last moment of 2020.

3.1 Politically Driven: Way in and Way Out

Although CAI has economic objectives, the treaty was created with a strong political presence. This presence is also demonstrated in the WTO treaty, the DSM of which has also been authorized in the CAI. The WTO treaty also builds up a community grounded on political, mutually recognized agreements to provide a general balance of rights and obligations to all member states via a dispute settlement mechanism.[73] The difference is that the SSDS in CAI is simpler, only regulating the rights and obligations between two parties, China and the EU, the political relation of which therefore deserves to be discussed.

International study of the CAI usually uses the agreement in principle available on the EU website, which is not the outcome of the agreement and will be final upon signature by both Parties.[74] The Parties still have many areas for further negotiation, notably ISDS. Concerning SSDS, the Parties must constitute the Investment Committee with lists of panellists.

On 20 May 2021, the European Parliament voted to freeze the CAI in response to the sanctions on European advocates made by the Chinese government.[75] No matter how many benefits the Parties may obtain, political tension must be released before the CAI is ratified. CAI seemed fated to experience many political challenges to its ratification, both internal and external.

---

[72] CAI, Art. 21.4.

[73] Ceva and Fracasso (2010), p. 461.

[74] European Commission, 'China' (22 January 2021) https://trade.ec.europa.eu/doclib/press/index.cfm?id=2237.

[75] Politico, 'European Parliament votes to 'freeze' investment deal until China lifts sanctions' (20 May 2021). https://www.politico.eu/article/european-parliament-freezes-china-investment-deal-vote/.

The cognitive splits towards China within the EU member states make ratification difficult. From an internal aspect, the EU member States have a distinct policy in their relationship with China. The distinction is more apparent between member States having close economic partnerships with China, and those with looser arrangements. For example, as one of the major beneficiaries of the CAI, Germany supports its ratification and Angela Merkel pushed for the CAI's conclusion during Germany's time in the EU presidency.[76] Another example is the downgraded bilateral diplomatic relationship between China and Lithuania because Lithuania allowed the Taiwanese authorities to set up a "Taiwanese Representative Office" in Lithuania.[77] The strained relationship between Lithuania and China further hits exports from Lithuania to China. As a consequence, Lithuania sought support from the EU for its alleged trade disputes with China. In its statement, the European Commission must balance unity and solidarity within the EU with its bilateral relation with China. In a recent statement, the EC declared that "the EU would also assess the compatibility of China's action with its obligations under the World Trade Organisation"[78] rather than a direct economic sanction against China.

The external relationship of China and the EU with a third country, in particular the US, may also impact the ratification of the CAI. Shortly after a rumour about the conclusion of the CAI spread, Jake Sullivan, the President-elect Biden's national security adviser (now the national security advisor of the US) called for "early consultations with our European partners on our common concerns about China's economic practices" quoted on Twitter.[79] This post epitomises the concerns of US officials. Although China overtook the US to become the largest EU import source for goods in 2021, the EU still recognizes the US as its largest trade and investment partner.[80] The EU and the US have a historically close relationship with common interests and core values in not only the economy but also international politics and

[76] Politico, 'Merkel Pushes EU-China Investment Deal Over the Finish Line Despite Criticism' (29 December 2020) https://www.politico.eu/article/eu-china-investment-deal-angela-merkel-pushes-finish-line-despite-criticism/.

[77] Euronews, 'Taiwanese Representative Office in Lithuania' (20 July 2021) https://www.euronews.com/2021/07/20/taiwan-to-open-de-facto-embassy-in-lithuania-under-own-name-prompting-rebuke-from-china; DW 'Taiwan opens representative office in Lithuania' (18 November 2021) https://www.dw.com/en/taiwan-opens-representative-office-in-lithuania/a-59853874.

[78] European Commission, 'Joint Statement by High Representative/Vice-President Josep Borrell and Executive Vice-President Valdis Dombrovskis on China's measures against Lithuania' (8 December 2021) https://trade.ec.europa.eu/doclib/press/index.cfm?id=2340.

[79] VOA News, 'EU-China Investment Talks Near Completion, Raising Concerns' (25 December 2020) https://www.voanews.com/a/east-asia-pacific_voa-news-china_eu-china-investment-talks-near-completion-raising-concerns/6200011.html; Financial Times, 'Biden Team Voices Concern Over EU-China Investment Deal' (22 December 2020) https://www.ft.com/content/2f0212ab-7e69-4de0-8870-89dd0d414306.

[80] European Commission, 'United States' https://ec.europa.eu/trade/policy/countries-and-regions/countries/united-states/.

the military.[81] Even though the EU-US relation suffered a trust crisis, in particular for trade, under the Trump administration, the bilateral relation has gradually warmed again under the Biden administration. However, it would be too simple to conclude that the EU and the US have the same interests in respect of global economic partnerships. An economic partnership should be examined and measured together with other military, security and territory interests. A gradually increasing number of global political events added uncertainty to the interactions and fundamental trust between the EU and the US, such as the withdrawal of American troops from Afghanistan, the creation of AUKUS,[82] and the invasion of Ukraine. The situation becomes tougher when it comes to the economic partnership between the US and China. China and the US may never come back to their honeymoon period but escalate and enter an era of economic competition and threat.[83] Considering all this complexity, the EU need to balance its core interests between the US and China and stipulate its positions on the ratification of the CAI.

3.2 Bargaining Power and Joint Effort

The text of CAI shows that the EU and China stand on a relatively equal footing to agree on a DSM for disputed matters. Such equal footing is important for both sides to apply, secure and consolidate a long-lasting and mutually trusted DSM. Investors from both sides may see SSDS as an alternative option for resolving disputes.

Since the Lisbon Treaty,[84] the EU has concluded several trade and investment protection agreements with third countries.[85] Among these concluded treaties, China is the largest economy with which the EU concluded a unified investment treaty,

[81] European Parliament, 'State of EU-US Relations' (September 2018) https://www.europarl.europa.eu/RegData/etudes/ATAG/2018/625167/EPRS_ATA(2018)625167_EN.pdf.

[82] An enhanced trilateral security: "AUKUS", meaning Australia, the UK and the US.

[83] The Chicago Council Survey (7-26 July 2021) https://www.thechicagocouncil.org/commentary-and-analysis/blogs/americans-and-us-china-trade-relations.

[84] Treaty on the Functioning of the European Union (2009).

[85] The treaties signed by the EU with other countries include EU-Cameroon Economic Partnership Agreement (EPA) on 15 January 2009 (not in force); the EU-SADC Interim Agreement on 22 January 2009 (not in force); EU-Eastern and Southern Africa States Interim EPA on 29 August 2009 (not in force); force); the EU-Korea FTA on 6 October 2010; the EU-Iraq Cooperation Agreement on 11 May 2011; Colombia-Ecuador-EU-Peru Trade Agreement on 26 June 2012; Central American Common Market-EU Agreement on 29 June 2012; the EU-Ukraine Association Agreement on 27 June 2014, EU-Moldova Association Agreement on 27 June 2014; the EU-Georgia Association Agreement on 27 June 2014; the EU-Kazakhstan Economic Partnership and Cooperation Agreement on 21 December 2015 (not in force); The EU-SADC EPA Group Agreement on 10 June 2016 (not in force); the Canada-EU CETA on 30 October 2016 (not in force); Armenia-EU CEPA on 24 November 2017 (not in force); EU-Japan EPA on 17 July 2018; EU-Singapore Investment Protection Agreement on 15 October 2018 (not in force); EU-Viet Nam Investment Protection Agreement on 30 June 2019 (not in force) and EU-United Kingdom Trade and Cooperation Agreement on 30 December 2020 (not in force).

until the US recommences its trade and investment agreement with the EU. The CAI is also the only treaty concluded by the EU with third countries having relatively equal power. The power of nations is usually defined as the ability to shape world politics in line with national interests and has a wide range of indicators, including wealth and military power.[86] Although a systematic measure of the power of a nation is difficult, economic power is usually seen as one indicator.[87]

On economic performance in terms of Gross Domestic Product (GDP), the EU represents 13.53% of the global economy while China represented 13.04% in 2020.[88] GDP may not be the sole indicator of national power, but certainly can allow general inferences to be made. The power of a nation may influence its negotiating power with other nations. Nations with more power than other negotiating parties will rely on hard bargaining.[89] Conversely, it may be presumed that parties with equal power may have bargaining power on par. This conclusion also applies to investment treaty negotiations. The EU and China have similar levels of bargaining power in the CAI negotiation process. Thus, the CAI faithfully reflects the positions of both the EU and China.

Due to no additional information being disclosed regarding how the EU and China negotiated, we may not conclude which party is the drafter and which is the taker on the DSM in the CAI. The final provisions may indicate the positions of both sides. From the EU perspective, the EU has adopted a similar SSDS mechanism to the one in the CAI in its investment protection agreement with Vietnam. Despite the DSM in EU-Vietnam IPA being established for resolving trade disputes, the similar structure and content suggest the EU standards on formulating the SSDS. From the Chinese side, China is open to accepting a detailed and comprehensive DSM for resolving disputes. Consultation and mediation as a first step to resolve disputes is widely practised in China, both in Chinese courts[90] and in arbitration administered by Chinese institutions. Reaching a satisfactory agreement with both Parties and achieving harmony without being decided by arbitrators or judged by courts is part of Chinese juridical practice and culture. Therefore, the content of the current SSDS in the CAI is consistent with normal practice in China.

---

86 Beckley (2018), pp. 7–44.

87 Ibid.

88 Trading Economics https://tradingeconomics.com. Data available at the World Bank https://data.worldbank.org/country/.

89 <Author-Query xmlns:aid5="http://ns.adobe.com/AdobeInDesign/5.0/"><!--<QUERY ID="Q1">
The citation "Jensen (2016)" has been changed to "Jensen (1965)" to match the author name/date in the reference list. Please check if the change is fine in this occurrence and modify the subsequent occurrences, if necessary.-->Jensen (1965), pp. 155–163; Dür and Mateo (2010), pp. 557–578.

90 Civil Procedure Law of the People's Republic of China (last revised 24 December 2021).

3.3 From SSDS to ISDS? Necessity and Possibility

SSDS in CAI is formulated to put the parties in a position where they can reach a mutual agreement or understanding, regardless of the methods and timing of resolving the dispute. CAI emphasises dialogue between the EU and China on the disputed matters with an SSDS procedural commitment. This raises further discussions about whether SSDS is already sufficient for resolving the disputes arising from the CAI.

Several assumptions can be made according to the available SSDS while waiting for the final text of ISDS adopted by the Parties. Two concerns are addressed in this section. The first is whether there is any necessity for the EU and China to set up an ISDS mechanism; and the second is how an ISDS can be agreed to reflect the positions of both the EU and China.

Is there any urgent need to reach an agreement on ISDS? The answer might be "*No*" based on the negotiating calendar proposed by the EU and China. One practical reason would be that the ratification procedure is long, as the two sides face many political challenges. Even after the CAI comes into effect, ISDS disputes may only arise after a while. Another reason is an assumption that the EU and China are confident about the SSDS adopted in the CAI. The purpose of having a DSM is the contracting State of the treaty and *de facto* users of the treaty, investors, can use it to resolve investment disputes. SSDS under the CAI gives an outstanding focal point on the bilateral dialogue and mutual efforts from both the EU and China to facilitate the procedure, such as the establishment of an Investment Committee. Although the adoption of ISDS in the CAI is put on the calendar, the role of ISDS remains to be further defined.

All BITs signed between China and EU member states include the SSDS and ISDS as parallel DSMs from which investors can choose. Investors usually seek support from their home state to bring claims against the host state or bring direct investor-state arbitration claims against the host state. Nevertheless, SSDS under the CAI strengthens the structure and capacity of SSDS to become an alternative DSM for investors. It will further reinforce the sense of using SSDS for dispute settlement in the investors' minds. In particular, compared with ISDS where investors have to participate as one disputant party in the proceedings, bilateral dialogue or DSM between two States, with the mentorship from the Investment Committee, would be more manageable and cost-effective. Therefore, it is predictable that ISDS under the CAI should have a supplementary role accompanying the SSDS in resolving disputes.

Many studies suggest how the ISDS mechanism will be adopted in the CAI. Early studies examined the legal framework of the EU-China investment relation, covering the governing law of foreign investment and how international treaties become the essential instrument for promoting and protecting bilateral investment.[91] On the position of China on ISDS, discussions may be focused on a comparative analysis

---

[91] Shan (2005).

of the Chinese BITs in different generations to presume the model of BITs will be chosen in the EU-China CAI.[92] The position of the EU on the ISDS are also mentioned in much research but converge on the criticisms and shortcomings of the ISDS, including inconsistency, transparency, and legitimacy of ISDS.[93]

The EU is proposing the judicialization of the ISDS with the establishment of a multilateral investment court (MIC).[94] The European Commission has been working on the design of MIC since 2015 and in 2016 MIC was adopted into a signed treaty for the first time in the Canada-EU Comprehensive Economic and Trade Agreement (CETA).[95] In January 2021, Canada and the EU made additional steps to clarify how the MIC will operate under the CETA.[96] Although China is gradually participating in the ISDS, it still welcomes reform of ISDS. Several problems in ISDS were outlined by China, including no error-correcting mechanism for ISDS awards, lack of stability and predictability of ISDS awards, questions of the professionalism and independence of arbitrators, imbalances between the disputant Parties due to third-party funding (TPF), and the length and cost of the procedure.[97] To resolve these concerns, China is open to the reform of ISDS, including the establishment of a permanent appellate mechanism, rights of parties to appoint arbitrators, a code of conduct for arbitrators, alternative dispute resolution measures, pre-arbitration consultation procedures, and transparency for TPF.

From these proposals, we may conclude that China has much common ground with the EU concerning the ISDS reform. Many proposals have been negotiated between the EU and China and are reflected in the SSDS of the CAI. Firstly, both the EU and China agree on a monitoring system for the tribunal to make the decision-making process more consistent and predictable. In terms of the members of arbitration tribunals, it would be practical and reliable to compile a fixed list of names to ensure the quality and professionalism of the panellists. Under the SSDS of the CAI, the Investment Committee will work on a list of panellists with representatives from the EU, and China and any third countries and will also set up the rules for mentoring the panellists. Secondly, the rights of contracting states shall be legally respected under the ISDS as pointed out by both the EU and China. Even though ISDS is created to provide a direct remedy to investors against sovereign States,

---

[92] Abgaryan (2019).

[93] Brown and Gaarthuis (2020), pp. 71–86.

[94] Council of the European Union, 'Negotiating Directives for a Convention Establishing a Multilateral Court for the Settlement of Investment Disputes', 12981/17 ADD 1 DCL 1, 1 March 2018.

[95] The European Commission, 'The Multilateral Investment Court project' (21 December 2016, Last Updated November 2021).

[96] Canada, ' Decision No 001/2021 of the CETA Joint Committee of 29 January 2021 setting out the administrative and organisational matters regarding the functioning of the Appellate Tribunal' https://www.international.gc.ca/trade-commerce/trade-agreements-accords-commerciaux/agr-acc/ceta-aecg/appellate-tribunal-dappel.aspx?lang=eng.

[97] UNCITRAL, 'Possible reform of investor-State dispute settlement (ISDS)Submission from the Government of China. Note by the Secretariat' (14-18 October 2019) https://undocs.org/en/A/CN.9/WG.III/WP.177.

parties to the dispute shall be equally balanced no matter whether the parties are private investors or sovereign States. SSDS under the CAI may not reflect directly on this point, but the provisions emphasize how the procedures shall guarantee the rights of both parties. Thirdly, the core objective of any DSM should be given the highest prominence. The objective of DSM is to be established and used for resolving disputes in the most efficient and effective way. A costly, lengthy procedure may not contribute to a successful DSM, as ISDS is usually criticized. As long as the disputing Parties can reach a mutual agreement, the DSM is successful no matter whether and how DSM is finally used. In other words, DSM adopted in the treaty provision should serve as a tool to achieve the objectives of resolving disputes, instead of being exhaustively used for the final goal.

4 Conclusion

CAI is not easy to negotiate for either the EU or China and now it seems even more difficult to ratify. The speedy negotiation and rushed conclusion in 2020 was achieved by the political ambition from both internal promotion and external drive. However, politics cleared the way for the CAI but also bars the way, in that tension between the EU and China is freezing ratification. Analysis of the CAI should have a political element, rather than limiting it to a purely legal discussion.

The SSDS provisions indicate the general direction of the Parties on DSM in CAI. Reaching a mutual agreement for an effective and efficient solution is still the starting point for the DSM in the CAI, as demonstrated in the SSDS with conceivable adoption in the future ISDS. CAI is a new dish for both the EU and China in the investment treaty negotiation. This is not just because CAI makes a remarkable impact on bilateral investment and the global economy, but also because it represents the joint efforts made by the EU and China. CAI is a splendid feast but before enjoying those glorious cuisines, all *Cai* takes a while to be prepared.

References

Abgaryan S (2019) EU-China comprehensive agreement on investment in the context of chinese bilateral investment treaty program with the EU countries. Indian J Int Law 58:171–203

Beckley M (2018) The power of nations: measuring what matters. Int Secur 43(2):7–44

Brown MC, Gaarthuis E (2020) Juridicialization of ISDS: the European Union's approach to multilateral reform of investment dispute settlement. In: Li Y et al (eds) China, the EU and international investment law: reforming investor-state dispute settlement. Routledge, London, pp 71–86

Ceva E, Fracasso A (2010) Seeking mutual understanding: a discourse-theoretical analysis of the WTO Dispute Settlement System. World Trade Rev 457:461

Council of the European Union (2018, 1 March) Negotiating Directives for a Convention Establishing a Multilateral Court for the Settlement of Investment Disputes

Dür A, Mateo G (2010) Bargaining power and negotiation tactics: the negotiations on the EU's financial perspective, 2007–13. J Common Mark Stud 48(3):557–578

DW (2021, 18 November) Taiwan Opens Representative Office in Lithuania. https://www.dw.com/en/taiwan-opens-representative-office-in-lithuania/a-59853874
Euronews (2021, 20 July) Taiwanese Representative Office in Lithuania
European Commission (2020, 30 December) The EU-China Comprehensive Agreement on Investment-The Agreement in Principle. https://trade.ec.europa.eu/doclib/docs/2020/december/tradoc_159242.pdf
European Commission (2021a, November) The Multilateral Investment Court Project
European Commission (2021b, 22 January) China. https://trade.ec.europa.eu/doclib/press/index.cfm?id=2237
European Commission (2021c, 8 December) Joint Statement by High Representative/Vice-President Josep Borrell and Executive Vice-President Valdis Dombrovskis on China's measures against Lithuania. https://trade.ec.europa.eu/doclib/press/index.cfm?id=2340
European Commission, United States. https://ec.europa.eu/trade/policy/countries-and-regions/countries/united-states/
European Parliament (2018, September) State of EU-US Relations. https://www.europarl.europa.eu/RegData/etudes/ATAG/2018/625167/EPRS_ATA(2018)625167_EN.pdf
Financial Times (2020, 22 December) Biden Team Voices Concern Over EU-China Investment Deal. https://www.ft.com/content/2f0212ab-7e69-4de0-8870-89dd0d414306
Jensen L (1965) Military capabilities and bargaining behavior. J Confl Resolut 9(2):155–163
Politico (2020, 29 December) Merkel Pushes EU-China Investment Deal Over the Finish Line Despite Criticism. https://www.politico.eu/article/eu-china-investment-deal-angela-merkel-pushes-finish-line-despite-criticism/
Politico (2021, 20 May) European Parliament Votes to 'Freeze' Investment Deal until China Lifts Sanctions. https://www.politico.eu/article/european-parliament-freezes-china-investment-deal-vote
Shan W (2005) The legal framework of EU–China investment relations: a critical appraisal. Hart Publishing, London
The Chicago Council Survey (2021, 7-26 July). https://www.thechicagocouncil.org/commentary-and-analysis/blogs/americans-and-us-china-trade-relations
UNCITRAL (2019, 14–18 October) Possible reform of investor-State dispute settlement (ISDS) Submission from the Government of China, Note by the Secretariat. https://undocs.org/en/A/CN.9/WG.III/WP.177
VOA News (2020, 25 December) EU-China Investment Talks Near Completion, Raising Concerns. https://www.voanews.com/a/east-asia-pacific_voa-news-china_eu-china-investment-talks-near-completion-raising-concerns/6200011.html

Zhang Anran (PhD, LL.M, LL.B, B.A) is the Deputy Director of ICC Arbitration and ADR for North Asia. He forges strong relationship with stakeholders, advises ICC strategic development and organizes capacity building events across North Asian 17 jurisdictions. He holds a doctorate from Erasmus University Rotterdam. Anran worked as an international case counsel at AIAC in Malaysia, where he was responsible for arbitration and adjudication case management, rules revision, international cooperation and institutional initiatives. In addition to institutional experience, he was an academic researcher at Europa Institute, Leiden University, a visiting researcher at University of Cambridge, and worked a short-term consultant at ICSID. He regularly teaches at lawyers' associations, universities across the globe and speaks at international conferences. Anran obtained his LL.M degree from Uppsala University with IPK full scholarship and attended the summer course at the Hague Academy of International Law. He graduated from Southwest University of Political Science and Law (qualified in PRC) and Sichuan International Studies University with the TEM 8 certificate. This chapter was finalized before the author joined the ICC and it only reflects the opinions of the author and not of any of the author's current or previous affiliations. Any errors remain the author's own.

Never Fear to Negotiate: Options for Non-Adversarial Dispute Resolution in the EU-China Comprehensive Agreement on Investment

Sara Migliorini and Naina Gupta

Abstract The current tumultuous time in foreign relations has furthered the need for a reflection on the role of non-adversarial dispute resolution mechanisms in recent treaties, especially those that bind major economic powers such as the EU-China Comprehensive Agreement on Investment (CAI). This chapter analyses Arts. 3, 4 and 5 of Section V of CAI, which puts in place the system of non-adversarial dispute resolution. It finds that they are in line with the consistent efforts of the EU and China to incorporate processes of mediation and conciliation to resolve legal differences. After finding that non-adversarial dispute resolution mechanisms offer traditional advantages, that their weaknesses have been overcome in recent developments and that favourable jurisprudence has also emerged, the chapter concludes there are genuine prospects for the growth of non-adversarial dispute resolution in the China-EU context. This is enhanced by institutional moves encouraging mediations and consultations, other instances of the use of such processes in international disputes, and the traditional Chinese cultural preference for non-adversarial conflict handling.

1 Introduction

The current tumultuous time in foreign relations has furthered the need for a reflection on non-adversarial dispute resolution mechanisms in recent treaties, especially those that bind major economic powers such as the EU-China Comprehensive Agreement on Investment (CAI). At the time of writing, the finalization of the CAI has been suspended by the parties amid geopolitical tensions and tit-for-tat

S. Migliorini (✉)
University of Macau, Faculty of Law, Macao, SAR, China
e-mail: saramigliorini@um.edu.mo

N. Gupta
Arnold & Porter Kaye Scholer LLP, London, UK

© The Author(s), under exclusive license to Springer Nature Switzerland AG 2024

A. Svetlicinii, I.-J. Chen (eds.), *The EU-China Comprehensive Agreement on Investment*, European Yearbook of International Economic Law,
https://doi.org/10.1007/978-3-031-66862-3_13

sanctions.[1] This was despite the parties reaching an agreement in principle of the treaty text in December 2020. In addition, the Covid-19 pandemic has taken impetus away from international trade and cooperation, polarizing East and West. Hence, far from marking the renewal of an era of cooperation, the CAI has emerged at a time when the EU-China relationship is rocky.

However, it is precisely at times of increased tensions between states that opportunities arise for discussion, negotiation and even resolution of disputes in a non-adversarial way, leading to satisfactory outcomes for all parties involved. This chapter sees the non-adversarial options for dispute resolution in the CAI as part of the toolbox to bolster, rather than undermine, the prospects of international relations, and provide a more attractive and sustainable method of settling differences. We submit that non-adversarial methods can fill the gap for a consultative medium left by the various geopolitical tensions, and, as such, stand a fair chance of success, against the backdrop of the global ongoing movement to promote these dispute resolution methods in the fields of trade and investments.

By "non-adversarial dispute resolution", this chapter refers to the resolution of disputes via non-contentious methods, allowing for parties to come to an agreement via rule-based discussions that are less formal than adjudicatory methods, although not necessarily informal, with a view to reaching a compromise. In the literature, mediation, 'together with negotiation, good offices, conciliation, and inquiry, are usually grouped in the category of 'political' or 'diplomatic' dispute settlement methods',[2] and similarities among these methods are highlighted.[3] Due to these similarities, this chapter considers negotiation, consultation, conciliation and mediation as falling under the umbrella term of "non-adversarial dispute resolution methods".

Consultations or negotiations broadly refer to 'discussions at different levels of authority with a view to achieving common understanding or agreement'.[4] Negotiations may be conducted by party representatives, which makes this method of non-adversarial dispute resolution more politicised and less structured than conciliation or mediation. In the absence of neutral representatives, the parties communicate directly. Negotiation comes into the dispute resolution landscape in a distinct way from conciliation. Firstly, negotiations may commence at various stages; parties may negotiate before the initiation of the dispute as well as when the dispute is undergoing litigation. Secondly, this method allows parties to 'exchange [...] views',[5] and the process is often voluntary. Thirdly, due to the lack of formal structures, negotiation tends to enhance the 'communicative contact between the

[1] EP Press Office (2021) 'MEPs refuse any agreement with China whilst sanctions are in place'.

[2] Orrego Vicuña (2010), p. 1.

[3] See also Wang and Sharma (2021), p. 24; Zhao (2018), p. 116.

[4] Hakapää (2013), p. 1.

[5] Ibid., p. 16.

parties to explain and discuss their positions'[6] and ultimately is regarded as the most common, simple, and cost-efficient method of dispute resolution.[7]

Conciliation usually involves the parties setting up a commission, either on a permanent or on an *ad hoc* basis, to deal with a dispute.[8] The commission conducts an impartial examination of the matter and aims to determine the terms of a settlement.[9] The nominated commission members are independent parties and the commission acts strictly within the powers conferred upon the commission, which will normally include assessing the facts and applicable law, followed by drafting a solution. The role that conciliation plays in the dispute resolution process is unique as it is sometimes the mandatory first step in an adjudication system. Conciliation usually involves a legal assessment and thus is more "rule-based" than negotiation and mediation, which are intended to be facilitative processes.[10]

Finally, mediation is the process by which a neutral third party is appointed to aid the parties in discussing their views and arrive at a mutually satisfactory solution.[11] The procedure may be undertaken on a voluntary basis. The role of mediation in dispute resolution follows in the vein of conciliation and negotiation although with minor differences. Firstly, mediation is usually non-mandatory (unlike conciliation or negotiations which may be pre-requisites to commencing adjudication). Secondly, as mediation is structured yet informal, it forms a middle ground between the rule-based approach of conciliation and the flexibility of negotiation. In particular, the involvement of a neutral third party allows the parties to discuss their concerns in a more balanced manner (without power asymmetries) while seeking to reach a compromise.

Ultimately, the above non-adversarial dispute resolution methods have more in common than they have differences. Specifically, all methods are less-rule based and less formal than adjudication. In addition, they comprise of parties—whether the appointed neutral party or the disputing party themselves— adopting a persuasive stance to reach a settlement that is satisfactory to those involved. All three mechanisms are usually confidential and without prejudice to judicial proceedings.[12] While there may be a difference in the mandatory or non-mandatory nature of the procedures, this does not affect whether a dispute resolution mechanism is adversarial or not. Finally, the settlements or recommendations reached in the above-mentioned non-adversarial mechanisms do not carry legal authority and will only bind the parties contractually, unlike adjudicatory forms of dispute resolution like arbitration or litigation.

[6] Ibid., p. 21.

[7] Yeini (2020), p. 661.

[8] Cot (2006), p. 1.

[9] Ibid., pp. 2–3.

[10] Zhao (2018), p. 116.

[11] Orrego Vicuña (2010), pp. 1–2.

[12] Cot (2006), p. 2; Yeini (2020), p. 661; Orrego Vicuña (2010), p. 5.

This chapter focuses on Arts. 3, 4 and 5 of Section V of the CAI, which establish the regulatory framework of the non-adversarial dispute resolution mechanisms available to the parties under the CAI. The chapter will provide an overview of the provisions (Sect. 2). Subsequently, the chapter will analyse the practice of the EU and China in relation to non-adversarial dispute resolution mechanisms as included in their recent trade and investment agreements (Sect. 3). The authors find that while the CAI may not look out of the ordinary in light of the practice of the EU's recent agreements, it marks a step forward in light of prior Chinese practice and overall addresses some of the common shortcomings of non-adversarial procedures. The Chapter will illustrate the important international developments in the non-adversarial dispute resolution landscape, which allows the authors to maintain an optimistic position on the prospects of success of non-adversarial dispute resolution in the CAI. This optimism is derived from the traditional advantages of non-adversarial dispute resolution; the new developments that have partially overcome weaknesses of non-adversarial dispute resolution; favourable jurisprudence on this topic; increasing institutional support for mediation and conciliation; consideration of the successful instances of non-adversarial dispute resolution; and the importance of cultural factors in contributing to the likely success of non-adversarial dispute resolution in the CAI.

2 Overview of the Relevant Provisions

The dispute resolution system of the CAI comprises a preliminary phase of mandatory consultations, which, if unsuccessful, unlocks the right to start an arbitration. In addition, the resolution of disputes by mediation and good offices is encouraged at any time. Parties may start voluntary mediation by agreement and are encouraged to negotiate and reach a mutually agreed solution at any time. In line with other FTAs, the CAI seeks to establish an 'effective and efficient mechanism for avoiding and settling any disputes between the Parties [...] with a view to arriving at, where possible, a mutually agreed solution'.[13]

Art. 3 details the mandatory preliminary phase of consultations. The parties shall endeavour to resolve any dispute 'by entering into consultations in good faith with the aim of reaching a mutually agreed solution'. Consultations start with 'a written request delivered to the other Party', setting out 'the reasons for the request, including the identification of the measure at issue and an indication of the legal basis for the complaint' and the provisions of the CAI that are allegedly triggered by the measure at hand. The addressee party 'shall reply to the request within 10 days after the date of its receipt' and consultations are held within 30 days after the request unless mutually agreed otherwise. In order to avoid stagnation, Art. 3 provides that 'consultations shall be deemed concluded within 30 days after the date of receipt of

[13] CAI, Section V, Art. 1.

the request, unless both parties agree to continue consultations'. At this point, the party that initiated the consultations 'may proceed directly to request the establishment of an arbitration panel', including if consultations are actually not held within 30 days from receipt, or 'if consultations have been concluded and no mutually agreed solution has been reached'. The same party can also request the establishment of a Panel also in case the other party 'does not respond to the request for consultations within 10 days after its receipt'. On one reading the request can be made after the 10-day period is expired, without waiting for the 30-day timeframe that applies when such reply is submitted in time but consultations are otherwise unsuccessful. As in similar agreements, the consultations, and in particular of all information disclosed and positions taken by the parties, are to remain confidential. The consultations shall also be 'without prejudice to the rights of either Party in any further proceedings'.[14]

Art. 4 establishes a mechanism for voluntary mediation, which may only start when both parties consent. Mediation can be initiated at any time, i.e. before or during the consultation or arbitration phases. Art. 4 provides for broad choice regarding the rules applicable to the mediation process: 'upon initiation of the mediation procedure the Parties shall agree on the selection, tasks and powers of the mediator and on the rules governing the mediation procedure, including time-frame, termination and costs'.[15] In addition, Article 4 leaves it to the Joint Committee to adopt rules on the initiation, conduct and termination of mediation, which 'it shall endeavour to adopt' within three years after the entry into force of the CAI. Confidentiality is the default rule during mediation.

In line with many other trade agreements and according to general principles of international law, parties are encouraged to reach a shared solution at any time. Art. 5 provides that 'the Parties may reach a mutually agreed solution to a dispute [...], or to certain claims thereof, at any time'. When parties reach a mutually agreed solution during consultation, all claims covered by such a solution may not be submitted to arbitration. If the parties reach a mutually agreed solution during the arbitration or mediation procedures, 'the Parties shall jointly notify it to the arbitration panel or the mediator'. When notified, the mediator or the arbitration panel will terminate the whole procedure, or exclude the claims covered by the mutually agreed solution. As for implementation, Art. 5 imposes on the parties an obligation to 'comply with a mutually agreed solution[...] without delay and in good faith'. Parties are under an obligation to take all the measures that are necessary to implement the mutually agreed solution within the agreed time period, and to notify the other party in a timely fashion.

[14] CAI, Section V, Art. 3.

[15] CAI, Section V, Art. 4.

3 Setting the Non-Adversarial Methods in the Wider Context of International Practice

The process of non-adversarial dispute resolution methods must be considered in light of its long-established, intrinsic benefits as well as its novel developments. The primacy and importance of non-adversarial methods was famously stated by the ICJ in the case of the *Free Zones of Upper Savoy and the District of Gex*. Specifically, the court stated that 'the judicial settlement of international disputes[...] is simply an alternative to the direct and friendly settlement of such disputes between the parties'.[16] Despite the popularity of arbitration as a means to settle disputes in the fields of trade and investments, non-adversarial settlement of disputes is indeed the first and *par default* option open to the parties under general international law as well as sectoral treaties and Conventions.

In addition, the emphasis on legal and non-legal elements of a dispute allows for an outcome that is based on the overall interests of the parties as opposed to simply the legal merits.[17] In an observation by Judge Xue in her dissenting opinion in *Application of the Interim Accord of 13 September 1995 (the former Yugoslav Republic of Macedonia v. Greece)*, 'the imposition of a solution by a third party, or any direct or indirect involvement, even from this Court, is undesirable' when negotiation may be ongoing. In that case, Judge Xue felt that the decision of the Court would affect how the parties would settle a much bigger dispute between them than that settled by the judgment.[18] Conversely, an adverse compulsory ruling by a third party may sour the relationship between parties in a context broader than the initial dispute.

On a practical level, many advantages stem from non-adversarial methods. They are often less expensive and more expeditious than arbitral proceedings and (crucially) known to preserve the relationship between the parties, paving the way for more durable cooperation.[19] This last aspect is of particular importance to sovereign states engaging in dispute resolution due to the politicised nature and international relations context of their disputes, such as those regarding territorial sovereignty.[20] Via the involvement of a neutral third party without a compulsory decision-making ability, non-adversarial dispute resolution prevents an adverse impact on the power balance between the parties – a disadvantage that pertains to adversarial dispute resolution – and results in a consensual, win-win outcome.[21]

---

[16] *Free Zones of Upper Savoy and the District of Gex,* Order of 19 August 1929, PCIJ Series A, No. 22, p. 13.

[17] Zhao (2018), pp. 114–115.

[18] Application of the Interim Accord of 13 September 1995 (the former Yugoslav Republic of Macedonia v. Greece), Dissenting opinion by J. Xue Judgment of 5 December 2011 (2011), ICJ Reports, https://www.icj-cij.org/en/case/142/judgments, accessed 30 January 2023.

[19] Zhao (2018), pp. 114–115.

[20] Koh (2011), pp. 57–58.

[21] Ibid.

Furthermore, the inclusion of non-adversarial dispute resolution mechanisms is unlikely to be construed as barring jurisdiction over the dispute where the non-adversarial mechanisms are not successful. In the WTO case of *Mexico – Anti-Dumping Investigation Of High Fructose Corn Syrup (Hfcs) From The United States*, the Appellate Body clarified that, on the one hand, if a party does not raise the issue of a lack of consultation promptly, a panel may consider that they have waived their right to consultation and implicitly consented to proceed with the arbitration. On the other hand, and more importantly, the Appellate Body also found that 'the lack of prior consultations is not a defect that, by its very nature, deprives a panel of its authority to deal with and dispose of a matter, and that, accordingly, such a defect is not one which a panel must examine of its on motion'.[22] In this case, the Appellate Body conducted a review of the wording of the DSU (in particular Art. 4.1) to conclude that neither the consultation nor the obligation in Art. 6, that the request for the establishment of a Panel include a mention of 'whether consultation[s] have been held', can deprive the panel of its jurisdiction if lacking.[23] As the wording of Art. 4.2 of the DSU and Art. 6.2 of the CAI are identical, and it is possible that they are compared or interpreted similarly, non-adversarial dispute resolution will not bar jurisdiction over CAI disputes. On other occasions, courts have recommended or acknowledged the use of diplomatic methods like negotiation throughout the panel proceedings. In different cases, the ICJ encouraged the parties to settle their dispute through out-of-court negotiations.[24] In the WTO, parties have reached consensus on a mutually agreed solution at various stages of the proceedings.[25]

Furthermore, non-adversarial methods of dispute resolution may gain new traction after the successful mandatory conciliation between Timor Leste and Australia concerning their maritime boundary.[26] The case has been applauded as groundbreaking, blazing the trail for conciliation to be seen as a realistic means of international dispute settlement, including in highly complex cases.[27] In 2017, after two years of mandatory UNCLOS conciliation, the two states reached an agreement. The dispute concerned the interpretation and application of the UNCLOS in a number of instances referring to Arts. 74 and 83, which lay down rules on the delimitation of the exclusive economic zone and the continental shelf in cases where adjacent or opposite states have overlapping entitlements. The UNCLOS convention provides for, *inter alia*, a particular kind of compulsory conciliation that, in certain conditions, a state must accept. Timor Leste relied on this procedure and requested compulsory conciliation in 2016. The success of conciliation in this case derives

[22] *Mexico – Anti-Dumping Investigation* (2001), p. 64.

[23] Ibid., p. 62.

[24] See generally Hakapää (2013).

[25] See for example, WTO (2020a) Summary of DS7 European Communities – Trade Description of Scallops; WTO (2020b) United States – Anti-Dumping Duty on Dynamic Random Access Memory Semiconductors (DRAMS) from Korea.

[26] See further documents of *Timor-Leste v. Australia* at https://pca-cpa.org/en/cases/132/.

[27] See generally Le Moli and Viñuales (2020).

from various factors. Firstly, the Conciliation Commission achieved a high level of confidence of the parties in the process itself and in each other via arranging separate meetings as well as dedicating many hours to understand the positions, arguments and sensitivities of the parties. Despite initial distrust, the Commission recognised that 'the Parties did, through the conciliation, engage bilaterally in a constructive manner to achieve an equitable compromise'.[28] The compulsory nature of the conciliation prevented the defendant state from escaping the non-adversarial mechanism. Indeed, the compulsory character of non-adversarial methods plays a key role in changing the attitude of the defendant state to a more accommodating mindset. The UNCLOS mechanism of compulsory negotiation is certainly not unique, and other international conventions include similar ones.[29] It has been argued that these and other practices used and developed by the Conciliation Commission in the Timor Leste-Australia case could set a precedent for future conciliation processes.[30]

However, such mandatory mechanisms are lacking in trade or investment agreements. This means that, in the absence of political will, it will be challenging to initiate conciliation or mediation procedures. Hence, as of today, non-adversarial methods have not been used in WTO dispute settlement, which is something that the Director General office has been willing to correct for the past 20 years.[31] In one case,[32] three states jointly requested the Director-General to mediate. Though they did not consider the matter a hand a "dispute" within the meaning of the DSU, they used procedures similar to those envisaged for mediation under Art. 5 of CAI. The nominated mediator[33] drafted a report with undisclosed conclusions. Although minimal, the jurisprudence indicates that mandatory conciliation may lead to its more frequent invocation.[34]

Institutional promotion of non-adversarial dispute resolution is crucial to its development, as it enables the disputing parties to avail themselves of pre-agreed procedures. Therefore, it is relevant that the general movement of states in the fields of trade and investments is towards non-adversarial methods,[35] and is matched by movement on the institutional front, such as the extension of services to include

[28] *Report And Recommendations of the Compulsory Conciliation Commission Between Timor-Leste and Australia on the Timor Sea*, PCA Case N° 2016-10, 289.

[29] See for example, the Convention on Biological Diversity (1992), Art. 27.

[30] Duy Phan (2018).

[31] Communication from the Director-General, Art. 5 of the DSU.

[32] Communication from the Director-General, Request for Mediation by the Philippines, Thailand and the European Communities.

[33] The WTO Deputy Director, nominated by the WTO Director-General.

[34] See generally Orrego Vicuña (2010) referring to the Algeria hostage crisis in 1980 between Iran and the US which involved good offices and mediation, the involvement of Soviet Union in Kashmir in 1965 and the actions of US in relation to Yugoslavia that ultimately led to the signing of the Dayton Peace Agreement (1995).

[35] See for example Kessedjian et al. (2020) and Wang and Sharma (2021), pp. 22–27.

cross-border mediation by the ICC in Paris, LCIA and AIAC.[36] One such movement is the adoption of the UNCITRAL Model Law on Mediation (2018) which supports states in reforming their laws on mediation of commercial disputes.[37] In investment arbitration, UNCITRAL has also been working on a reform of ISDS that embraces mediation as an alternative to arbitration. Furthermore, ICSID is carrying out work to refine its rules, through a series of updates and amendments regarding, in particular, mediation and conciliation.[38] To encourage the use of mediation in investor-state-dispute-settlement (ISDS), ICSID also released different papers[39] regarding the background of mediation and reviewing the context of investment treaty clauses on mediation. Moreover, new institutions have emerged that offer expertise in non-adversarial dispute resolution, allowing disputants to benefit from the specialisation of such centres and their economies of scale. These include the Singapore International Mediation Centre and Japan International Mediation Centre.[40]

This impact is enhanced due to the increasing number of international treaties signed by both the EU and China that incorporate mediation provisions, regardless of their infrequent invocation. The incorporation of non-adversarial dispute resolution mechanisms in treaty texts is not meaningless, because it demonstrates increased political will. This political will is considered important and by some 'the most important factor [...] to find a just and durable compromise'[41] and consequently also important to the practices and approaches for maintaining international peace and security.[42]

---

[36] Alexander (2019), p. 408.

[37] Note by the Secretariat, UNCITRAL Working Group-III (Investor-State Dispute Settlement Reform), Thirty-Ninth Session, UN Doc. A/CN.9/WG.III/WP.190, ¶ 30 (Mar. 30-Apr. 3, 2020). See also Submission from the Government of China, UN Doc. A/CN.9/WG-III/WP.177, ¶ 5, as mentioned in the Note by the Secretariat, p. 30.

[38] ICSID (2021).

[39] See also ICSID, Working Paper #4, ICSID, Working Paper #5, and ICSID, Working Paper #6, all available at: https://icsid.worldbank.org/resources/rules-amendments.

[40] Alexander (2019), pp. 407–408.

[41] Koh (2017).

[42] Orrego Vicuña (2010), p. 43.

4 Review of the Practice of China and the EU in Recent Trade Agreements and Bilateral Investment Treaties

4.1 Practice of the EU in Recent Trade and Investment Agreements

The EU has concluded trade agreements with Canada,[43] the UK,[44] Japan,[45] Singapore,[46] and Vietnam,[47] which entered into force in the last five years (with the CETA entering into force provisionally). Their provisions on non-adversarial methods are largely similar: a mandatory consultation phase precedes the establishment of a panel. While mediation may be initiated and carried out at any moment, there are minor differences in the phrasing.[48]

Among these agreements, the EU-UK Trade Cooperation Agreement (TCA) adopts a slightly different format. The TCA stands out as its dispute resolution mechanism is restricted to a WTO-style state-to-state arbitration. This is a 'striking move away from recent treaties concluded by the EU with third states, such as CETA with Canada or the recently agreed in principle Comprehensive Agreement on Investment ("CAI") with China'.[49] Notably, the TCA does not contain a designated mediation provision.

CETA permits parties to bring a dispute under the WTO's DSU rules, by constituting an arbitration panel or as per any other agreement.[50] The agreement still encourages non-adversarial dispute resolution by stating that the parties may initiate good faith consultations regarding trade or investment measures; consultations will last 30 days and may be prolonged further or succeeded by referring the matter to an arbitration.[51] Its objective is to endeavour to reach, 'where possible, a mutually agreed solution.'[52] To request consultations, the complaining party must submit a written request identifying the measures at issue and the legal basis for the request, and the provisions it considers applicable.[53] Consultations on matters of urgency must be held in 15 or 20 days and consultations are confidential and "without

[43] CETA (2016).

[44] EU-UK TCA (2020).

[45] EU-Japan FTA (2018).

[46] EU-Singapore FTA (2018).

[47] EU-Vietnam FTA (2019).

[48] For example, in the EU-Vietnam FTA and EU-Japan FTA, the conciliation phase may be slightly longer than in the CAI, i.e., 45 days instead of 30.

[49] Schwedt et al. (2021).

[50] CETA (2016), Art. 29.3(3).

[51] EU-UK TCA (2020), Arts. 738, 734, CETA (2016) Arts. 29.1, 29.4.

[52] EU-UK TCA (2020), Art. 734. See also CETA (2016), Art. 29.1.

[53] EU-UK TCA (2020), Art. 738, CETA (2016) Art. 29.4.

prejudice to the rights of either Party in any further proceedings".[54] If the parties agree a mutual solution, ongoing arbitration proceedings will be terminated and the parties shall implement the measures agreed upon.[55] The agreement incorporates flexibility regarding time periods, by allowing parties to modify time limits upon agreement. These provisions on consultations are largely replicated in the EU-Vietnam FTA, EU-Japan FTA and EU-Singapore FTA.[56]

In addition to providing for good faith consultations for achieving a mutually agreed solution, CETA, the EU-Vietnam, EU-Japan and EU-Singapore FTAs go further and have provisions for mediation allowing recourse to mediation for measures affecting trade or investment in combination with a separate part on mediation rules (all agreements except for the EU-Japan FTA have the latter).[57] The differences between the sets of rules are negligible. The agreements emphasise that the objective of the mediation rules is to foster a mutually agreed solution.[58] The mediation procedure may start at any time via a request to the other party and it requires the consent of both parties.[59] This request has to identify the specific measure at issue, its alleged adverse effects on trade or investment between the parties, and 'explain how the requesting Party considers that those effects are linked to the measure'.[60]

If the requested party agrees to initiate the mediation procedure, both parties are obliged to agree on a mediator within the next 15 days.[61] Unless the parties agree differently, the selected mediator cannot be a national of either party, and the mediation procedure shall take place in the territory of the party to which the request was addressed.[62] Mediators are required to abide by the code of conduct for arbitrators (and mediators)[63] that will apply to the extent that it is compatible with mediation and having regard to its particular nature. The agreements also outline the general

[54] EU-UK TCA (2020), Art. 738, CETA (2016) Art. 29.4.

[55] EU-UK TCA (2020), Art. 756, CETA (2016) Art. 29.19.

[56] EU-Singapore FTA (2018), Art. 14.3; EU-Vietnam FTA (2019), Art. 15.3; EU-Japan FTA (2018), Art. 21.5.

[57] CETA (2016), Art. 29.5 and Annex 29-C; EU-Singapore FTA (2018) , Art. 15.1; EU-Vietnam FTA (2019), Art. 15.4 and Annex 15-C; EU-Japan FTA (2018), Art. 21.6.

[58] CETA (2016), Annex 29-C, Art. 1; EU-Singapore FTA (2018), Art. 15.1; EU-Vietnam FTA (2019), Annex 15-C, Art. 1; EU-Japan FTA (2018), Art. 21.26.

[59] CETA (2016), Annex 29-C, Art. 2; EU-Singapore FTA (2018), Art. 15.3; EU-Vietnam FTA (2019), Annex 15-C, Art. 3.

[60] CETA (2016), Annex 29-C, Art. 2; EU-Singapore FTA (2018), Art. 15.3; EU-Vietnam FTA (2019), Annex 15-C, Art. 3.

[61] CETA (2016), Annex 29-C, Art. 3; EU-Singapore FTA (2018), Art. 15.4; EU-Vietnam FTA (2019), Annex 15-C, Art. 4.

[62] CETA (2016), Annex 29-C, Art. 3-4; EU-Singapore FTA (2018), Art. 15.4; EU-Vietnam FTA (2019), Annex 15-C, Art. 4.

[63] CETA (2016), Annex 29-C, Arts. 3-4; EU-Singapore FTA (2018) Annex 14-B; EU-Vietnam FTA (2019), Annex 15-B; EU-Japan FTA (2018), Art. 21.30.

powers of mediators.[64] The mediator is empowered to 'decide on the most appropriate way of bringing clarity to the measure concerned and its possible adverse effects on trade and investment'. To this end, they may meet or consult the parties together or separately. The mediator may also consult with 'relevant experts and stakeholders'. The mediator may offer advice and may propose a solution for the consideration of the parties, but the proposed solution is not binding. Parties are under an obligation to endeavour to reach a mutually agreed solution within 60 days of the appointment of the mediator. The adoption of a mutually agreed solution brings a formal end to the mediation procedure.[65] The mediation procedure is also terminated if the parties mutually agree so, or if the mediator, after having consulted with the parties, makes a written declaration that further efforts at mediation would be to no avail. As to the implementation of a mutually agreed solution, each party is under an obligation to take the measures necessary to implement it within the agreed timeframe.[66]

On a procedural note, the mediation procedure is confidential, which is consistent with international practice.[67] Information submitted by the parties during the mediation procedure, either to each other or to the mediator, and all steps of the procedure, including any advice that may be given or solution that may be proposed by the mediator, is confidential. More generally, the mediation procedure itself is without prejudice to the parties' rights and obligations under the dispute settlement procedures. In addition, the mediation procedure cannot serve as a basis for dispute settlement procedures under any agreement. All time limits may be modified by mutual agreement between the parties.[68]

In regards to investment agreements of the EU supporting non-adversarial dispute resolution, it should firstly be noted that the CETA, EU-Singapore FTA, EU-Vietnam FTA, and EU-Japan FTA provide that their mediation mechanisms cover investments as well (though not the remainder of the dispute resolution chapter or consultation provisions).[69] The TCA is unique in that it does not distinguish a dispute settlement mechanism for investment disputes and instead includes ISDS within the scope of the general disputes resolution chapter.[70]

[64] CETA (2016), Annex 29-C, Art. 4. EU-Singapore FTA (2018), Art. 15.5, EU-Vietnam FTA (2019), Annex 15-C, Art. 5.

[65] See EU-Singapore FTA (2018), Art. 14.15; EU-Vietnam FTA (2019), Annex 15-C, Art. 5; EU-Japan FTA (2018), Art. 21.26.

[66] CETA (2016), Annex 29-C, Art. 5, EU-Singapore FTA (2018), Art. 15.6; EU-Vietnam FTA (2019), Annex 15-C, Art. 6; EU-Japan FTA (2018), Art. 21.26.

[67] CETA (2016), Annex 29-C, Art. 6, EU-Singapore FTA (2018), Art., 15.7; EU-Vietnam FTA (2019), Annex 15-C, Art. 7.

[68] CETA (2016), Annex 29-C, Arts. 6-7, EU-Singapore FTA (2018), Arts. 15.7-15.8; EU-Vietnam FTA (2019), Annex 15-C, Arts. 7-8; EU-Japan FTA (2018), Arts. 21.27-21.28.

[69] CETA (2016), Art. 29.2, 29.4, 29.5; EU-Vietnam FTA (2019), Arts. 15.2, 15. 3, 15.4; EU-Japan FTA (2018), Arts 21.2, 21.4, 21.6; EU-Singapore FTA (2018), Art. 14.2, 14.3, 15.1.

[70] EU-UK TCA (2020), Art. 735.

In their separate dispute resolution chapters or agreements for ISDS, the CETA, the EU-Singapore Investment Protection Agreement (EU-Singapore IPA) and EU-Vietnam Investment Protection Agreement (EU-Vietnam IPA) provide for non-adversarial dispute settlement as well.[71] Specifically, they provide that disputes should be amicably settled within a 45–60 day period, unless a longer period is agreed, after the registration of a dispute.[72] Among other items, the written request for consultation must lay out the allegedly breached provisions, the legal and factual basis for the claim and the relief sought.[73] Parties may also resort to mediation at any time.[74] Recourse to mediation is without prejudice to the position and rights of the parties and the governing rules are as agreed by both parties.[75] The EU-Vietnam IPA provides specific mediation rules to apply to its ISDS disputes in Annex 10 of the EU-Vietnam IPA. Similarly, the EU-Singapore IPA sets out that the governing rules for mediation may be those set out in Annex 6 of the agreement or as otherwise agreed by parties. The mediator is appointed by agreement of the parties or third parties, for instance the Secretary General of ICSID, within 15 days of the dispute and the parties are to endeavour to reach a resolution within 60 days of appointing the mediator.[76] The mediator is empowered to 'decide on the most appropriate way of bringing clarity to the measure concerned and its possible adverse effects on trade and investment'.[77] To this end, they may meet or consult the parties together or separately. The mediator may also consult with 'relevant experts and stakeholders'. With a view to resolving the dispute at hand, the mediator may offer advice and may propose a solution for the consideration of the parties. The solution proposed by the mediator is not binding on the parties. Mediation may be terminated by a single party's decision.[78] Aside from this, parties may adopt a mutually agreed solution at any time and notify the relevant committees or arbitration panels to terminate the ongoing proceedings.[79]

The wording in both the investment and trade agreements of the EU in relation to the non-adversarial provisions have thus been, by and large, similar.

[71] A separate EU-Japan investment agreement has not yet been negotiated or signed and has thus been excluded from this section.

[72] CETA (2016), Art. 8.19; EU-Vietnam IPA (2019), Art. 3.29; EU-Singapore IPA (2018), Art. 3.3.

[73] CETA (2016), Art. 8.19; EU-Vietnam IPA (2019), Art. 3.30; EU-Singapore IPA (2018), Art. 3.3.

[74] CETA (2016), Art. 8.20; EU-Vietnam IPA (2019), Art. 3.31; EU-Singapore IPA (2018), Art. 3.4.

[75] CETA (2016), Art. 8.20; EU-Vietnam IPA (2019), Art. 3.31, Annex 10, Art. 6; EU-Singapore IPA (2018), Art. 3.4.

[76] CETA (2016), Art. 8.20; EU-Vietnam IPA (2019), Art. 3.31, Annex 10, Art. 3-4; EU-Singapore IPA (2018), Art. 3.4, Annex 6, Art. 3.

[77] EU-Vietnam IPA (2019), Annex 10, Art. 4; EU-Singapore IPA (2018), Annex 6, Art. 4.

[78] CETA (2016), Art. 8.20; EU-Vietnam IPA (2019), Annex 10, Art. 4; EU-Singapore IPA (2018), Annex 6, Art. 4.

[79] CETA (2016), Art. 29.19; EU-Vietnam IPA (2019), Art. 3.19; EU-Singapore IPA (2018), Annex 6, Art. 4.

4.2 Practice of China in Recent Trade and Investment Agreements

China has consistently included non-adversarial dispute resolution provisions in its recent trade agreements, such as the China-Australia FTA, China-Iceland FTA, China-Cambodia FTA, China-Georgia FTA and China-Korea FTA. The provisions overlap and provide outright that the parties 'shall make every attempt through cooperation to arrive at a mutually satisfactory resolution'.[80] While China refers to the solution as 'mutually satisfactory' rather than the EU's consistent 'mutually agreed', this terminology is not materially different. The choice of forum for disputes is without prejudice to the parties' rights to bring disputes under other fora as per other agreements, unless otherwise provided.[81]

The non-adversarial dispute resolution provisions firstly provide for non-mandatory consultations (with the exception of Art. 109 in the China-Iceland FTA and Art. 20.6 of the China-Korea FTA, which conditions the establishment of an arbitral tribunal on the exhaustion of consultation). Parties may request consultation via a written notice containing the reasons for the request, identifying the measure at issue, and indicating the factual and legal basis for the complaint.[82] Upon receiving the request, the receiving party must engage in good faith, confidential consultations with a view to achieving a mutually satisfactory solution.[83]

Some of China's FTAs go a step further and also permit the parties to, at any time, agree to confidential good offices, conciliation or mediation, without prejudice to the rights of any party.[84] Unfortunately, no further detail is provided in the China-Australia FTA nor China-Cambodia FTA regarding the procedure for mediation, appointment of the mediator or the rules governing the mediation. The China-Korea FTA provides additional details by specifying that the parties

> should endeavour to participate in the mediation procedure provided for . . . in an expeditious way and with the aim to reach a mutually agreed solution within a reasonable period of time with the assistance of a mediator designated or appointed by the Parties . . . Where the Parties have agreed to a solution, each Party should take any measure necessary to implement the mutually agreed solution.[85]

---

[80] China-Australia FTA (2015), Art. 15.1; China-Cambodia FTA (2020), Art. 14.1; China-Georgia FTA (2017), Art. 15.1; China-Iceland FTA (2013), Art. 105; China-Korea FTA (2015), Art. 20.1.

[81] China-Australia FTA (2015), Art. 15.4; China-Cambodia FTA (2020), Art. 14.3; China-Georgia FTA (2017), Art. 15.3; China-Iceland FTA (2013), Art. 107; China-Korea FTA (2015), Art. 20.3.

[82] China-Australia FTA (2015), Art. 15.5; China-Cambodia FTA (2020), Art. 14.4; China-Georgia FTA (2017), Art. 15.4; China-Iceland FTA (2013), Art. 108; China-Korea FTA (2015), Art. 20.4.

[83] China-Australia FTA (2015), Art. 15.5; China-Cambodia FTA (2020), Art. 14.4; China-Georgia FTA (2017), Art. 15.4; China-Korea FTA (2015), Art. 20.4.

[84] China-Australia FTA (2015), Art. 15.5, China-Cambodia FTA (2020), Art. 14.4; China-Iceland FTA (2013), Art. 108; China-Korea FTA (2015), Art. 20.4.

[85] China-Korea FTA (2015), Art. 20.5.

Moreover, it also contains a Code of Conduct for Panelists and Mediators in Annex 20-B that comprises the procedural obligations and duties of mediators. Therefore, except for the China-Korea FTA, the FTAs of China do not refer to a specific set of rules and it will be for the parties in each dispute to set the rules of the non-adversarial procedure, either by adopting *ad hoc* rules, or referring to institutions.

Regarding investments, China's practice has excluded investments from the general FTA dispute resolution chapter in favour of its own bespoke dispute resolution mechanism.[86] Nonetheless, the China-Australia FTA and the China-Korea FTA contain a chapter on investment. In this chapter, the treaties provides that a party may submit a written request for consultations containing the legal and factual basis for the claim and the estimated damages, among other information.[87] Parties are under an obligation to 'initially seek to resolve the dispute through consultations' and a mutually agreed solution may be reached consequently.[88] The chapter on investment in the China-Australia FTA does not mention other non-adversarial methods of dispute resolution like mediation, good offices or conciliation.

China's BITs do not tend to outline non-adversarial dispute resolution procedures in detail. They simply state that disputing parties in ISDS 'shall initially seek to resolve the dispute by consultations and negotiations' or via diplomatic channels.[89] If the dispute is not settled within three to six months from the date, either party may initiate proceedings before a competent authority.[90] Some BITs, such as the China-Australia BIT, provide that where there is a state-to-state investment dispute, the parties shall endeavour to resolve disputes by 'prompt and friendly negotiations and consultations'.[91] Where this is not successful within 60 days, the matter may be submitted to a tribunal.[92]

5 Assessing the Prospect of non-Adversarial Methods in China-EU Trade Relations

As highlighted by the two previous sections, observers familiar with recent FTAs signed by China or the EU with other partners may be unimpressed by the provisions of the CAI regarding the non-adversarial methods of dispute resolution. Indeed, the rules of Section V of the CAI fall within the widespread practice of both

[86] China-Australia FTA (2015), Art. 15.2; China-Cambodia FTA (2020), Art. 14.2.

[87] China-Australia FTA (2015), Art. 9.11; China-Korea FTA (2015), Art. 12.12.

[88] China-Australia FTA (2015), Art. 9.11; China-Korea FTA (2015), Art. 12.12.

[89] China-Australia BIT (1988), Art. 12; China-Cambodia BIT (1996), Art. 9; China-Georgia BIT (1993), Art. 9; China-Iceland BIT (1994), Art. 8; China-Korea BIT (2007), Art. 9.

[90] China-Australia BIT (1988), Art. 12.2–12.3; China-Cambodia BIT (1996), Art. 9; China-Georgia BIT (1993), Art. 9; China-Iceland BIT (1994), Art. 8; China-Korea BIT (2007), Art. 9.

[91] China-Australia BIT (1998), Art. 13.2.

[92] Ibid.

trade giants, which routinely include them along with the adversarial option of setting up an arbitration panel. Admittedly, the provisions of CAI bears similarity with some recent EU agreements, while they seem broader than the provisions found in China's recent agreements. Nonetheless, much of the content may be considered classic: Section V makes preliminary consultations mandatory, but does not extend this obligation to mediation, which remains voluntary. As it stands, Section V also does not include rules on mediation (although it mentions the Code of Conduct of Arbitrators[93] which is yet to be developed and will apply to the extent it is compatible with mediation). Art. 4.4 empowers the Joint Committee to 'adopt rules on the initiation, conduct and termination of mediation' within three years after the entry into force of the CAI", although at the moment of writing, no speculations can be made as to what these rules may look like if and when the CAI is finalized.

Yet, some known weaknesses of non-adversarial dispute resolution have been addressed in the CAI. Firstly, the use of shorter time limits for the parties to respond, engage in consultation, and eventually reach an agreement avoids stagnation. This ensures that while parties may agree to prolong the consultation phase when it is yielding positive results and more time is necessary to reach an agreement, sharp time limits make it possible for the complaining party to move forward and request the setting up of an arbitration panel when the consultation procedure is not fruitful. Secondly, since solving a dispute through conciliation is far from being an obligation, the parties are only subject to the obligation to approach the procedure in good faith and give sympathetic consideration to the arguments of the other party. This also means that the jurisdiction of the arbitration panel does not depend on the actual consultation taking place.

In addition, as mentioned above, the international context has overall grown favourable to the use of non-adversarial methods. A significant weakness of mediated solutions was the lack of enforcement certainty of settlement agreements.[94] This weakness has been remedied by the UN Convention on International Settlement Agreements Resulting From Mediation (the Singapore Convention). As per this convention, even a party from a non-signatory state can enforce a mediation settlement agreement in a country that is a signatory, as 'there is no connection between the seat of mediation and the application of the Singapore Convention'.[95] Although 'some argue that investors may still prefer not to mediate because a state may make a reservation to not apply the Singapore Convention with respect to the state or state entities [...] such concerns may not be well founded'.[96] This is especially evident given that, out of the 53 signatory states of the Convention, only 4 states have made reservations of this type.

Finally, China, in particular, has a deep-rooted culture of dispute resolution through non-conflictual methods, on which the prospects of success of CAI's

[93] CAI, Art. 8.

[94] Wang and Sharma (2021), p. 24; Alexander (2019), pp. 415–416.

[95] Wang and Sharma (2021), p. 24.

[96] Ibid.

non-adversarial dispute resolution mechanisms could build. Mediation is integrated into other dispute settlement mechanisms in China, including arbitration and litigation, which has widened its the use.[97] Mediation has also been immensely successful, with a success rate of 94.8% in 2000, representing more than 5 million civil disputes resolved.[98] Domestic factors in China have yielded a fertile ground for non-adversarial dispute resolution also in the context of international disputes. For foreign investments, mediation has played a significant role as both independent and mixed mediation mechanisms are available and investors can resort to independent mediation hosted by a branch of the State Administration of Industry and Commerce.[99]

While the current geopolitical climax seems hostile to any compromise, a more long-term view allows us to see how the EU's trade strategy in China and Asia would be better built on engagement and dialogue, rather than conflict. Various commentators have stated that Asian nations, and especially China, have a successful tradition of using non-adversarial methods of dispute resolution, which preserve the relationship between the parties and social stability. A review of existing literature suggests that Confucian values preferring a socially acceptable dispute resolution mechanism, the communist ideology that is hostile to litigation, and socio-legal factors have led to a preference for non-adversarial dispute resolution methods.[100] As has been affirmed, 'the reason mediation is preferred in APEC is because it is in line with the growing sense of community rather than the 'win or lose' confrontation in the WTO'.[101] China, specifically due to its social and cultural, political past, has viewed international law as an instrument of state power rather than a constraint, and has rejected the rulings of international courts on what it considers political disputes; for this reason it has been averse to initiating legal disputes regarding political acts, and it is culturally suitable for non-adversarial dispute resolution mechanisms.[102] Building on this heritage, non-adversarial methods in EU-China relations have the potential to make this route of dispute resolution more attractive and fruitful for both parties.

References

Alexander N (2019) Ten trends in international mediation. Singapore Acad Law J (Special Issue) 31:373–746

[97] Zhao (2018), pp. 125–126.

[98] Kaufmann-Kohler and Kun (2018), p. 484.

[99] Zhao (2018), pp. 125–126.

[100] See for example Kaufmann-Kohler and Kun (2018), pp. 479–492; Wang (1996, 2009); Cohen (1966), pp. 1201–1223; Wang and He (2012), pp. 220–221.

[101] Lo et al. (2020), p. 247.

[102] Chesterman (2016), pp. 951–953.

Chesterman S (2016) Asia's ambivalence about international law and institutions: past, present and futures. EJIL 27(4):877–1182

Cohen JA (1966) Chinese mediation on the eve of modernization. Calif Law Rev:1201–1223

Cot J-P (2006) Max Planck Encyclopaedias of International Law, "Conciliation"

Duy Phan H (2018) Australia and Timor-Leste's Landmark Maritime Boundary Conciliation Process, The Diplomat, https://thediplomat.com/2018/05/australia-and-timor-lestes-landmark-maritime-boundary-conciliation-process/ Accessed 28 Jan 2023

EP Press Office (2021) MEPs refuse any agreement with China whilst sanctions are in place. 20210517IPR04123 https://www.europarl.europa.eu/news/en/press-room/20210517IPR04123/meps-refuse-any-agreement-with-china-whilst-sanctions-are-in-place Accessed 26 Jan 2023

Hakapää K, (2013) Max Planck Encyclopedias of International Law, "Negotiation"

ICSID (2021) Background Paper on Investment Mediation, available at https://icsid.worldbank.org/sites/default/files/publications/Background_Paper_on_Investment_Mediation.pdf

Kaufmann-Kohler G, Kun F (2018) Integrating mediation into arbitration: why it works in China. J Int Arbitr 25(4):421–528

Kessedjian C. et al. (2020) Mediation in future investor-state dispute settlement. Academic Forum on ISDS Concept Paper 2020/16

Koh T (2011) International law and the peaceful resolution of disputes: Asian perspectives, contributions, and challenges. AJIL 1:1–104

Koh T (2017) Maritime boundary conciliation between Timor-Leste and Australia: a success story. Tembusu College News & Events, https://tembusu.nus.edu.sg/news/2017/by-prof-tommy-koh-maritime-boundary-conciliation-between-timor-leste-and-australia-a-success-story. Accessed 30 Jan 2023

Le Moli G, Viñuales JE (2020) A foundational experiment: the Timor Leste-Australia conciliation. In: Tomuschat C, Kohen M (eds) Flexibility in international dispute settlement. Brill, Amsterdam, pp xvi–291

Lo C, Nakagawa J, Chen T (eds) (2020) The appellate body of the WTO and its reform. Springer, Singapore

Orrego Vicuña F (2010) Max Planck Encyclopaedias of International Law, "Mediation"

Schwedt K et al (2021) Investment protection in the EU-UK trade and cooperation agreement. Kluwer Arbitration Blog

Wang G (1996) The unification of the dispute resolution system in China cultural economic and legal contributions. J Int Arbitr 13:5–170

Wang G (2009) Mediation in the globalized business environment. Asia Pacific Law Rev 17(Issue supplement):1–204

Wang G, He X (2012) Mediation and international investment: Chinese Perspective. Maine Law Rev 65(1):215–236

Wang G, Sharma R (2021) The international commercial dispute prevention and settlement organization: a global laboratory of dispute resolution with an Asian flavor. AJIL Unbound 115. https://doi.org/10.1017/aju.2020.82

WTO (2020a) Summary of DS7 Scallops (Canada) Panel Report, European Communities — Trade Description of Scallops. https://www.wto.org/english/tratop_e/dispu_e/cases_e/ds7_e.htm. Accessed 28 Jan 2023

WTO (2020b) Summary of DS99 United States – Anti-Dumping Duty on Dynamic Random Access Memory Semiconductors (DRAMS) of One Megabit or Above from Korea, https://www.wto.org/english/tratop_e/dispu_e/cases_e/ds99_e.htm. Accessed 28 Jan 2023

Yeini SA (2020) Promoting peace in international law: bringing states to the mediation table. Colum J Transnatl Law 58(3):531–748

Zhao C (2018) Investor-state mediation in a China-EU bilateral investment treaty: talking about being in the right place at the right time. CJIL 17(1):1–205

Sara Migliorini is an Assistant Professor at the Faculty of Law – University of Macau. She is a Doctor of Laws, from the European University Institute (EUI), Florence, and her research interests include the field of Artificial Intelligence and Big Data, as well as the area of International Litigation and Arbitration. In the past, Dr. Sara Migliorini has worked in research at the British Institute of International and Comparative Law, as well as at the University of Lausanne. She has also experience working for an international law firm. Dr. Sara Migliorini has earned several grants and awards throughout her career.

Naina Gupta is an LLB and LLM (Public International Law) graduate from the London School of Economics. She is a trainee lawyer at Arnold & Porter Kaye Scholer LLP. Previously, she was an International Arbitration Clerk at Arnold & Porter Kaye Scholer LLP and a trainee at the European Commission's trade dispute settlement unit (DG TRADE). Naina has also been a Private International Law intern at BIICL and she is one of the founding committee members of the Young Investment Treaty Forum. She has contributed to this chapter in her personal capacity.

SPRINGER NATURE

GPSR Compliance

The European Union's (EU) General Product Safety Regulation (GPSR) is a set of rules that requires consumer products to be safe and our obligations to ensure this.

If you have any concerns about our products, you can contact us on ProductSafety@springernature.com

In case Publisher is established outside the EU, the EU authorized representative is:

Springer Nature Customer Service Center GmbH
Europaplatz 3
69115 Heidelberg, Germany

The manufacturer's authorised representative in the EU is Springer Nature Customer Service Centre GmbH, Europaplatz 3, 69115 Heidelberg, Germany. If you have any concerns regarding our products, please contact ProductSafety@springernature.com

Printed and bound by CPI Group (UK) Ltd, Croydon, CR0 4YY
01/10/2026
02225910-0008